BAKEMONOGATARI
volume 14

A Vertical Comics Edition

Editing: Ajani Oloye
Translation: Ko Ransom
Production: Grace Lu
　　　　　 Shirley Fang
　　　　　 Hiroko Mizuno
　　　　　 Eve Grandt

First published in Japan in 2021 by Kodansha, Ltd., Tokyo
Publication for this English edition arranged through Kodansha, Ltd., Tokyo
English language version produced by Vertical Comics,
an imprint of Kodansha USA Publishing, LLC

Translation provided by Vertical Comics, 2022
Published by Kodansha USA Publishing, LLC, New York

Originally published in Japanese as *BAKEMONOGATARI 14* by Kodansha, Ltd.
BAKEMONOGATARI first serialized in *Weekly Shonen Magazine*,
Kodansha, Ltd., 2017-

This is a work of fiction.

ISBN: 978-1-64729-088-7

Manufactured in the United States of America

First Edition

Kodansha USA Publishing, LLC
451 Park Avenue South
7th Floor
New York, NY 10016
www.kodansha.us

Vertical books are distributed through Penguin-Random House Publisher Services.

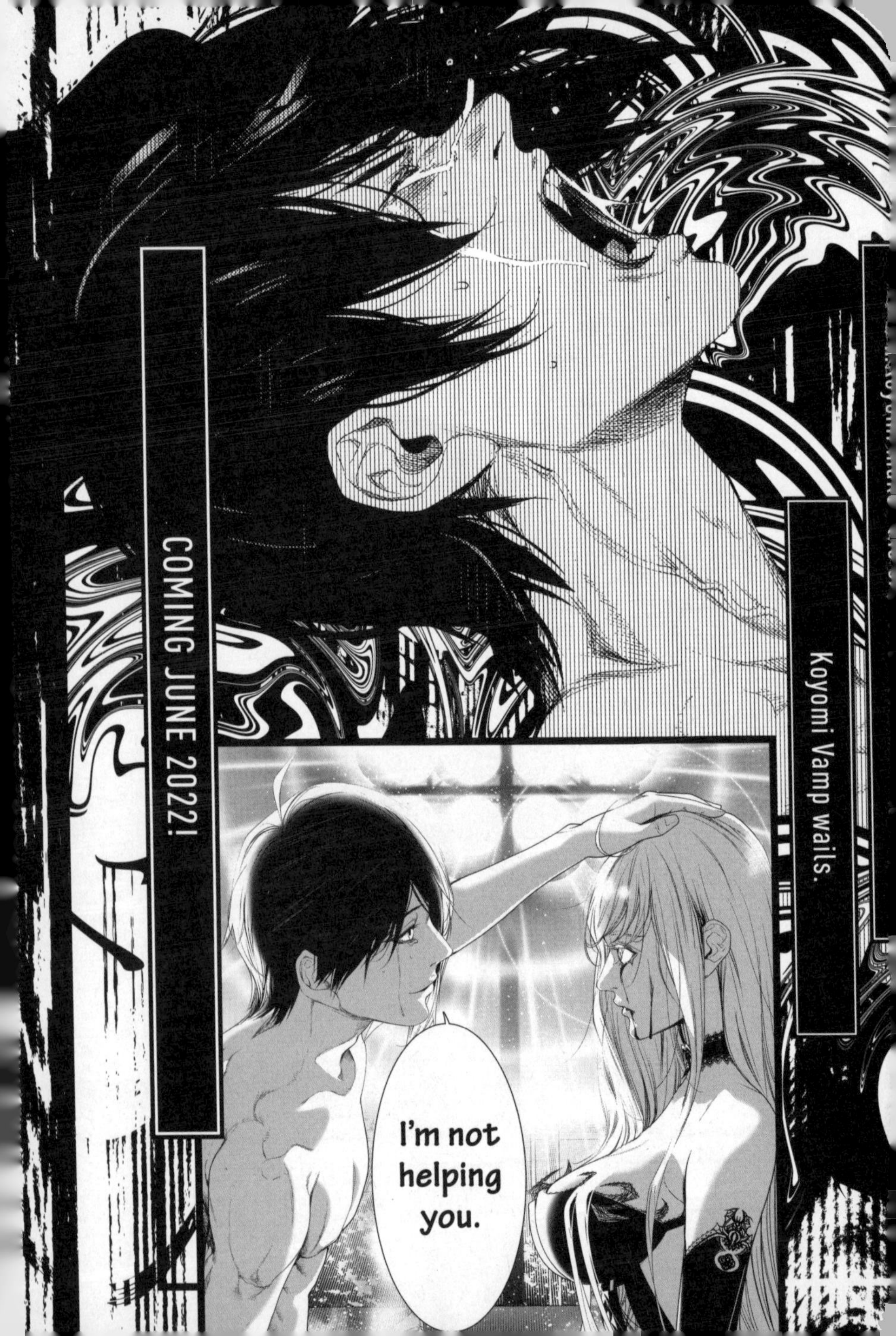
Koyomi Vamp wails.
I'm not helping you.
COMING JUNE 2022!

BAKEMONOGATARI

OH!GREAT

ORIGINAL STORY: NISIOISIN

ORIGINAL CHARACTER
DESIGN: VOFAN

14

MAIN CHARACTERS

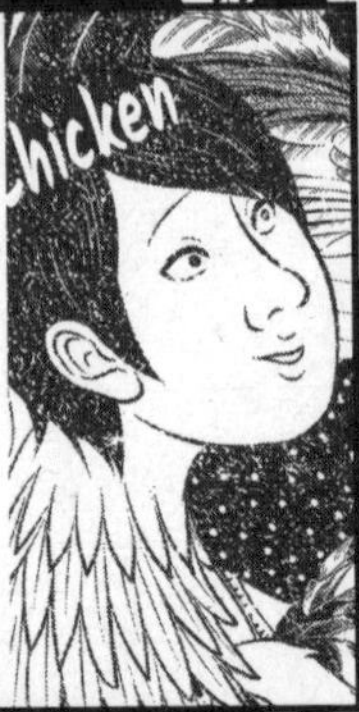
Chicken

Koyomi Araragi

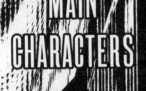

A boy who became Kiss-Shot's thrall after saving her. He now fights to become human again and to put a stop to Kiss-Shot.

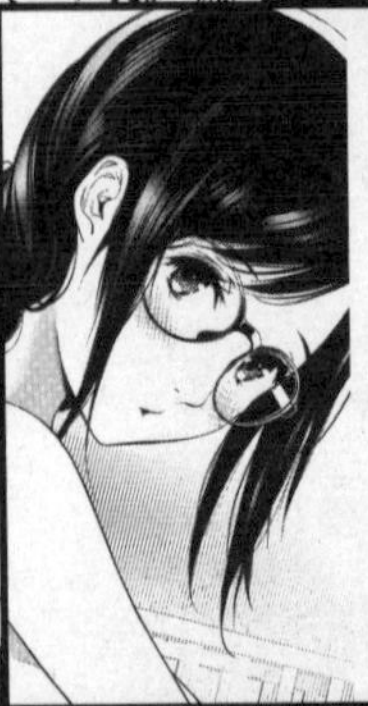

Tsubasa Hanekawa

Koyomi's friend who goes to the same school as him, and an honor student that few honors could sufficiently describe. She's dedicated to supporting Koyomi without any regard for her own safety.

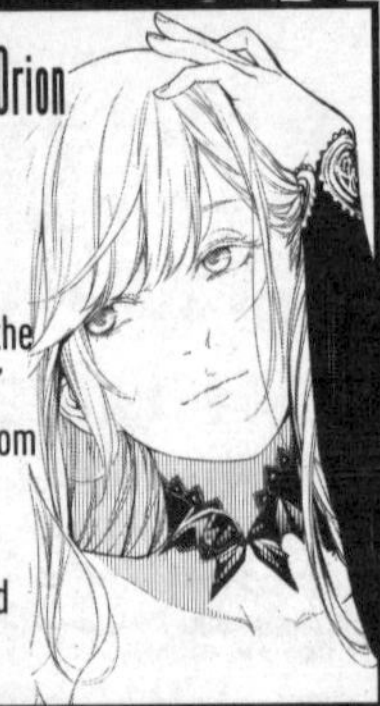

Kiss-Shot Acerola-Orion Heart-Under-Blade

A vampire powerful enough to be called the "king of aberrations" who Koyomi saved from near-certain death. Thanks to Koyomi, she has now returned to her original form.

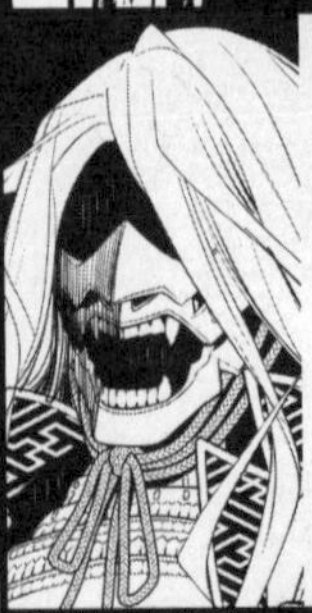

Seishiro Shishirui

Kiss-Shot's first thrall. He took his own life.

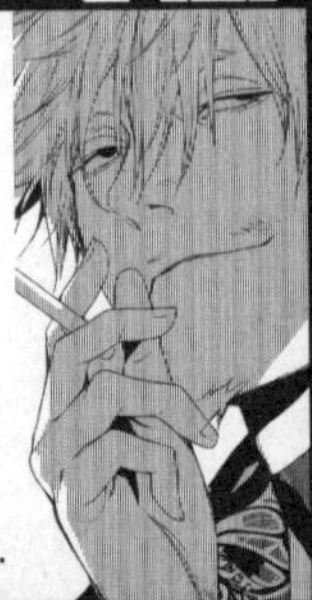

Mèmè Oshino

A self-described expert on aberrations who appeared in front of Koyomi one day.

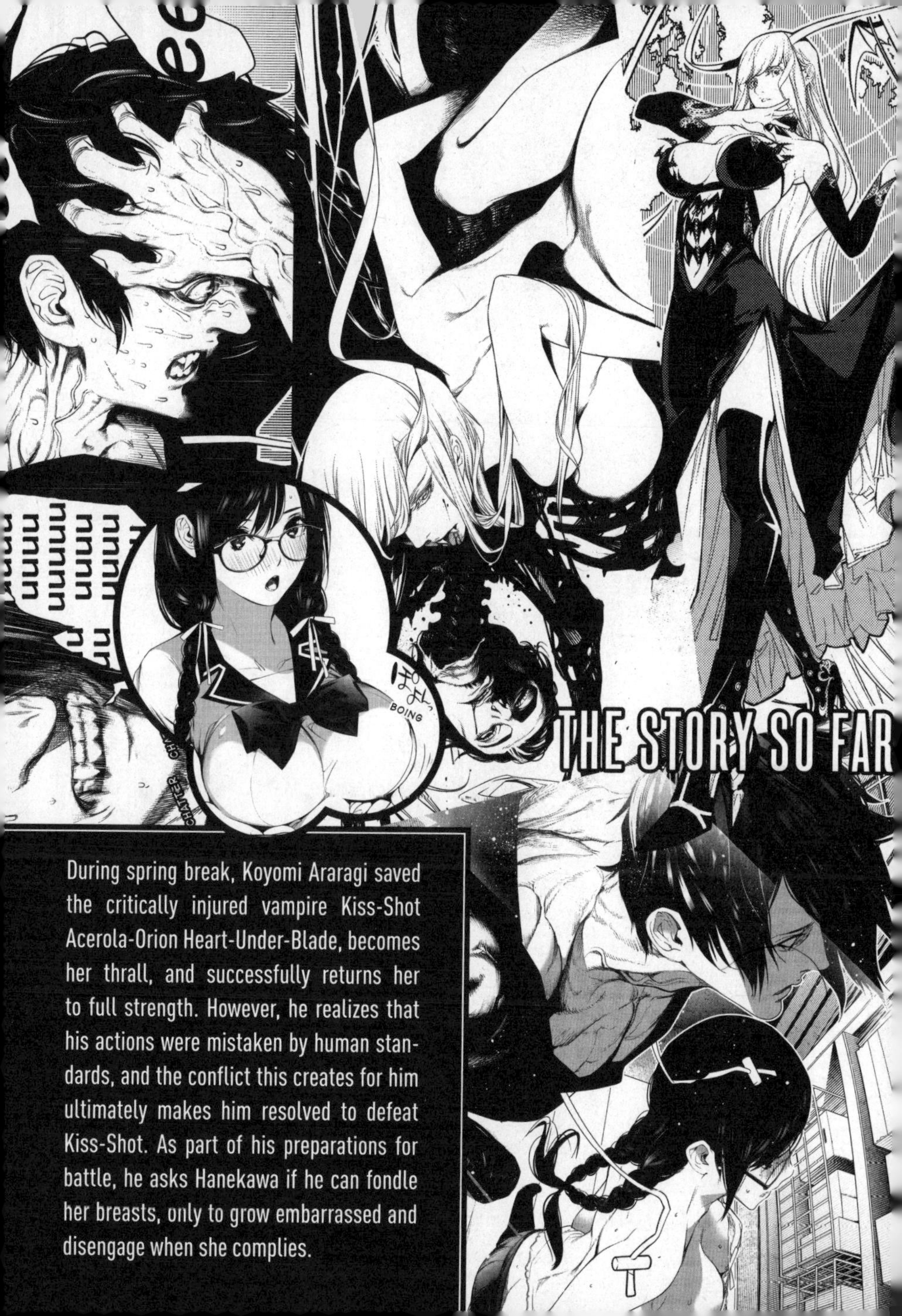
BOING
CHATTER

THE STORY SO FAR

During spring break, Koyomi Araragi saved the critically injured vampire Kiss-Shot Acerola-Orion Heart-Under-Blade, becomes her thrall, and successfully returns her to full strength. However, he realizes that his actions were mistaken by human standards, and the conflict this creates for him ultimately makes him resolved to defeat Kiss-Shot. As part of his preparations for battle, he asks Hanekawa if he can fondle her breasts, only to grow embarrassed and disengage when she complies.

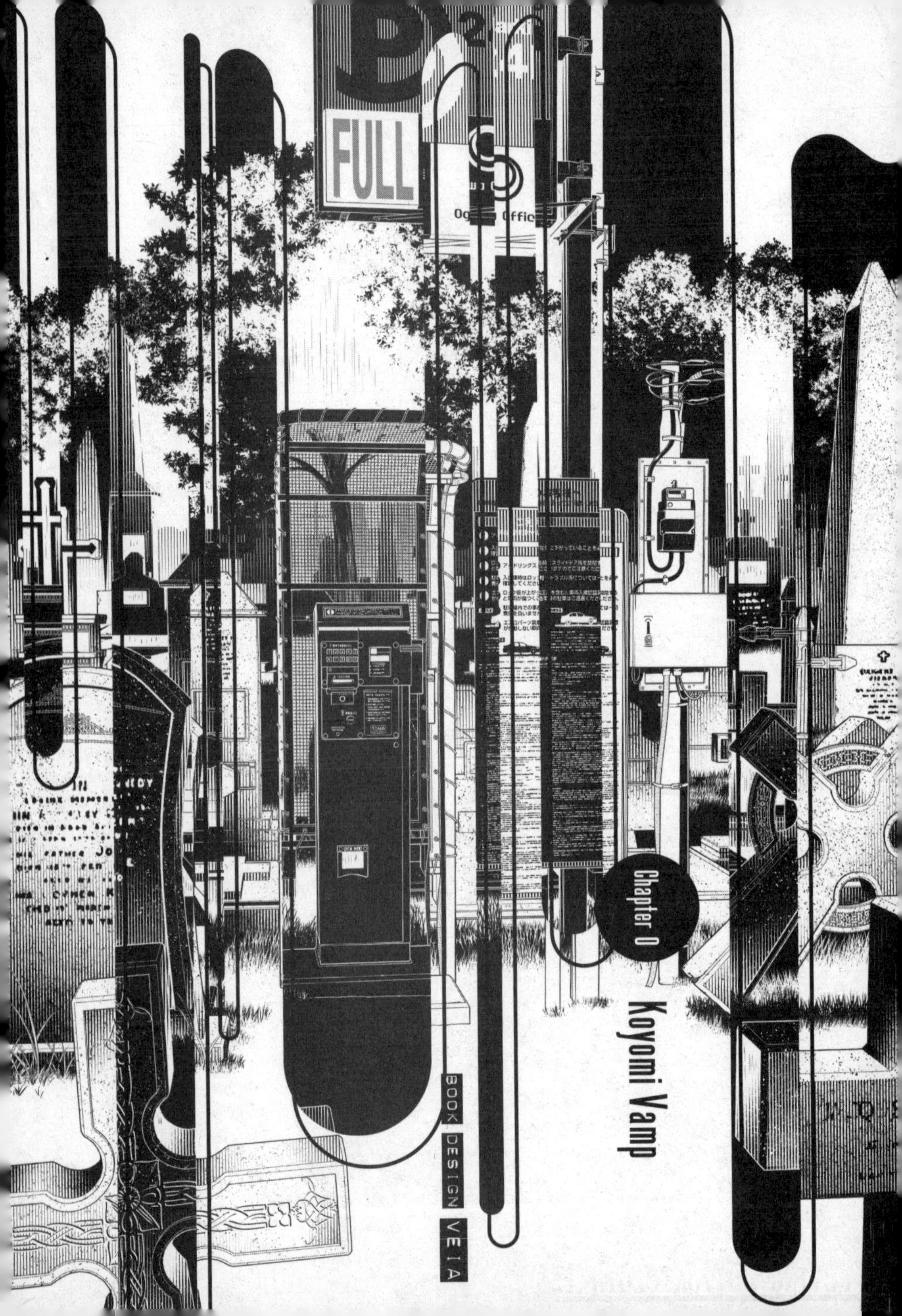
Chapter 0
Koyomi Vamp
BOOK DESIGN VEIA
FULL

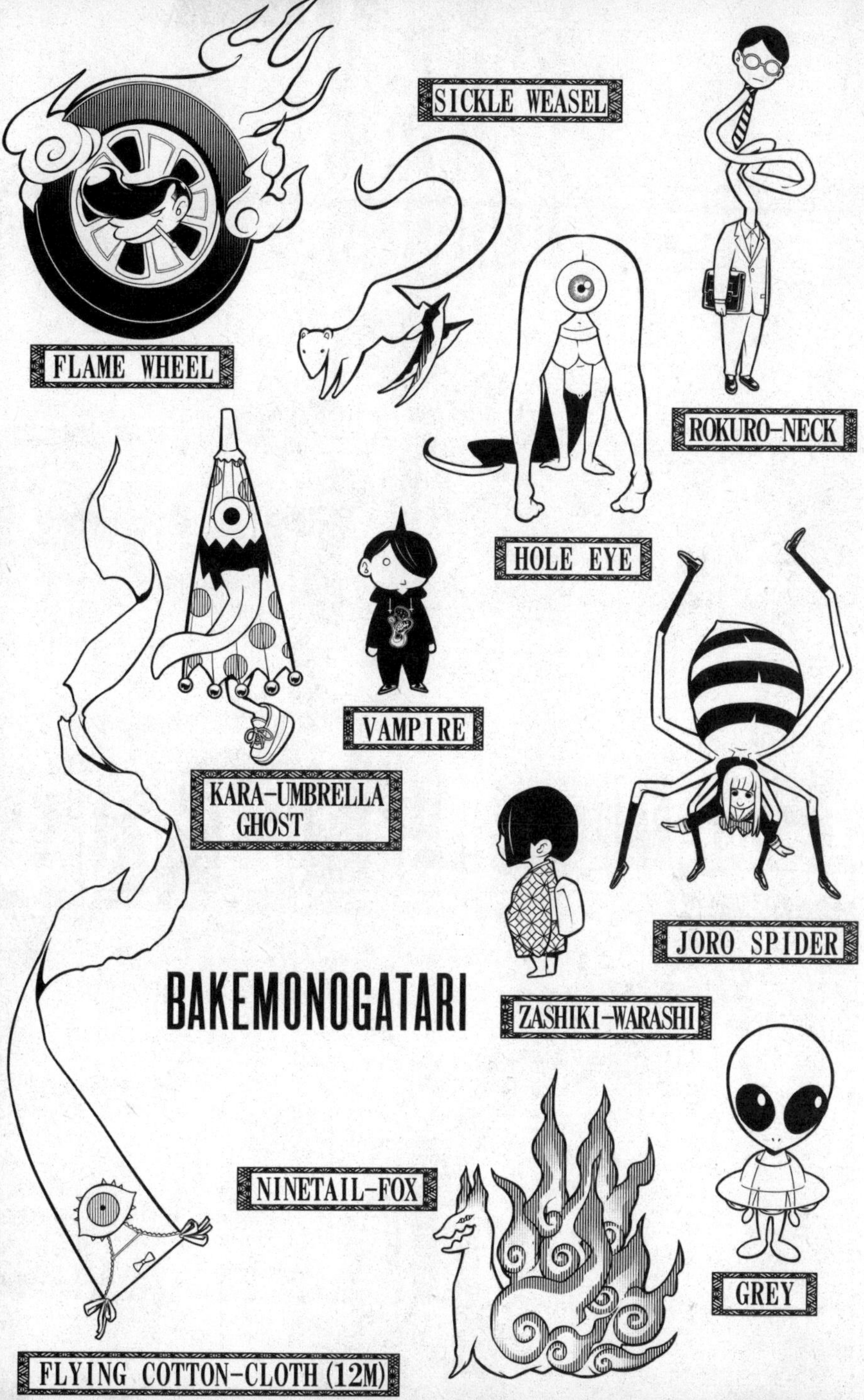
SICKLE WEASEL
FLAME WHEEL
ROKURO-NECK
HOLE EYE
VAMPIRE
KARA-UMBRELLA GHOST
JORO SPIDER
BAKEMONOGATARI
ZASHIKI-WARASHI
NINETAIL-FOX
GREY
FLYING COTTON-CLOTH (12M)

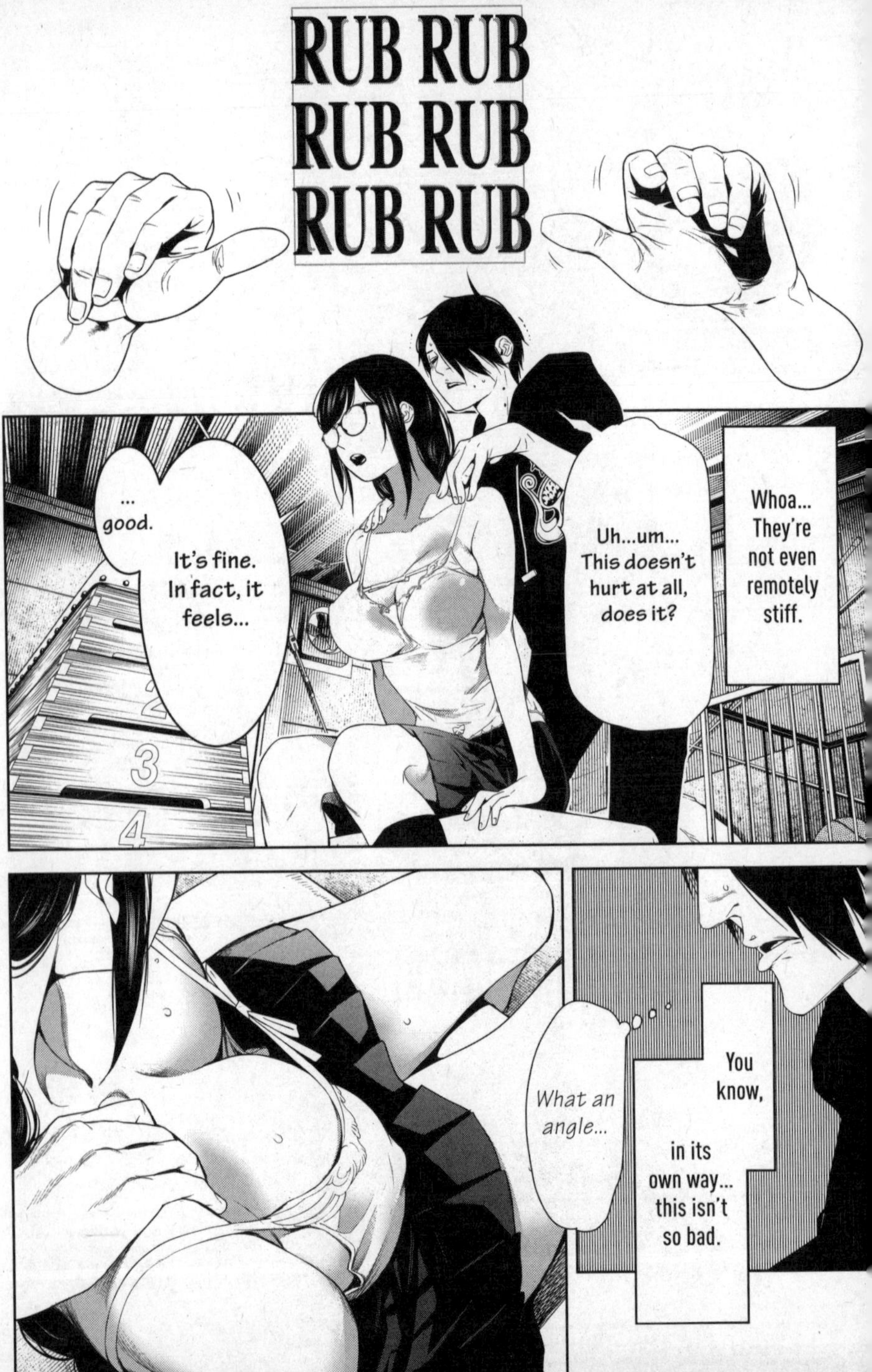
RUB RUB
RUB RUB
RUB RUB
Whoa... They're not even remotely stiff.
Uh...um... This doesn't hurt at all, does it?
It's fine. In fact, it feels...
... good.
You know,
in its own way... this isn't so bad.
What an angle...

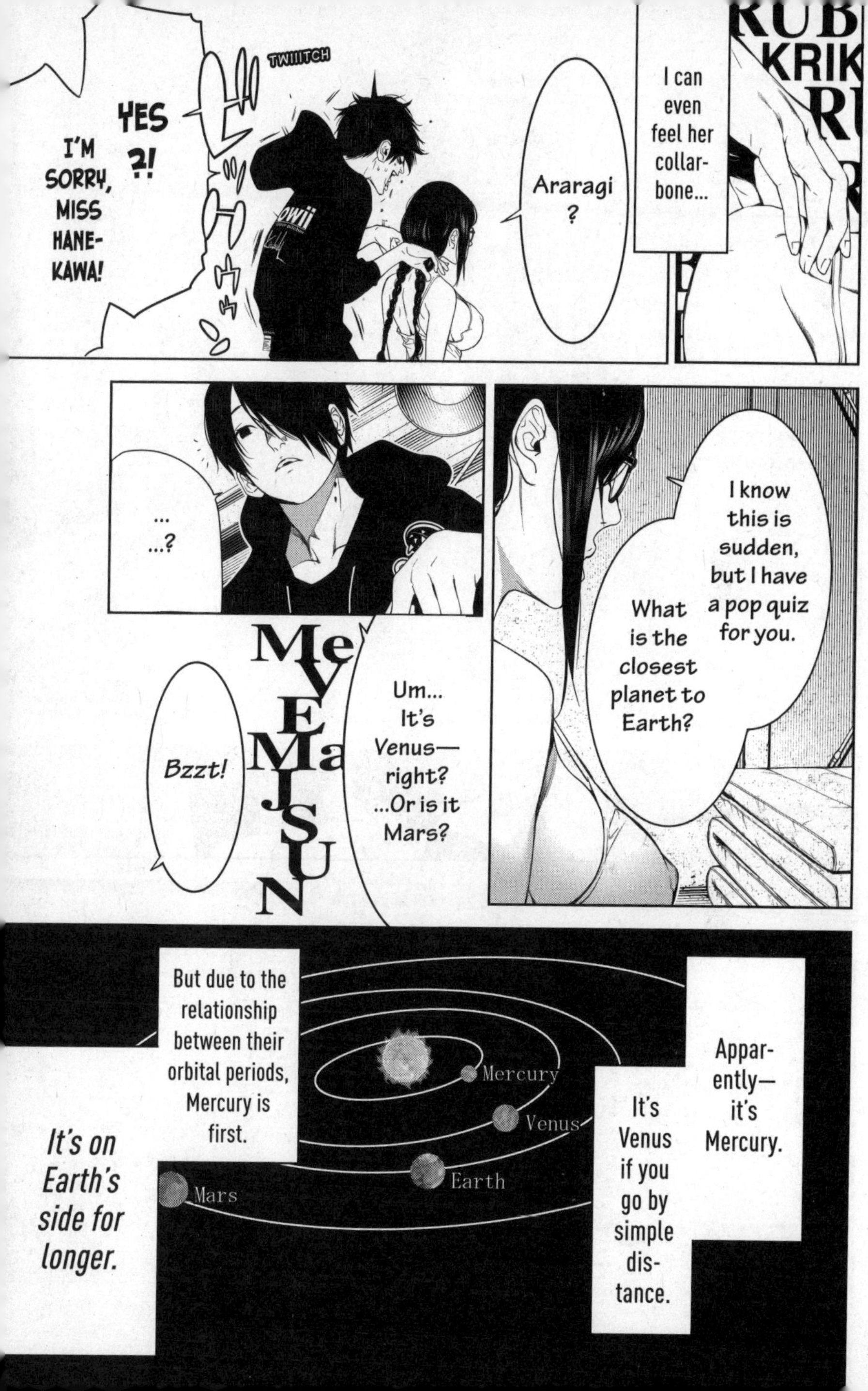
I can even feel her collar-bone...
Araragi?
TWIIITCH
YES?!
I'M SORRY, MISS HANE-KAWA!
I know this is sudden, but I have a pop quiz for you.
What is the closest planet to Earth?
...
...?
Um... It's Venus—right? ...Or is it Mars?
Bzzt!
Apparently—it's Mercury.
It's Venus if you go by simple distance.
But due to the relationship between their orbital periods, Mercury is first.
Mercury
Venus
Earth
Mars
It's on Earth's side for longer.

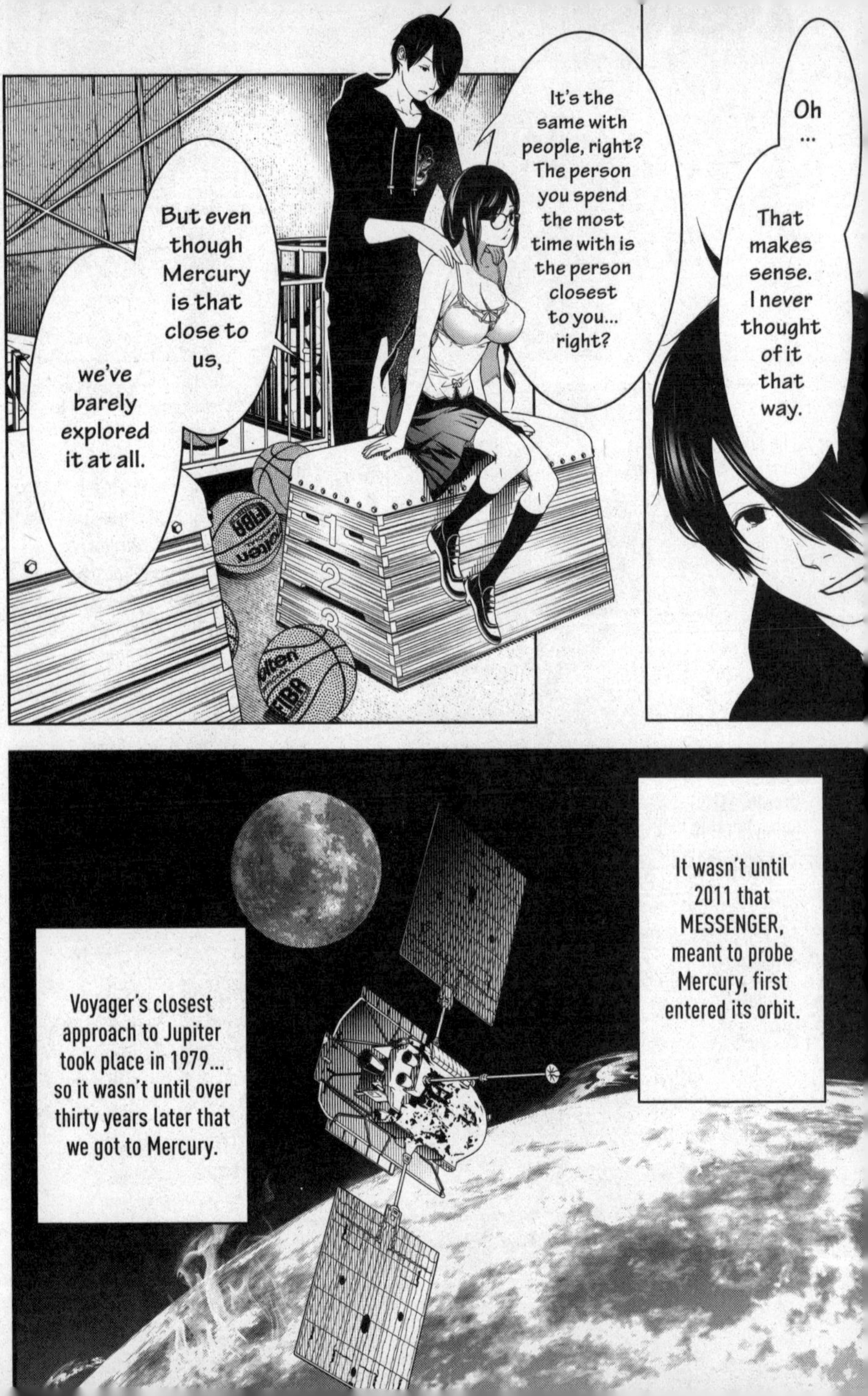
Oh ...
That makes sense. I never thought of it that way.
It's the same with people, right? The person you spend the most time with is the person closest to you... right?
But even though Mercury is that close to us,
we've barely explored it at all.
It wasn't until 2011 that MESSENGER, meant to probe Mercury, first entered its orbit.
Voyager's closest approach to Jupiter took place in 1979... so it wasn't until over thirty years later that we got to Mercury.

I guess maybe you could say... It's kind of like your relationship to my breasts?
HUH ?!
Maybe there's a really significant reason that you can't come into contact with them.
Her breasts draw me in with an irresistible force...
Desire
Gravity
SUN
Earth
Centrifugal force
CHICKEN
...and at the same time, the inertia created from being in orbit around her breasts consistently acts upon me to keep me away from them.
And so, trying to force myself to get close to them—is the wrong approach.
The more strength I exert...
CHICKEN
CHICKEN
CHICKEN
CHICKEN
Centrifugal force + Force
NERVES
VIRGINITY
Gravity
BREASTS
...the farther away I get from her breasts.

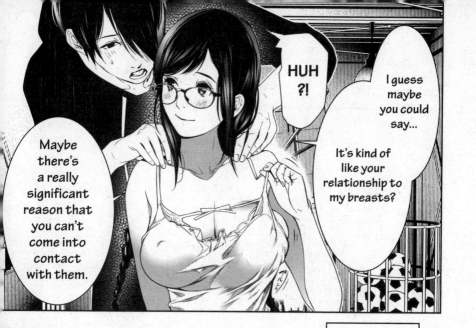

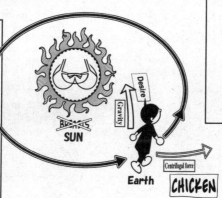

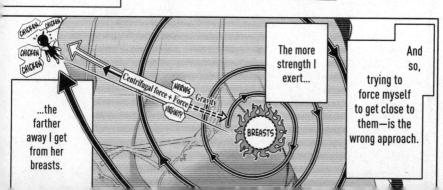

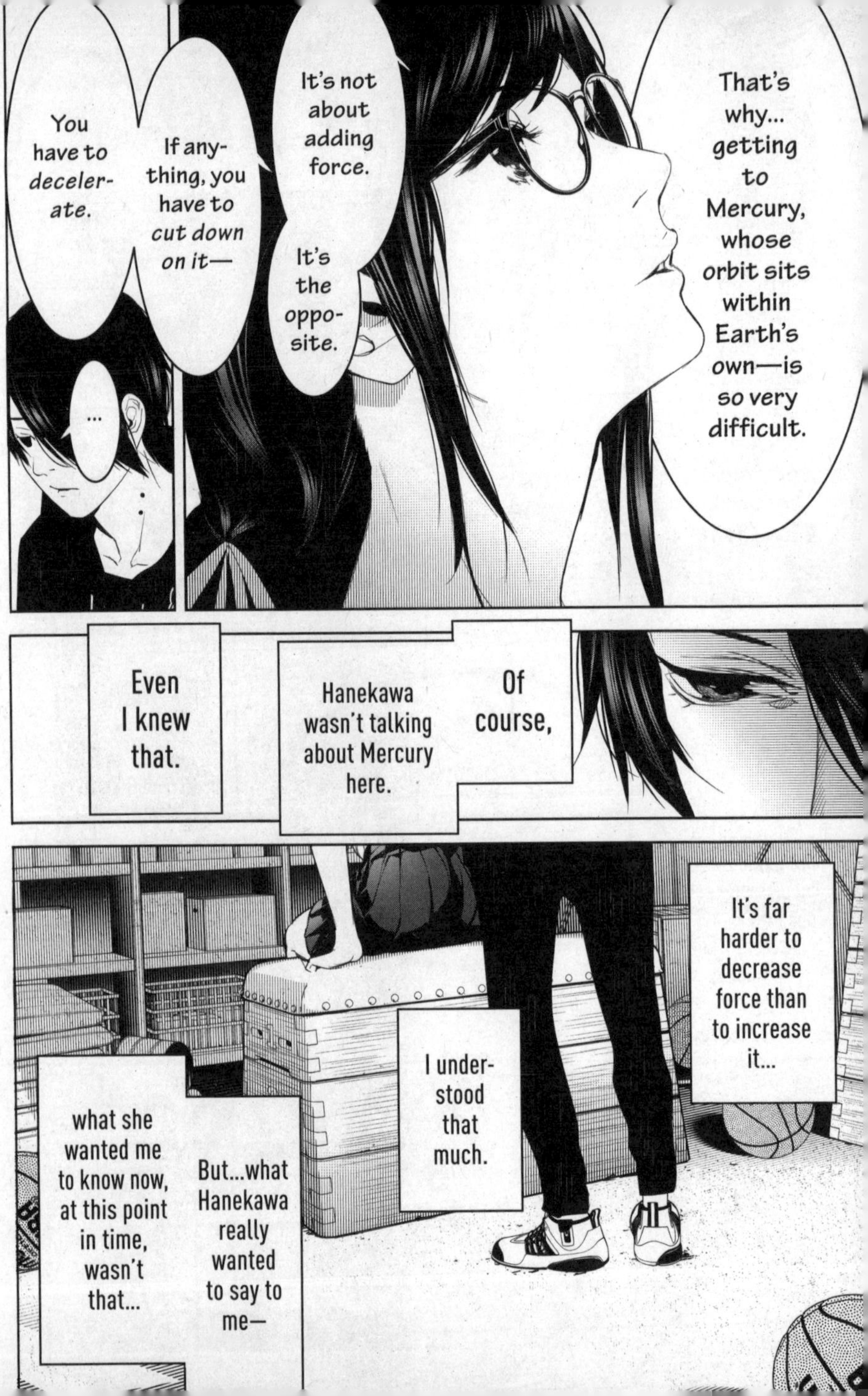
That's why... getting to Mercury, whose orbit sits within Earth's own—is so very difficult.
It's not about adding force.
It's the opposite.
If anything, you have to cut down on it—
You have to decelerate.
...
Of course,
Hanekawa wasn't talking about Mercury here.
Even I knew that.
It's far harder to decrease force than to increase it...
I understood that much.
But...what Hanekawa really wanted to say to me—
what she wanted me to know now, at this point in time, wasn't that...

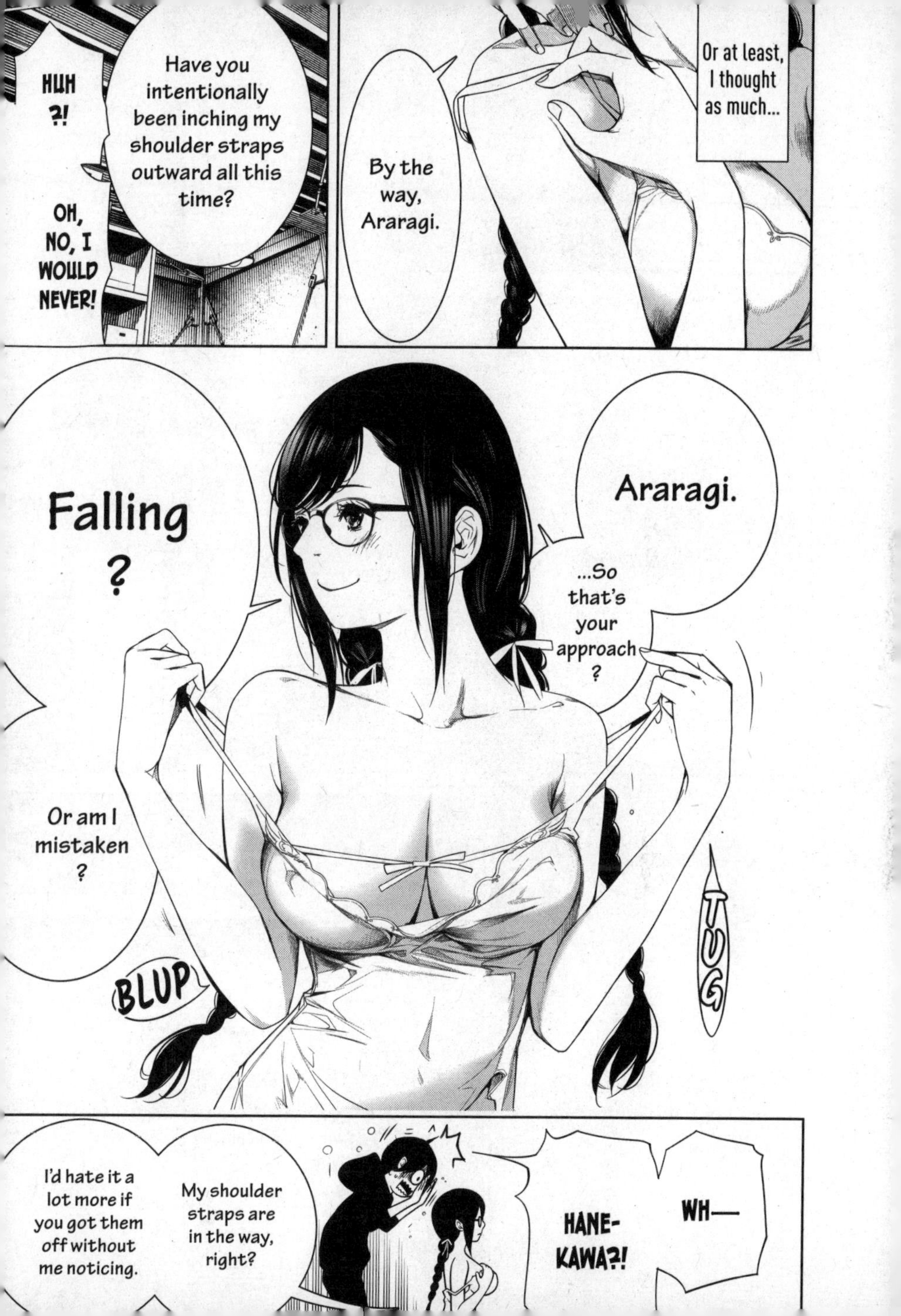
Or at least, I thought as much...
By the way, Araragi.
Have you intentionally been inching my shoulder straps outward all this time?
HUH ?!
OH, NO, I WOULD NEVER!
Araragi.
...So that's your approach ?
Falling ?
Or am I mistaken ?
TUG
BLUP
WH—
HANE-KAWA?!
My shoulder straps are in the way, right?
I'd hate it a lot more if you got them off without me noticing.

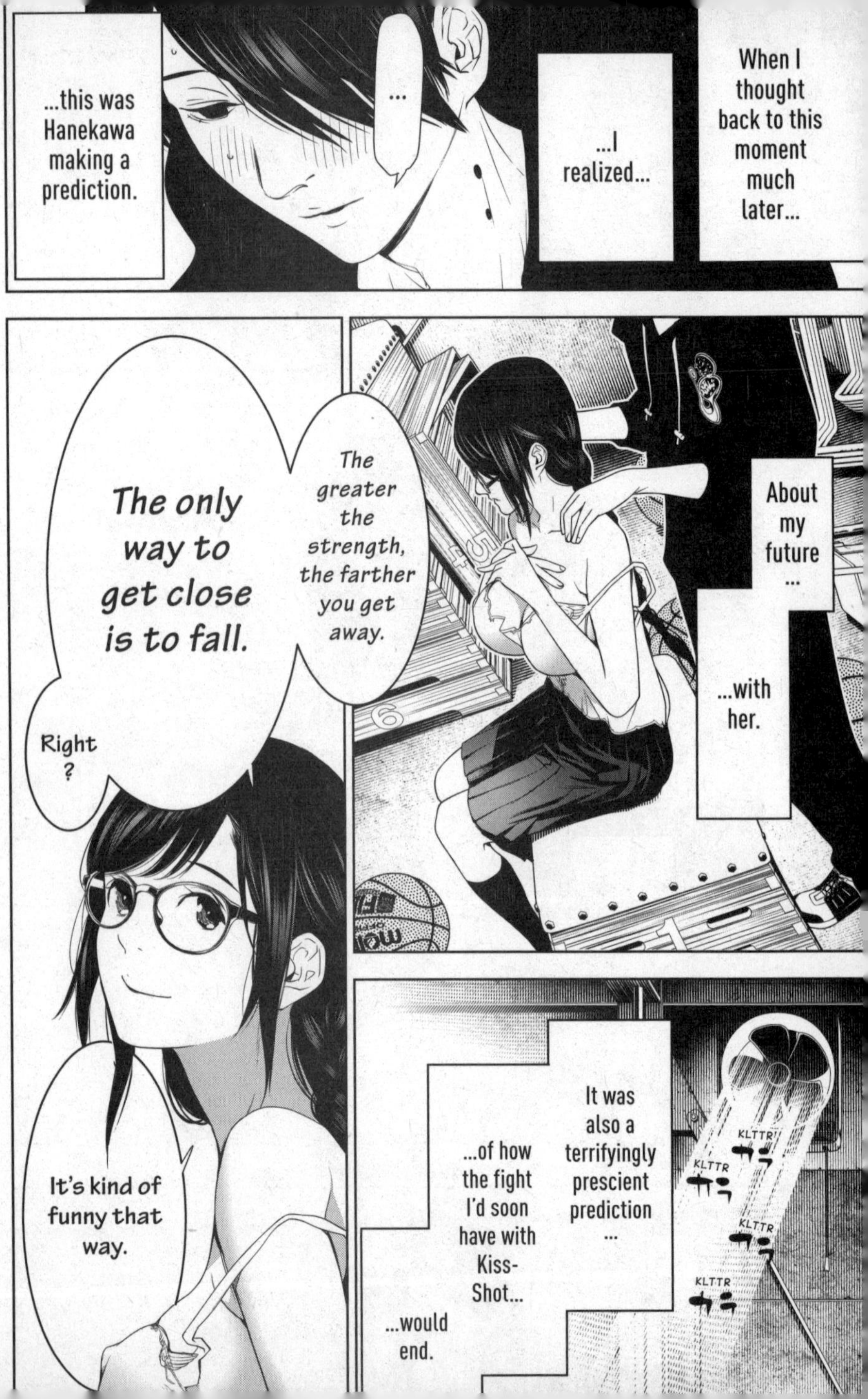
When I thought back to this moment much later...
...I realized...
...
...this was Hanekawa making a prediction.
About my future...
...with her.
KLTTR
KLTTR
KLTTR
KLTTR
It was also a terrifyingly prescient prediction...
...of how the fight I'd soon have with Kiss-Shot...
...would end.
The greater the strength, the farther you get away.
The only way to get close is to fall.
Right?
It's kind of funny that way.

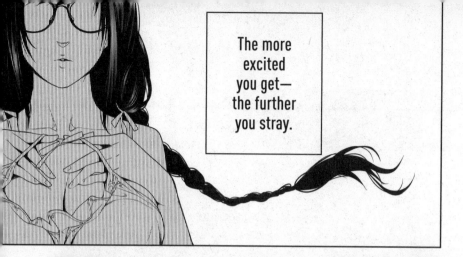

The more excited you get—the further you stray.
From victory.
From truth.
—So calm your mind.
Sink.
Sink deep.
Search for something beyond sight at the bottom of that cold, dark sea of thought.

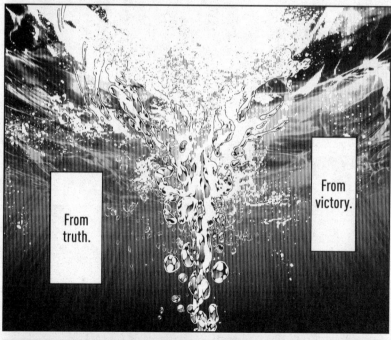

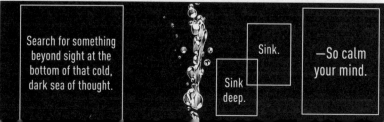

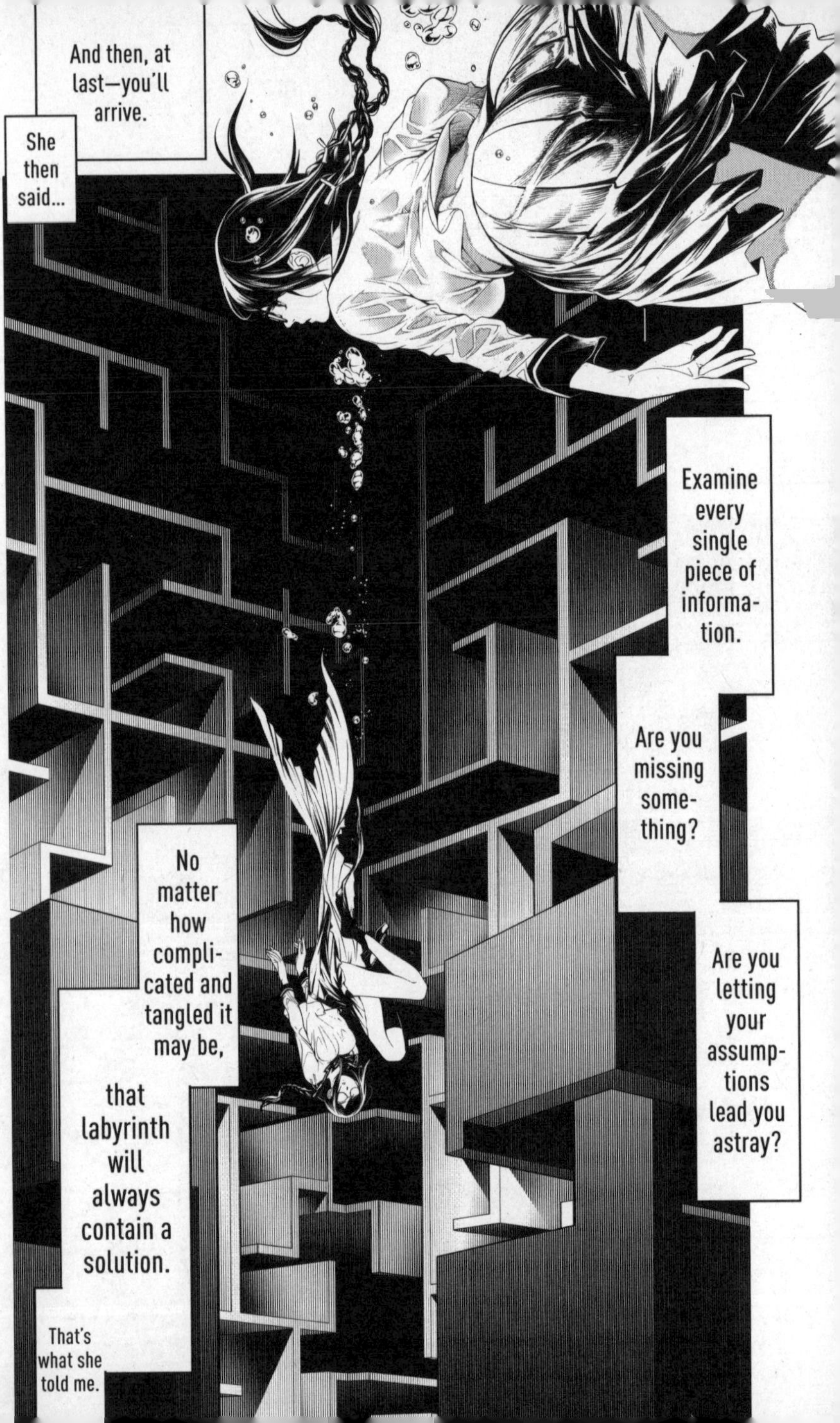

And then, at last—you'll arrive.
She then said...
Examine every single piece of information.
Are you missing something?
Are you letting your assumptions lead you astray?
No matter how complicated and tangled it may be,
that labyrinth will always contain a solution.
That's what she told me.

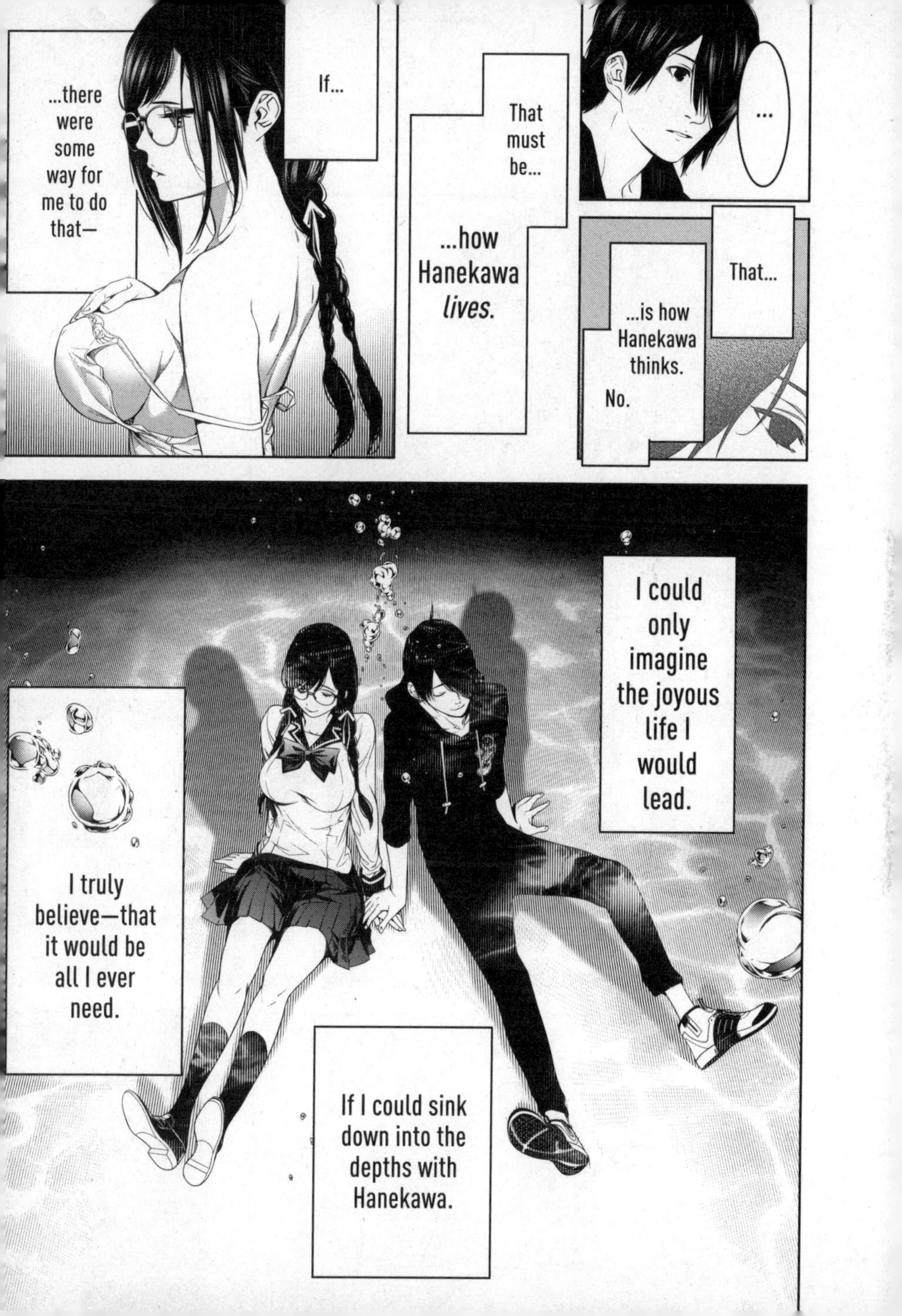
...
That...
...is how Hanekawa thinks.
No.
That must be...
...how Hanekawa *lives.*
If...
...there were some way for me to do that—
I could only imagine the joyous life I would lead.
I truly believe—that it would be all I ever need.
If I could sink down into the depths with Hanekawa.

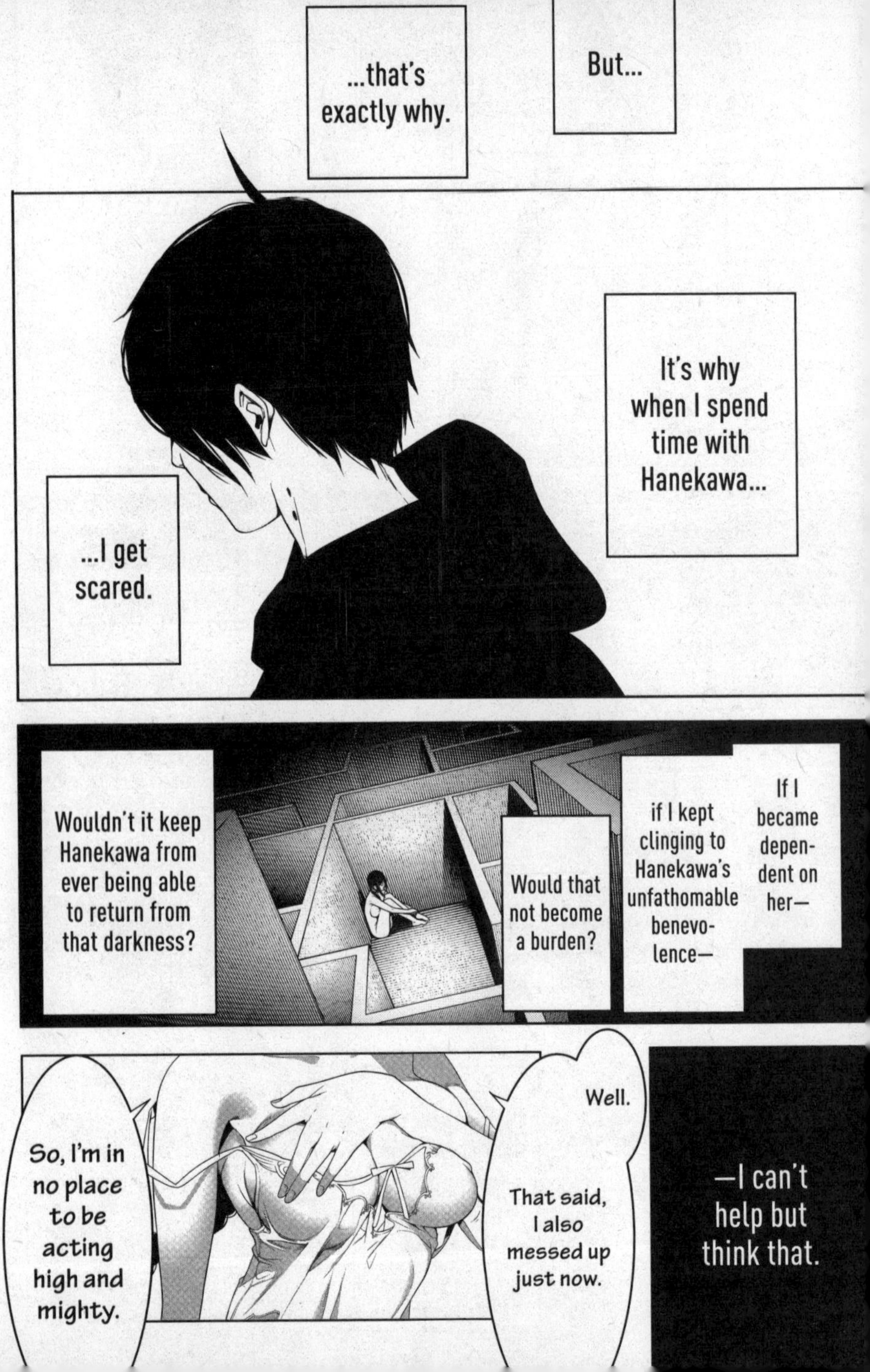
But...
...that's exactly why.
It's why when I spend time with Hanekawa...
...I get scared.
If I became depen-dent on her—
if I kept clinging to Hanekawa's unfathomable benevo-lence—
Would that not become a burden?
Wouldn't it keep Hanekawa from ever being able to return from that darkness?
—I can't help but think that.
Well.
That said, I also messed up just now.
So, I'm in no place to be acting high and mighty.

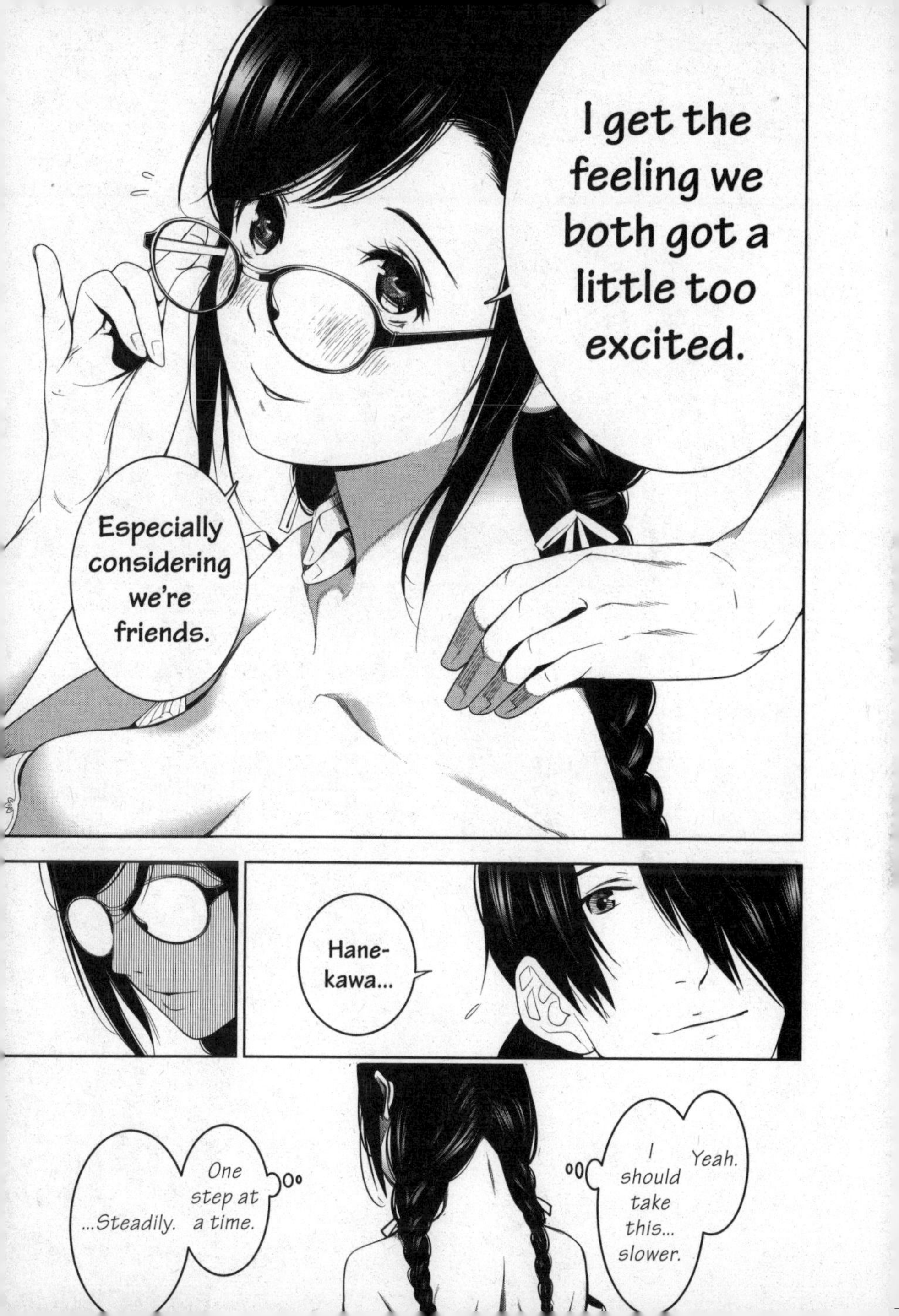
I get the feeling we both got a little too excited.
Especially considering we're friends.
Hane-kawa...
Yeah.
I should take this... slower.
One step at a time.
...Steadily.

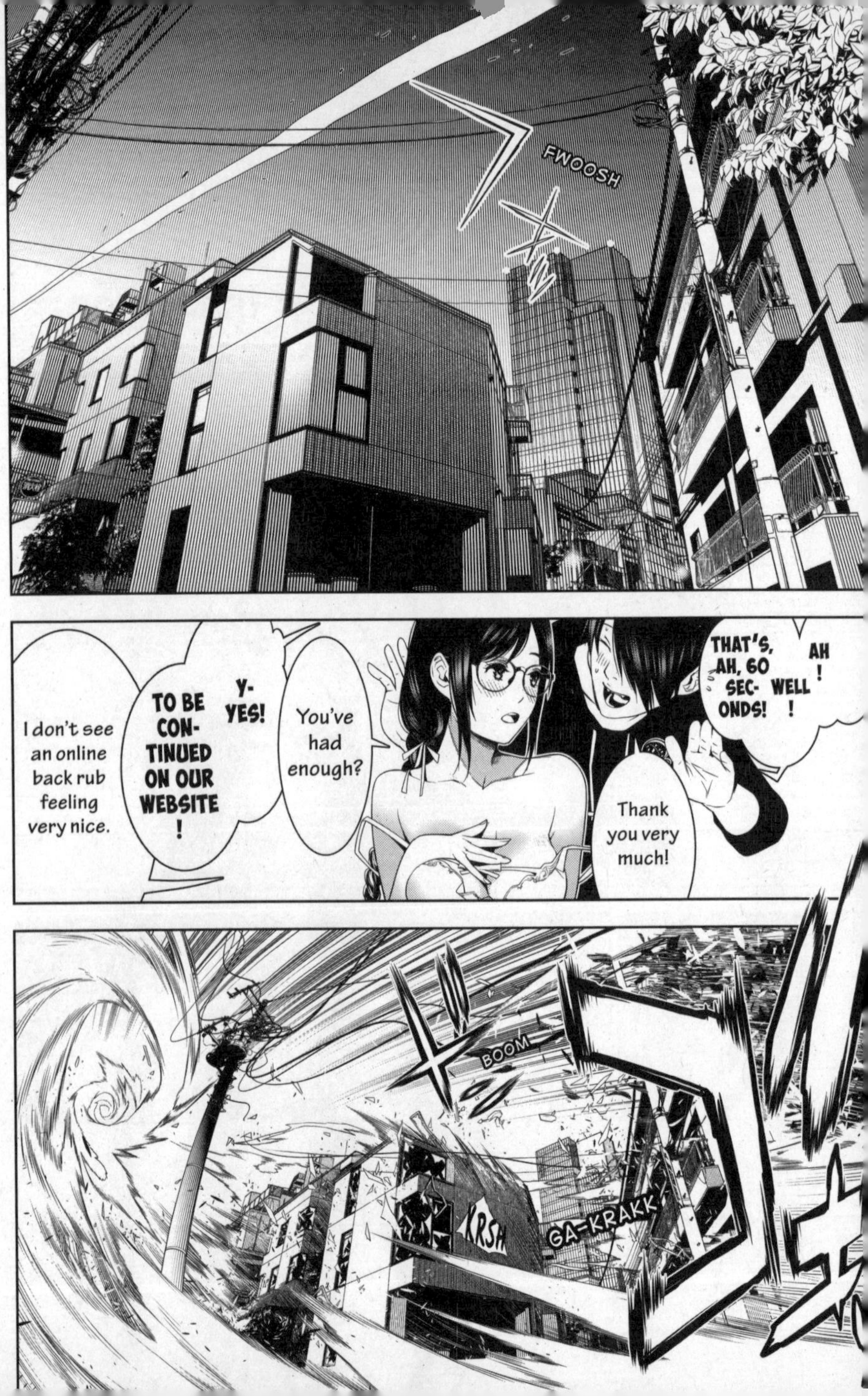
FWOOSH
AH! WELL!
THAT'S, AH, 60 SEC-ONDS!
Thank you very much!
You've had enough?
Y-YES!
TO BE CON-TINUED ON OUR WEBSITE!
I don't see an online back rub feeling very nice.
BOOM
GA-KRAKK
KRSH

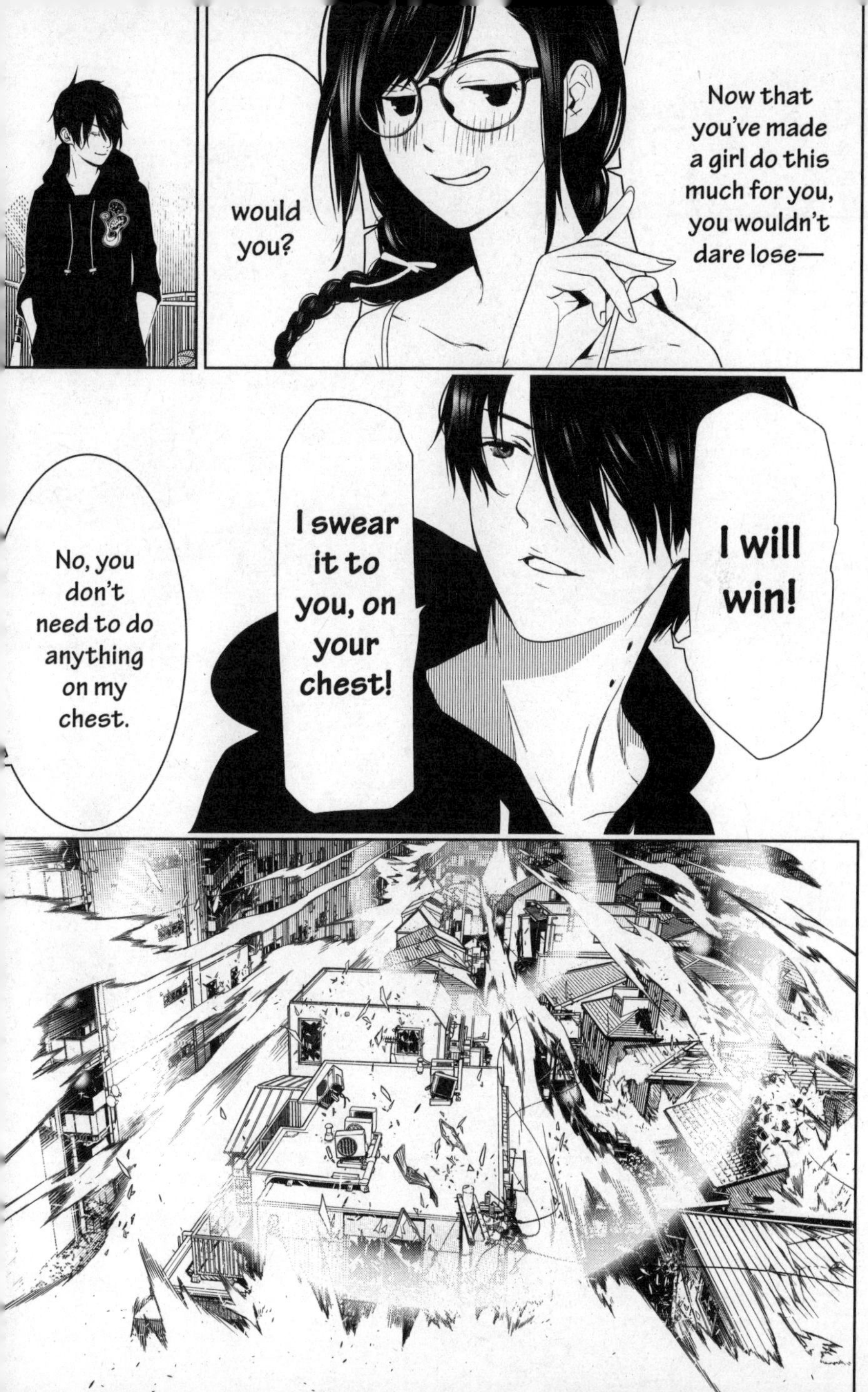
Now that you've made a girl do this much for you, you wouldn't dare lose—
would you?
I will win!
I swear it to you, on your chest!
No, you don't need to do anything on my chest.

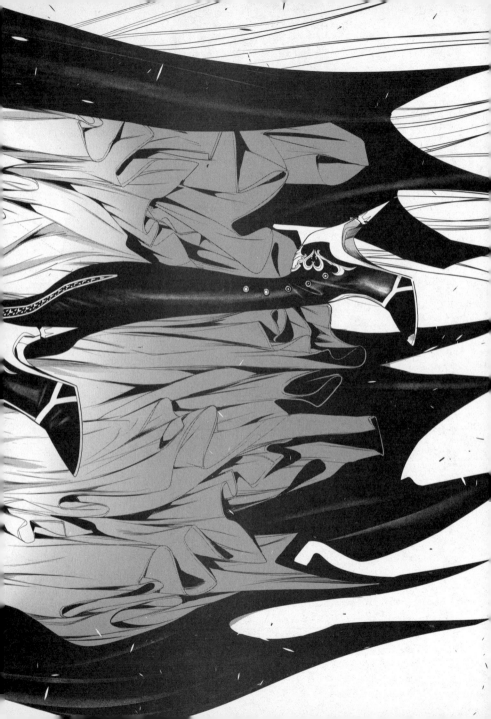

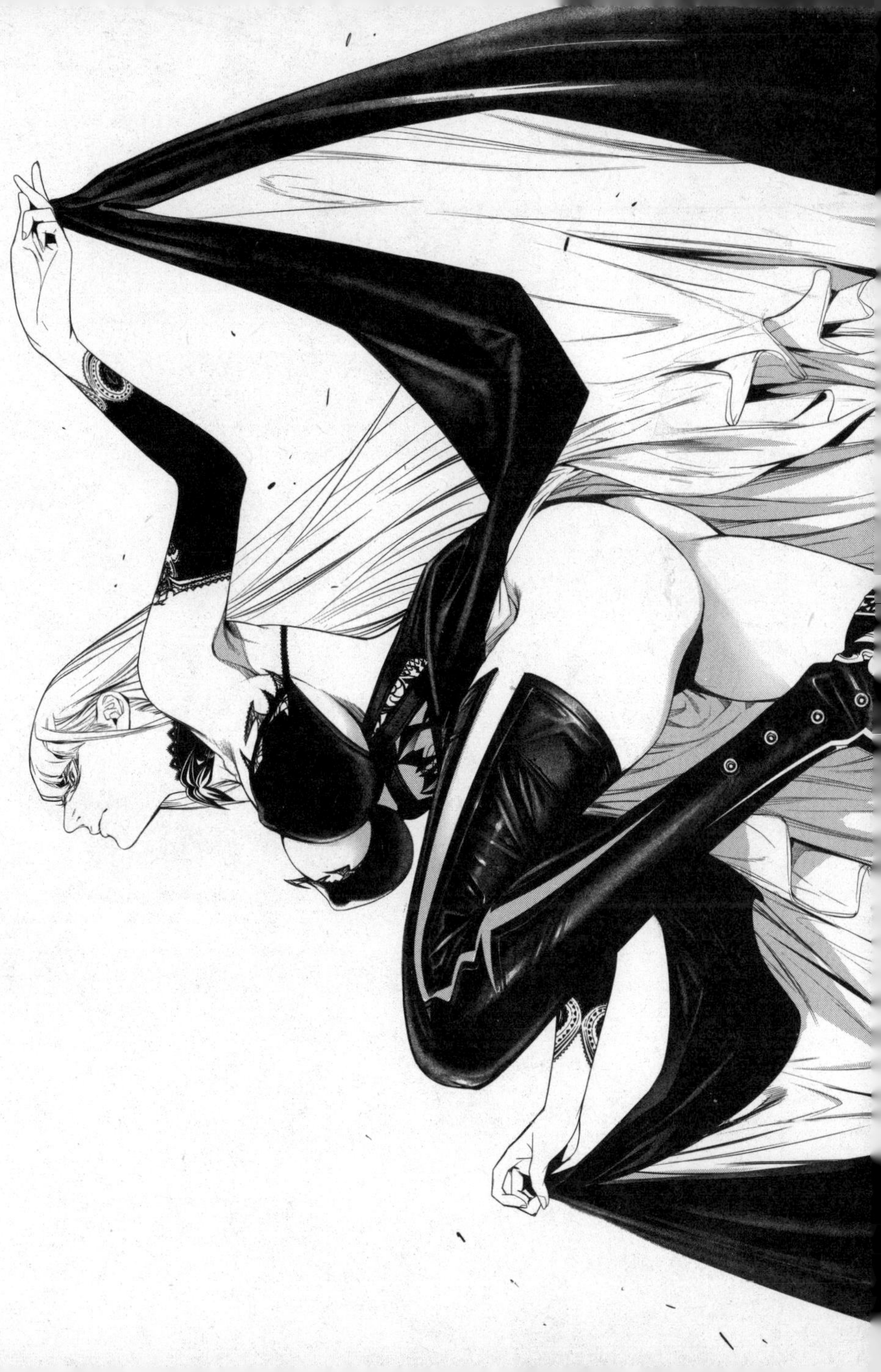

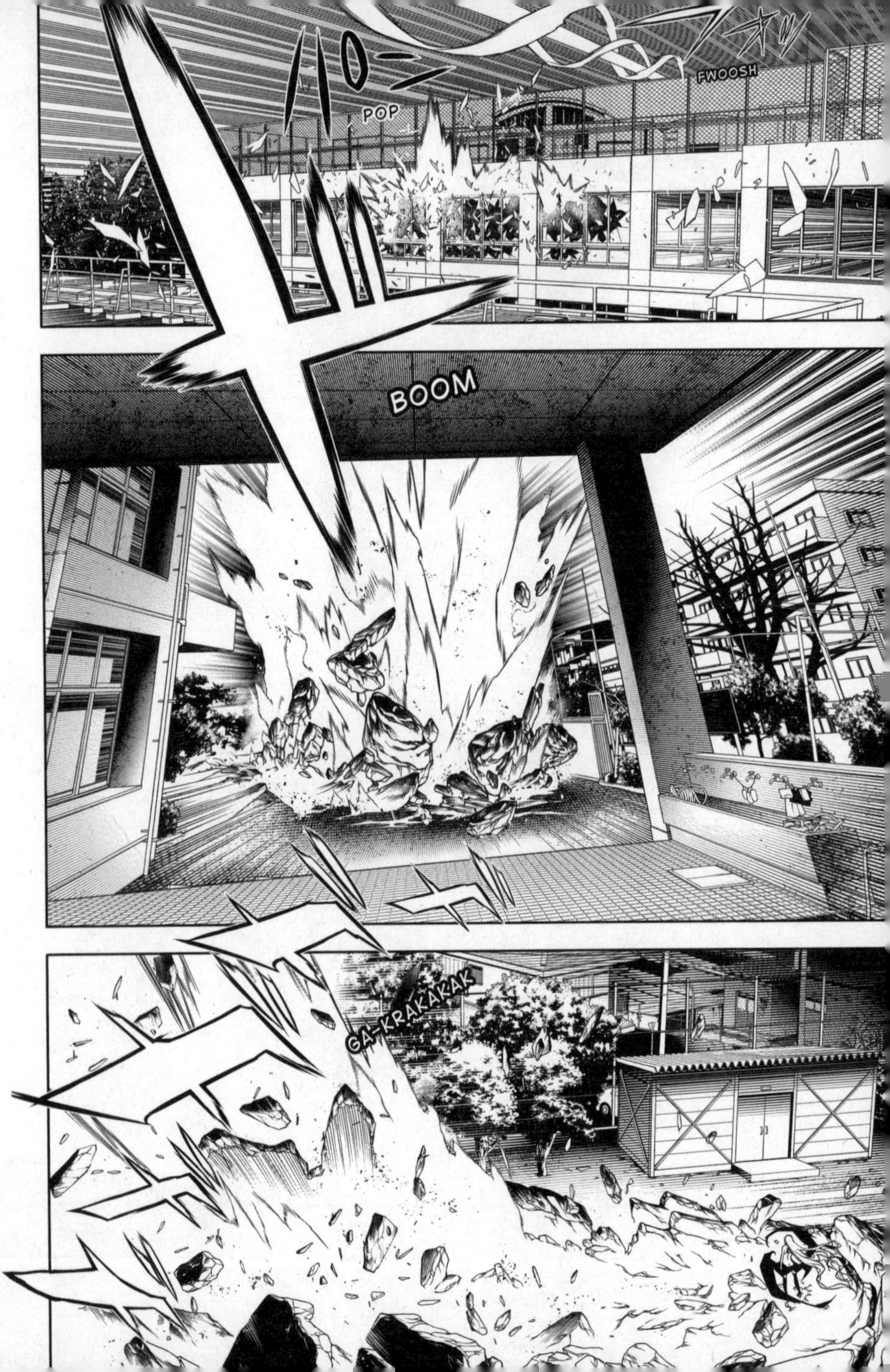
FWOOSH
POP
BOOM
GA-KRAKAKAK

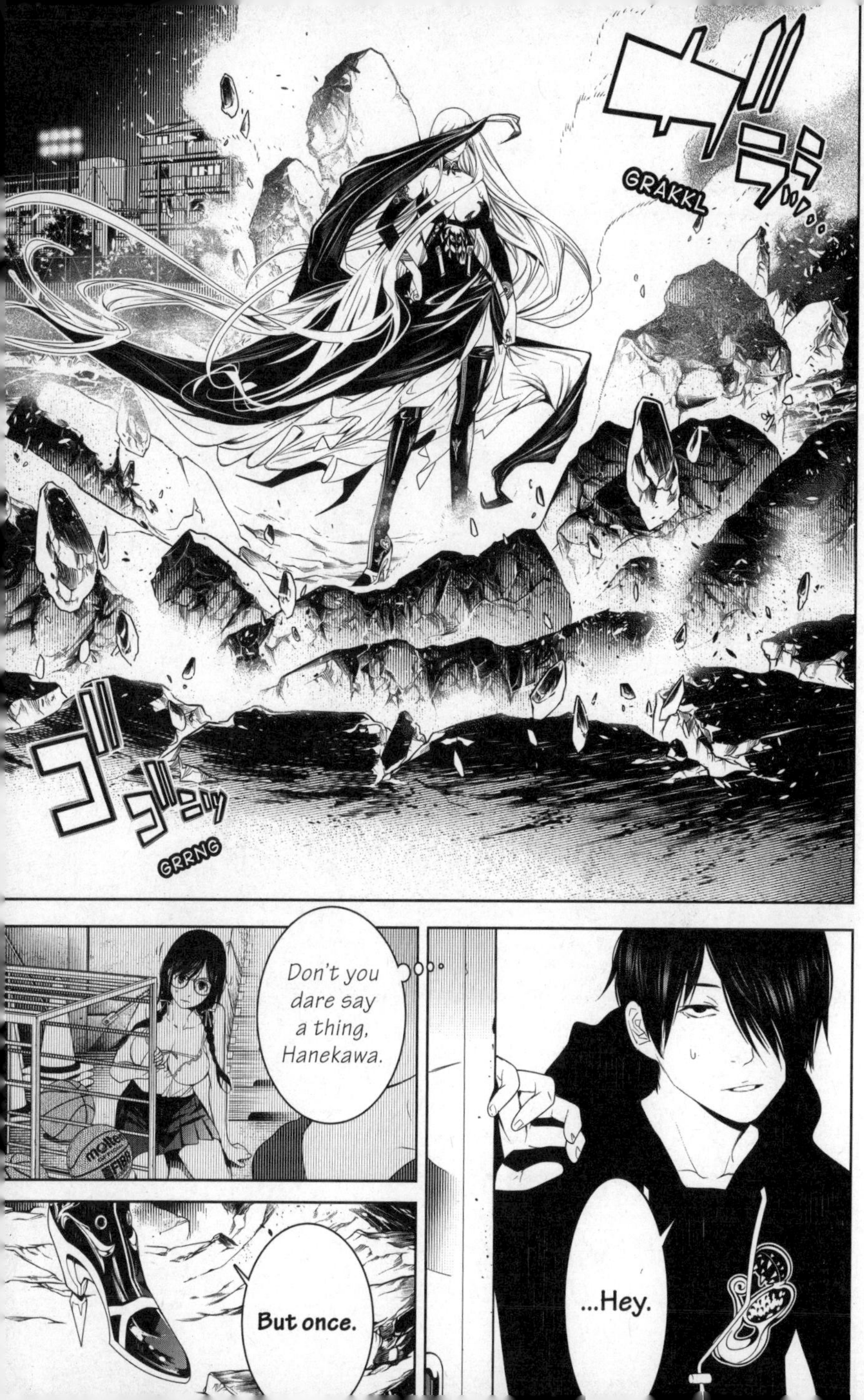
GRAKKL
GRRNG
...Hey.
Don't you dare say a thing, Hanekawa.
But once.

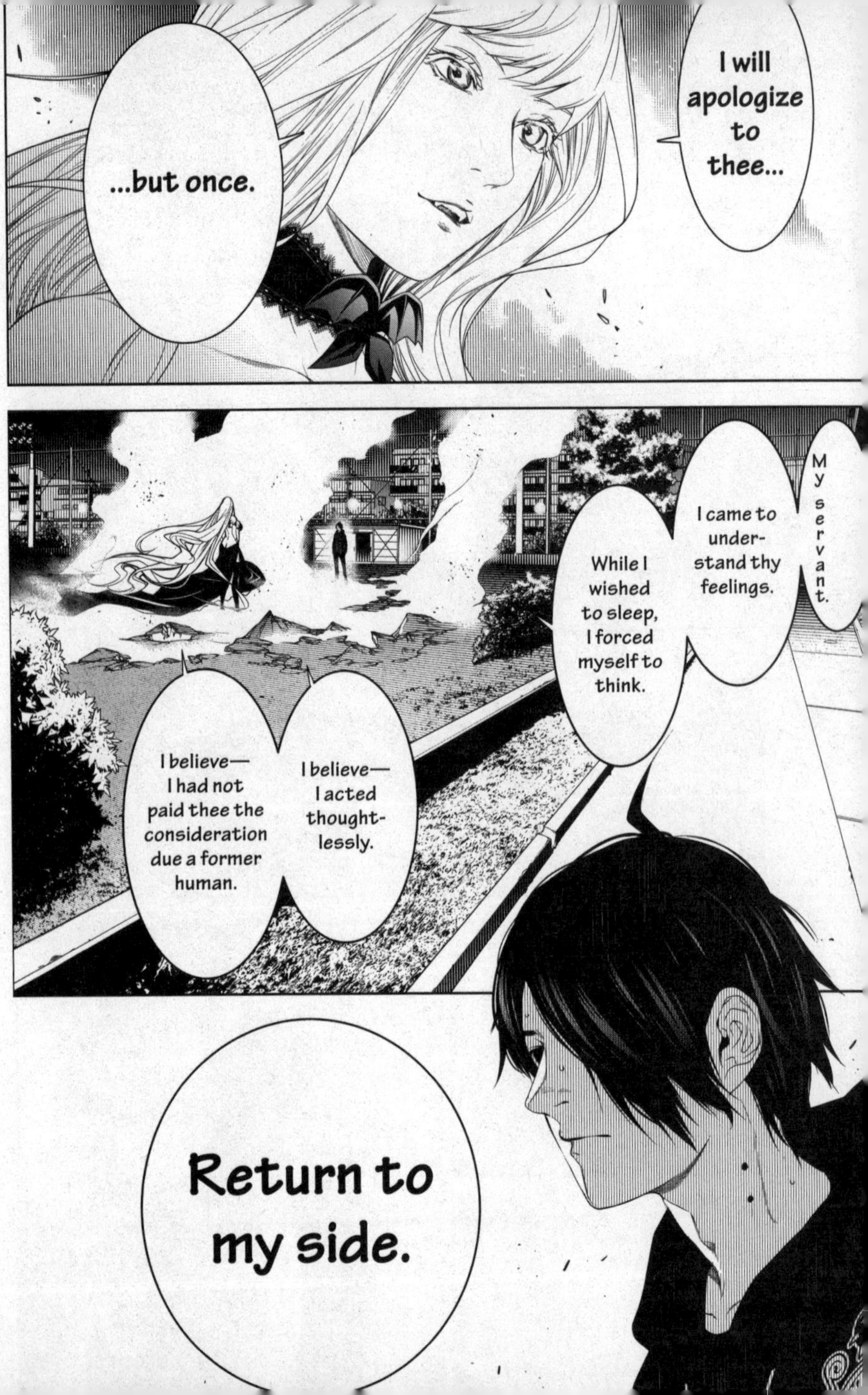
I will apologize to thee...
...but once.
My servant.
I came to under-stand thy feelings.
While I wished to sleep, I forced myself to think.
I believe— I acted thought-lessly.
I believe— I had not paid thee the consideration due a former human.
Return to my side.

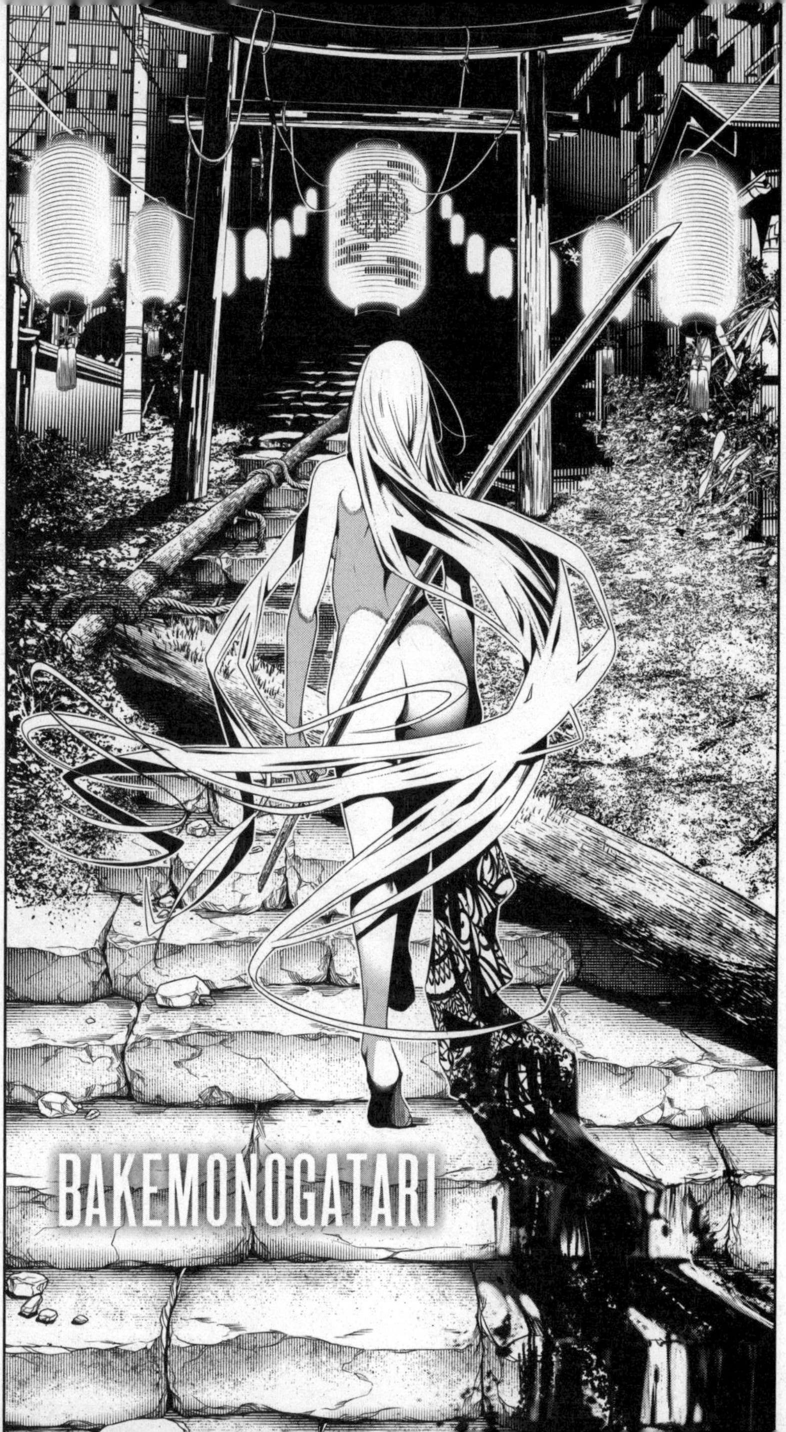
BAKEMONOGATARI

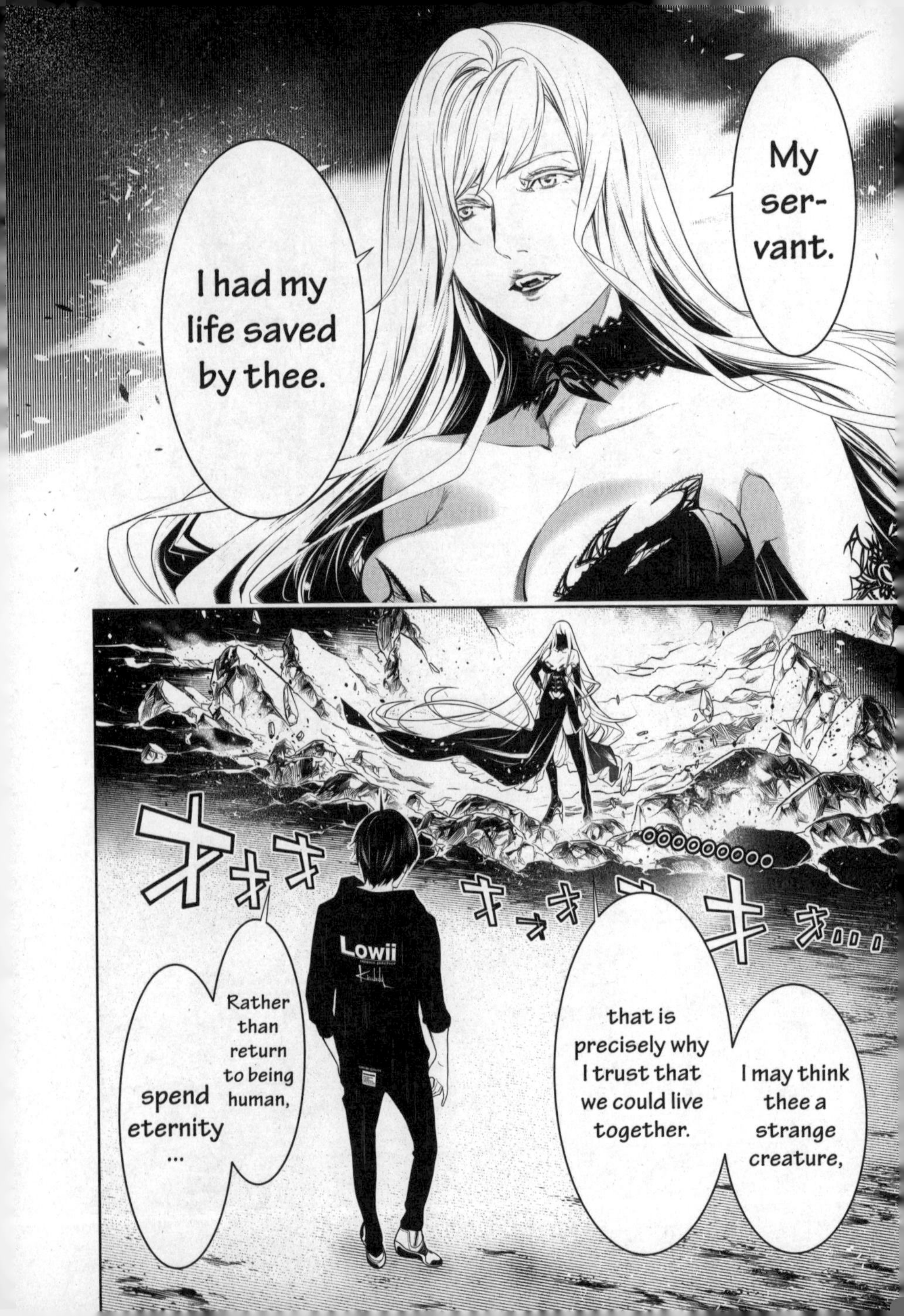
My ser-vant.
I had my life saved by thee.
I may think thee a strange creature,
that is precisely why I trust that we could live together.
Rather than return to being human,
spend eternity ...

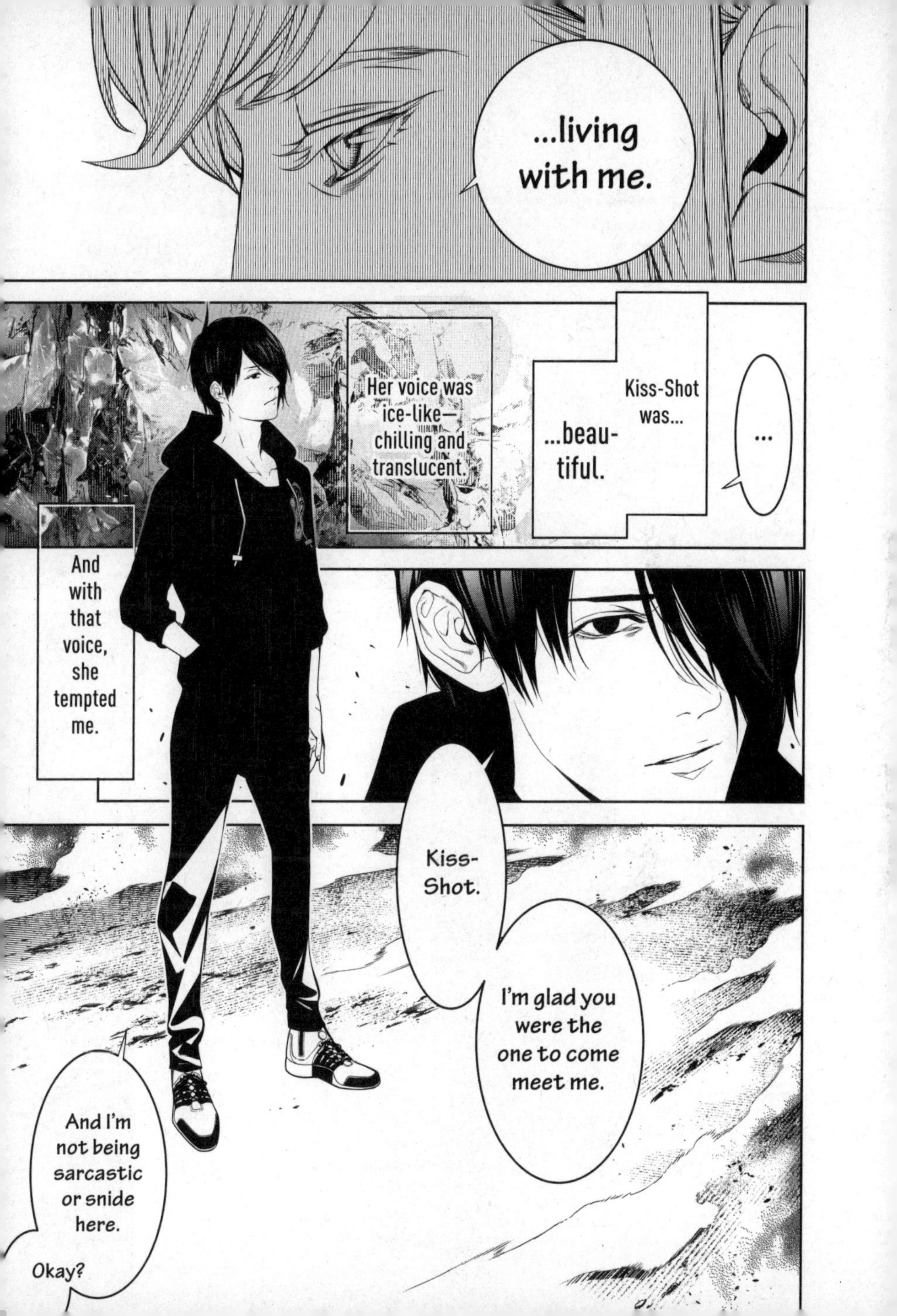
...living with me.
...
Kiss-Shot was...
...beau-tiful.
Her voice was ice-like—chilling and translucent.
And with that voice, she tempted me.
Kiss-Shot.
I'm glad you were the one to come meet me.
And I'm not being sarcastic or snide here.
Okay?

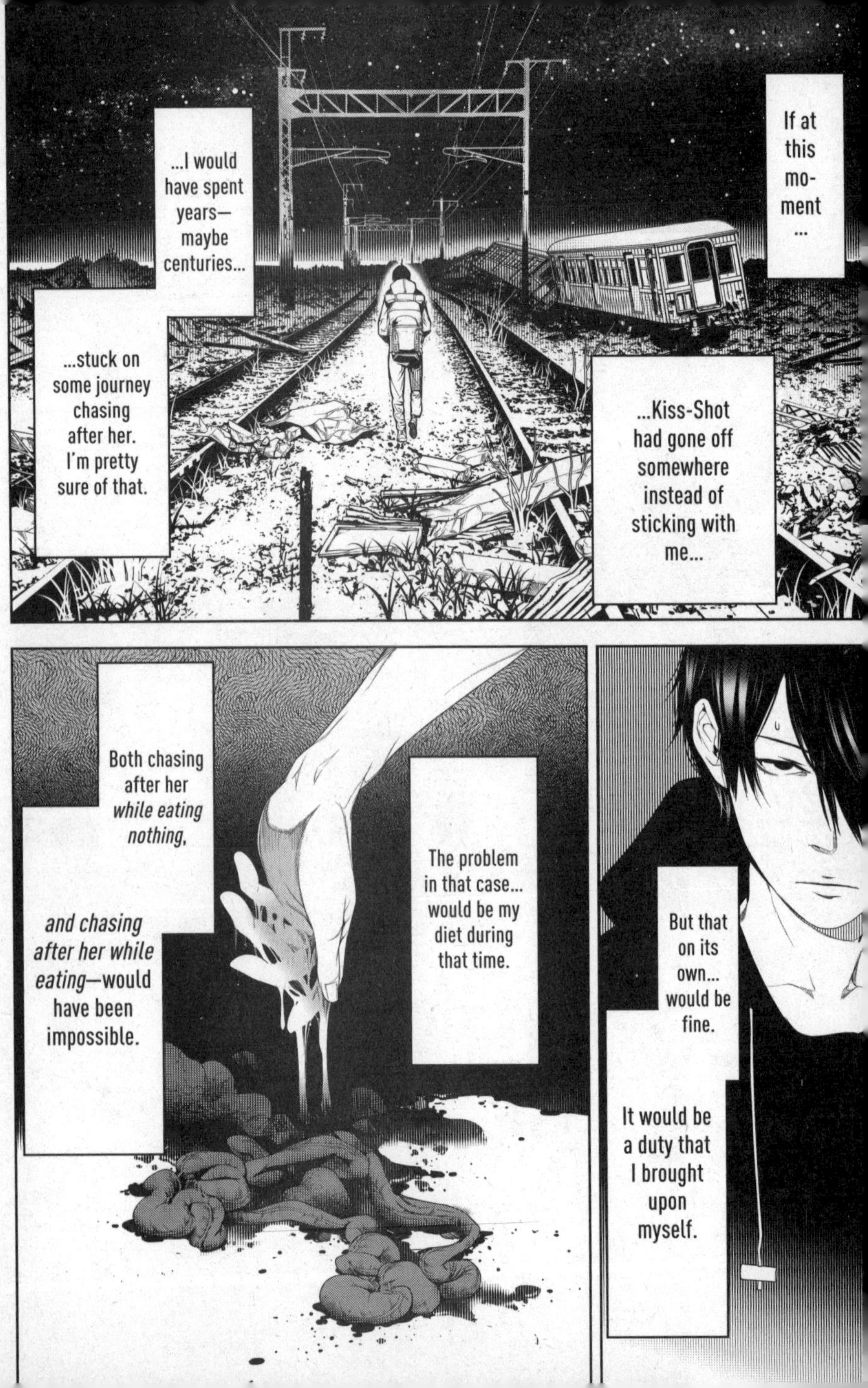
If at this moment...
...Kiss-Shot had gone off somewhere instead of sticking with me...
...I would have spent years—maybe centuries...
...stuck on some journey chasing after her. I'm pretty sure of that.
But that on its own... would be fine.
It would be a duty that I brought upon myself.
The problem in that case... would be my diet during that time.
Both chasing after her *while eating nothing*,
and chasing after her while eating—would have been impossible.

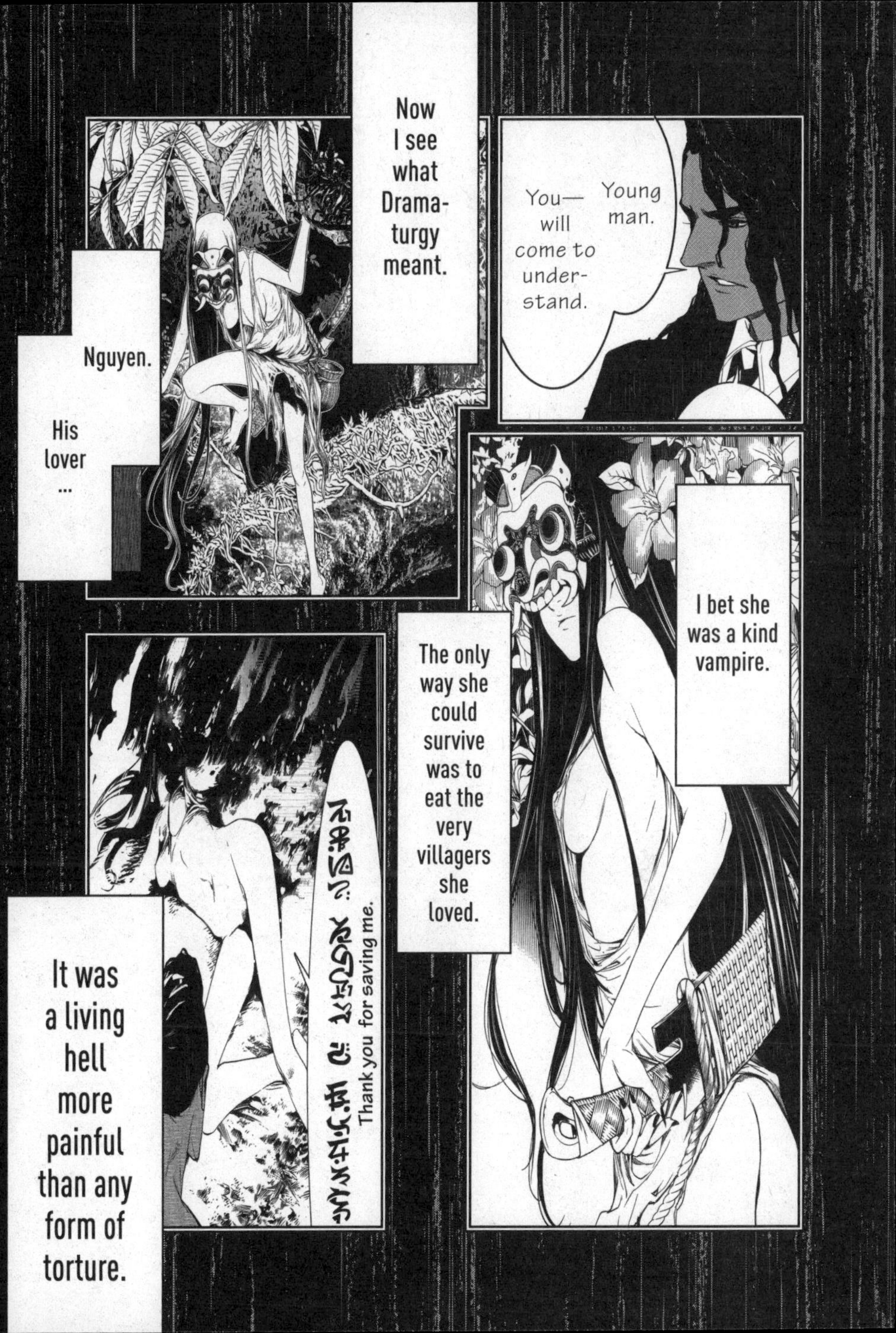
Young man.
You— will come to understand.
Now I see what Dramaturgy meant.
Nguyen.
His lover ...
I bet she was a kind vampire.
The only way she could survive was to eat the very villagers she loved.
Thank you for saving me.
It was a living hell more painful than any form of torture.

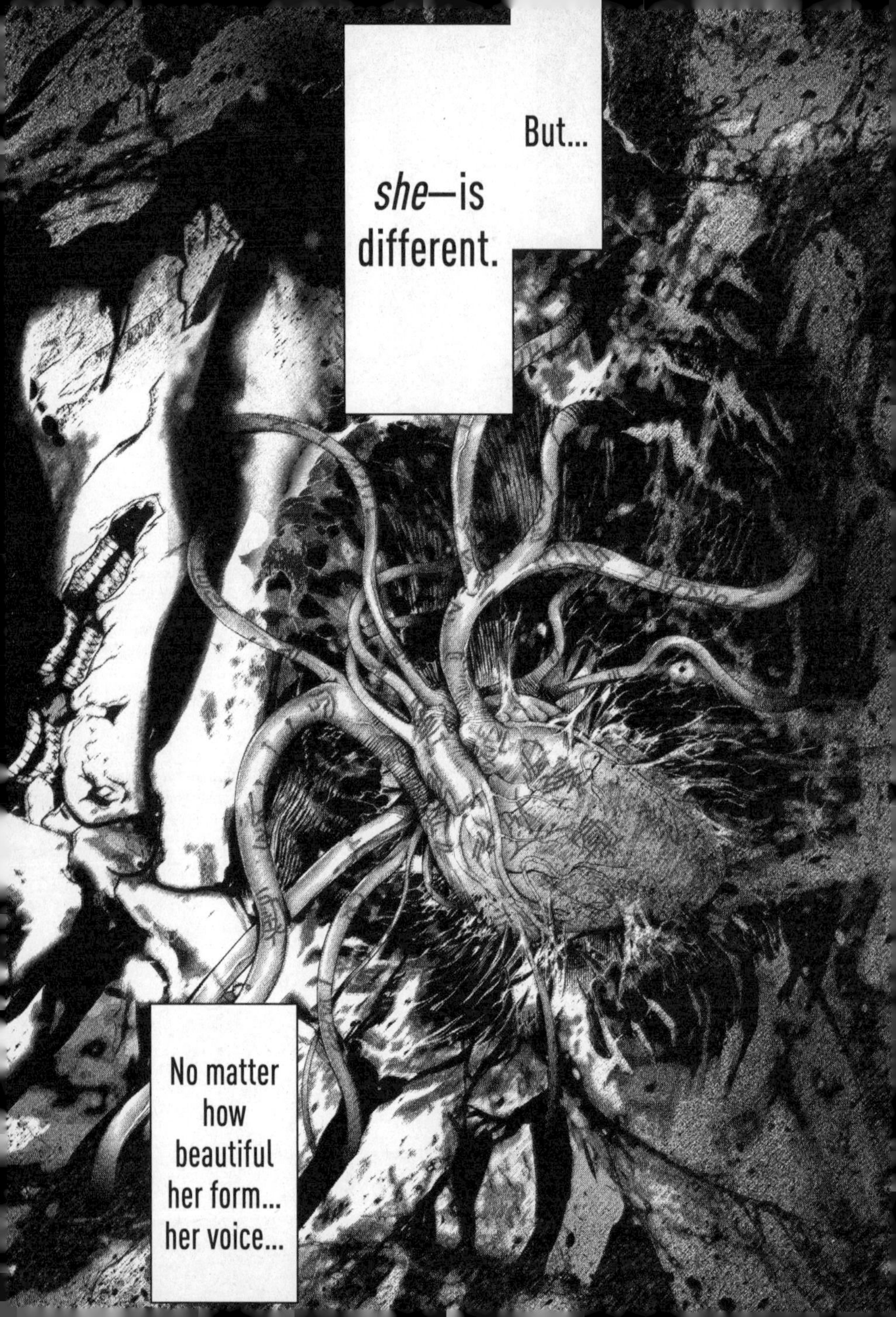
But...
she—is different.
No matter how beautiful her form... her voice...

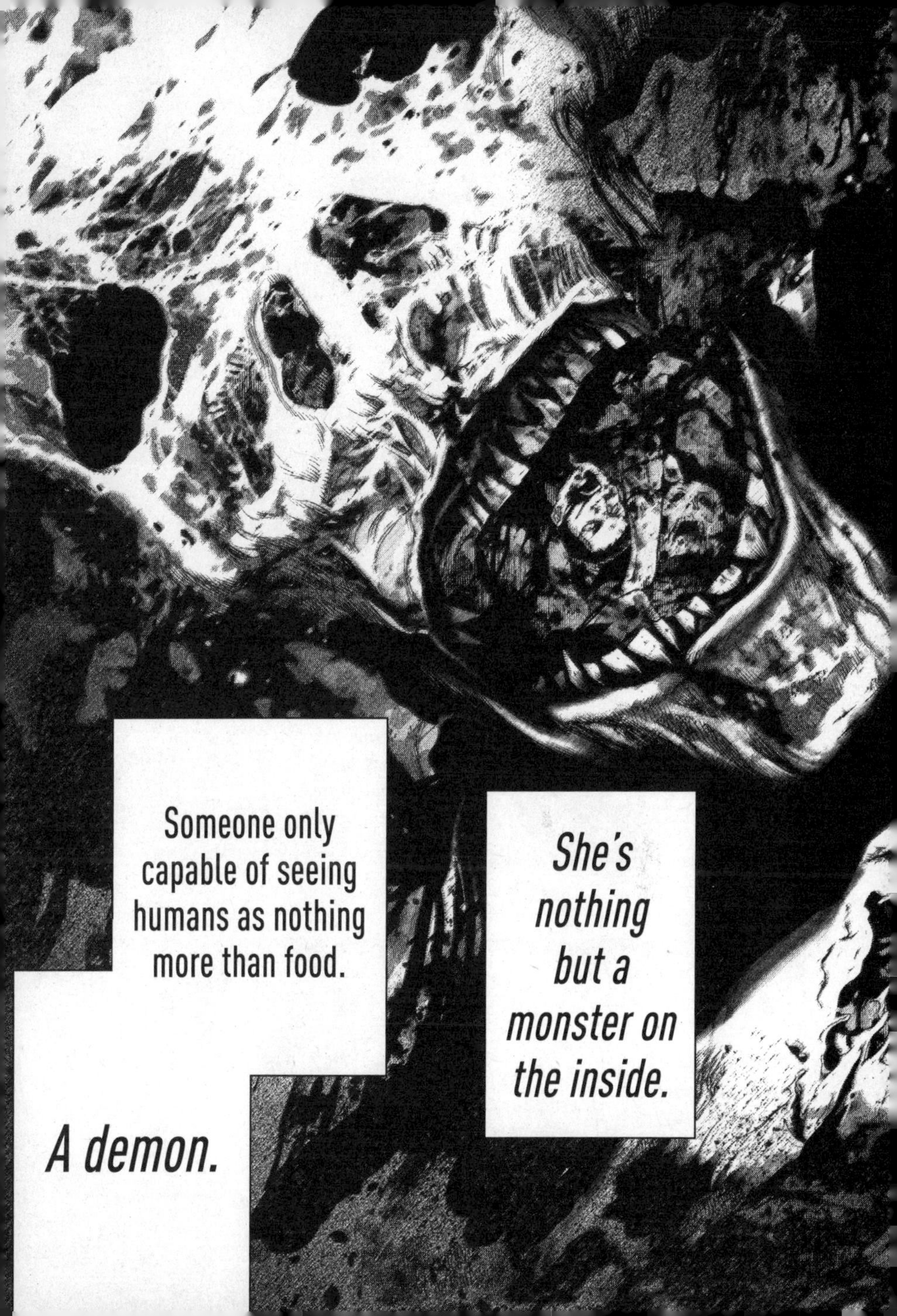
She's nothing but a monster on the inside.
Someone only capable of seeing humans as nothing more than food.
A demon.

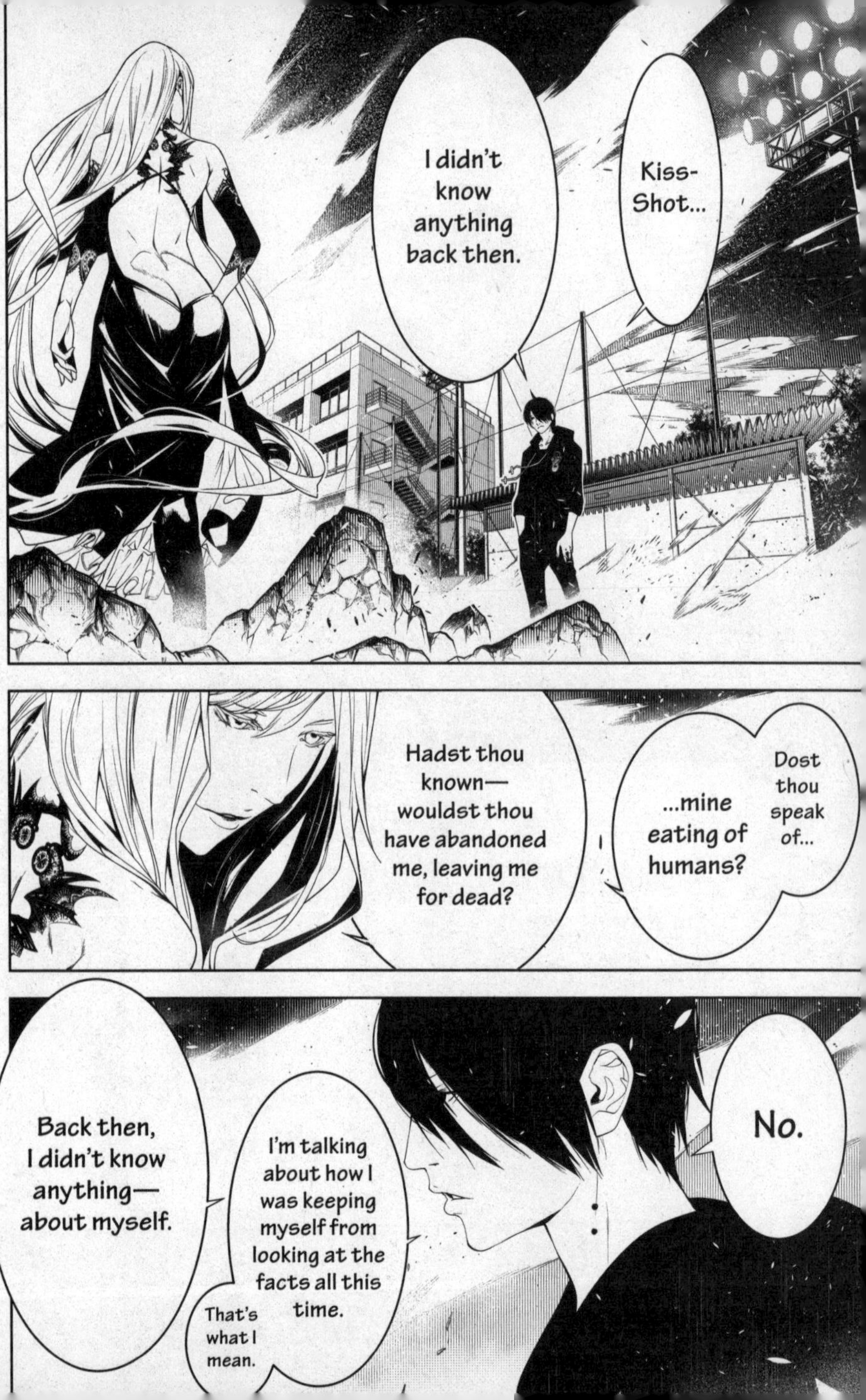
Kiss-Shot...
I didn't know anything back then.
Dost thou speak of...
...mine eating of humans?
Hadst thou known—wouldst thou have abandoned me, leaving me for dead?
No.
I'm talking about how I was keeping myself from looking at the facts all this time.
That's what I mean.
Back then, I didn't know anything—about myself.

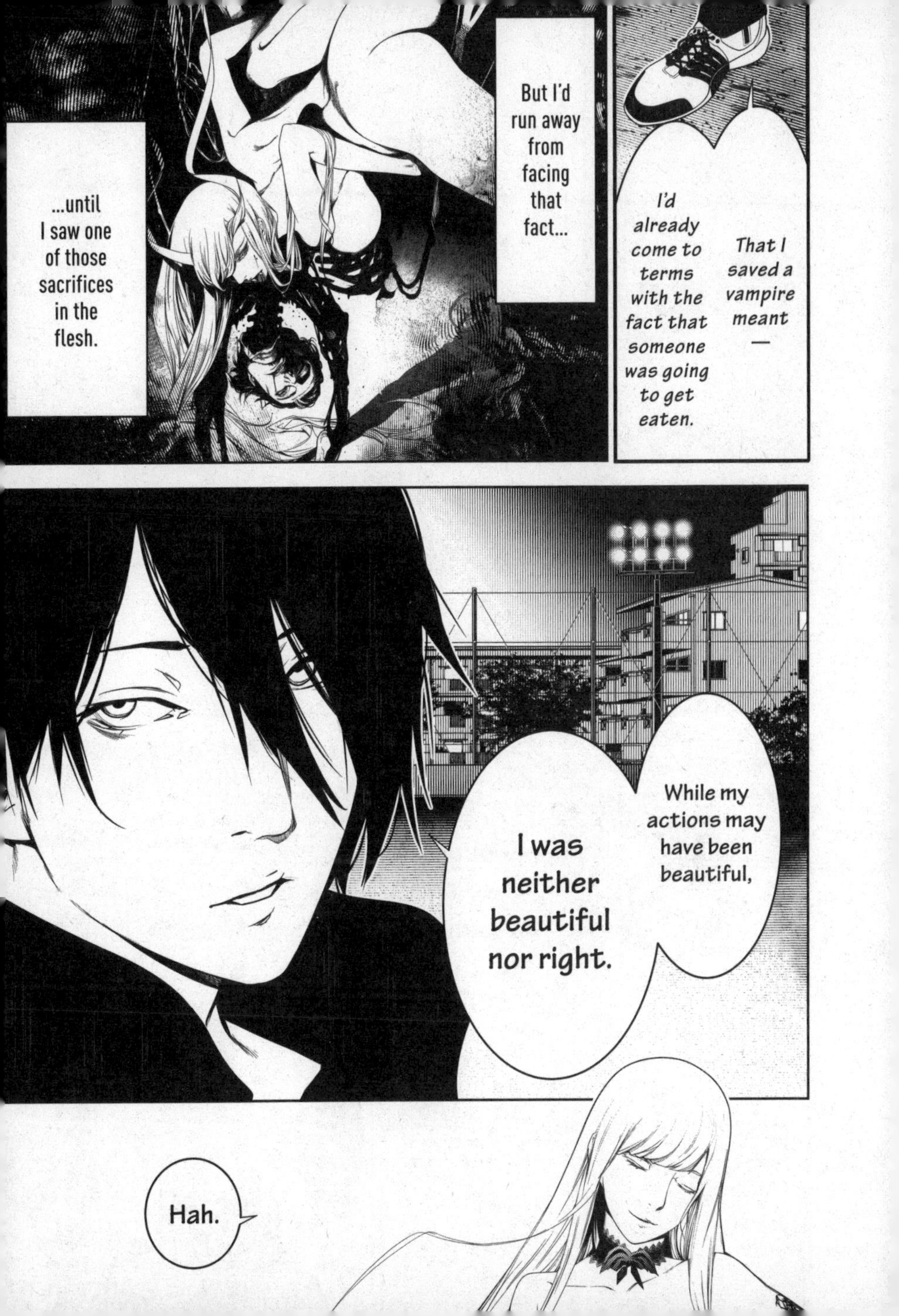
That I saved a vampire meant—
I'd already come to terms with the fact that someone was going to get eaten.
But I'd run away from facing that fact...
...until I saw one of those sacrifices in the flesh.
While my actions may have been beautiful,
I was neither beautiful nor right.
Hah.

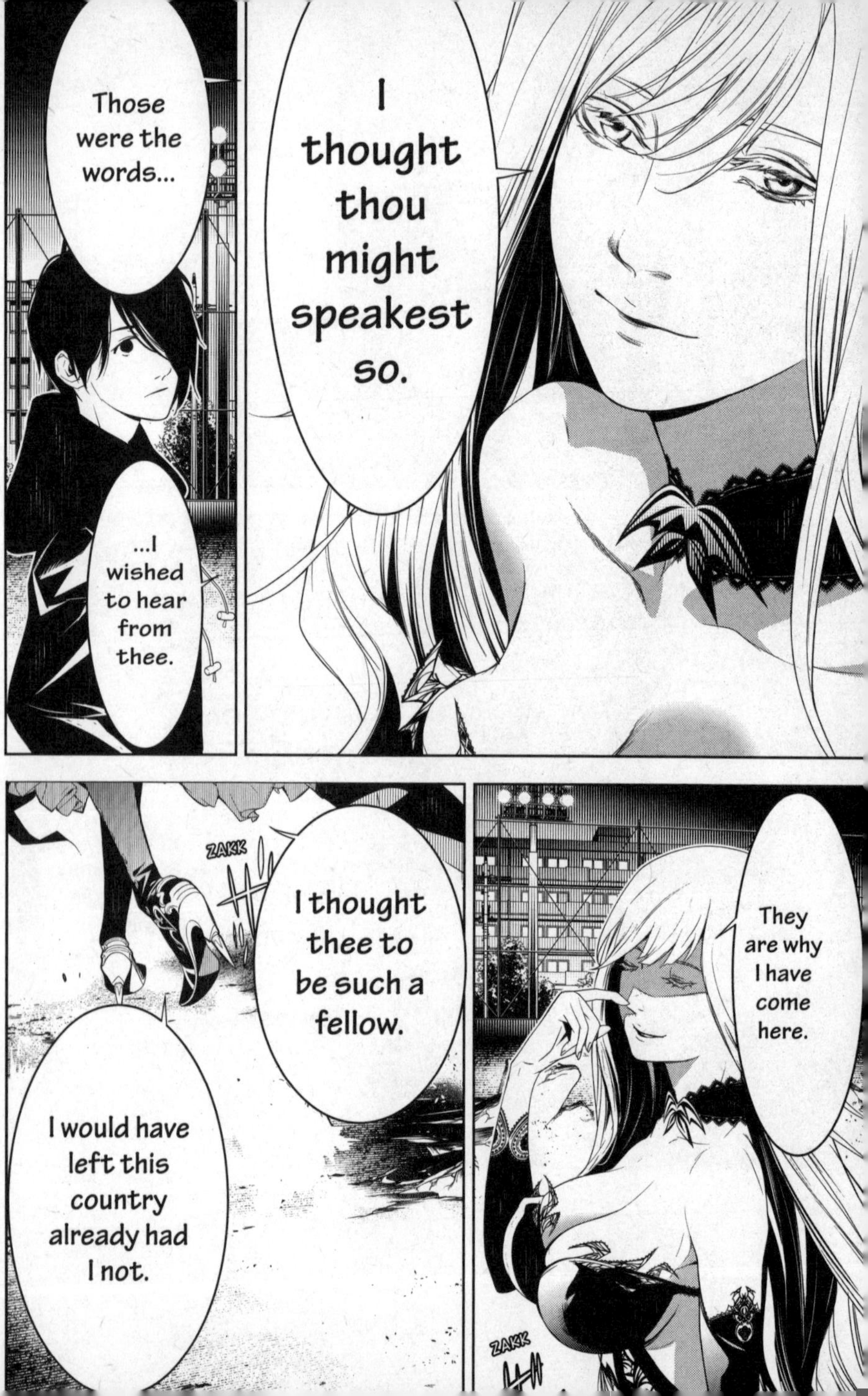
I thought thou might speakest so.
Those were the words...
...I wished to hear from thee.
They are why I have come here.
ZAKK
ZAKK
I thought thee to be such a fellow.
I would have left this country already had I not.

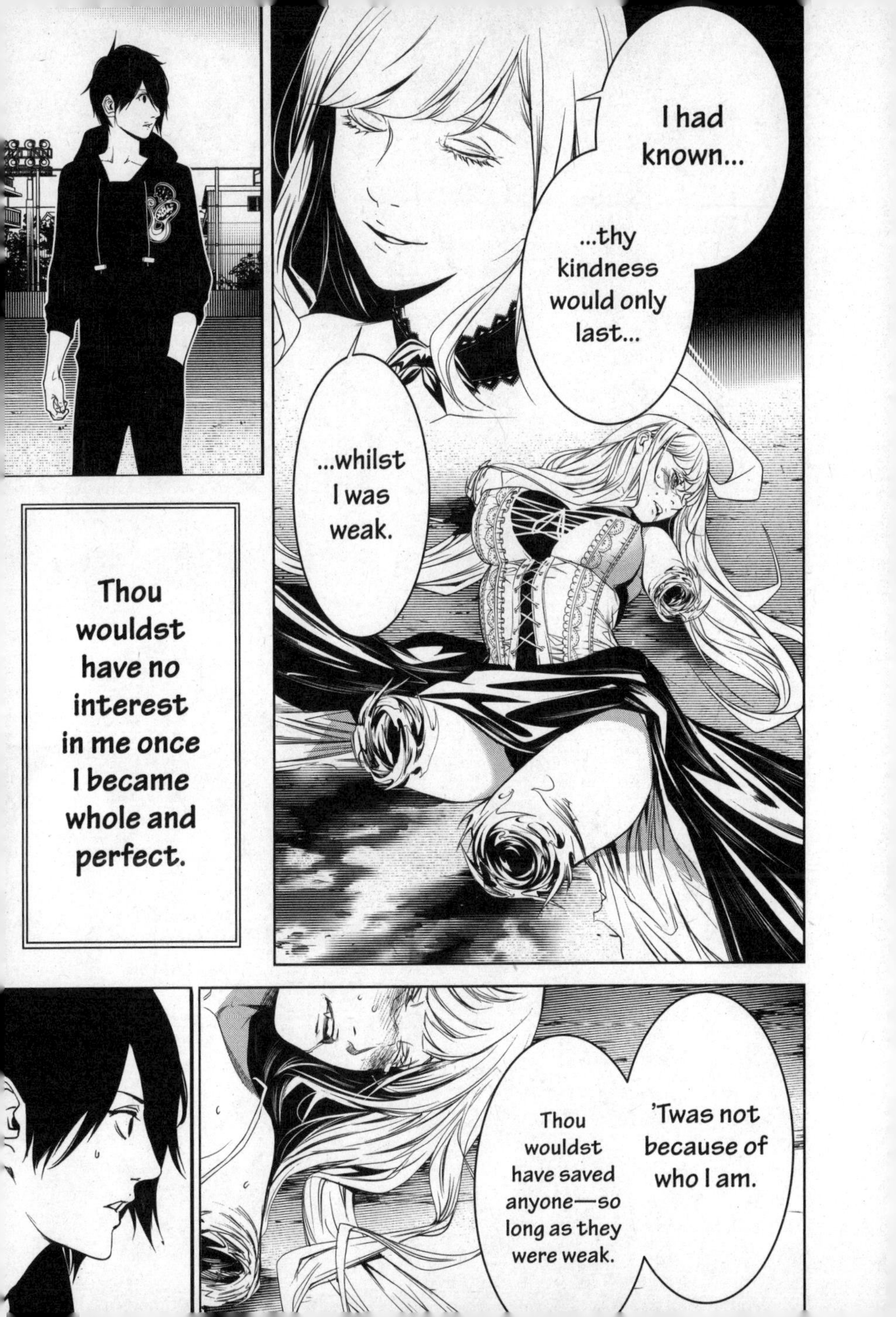
I had known...
...thy kindness would only last...
...whilst I was weak.
Thou wouldst have no interest in me once I became whole and perfect.
'Twas not because of who I am.
Thou wouldst have saved anyone—so long as they were weak.

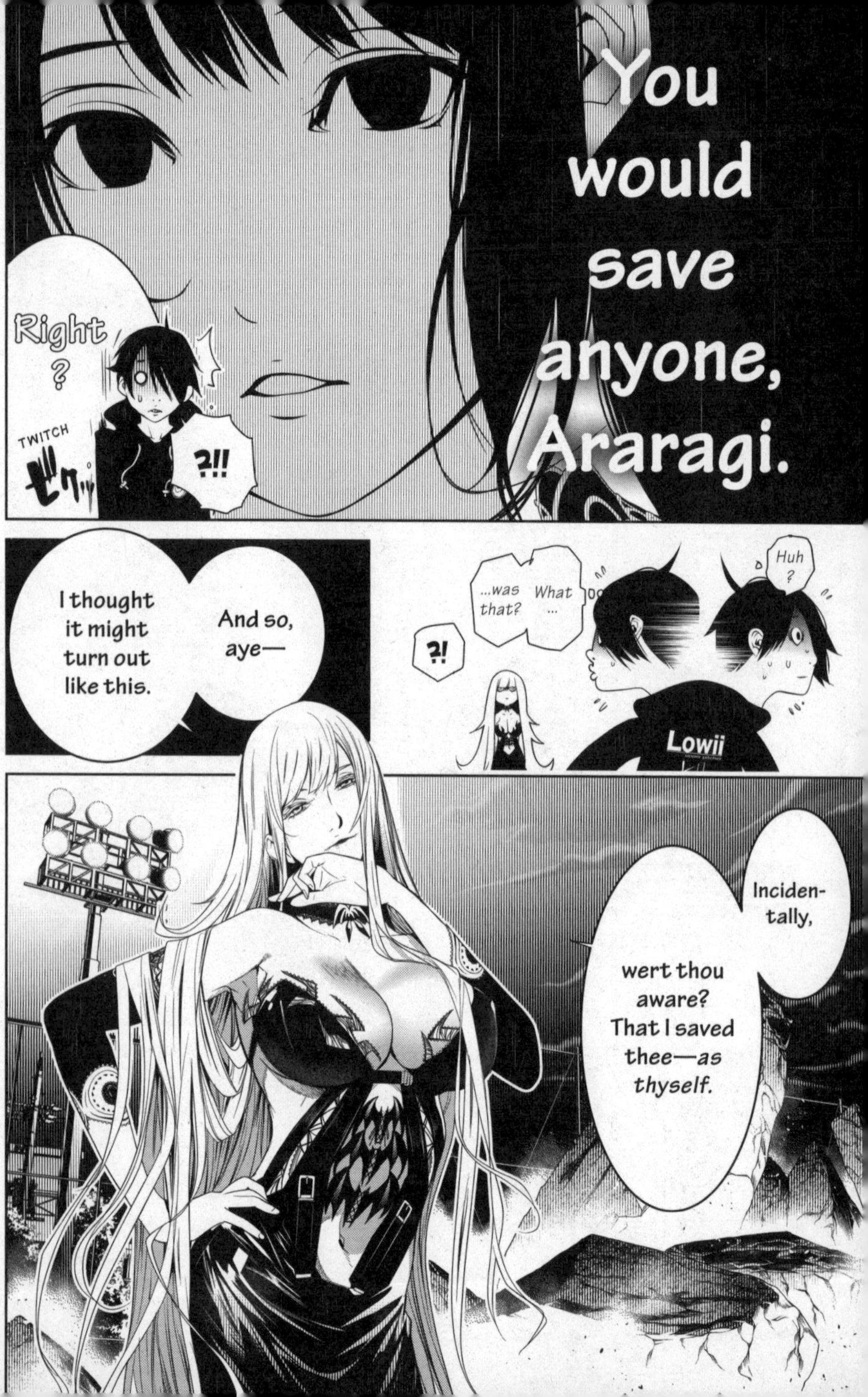
You would save anyone, Araragi.
Right?
TWITCH
ビクッ
?!!
Huh?
What... ...was that?
?!
Lowii
And so, aye—
I thought it might turn out like this.
Incidentally,
wert thou aware? That I saved thee—as thyself.

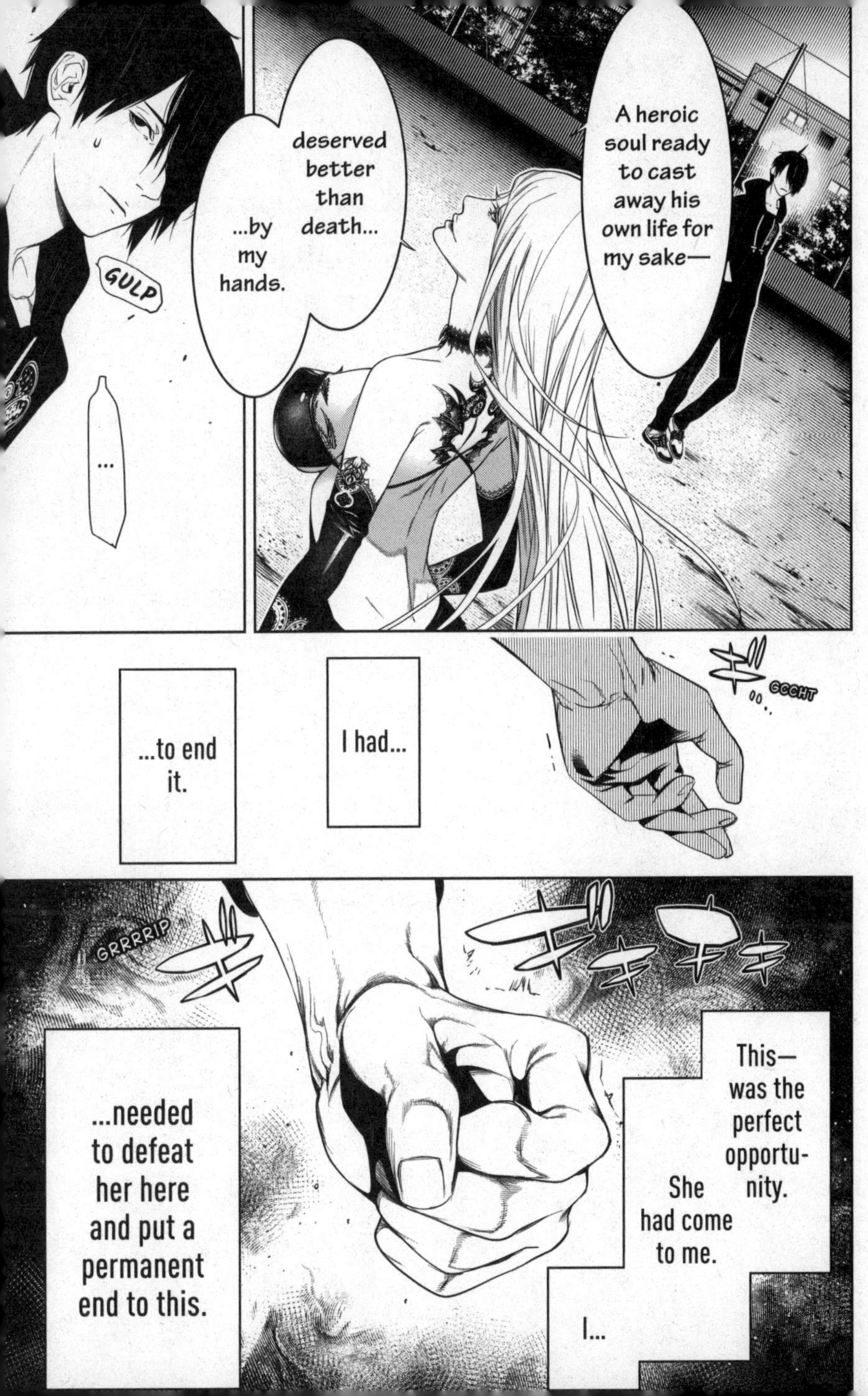
A heroic soul ready to cast away his own life for my sake—
deserved better than death...
...by my hands.
GULP
...
GGCHT
I had...
...to end it.
This— was the perfect opportunity.
She had come to me.
I...
GRRRRIP
...needed to defeat her here and put a permanent end to this.

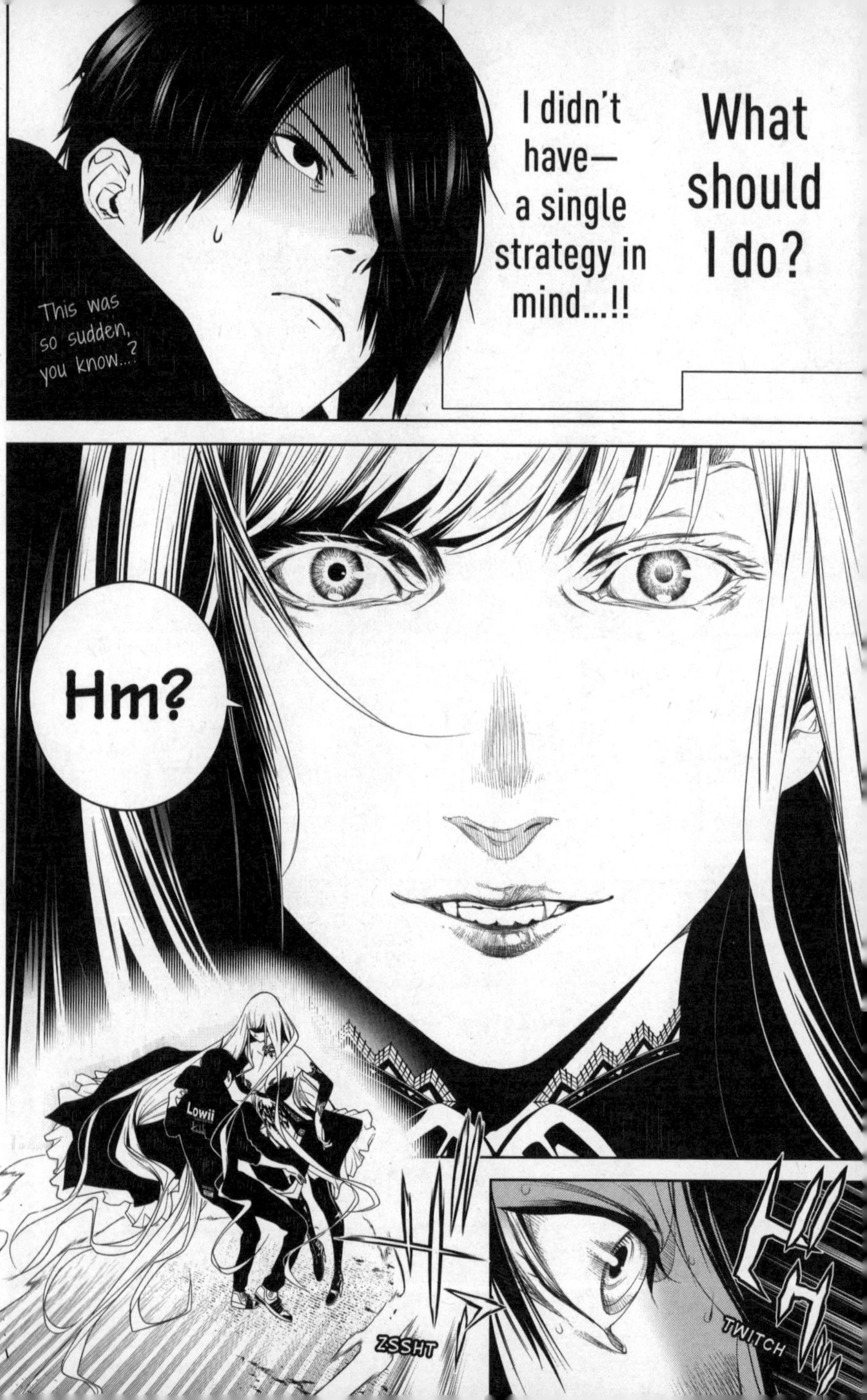
What should I do?
I didn't have— a single strategy in mind...!!
This was so sudden, you know...?
Hm?
TWITCH
ZSSHT

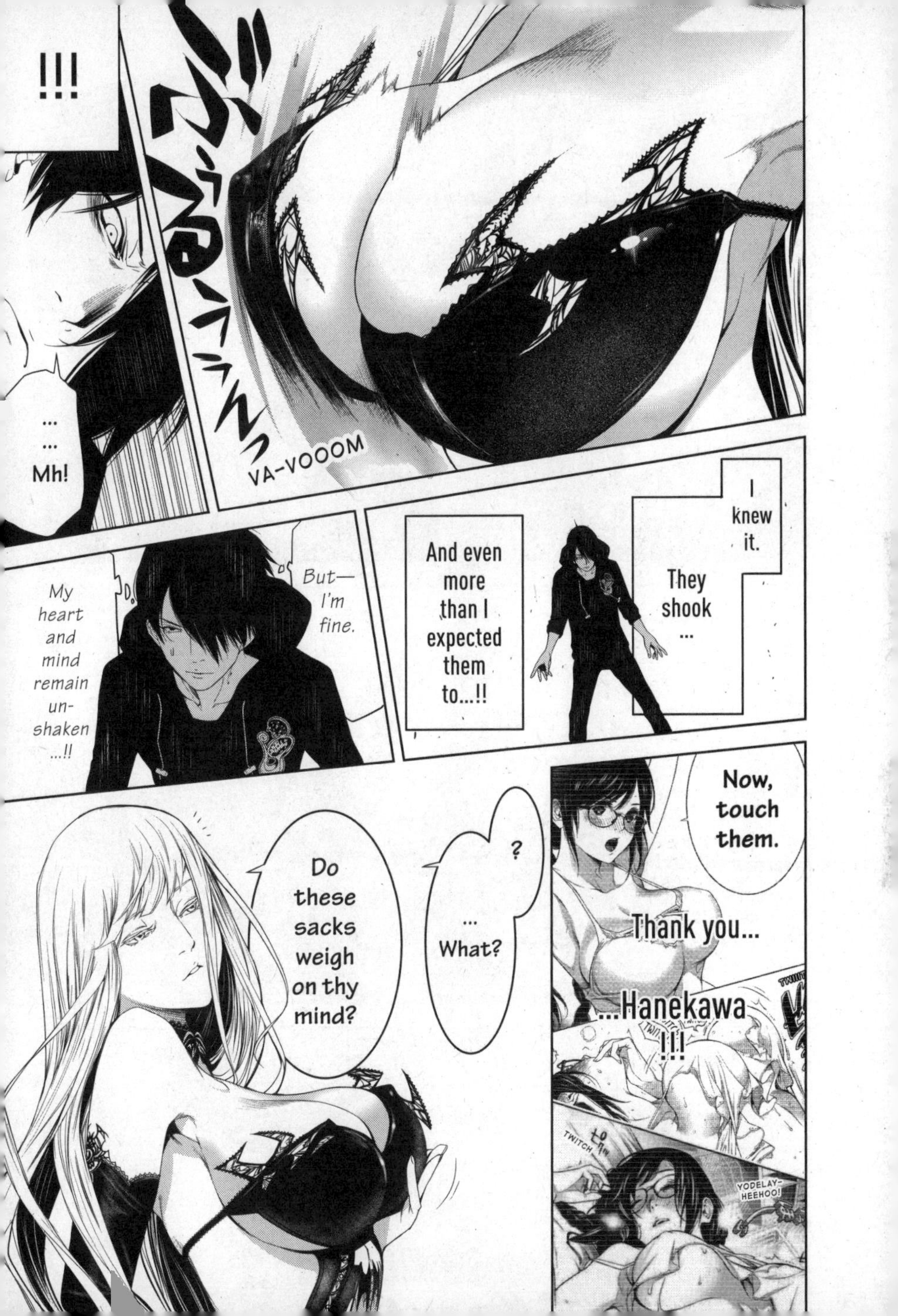
VA-VOOOM
!!!
... ... Mh!
I knew it.
They shook ...
And even more than I expected them to...!!
But— I'm fine.
My heart and mind remain un-shaken ...!!
Now, touch them.
Thank you...
...Hanekawa !!!
TWITCH
YODELAY-HEEHOO!
?
... What?
Do these sacks weigh on thy mind?

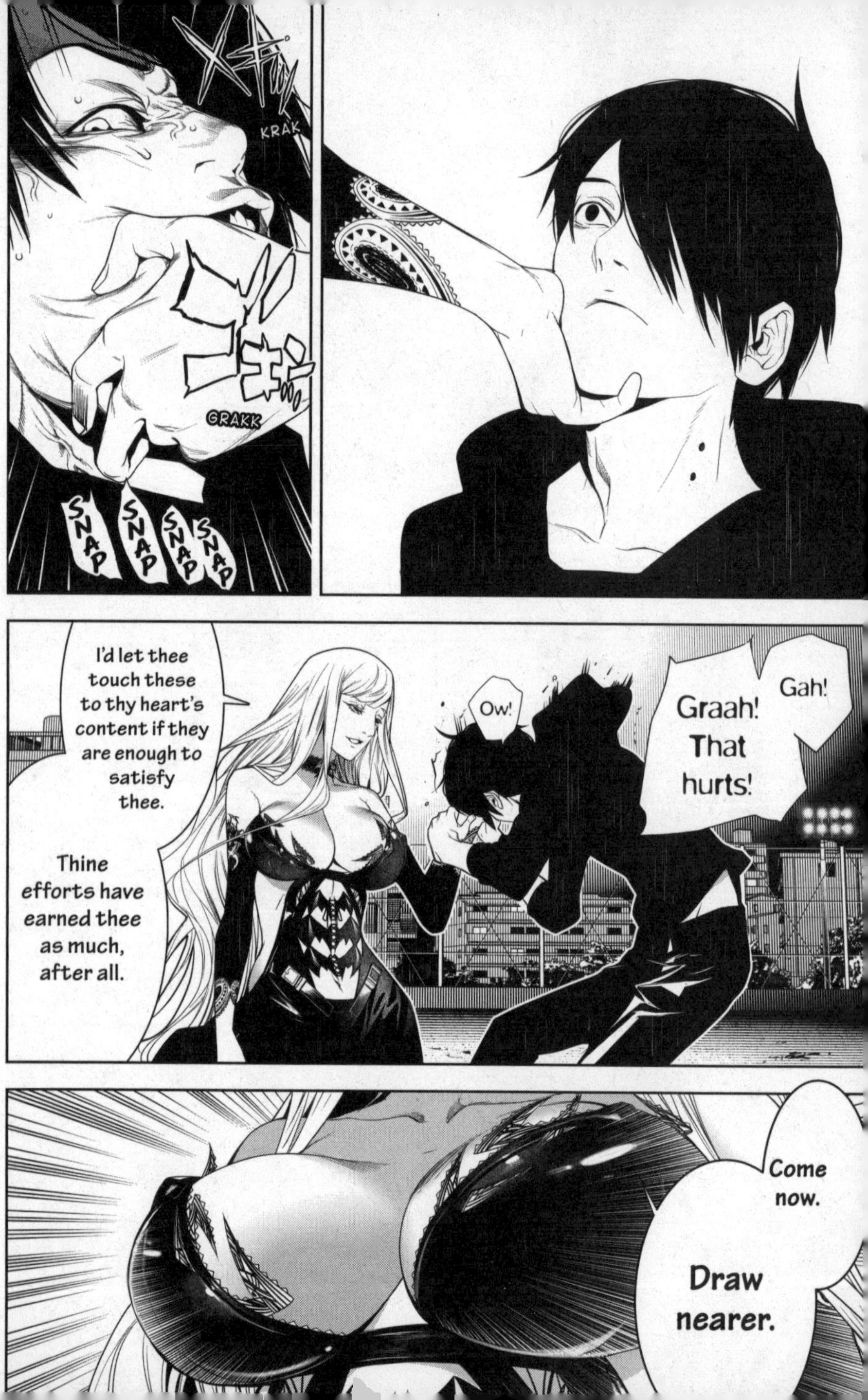
KRAK
GRAKK
SNAP
SNAP
SNAP
SNAP
Gah!
Graah! That hurts!
Ow!
I'd let thee touch these to thy heart's content if they are enough to satisfy thee.
Thine efforts have earned thee as much, after all.
Come now.
Draw nearer.

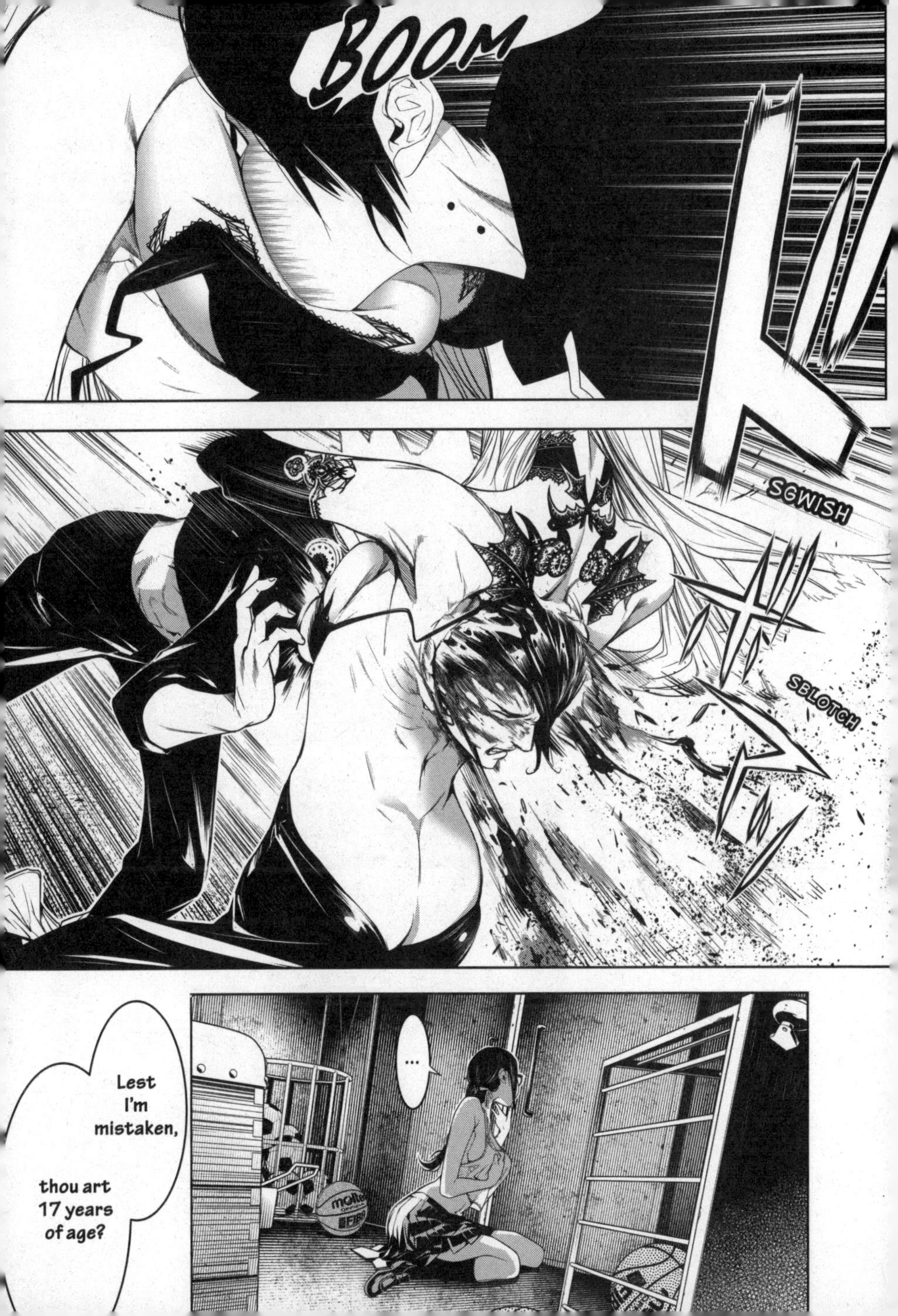
BOOM
SGWISH
SBLOTCH
...
Lest I'm mistaken,
thou art 17 years of age?

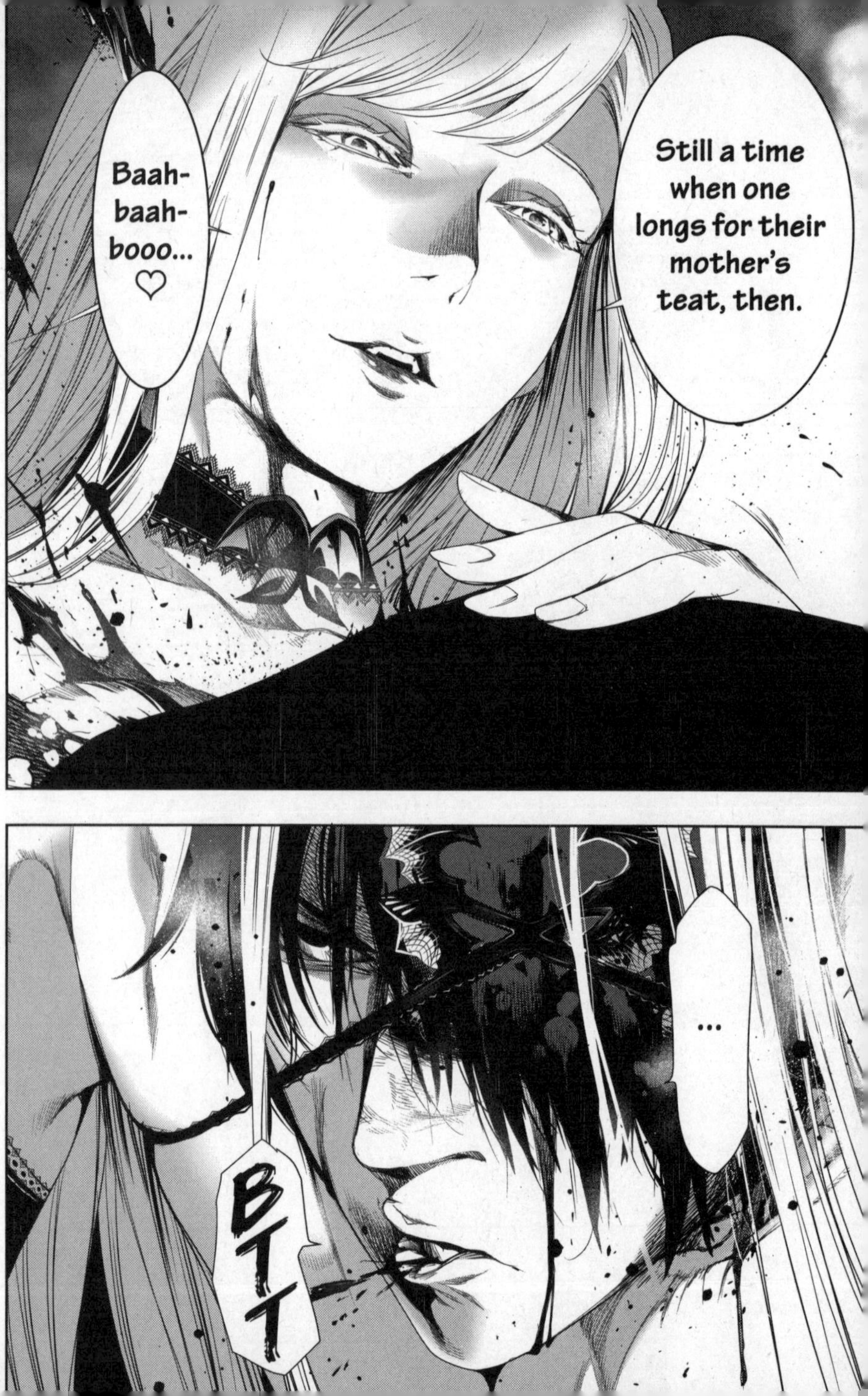
Still a time when one longs for their mother's teat, then.
Baah-baah-booo... ♡
...
BTT

[Puff-Puff]

1. A phrase representing the sound or appearance of being squeezed between soft objects.
2. The name of an ability or action that appears in games, particularly the *Dragon Quest* series.
3. A rewarding act given by women to men. [In the manga *Dragon Ball*, actions performed upon Master Roshi.]

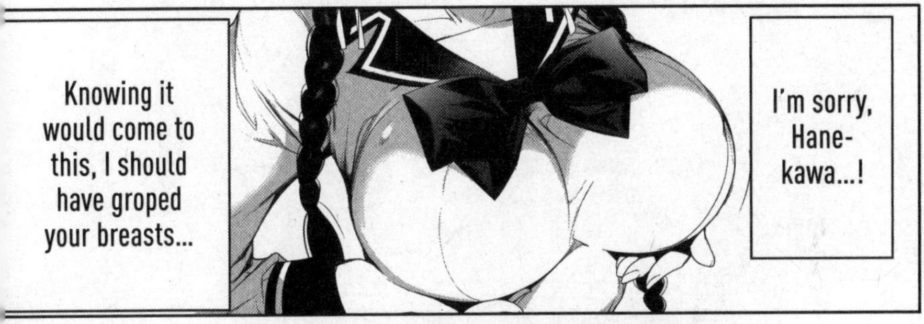

I'm sorry, Hane-kawa...!
Knowing it would come to this, I should have groped your breasts...

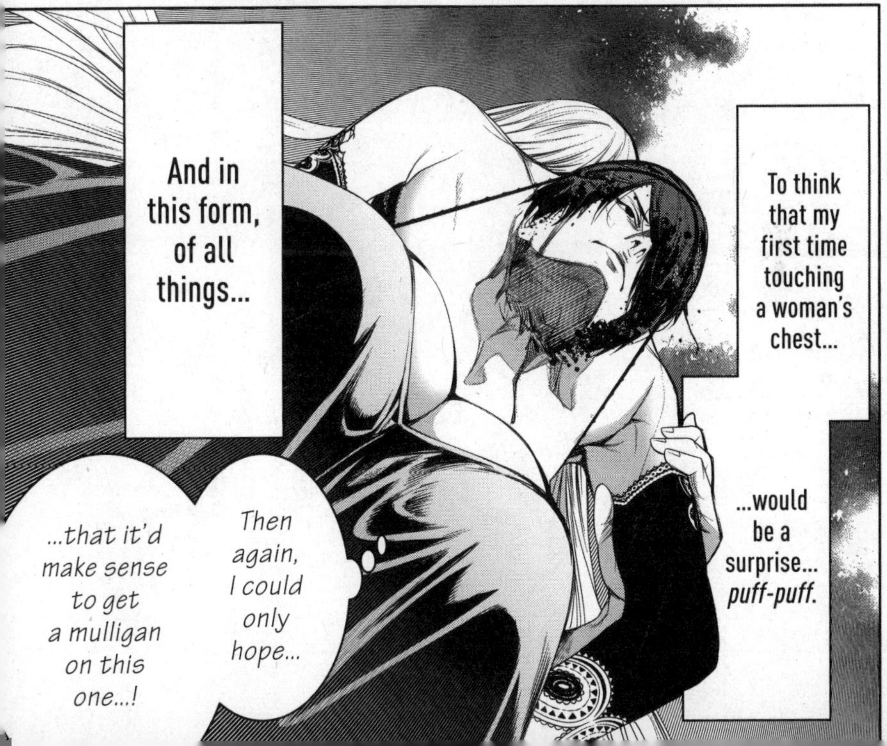

To think that my first time touching a woman's chest...
And in this form, of all things...
...would be a surprise... *puff-puff.*
Then again, I could only hope...
...that it'd make sense to get a mulligan on this one...!

BAKEMONOGATARI

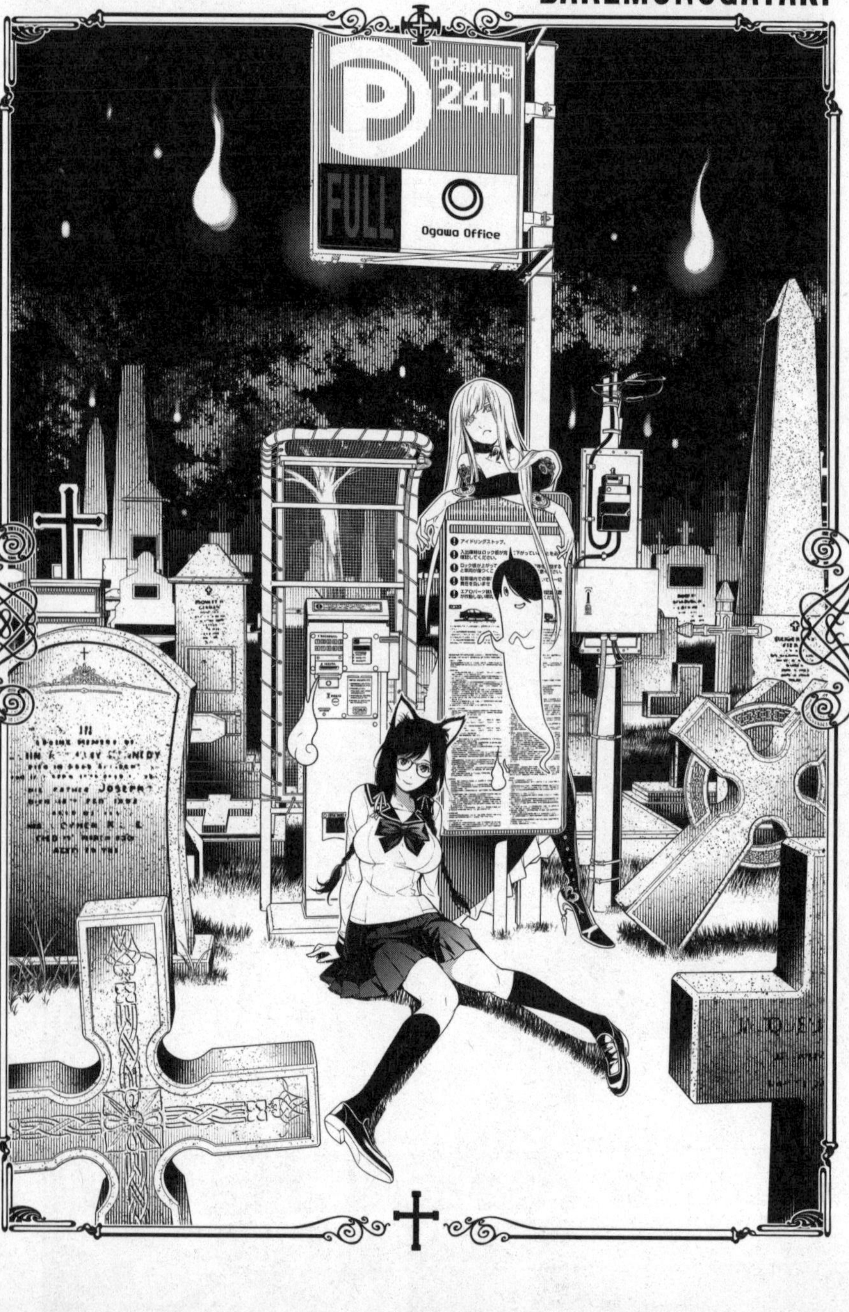
O-Parking
24h
FULL
Ogawa Office

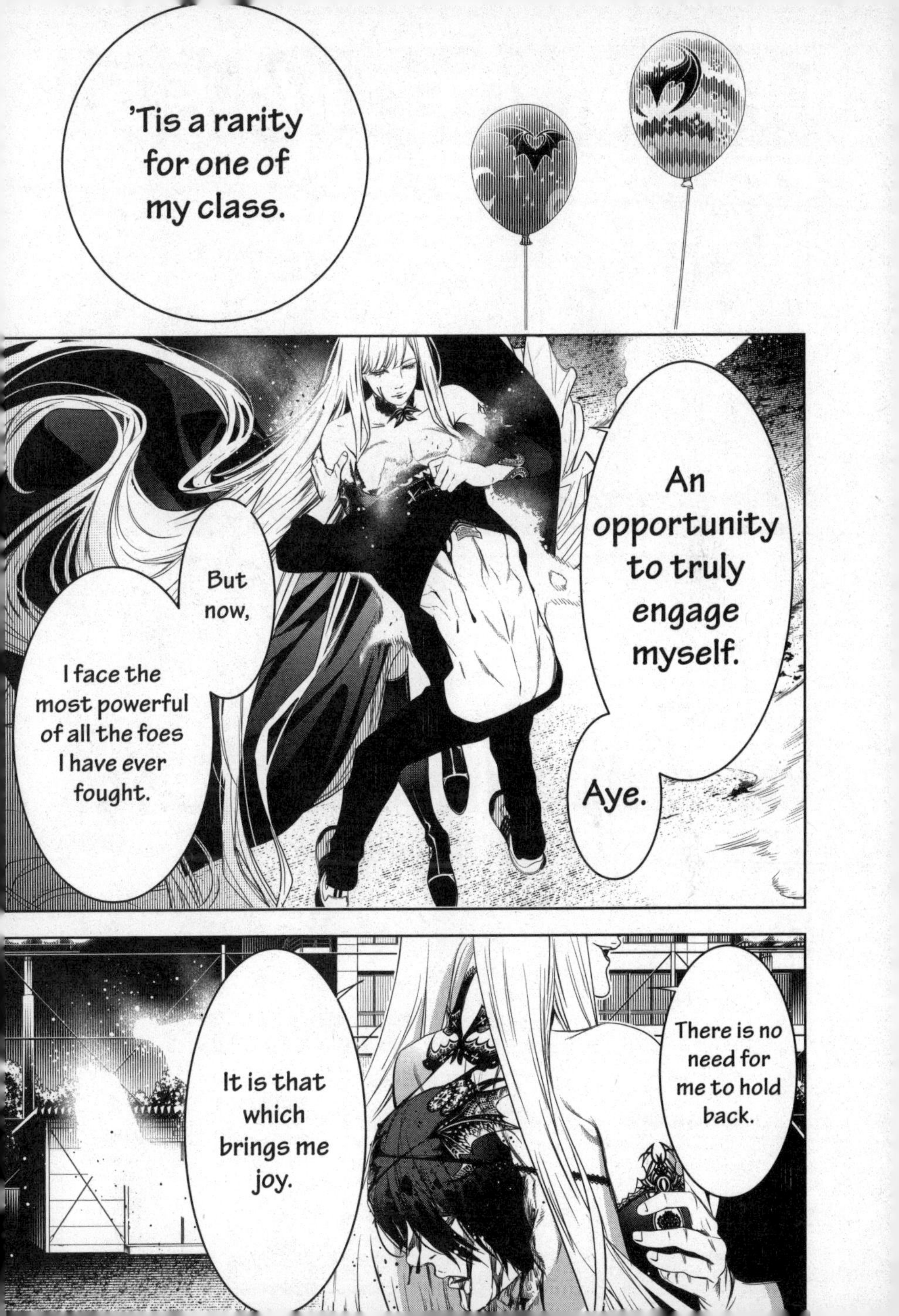
'Tis a rarity for one of my class.
An opportunity to truly engage myself.
Aye.
But now,
I face the most powerful of all the foes I have ever fought.
There is no need for me to hold back.
It is that which brings me joy.

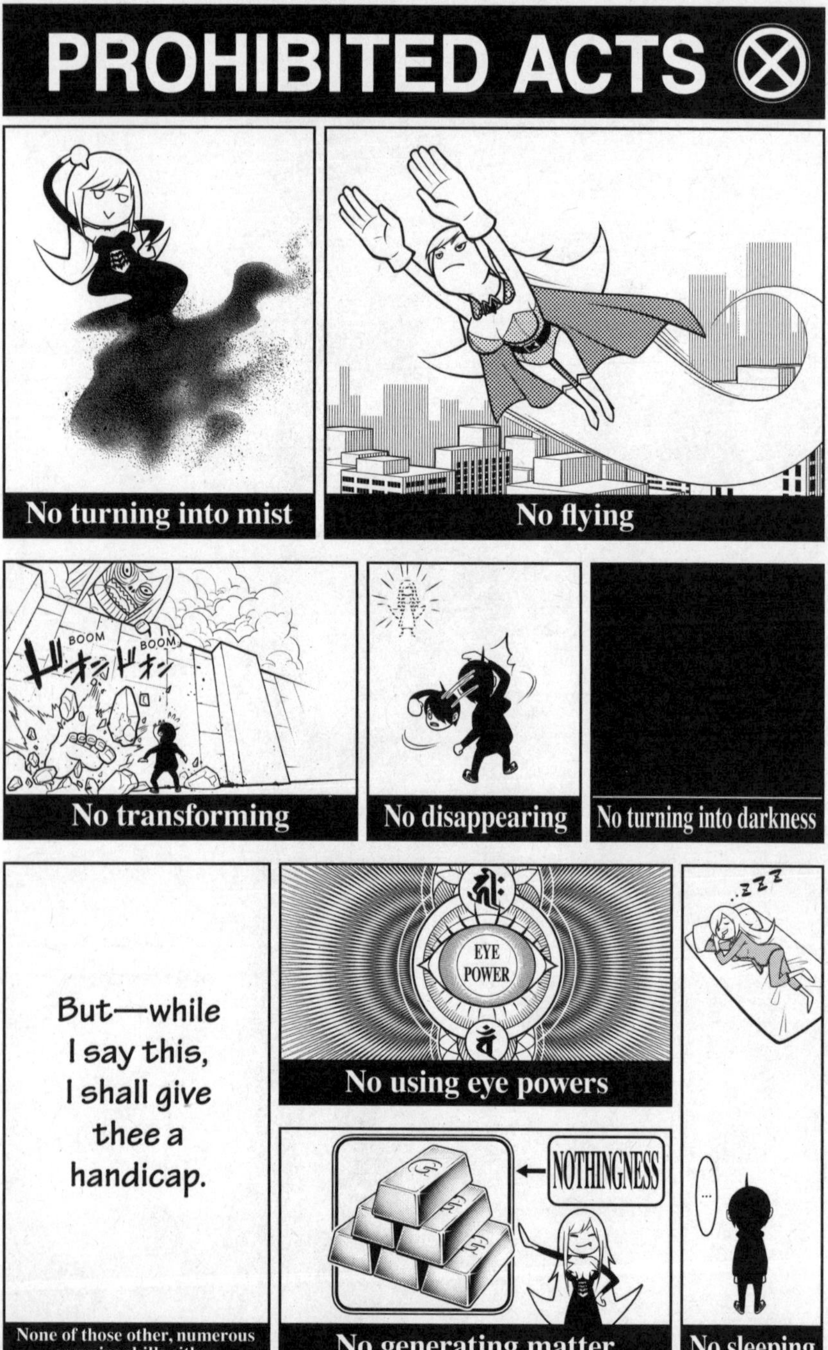
PROHIBITED ACTS
No flying
No turning into mist
No turning into darkness
No disappearing
BOOM
BOOM
ドオン ドオン
No transforming
ZZZ
...
No sleeping
EYE POWER
No using eye powers
NOTHINGNESS
No generating matter
But—while I say this, I shall give thee a handicap.
None of those other, numerous vampire skills either

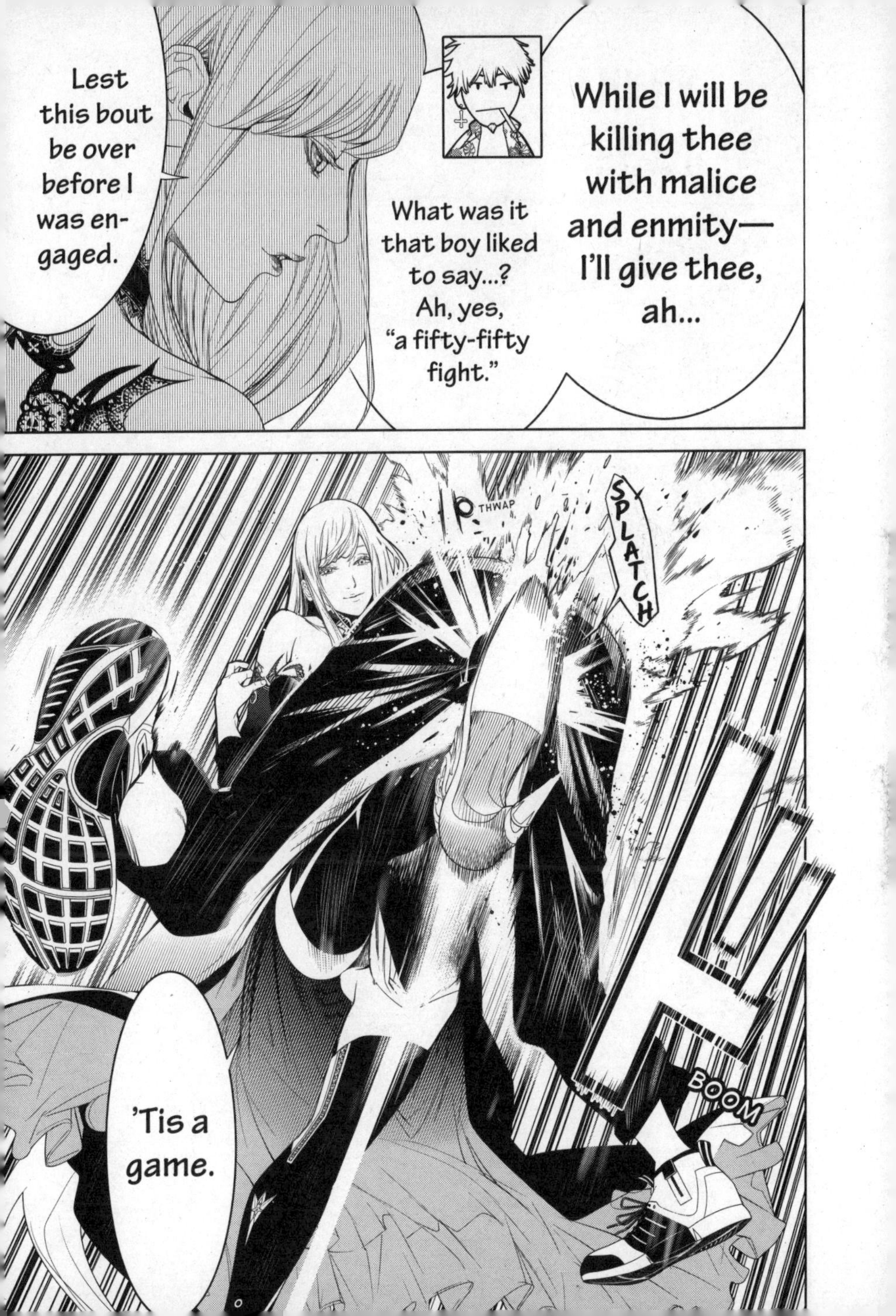
While I will be killing thee with malice and enmity— I'll give thee, ah...
What was it that boy liked to say...? Ah, yes, "a fifty-fifty fight."
Lest this bout be over before I was engaged.
SPLATCH
THWAP
BOOM
'Tis a game.

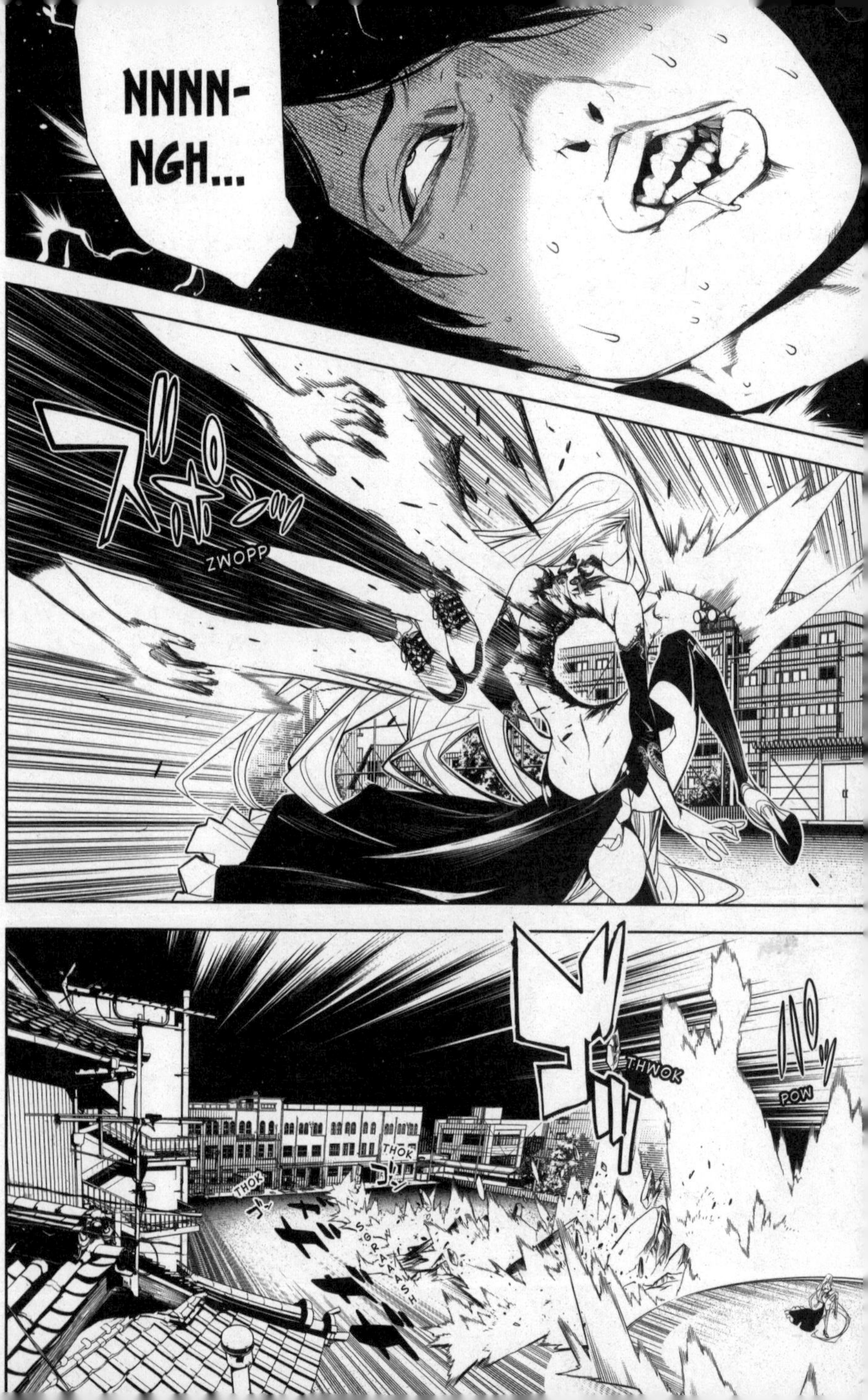
NNNN-NGH...
ZWOPP
POW
THWOK
THOK
THOK
SGRAASH

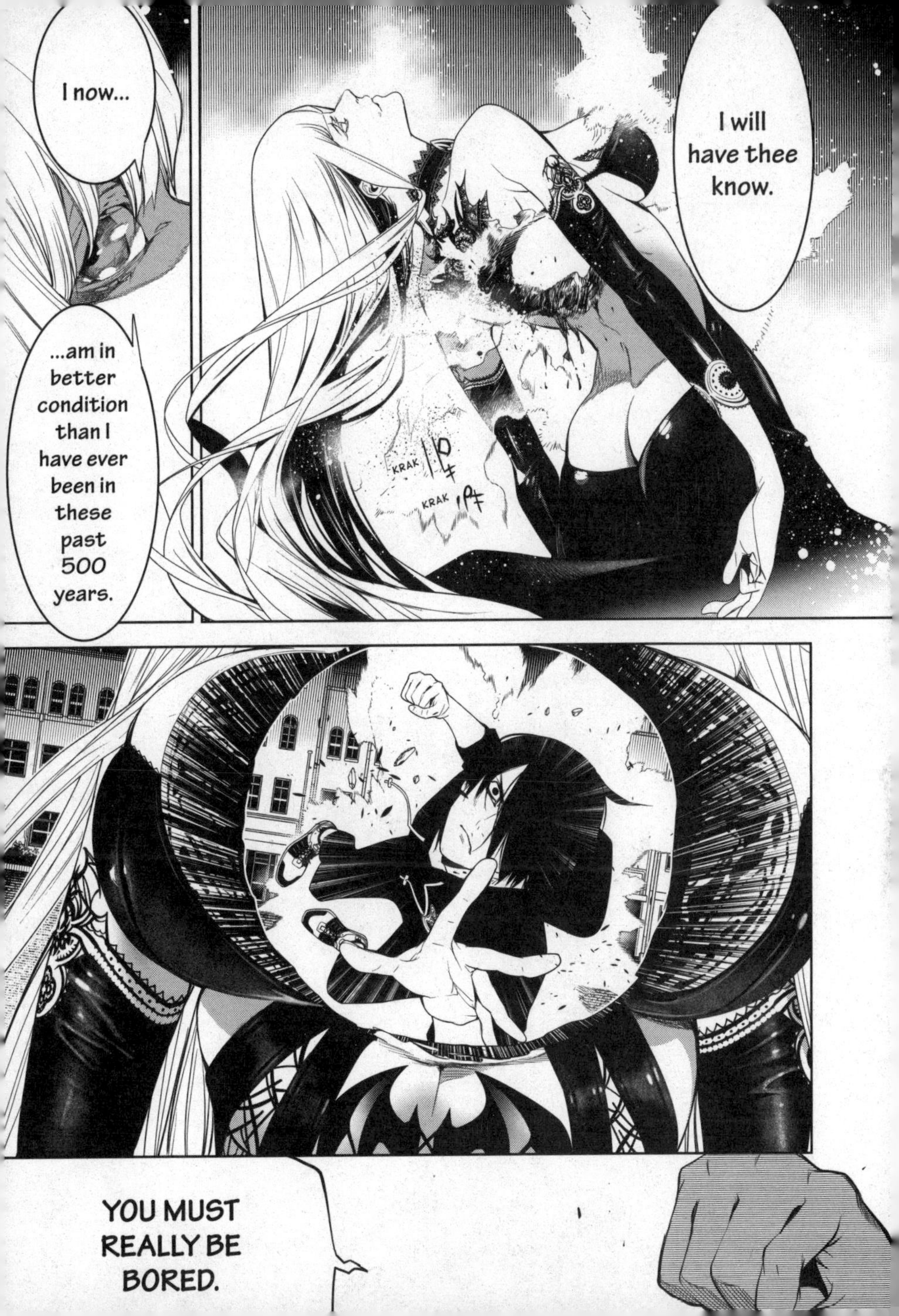
I will have thee know.
KRAK
KRAK
I now...
...am in better condition than I have ever been in these past 500 years.
YOU MUST REALLY BE BORED.

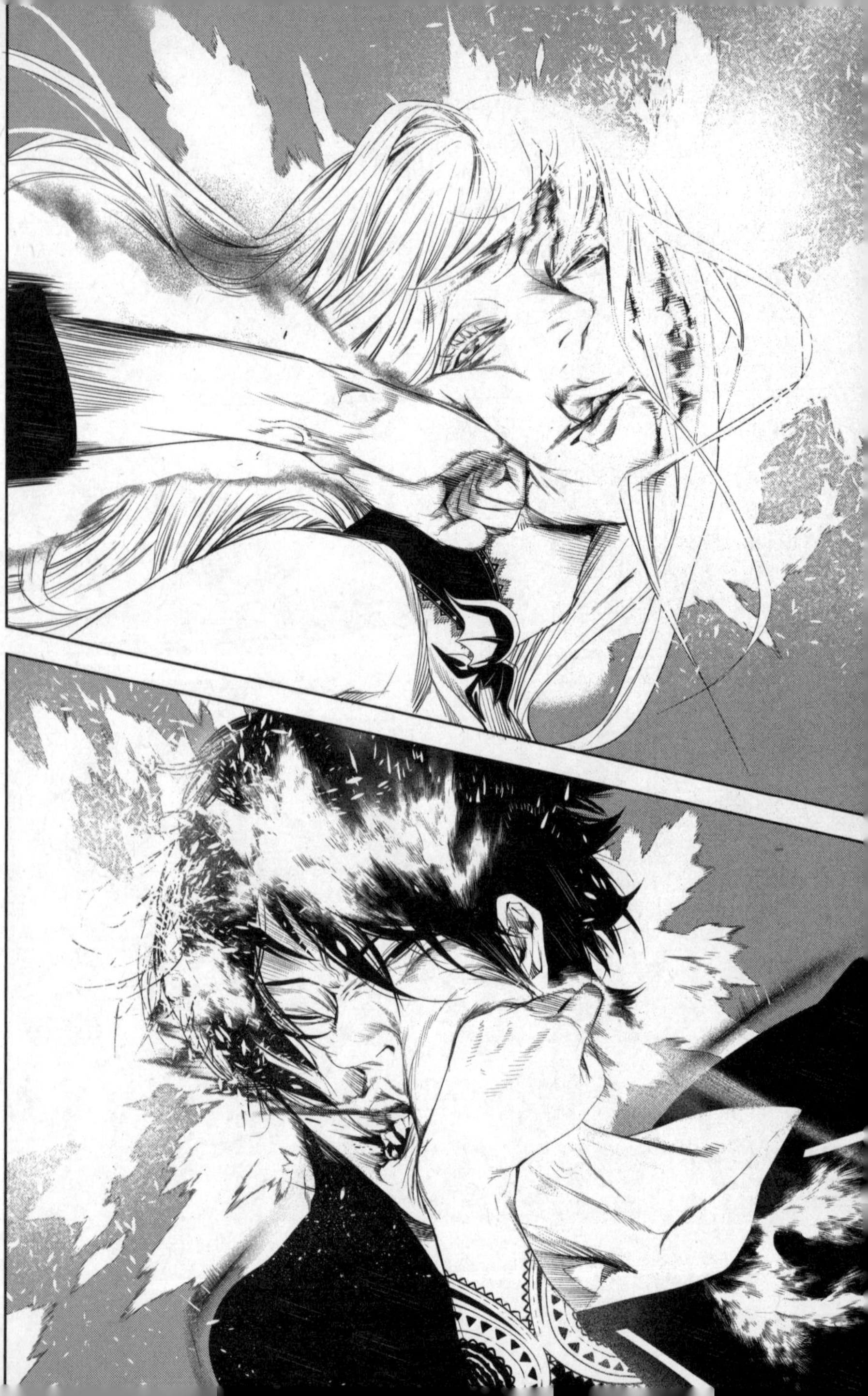

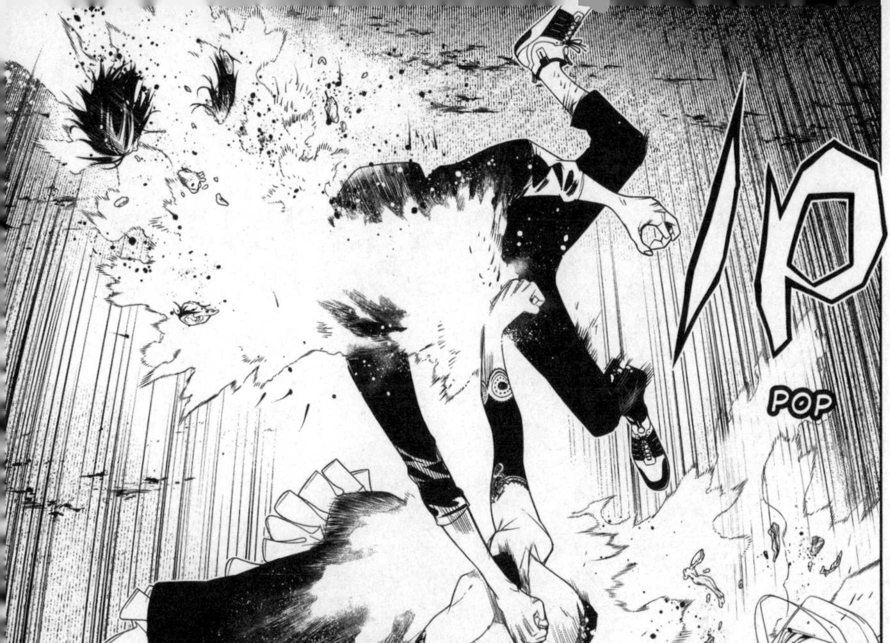
POP
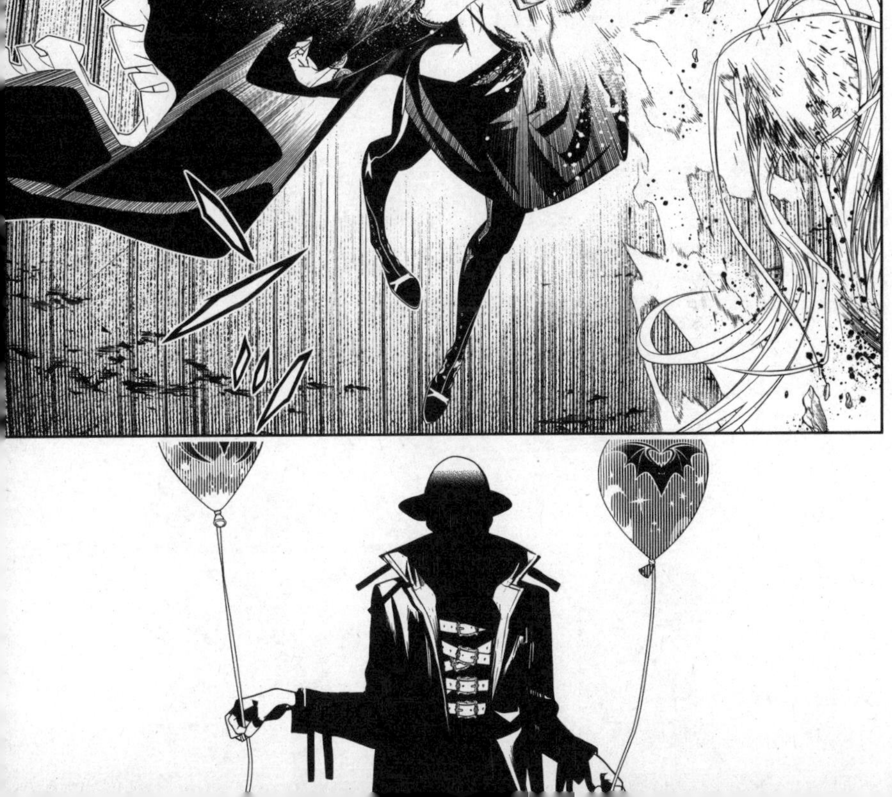

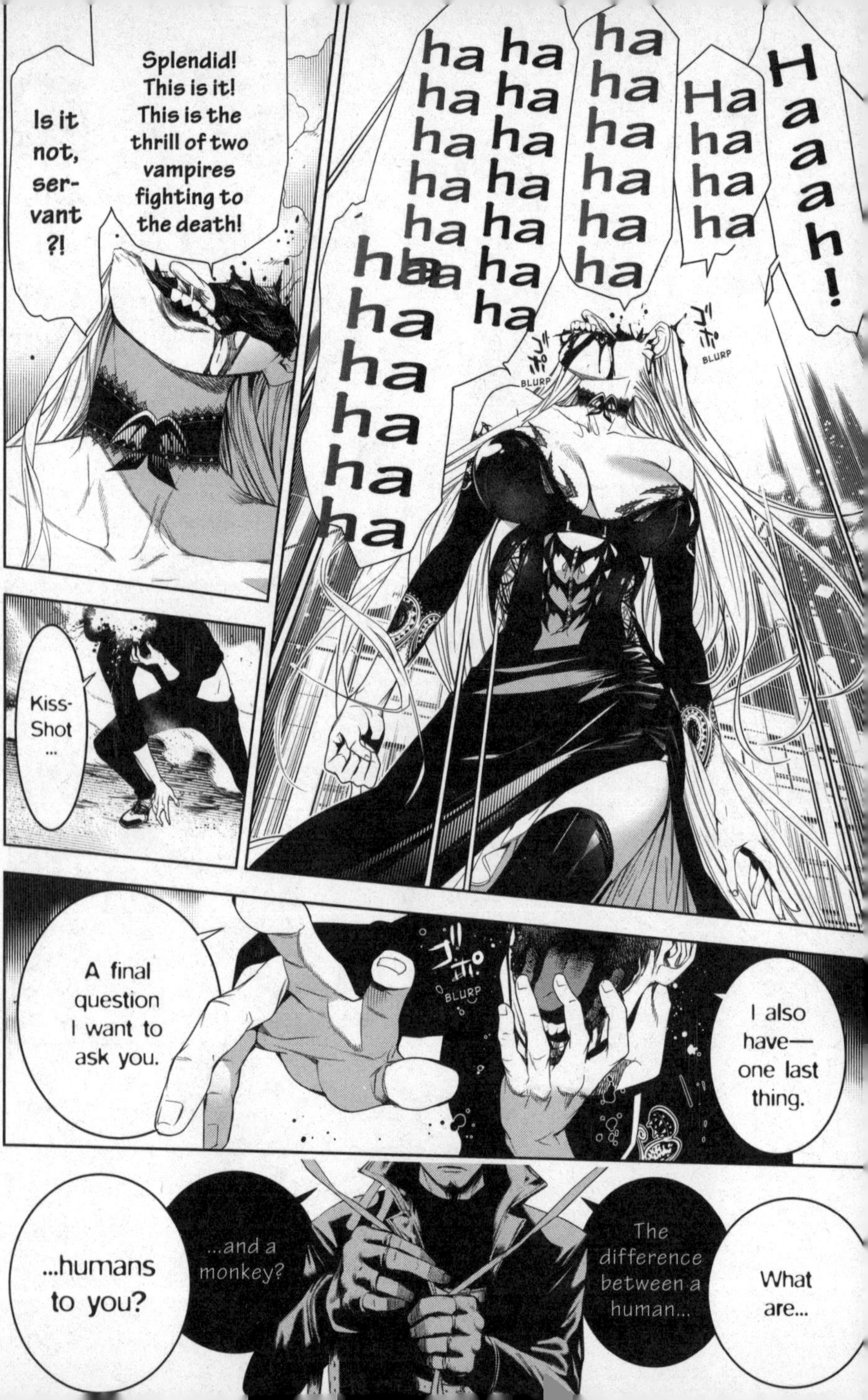
Haaaah!
Ha ha ha ha
ha ha ha ha ha ha
ha ha ha ha ha ha ha
ha ha ha ha ha ha
ha ha ha ha ha ha
BLURP
BLURP
Splendid! This is it! This is the thrill of two vampires fighting to the death!
Is it not, ser-vant?!
Kiss-Shot...
I also have— one last thing.
BLURP
A final question I want to ask you.
What are...
The difference between a human...
...and a monkey?
...humans to you?

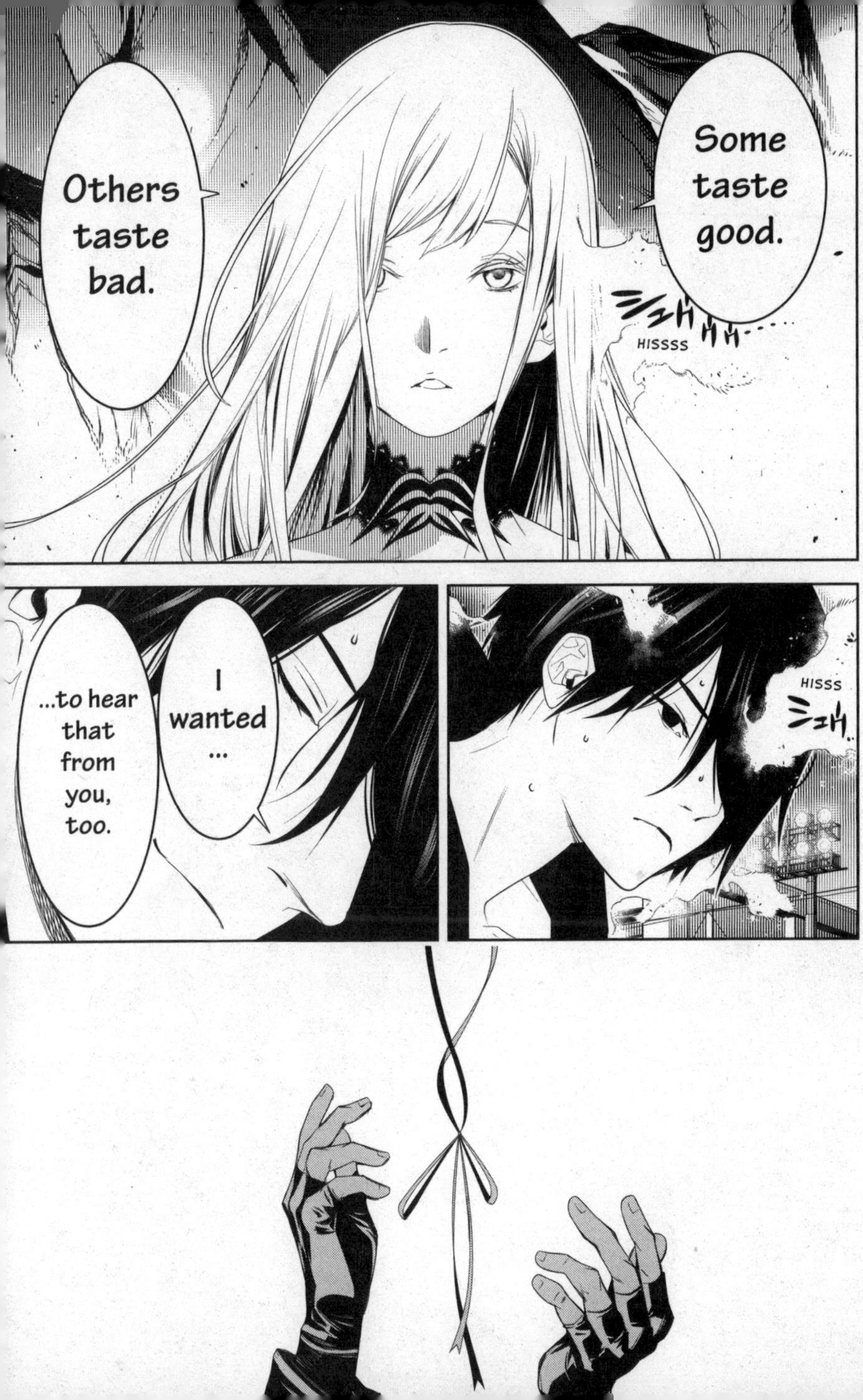
Some taste good.
Others taste bad.
HISSSS
HISSS
I wanted...
...to hear that from you, too.

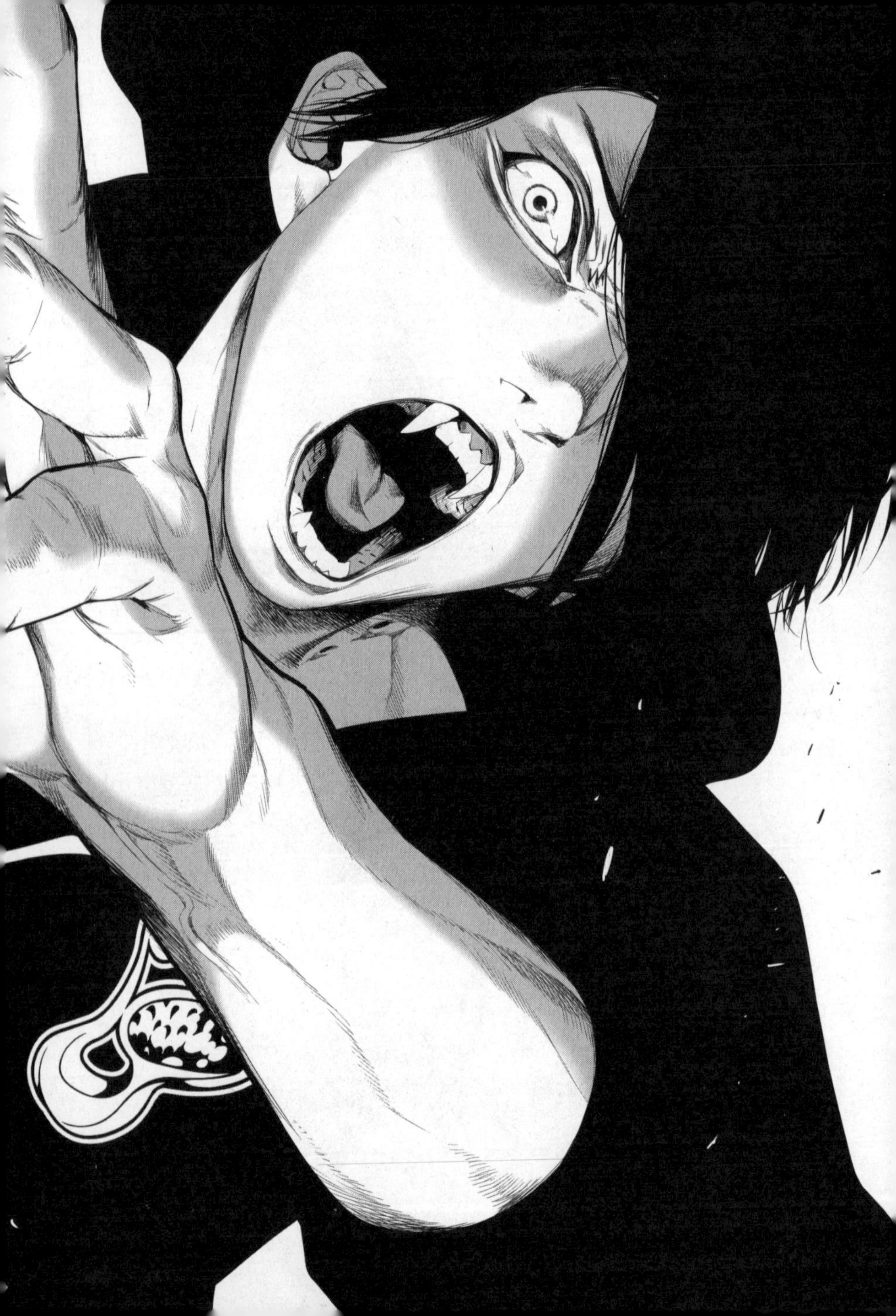

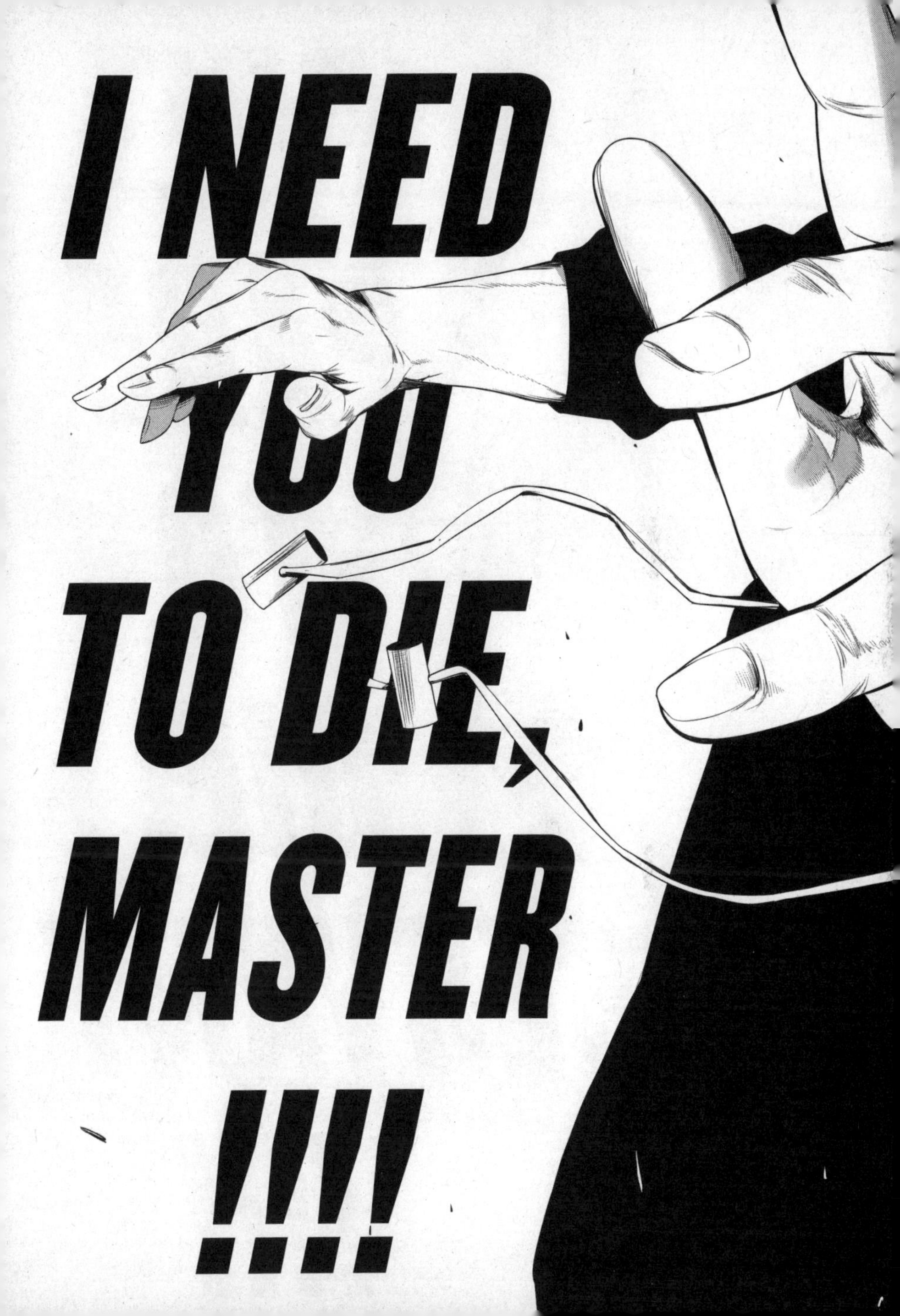
I NEED YOU TO DIE, MASTER !!!!

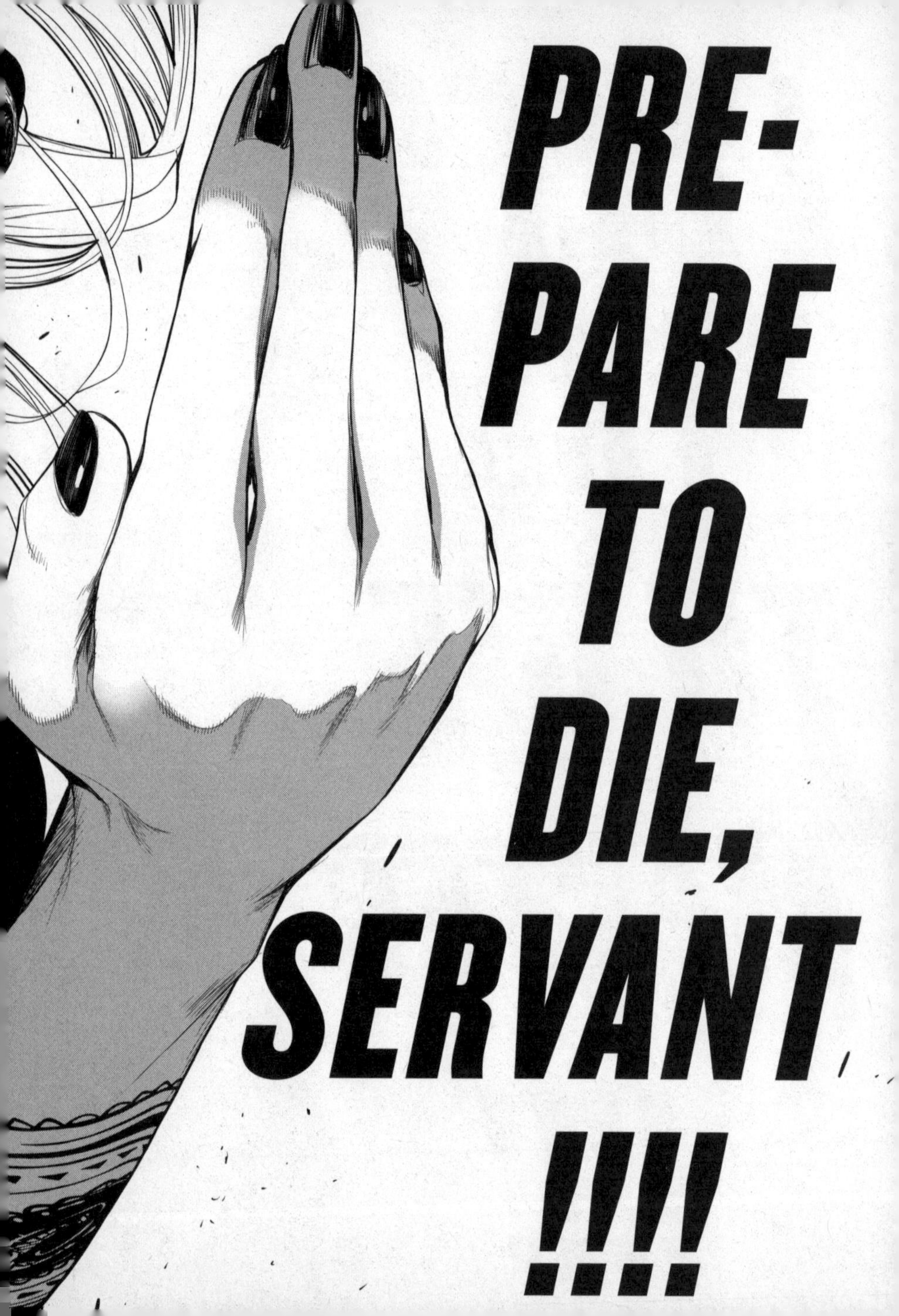
PRE-PARE TO DIE, SERVANT!!!!

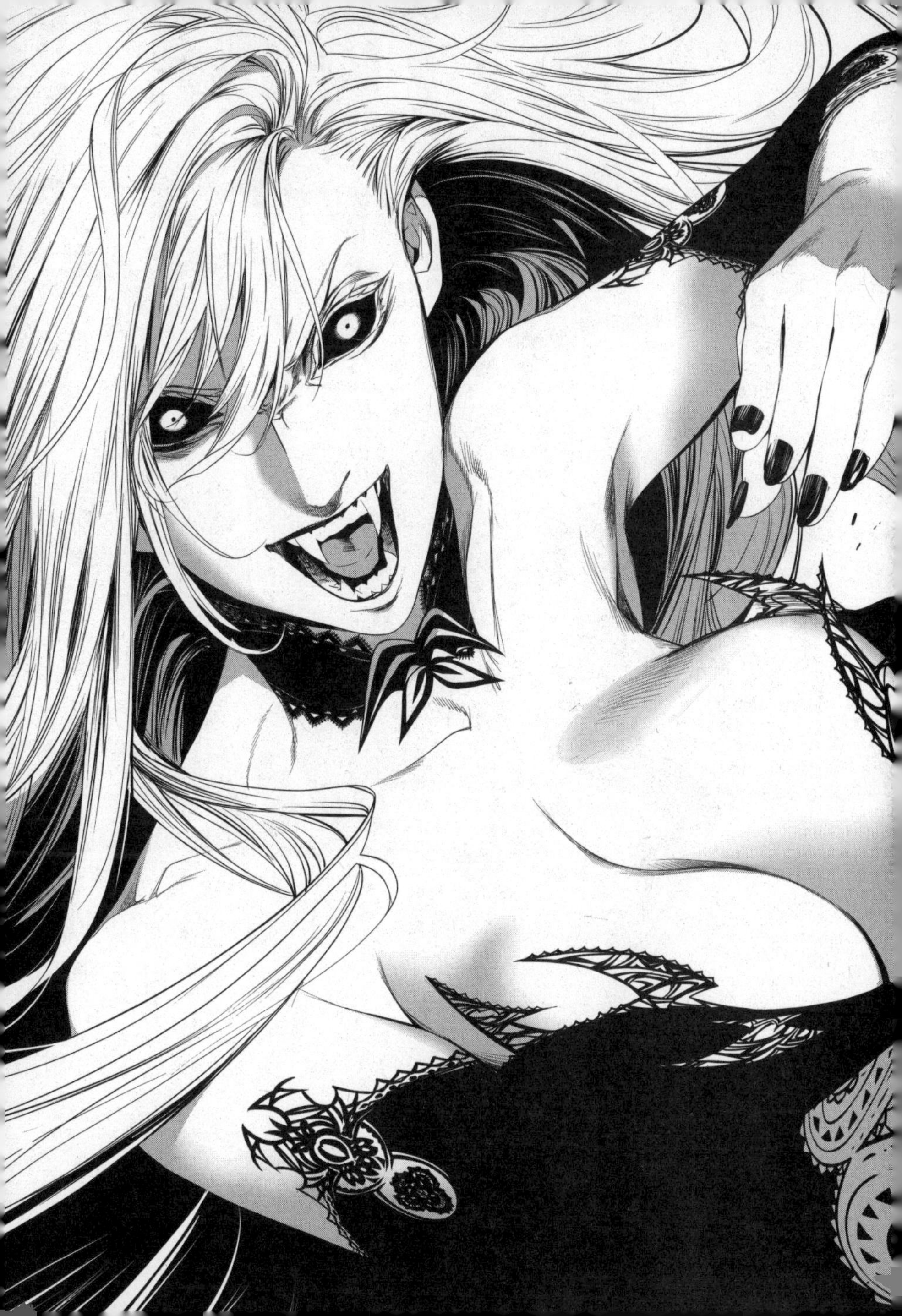

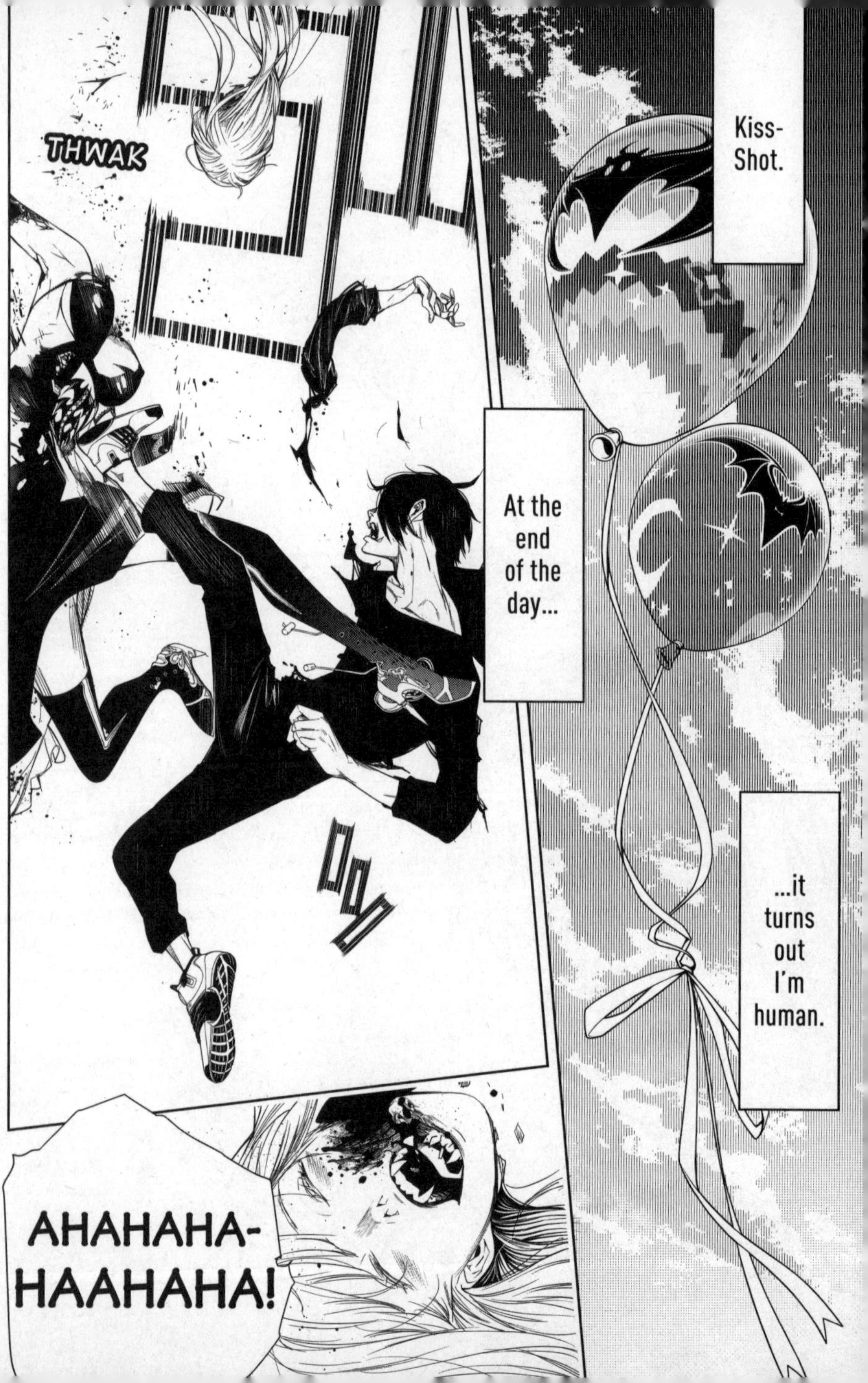
Kiss-Shot.
At the end of the day...
...it turns out I'm human.
THWAK
AHAHAHA-HAAHAHA!

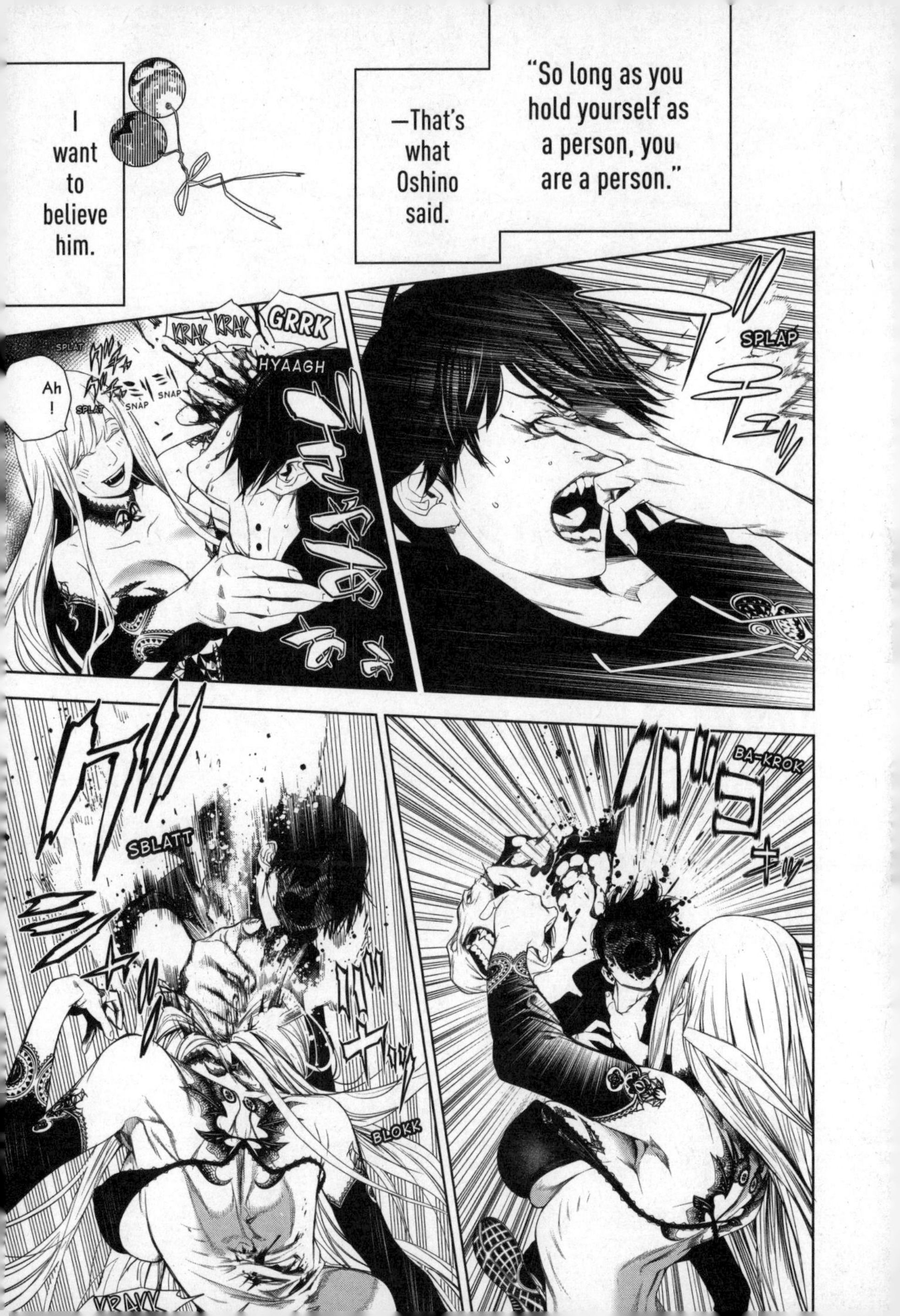
"So long as you hold yourself as a person, you are a person."
—That's what Oshino said.
I want to believe him.
SPLAP
GRRK
KRAK
KRAK
HYAAGH
SNAP
SNAP
SPLAT
SPLAT
Ah!
BA-KROK
SBLATT
BLOKK

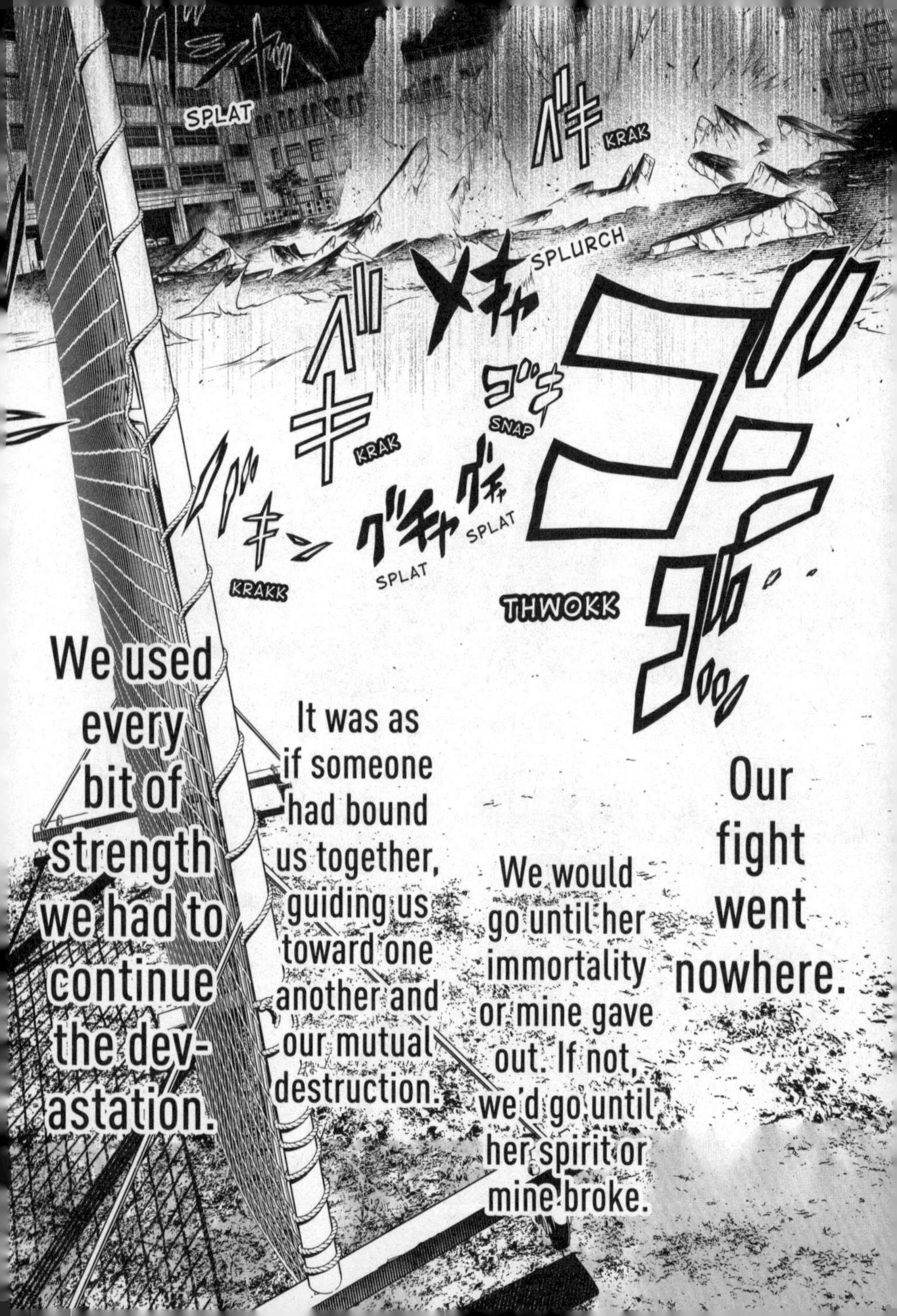
KRAK
SPLAT
SPLURCH
SNAP
KRAK
SPLAT
SPLAT
THWOKK
KRAKK
Our fight went nowhere.
We would go until her immortality or mine gave out. If not, we'd go until her spirit or mine broke.
It was as if someone had bound us together, guiding us toward one another and our mutual destruction.
We used every bit of strength we had to continue the dev-astation.

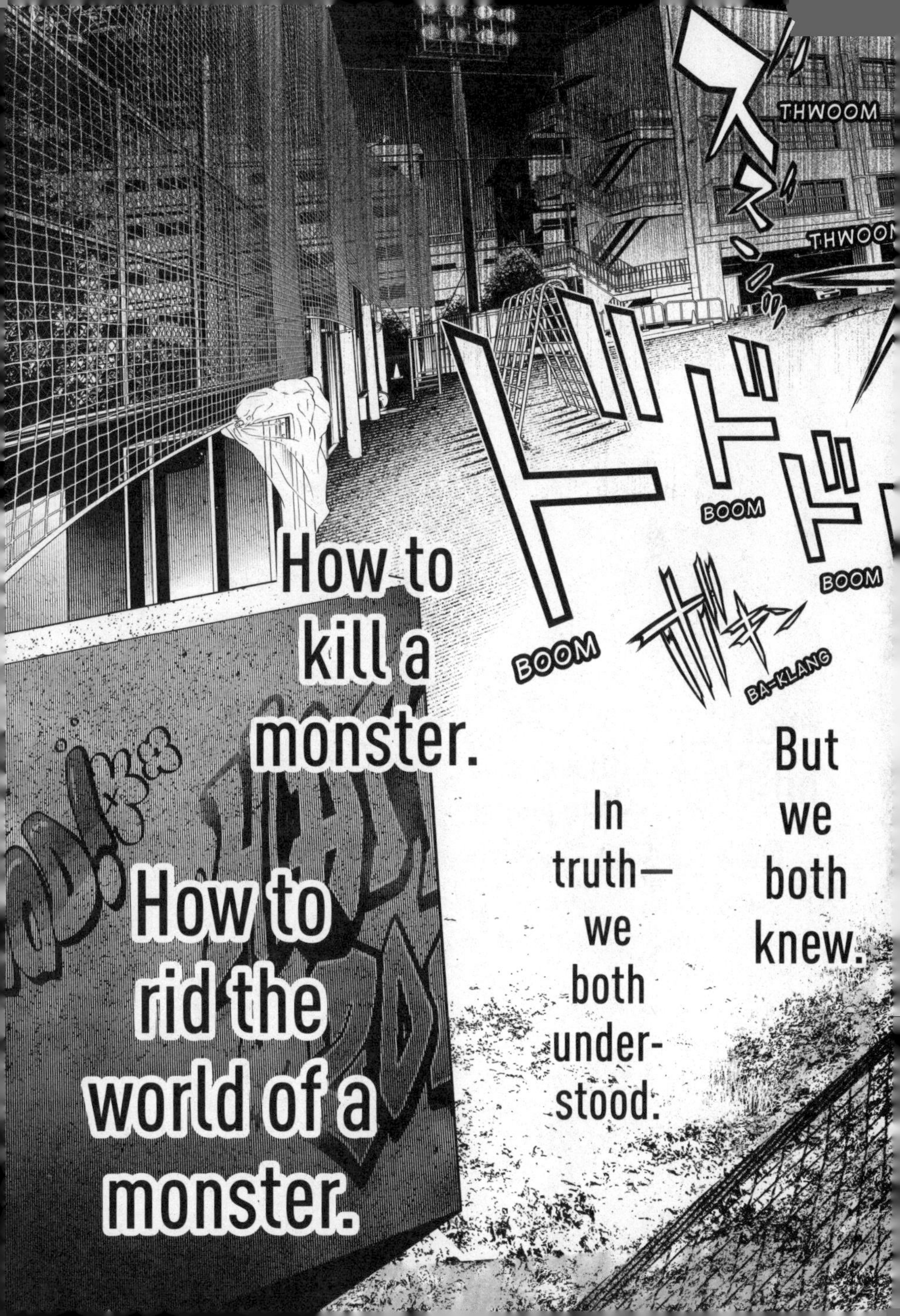
THWOOM
THWOOM
BOOM
BOOM
BOOM
BA-KLANG
But we both knew.
In truth— we both under-stood.
How to kill a monster.
How to rid the world of a monster.

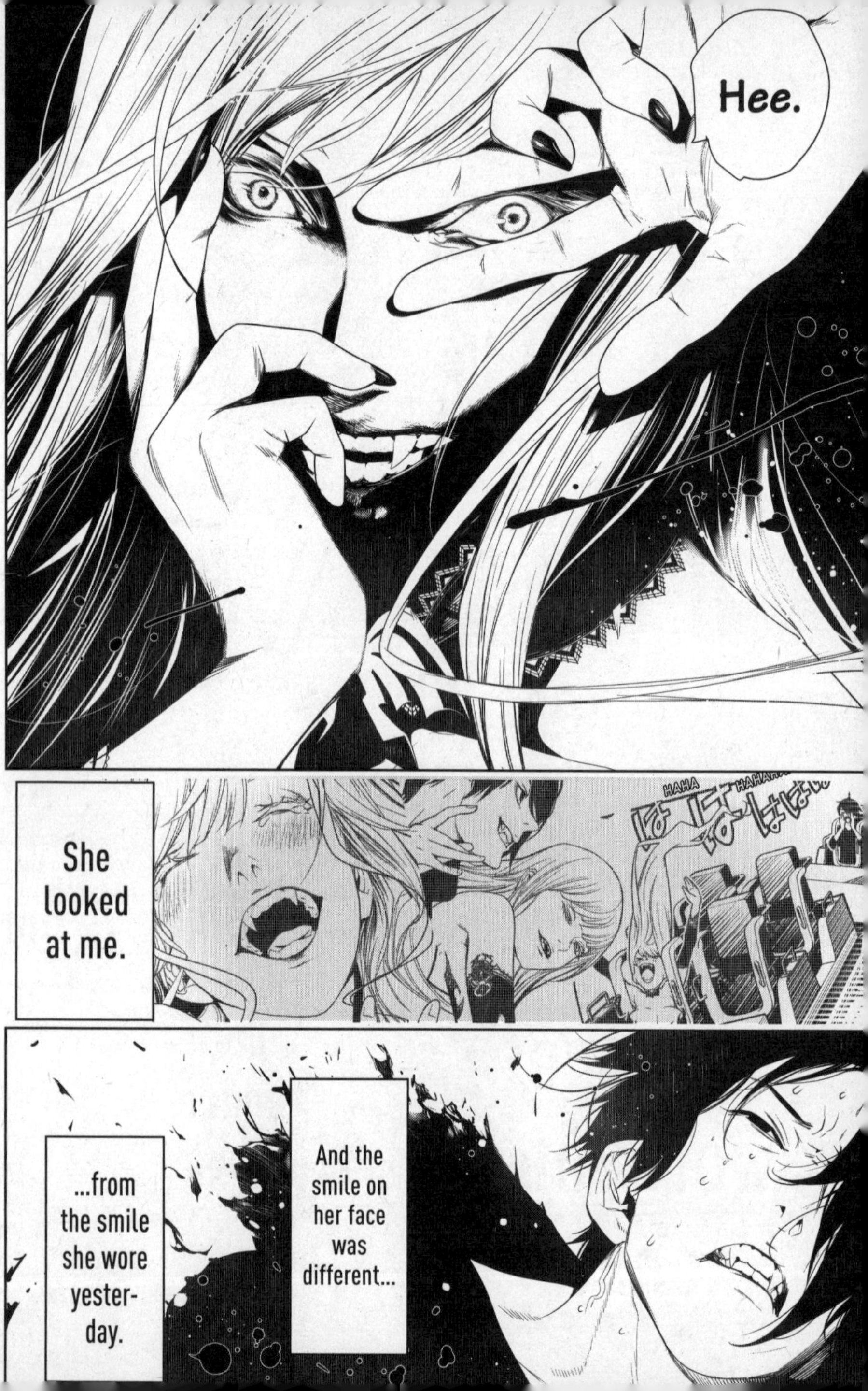
Hee.
HAHA
She looked at me.
And the smile on her face was different...
...from the smile she wore yesterday.

化 bake

物 mono

KOYOMIvamp

14

語 gatari

bake

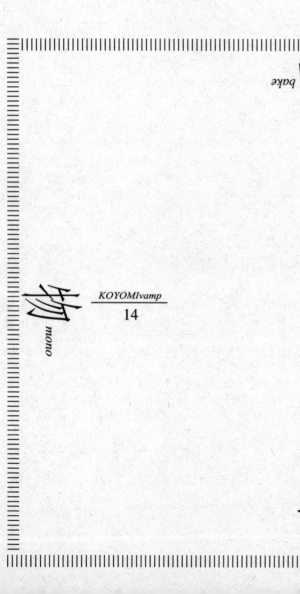
mono

KOYOMIvamp
14

gatari

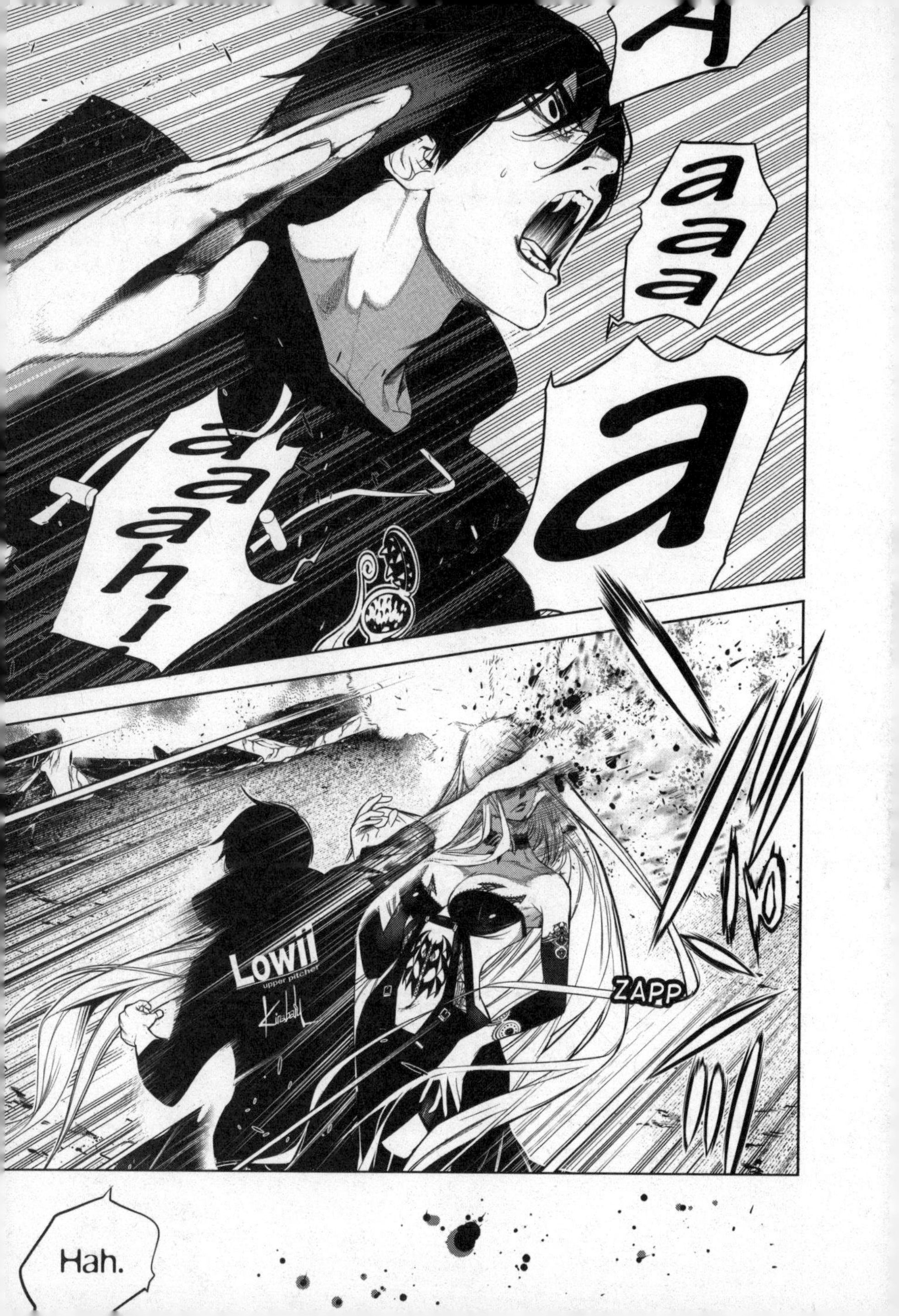

Aaaaa
aaaah!
ZAPP
Lowii
upper pitcher
Hah.

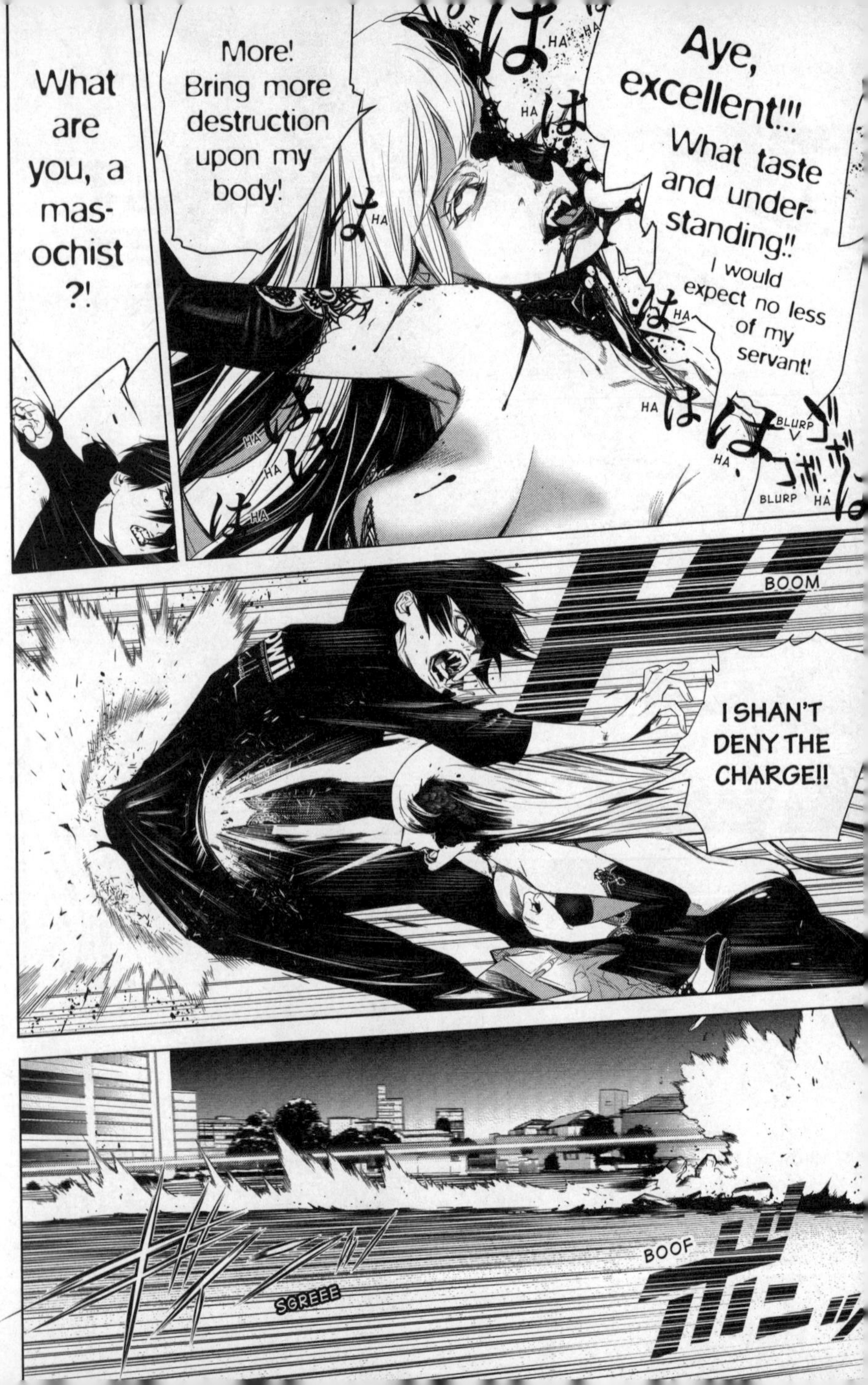
Aye, excellent!!! What taste and under-standing!! I would expect no less of my servant!
More! Bring more destruction upon my body!
HA HA HA HA HA HA HA HA HA HA HA
BLURP
BLURP
What are you, a mas-ochist ?!
BOOM
I SHAN'T DENY THE CHARGE!!
BOOF
SCREEE

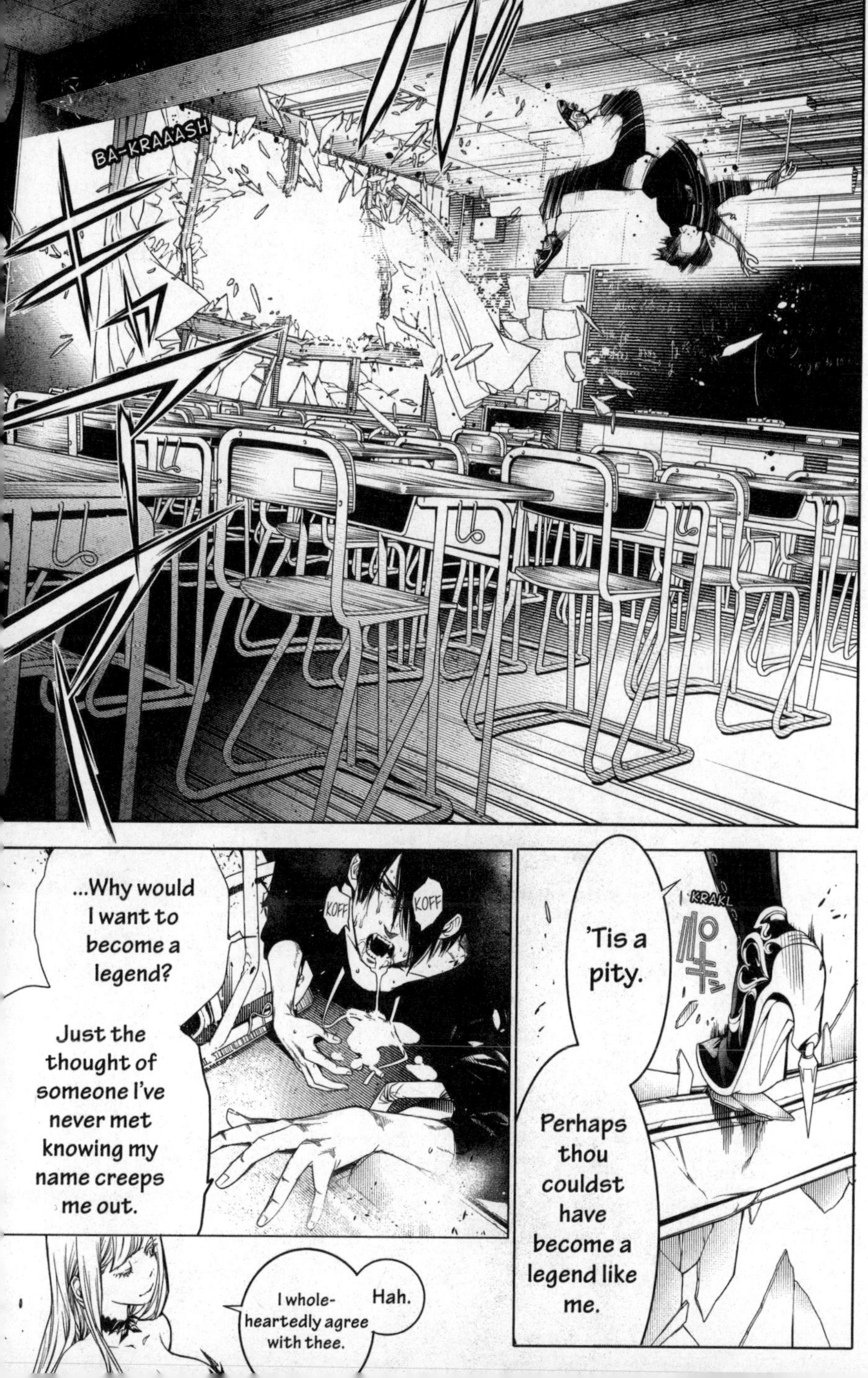
BA-KRAAASH
'Tis a pity.
KRAKL
Perhaps thou couldst have become a legend like me.
KOFF
KOFF
...Why would I want to become a legend?
Just the thought of someone I've never met knowing my name creeps me out.
Hah.
I whole-heartedly agree with thee.

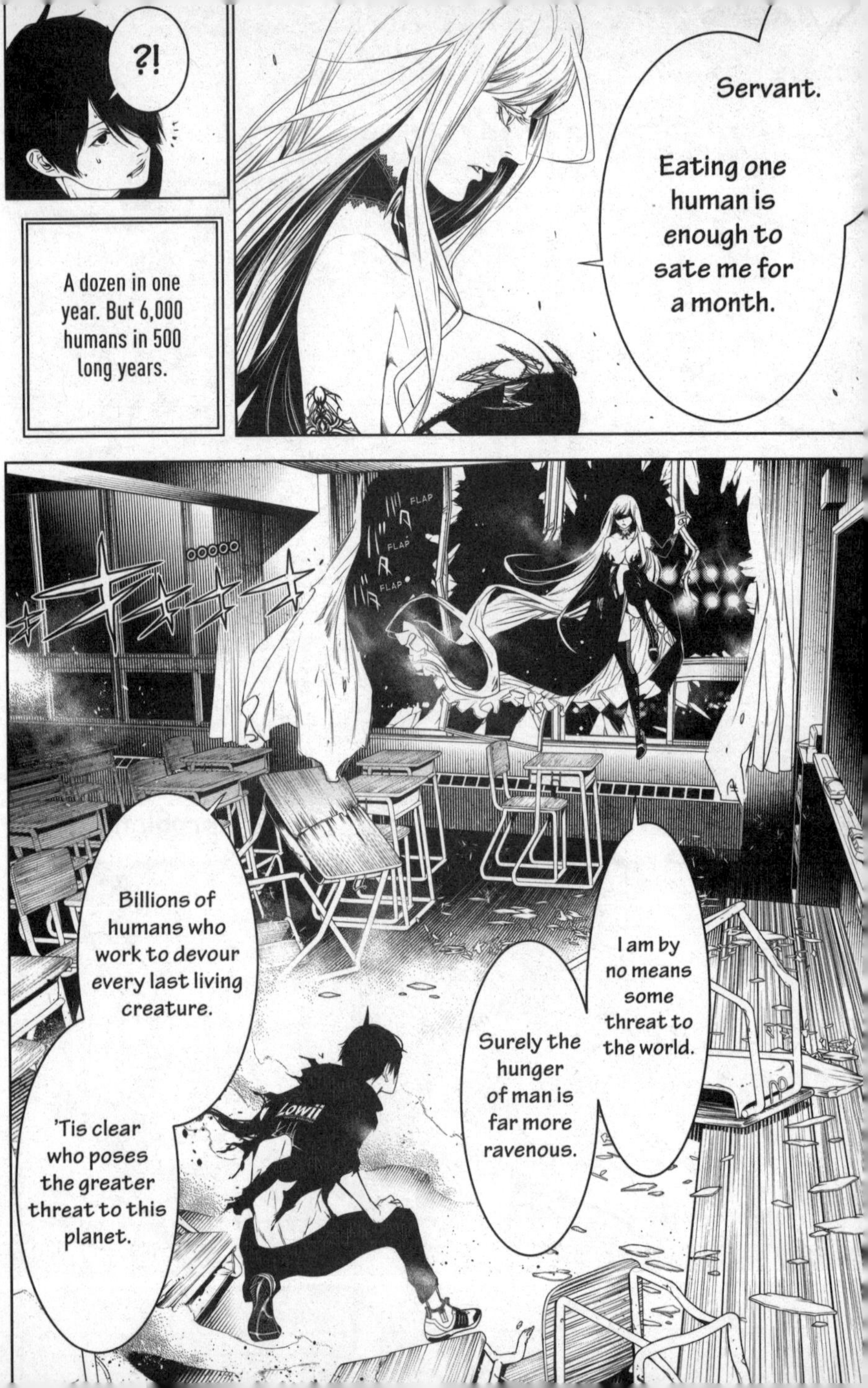
Servant.
Eating one human is enough to sate me for a month.
?!
A dozen in one year. But 6,000 humans in 500 long years.
FLAP
FLAP
FLAP
I am by no means some threat to the world.
Surely the hunger of man is far more ravenous.
Billions of humans who work to devour every last living creature.
'Tis clear who poses the greater threat to this planet.
Lowii

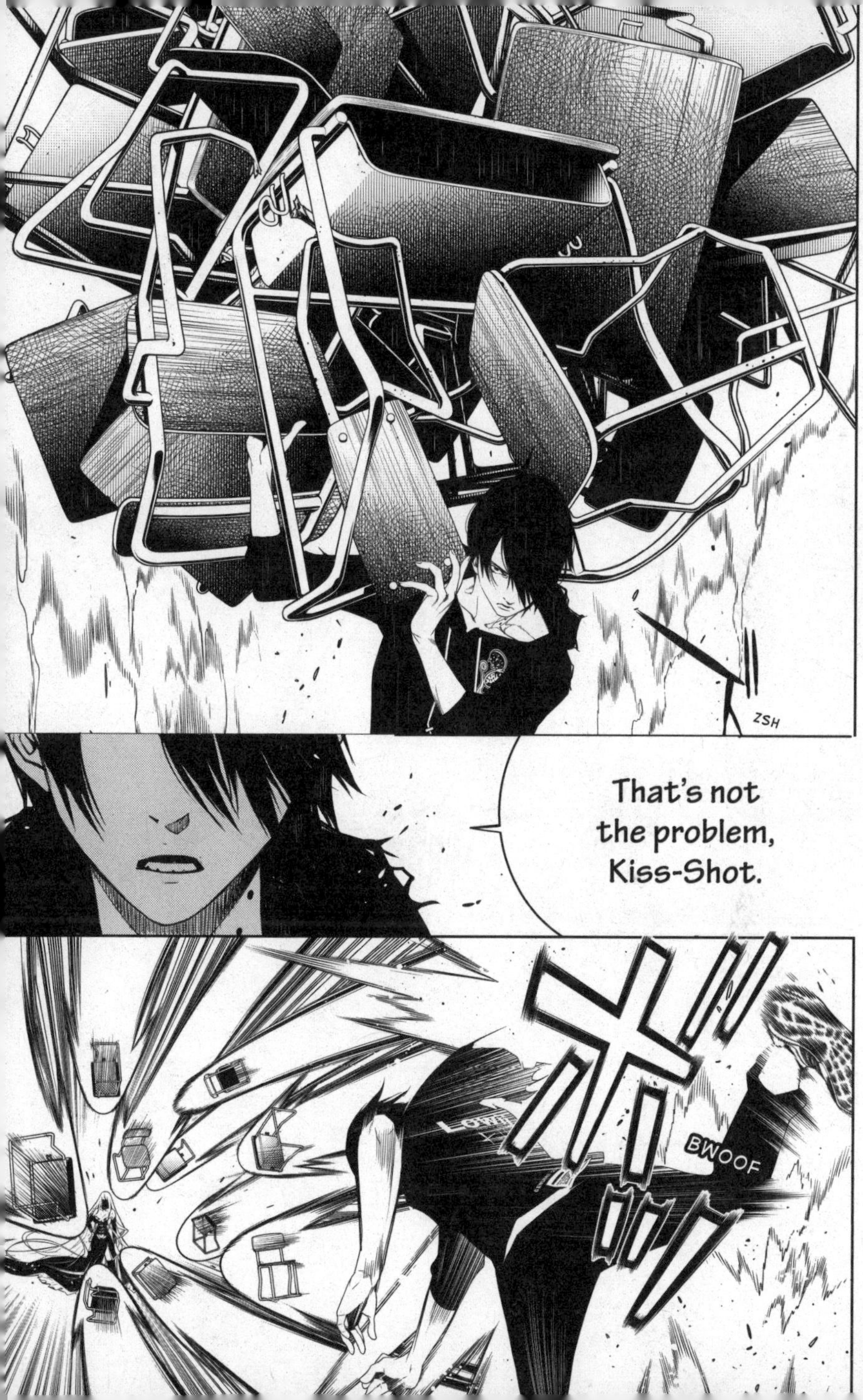
ZSH
That's not the problem, Kiss-Shot.
BWOOF

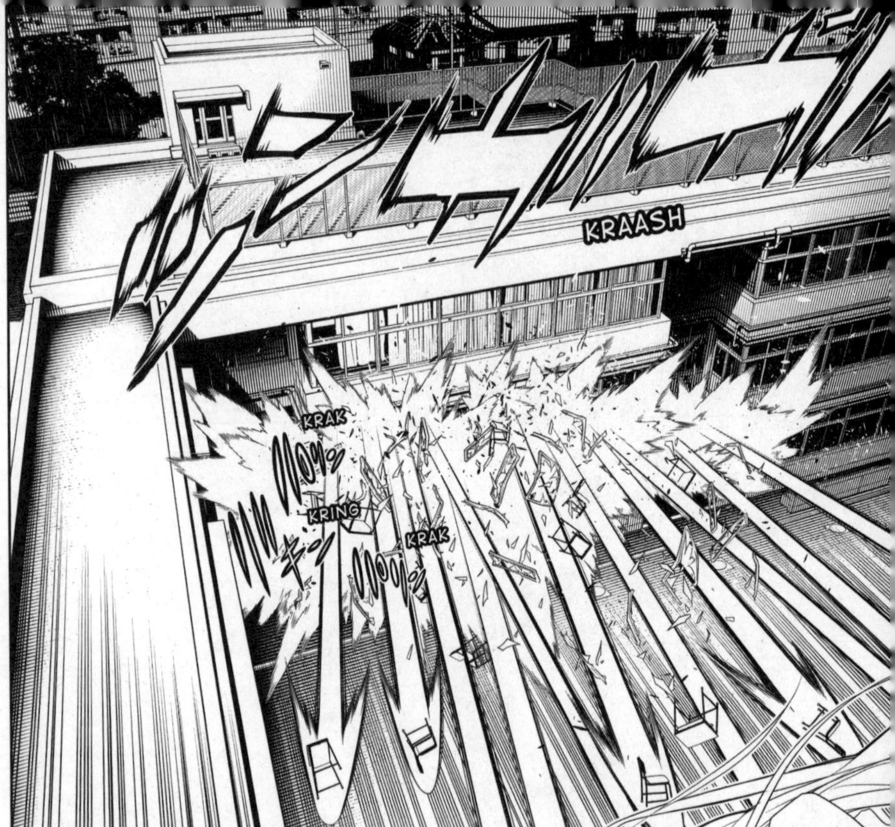
KRAASH
KRAK
KRING
KRAK
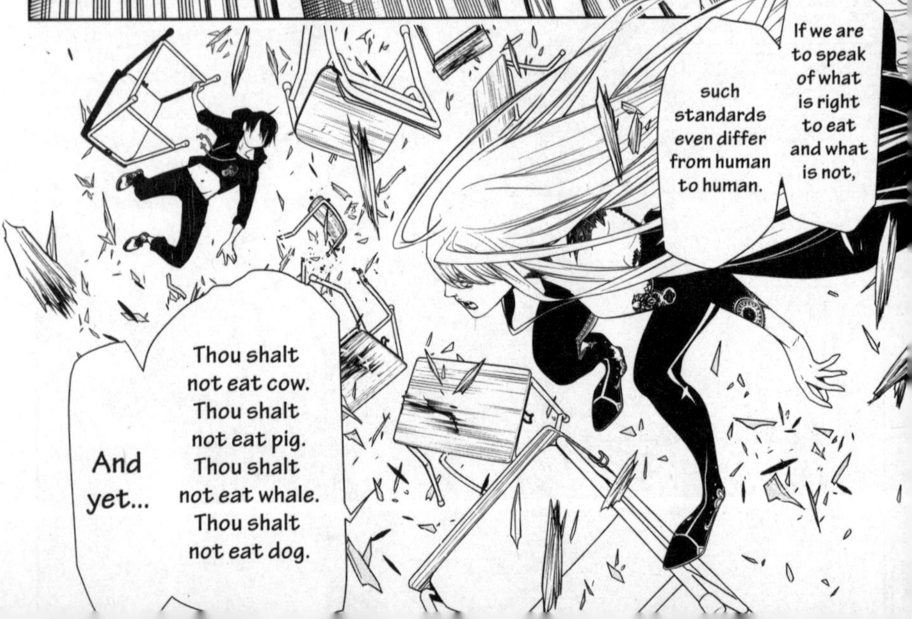
If we are to speak of what is right to eat and what is not,
such standards even differ from human to human.
Thou shalt not eat cow. Thou shalt not eat pig. Thou shalt not eat whale. Thou shalt not eat dog.
And yet...

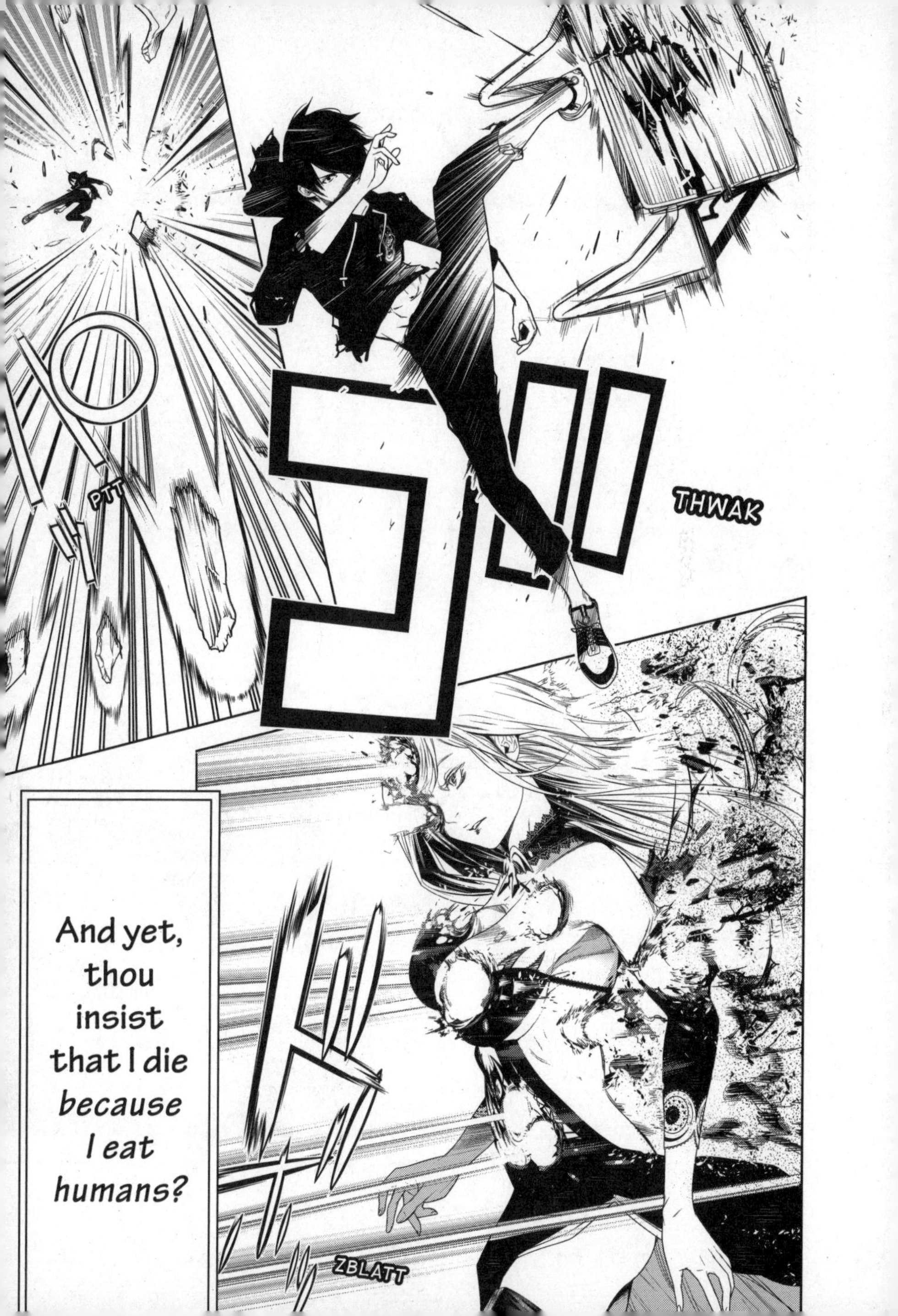
THWAK
PTT
And yet, thou insist that I die *because* I eat humans?
ZBLATT

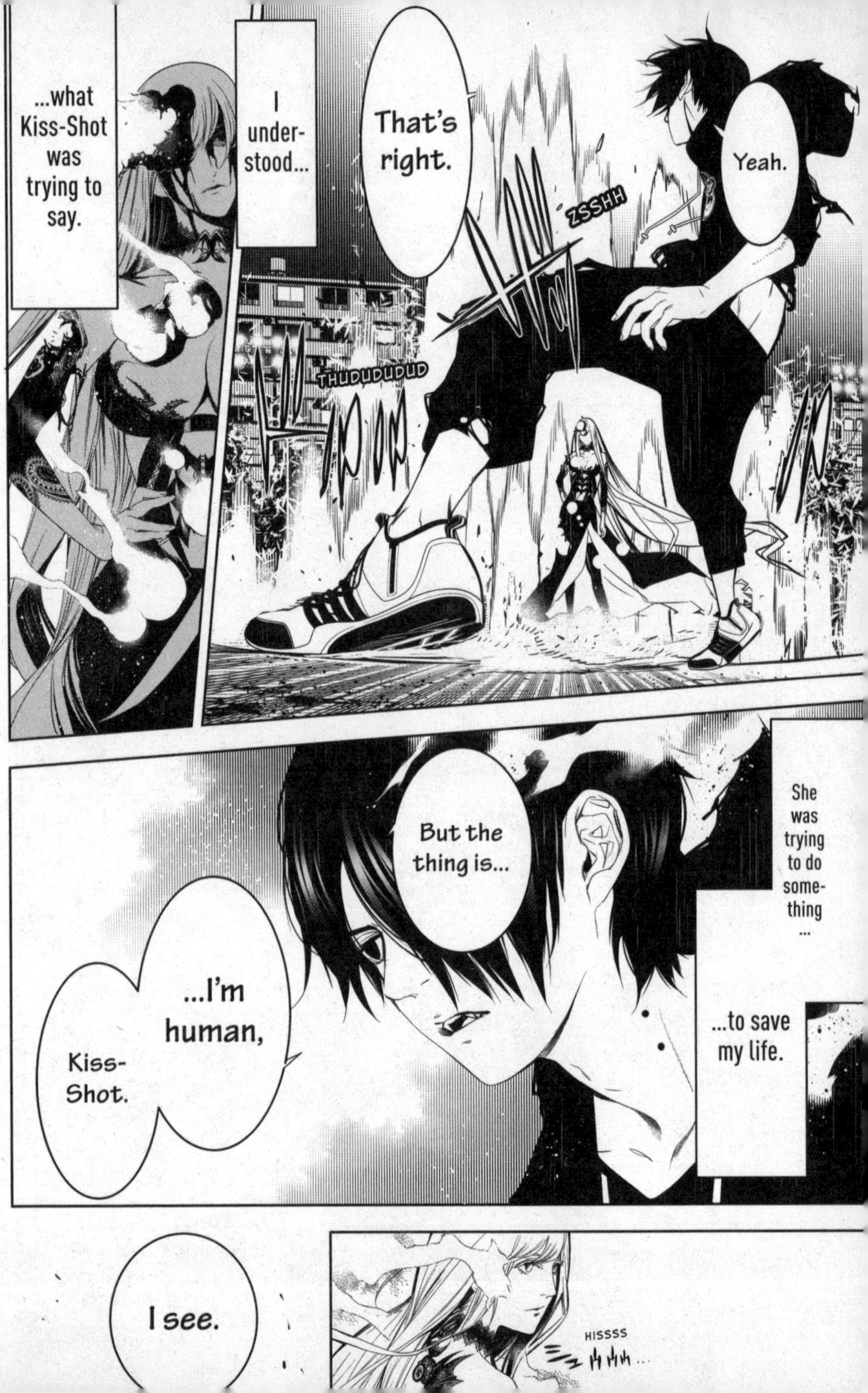
Yeah.
That's right.
ZSSHH
THUDUDUDUD
I understood...
...what Kiss-Shot was trying to say.
She was trying to do something...
...to save my life.
But the thing is...
...I'm human, Kiss-Shot.
HISSSS
I see.

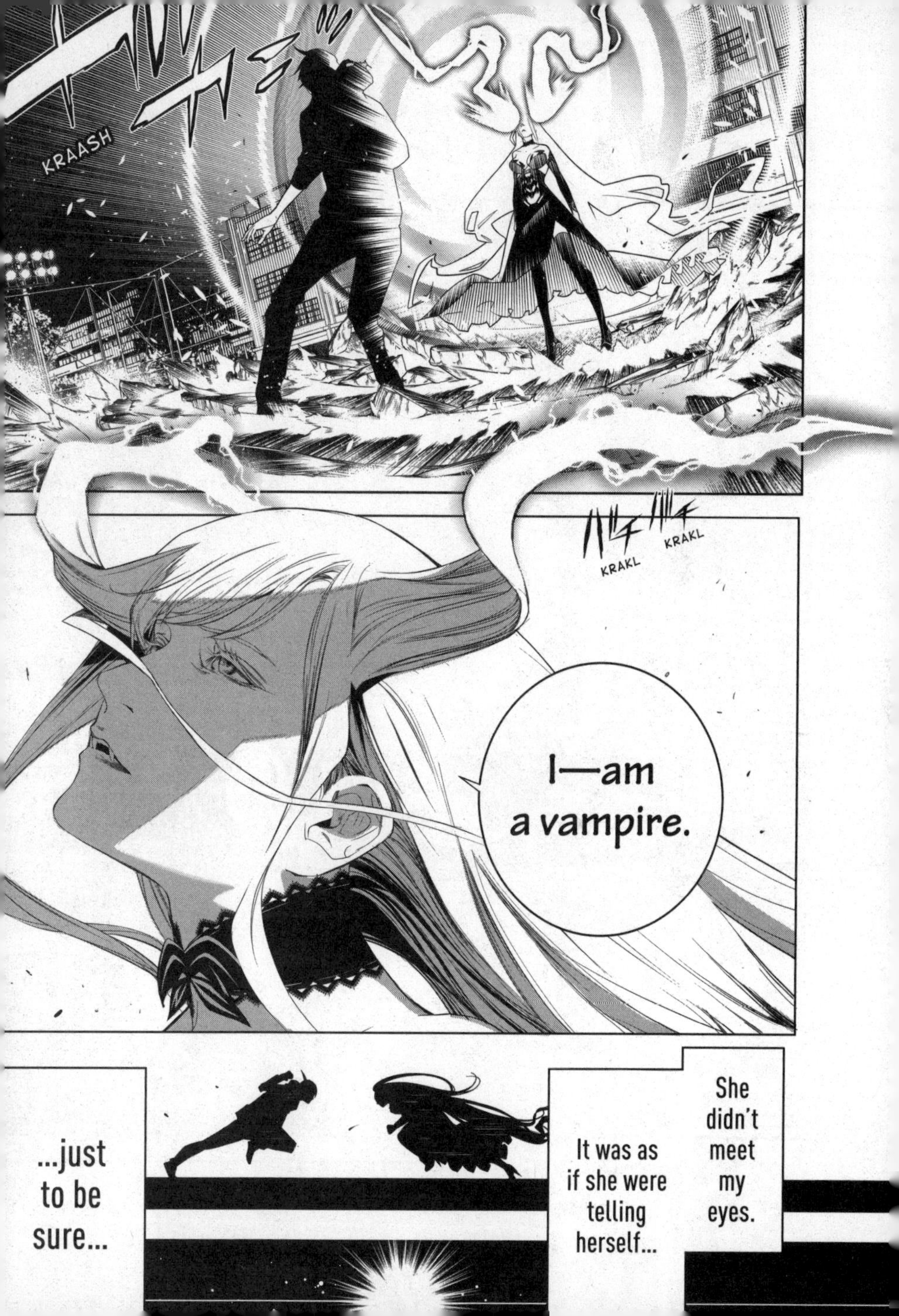
KRAASH
KRAKL
KRAKL
I—am a vampire.
She didn't meet my eyes.
It was as if she were telling herself...
...just to be sure...

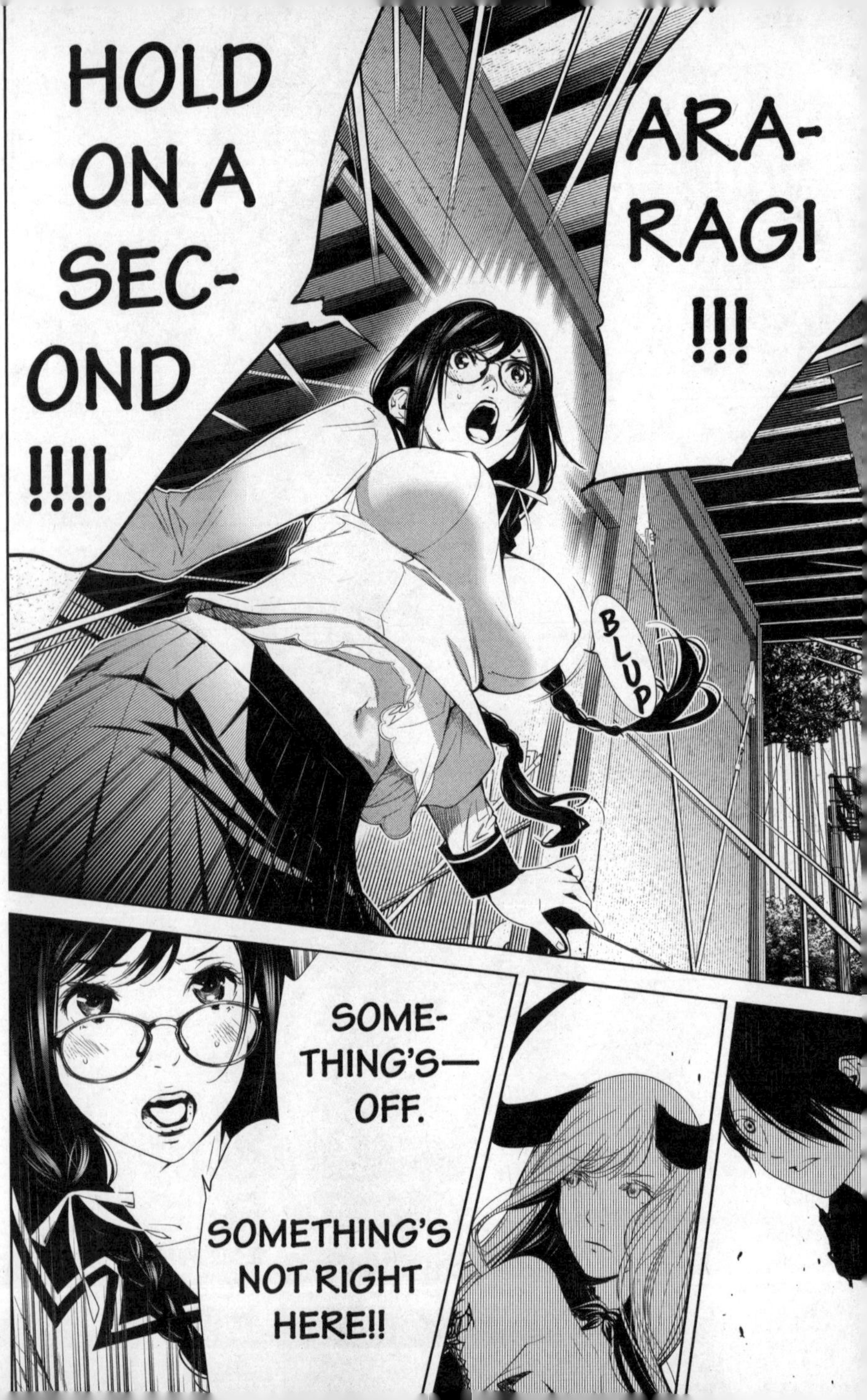
ARARAGI!!!
HOLD ON A SECOND!!!!
BLUP
SOMETHING'S— OFF.
SOMETHING'S NOT RIGHT HERE!!

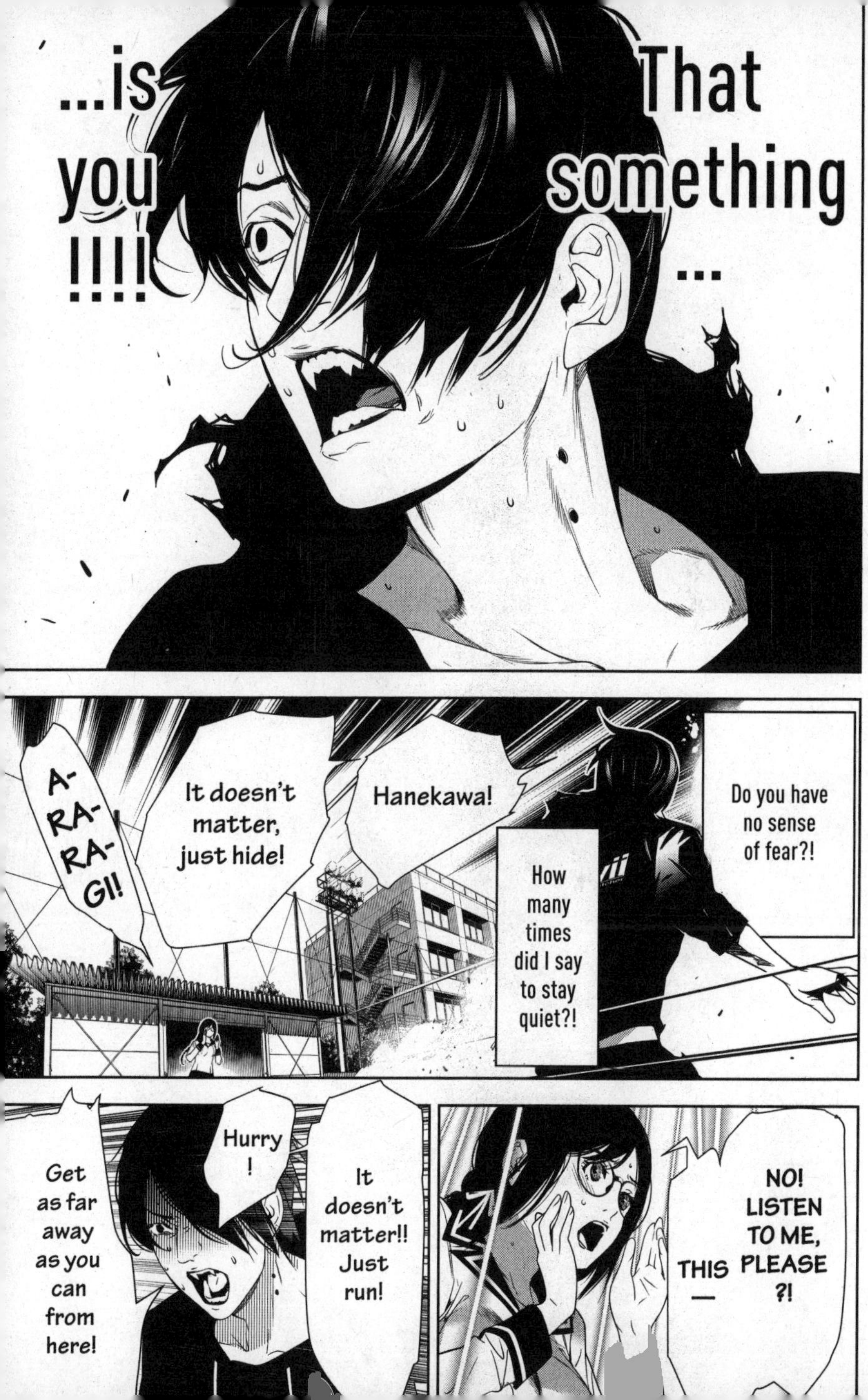
That something ...
...is you !!!!
Do you have no sense of fear?!
How many times did I say to stay quiet?!
Hanekawa!
It doesn't matter, just hide!
A-RA-RA-GI!
NO! LISTEN TO ME, PLEASE ?!
THIS —
Hurry!
It doesn't matter!! Just run!
Get as far away as you can from here!

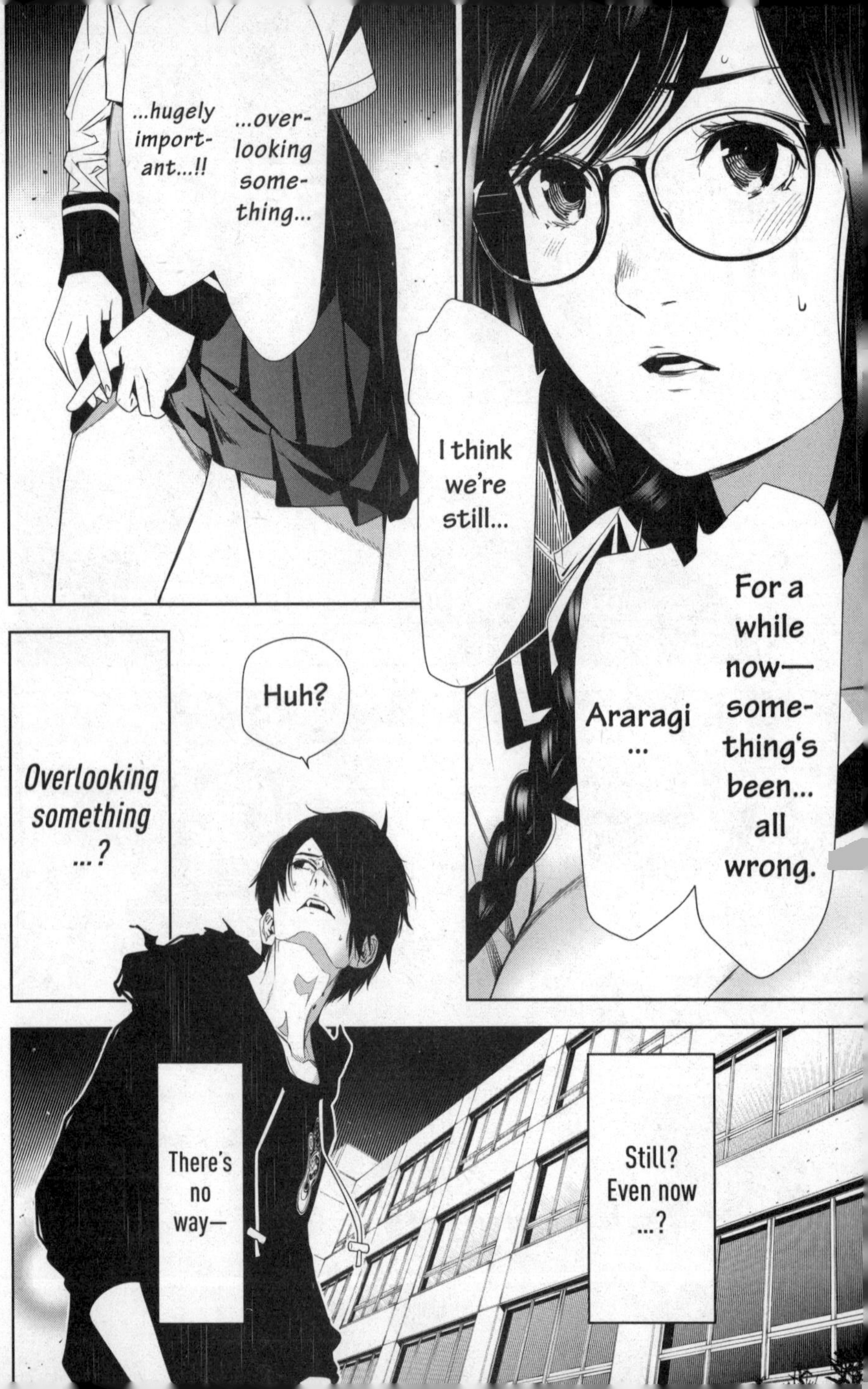
For a while now— some-thing's been... all wrong.
Araragi ...
I think we're still...
...over-looking some-thing...
...hugely import-ant...!!
Huh?
Overlooking something ...?
Still? Even now ...?
There's no way—

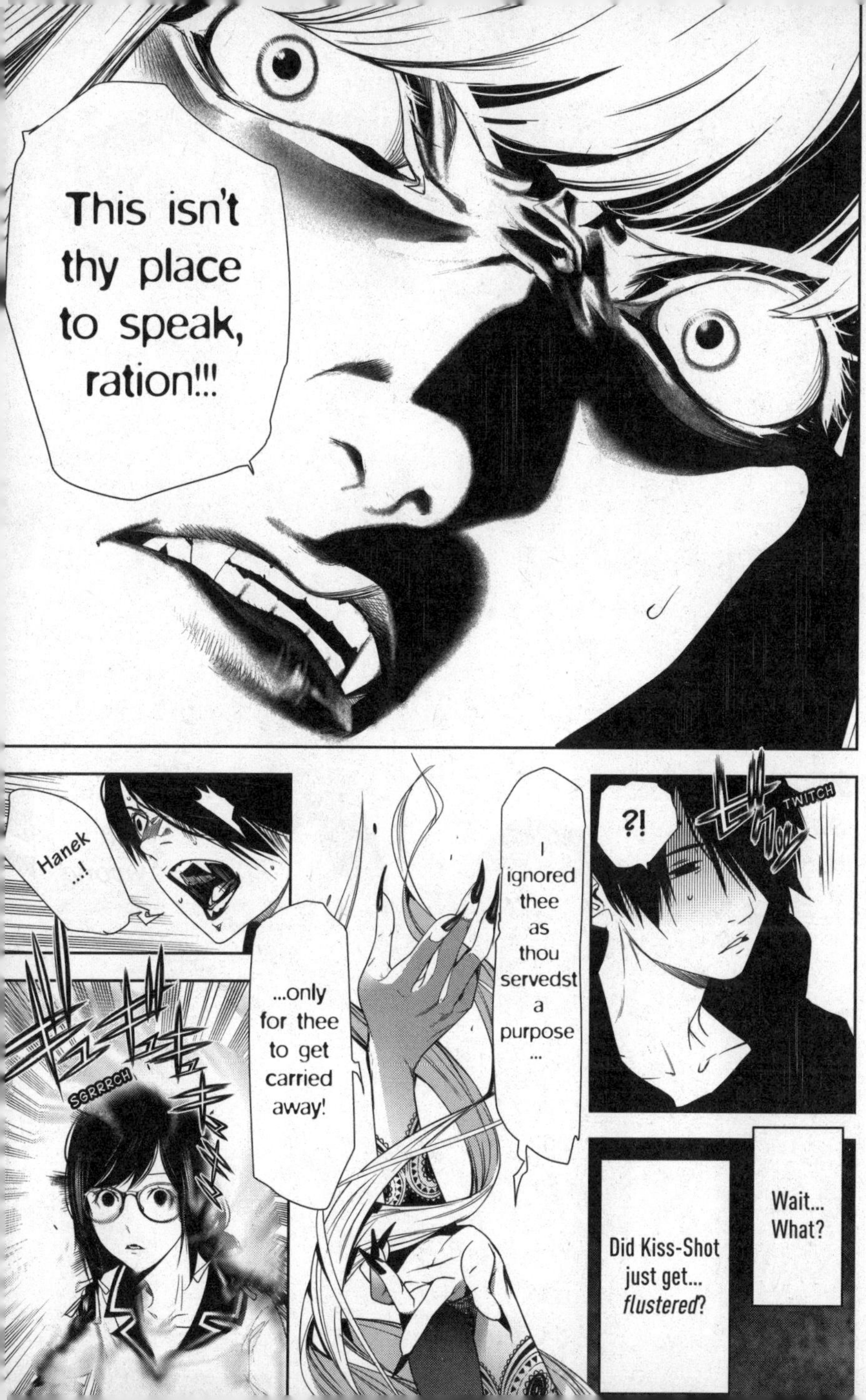
This isn't thy place to speak, ration!!!
?!
TWITCH
Wait... What?
Did Kiss-Shot just get... *flustered*?
I ignored thee as thou servedst a purpose...
...only for thee to get carried away!
Hanek ...!
SCRRRCH

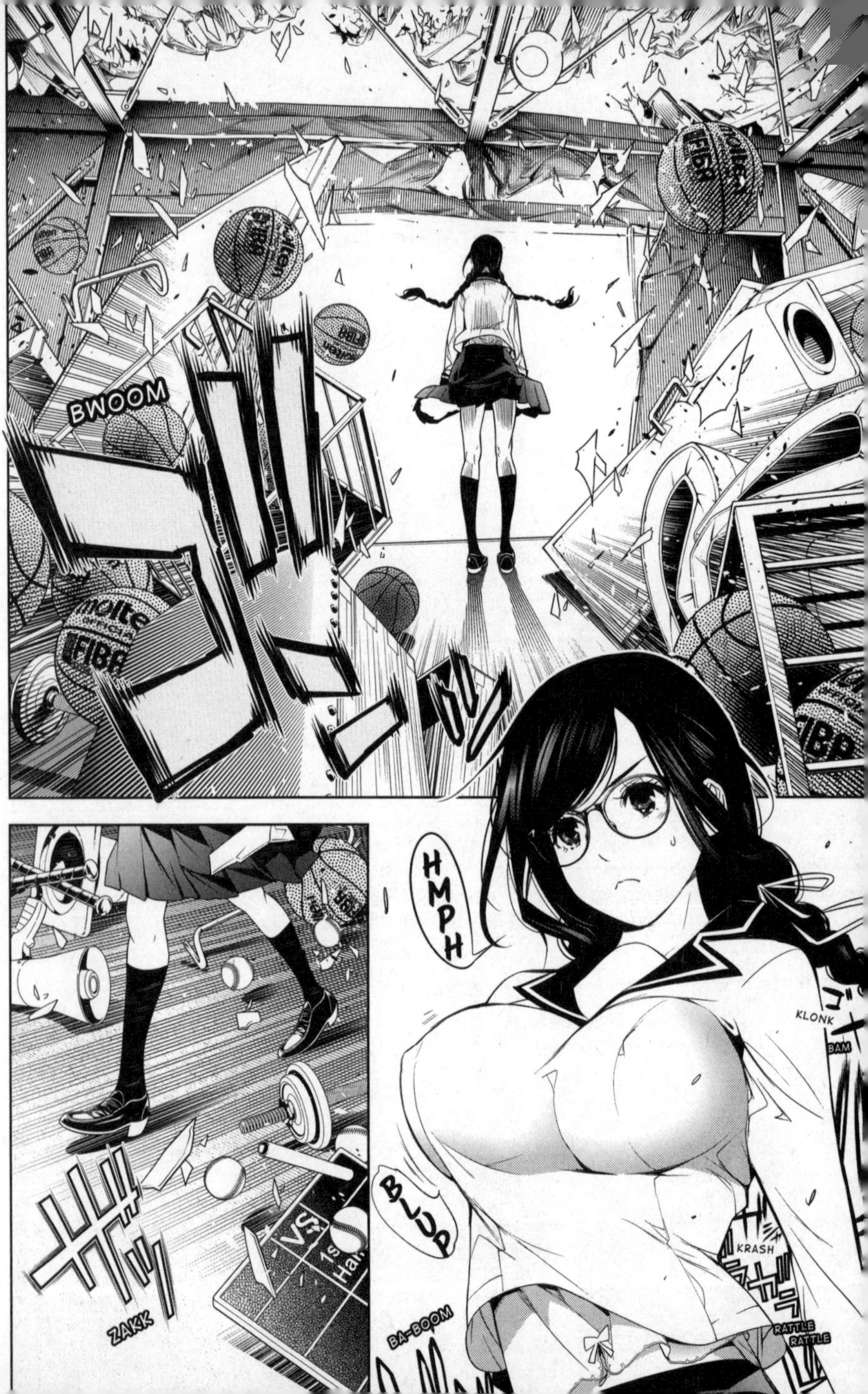
BWOOM
HMPH
KLONK
BAM
BLUP
KRASH
BA-BOOM
RATTLE RATTLE
VS.
ZAKK

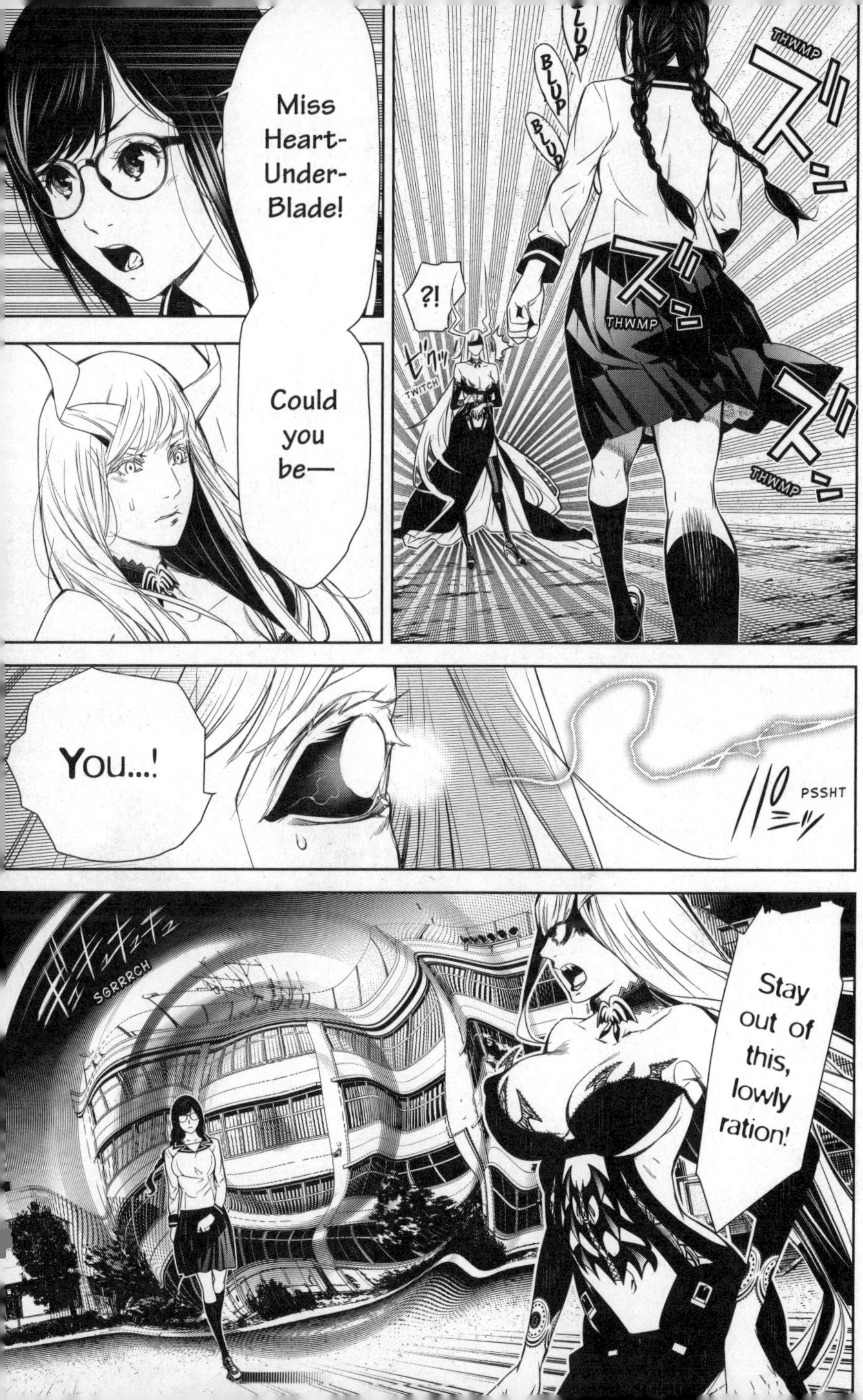
BLUP
BLUP
BLUP
BLUP
THWMP
THWMP
THWMP
?!
TWITCH
Miss Heart-Under-Blade!
Could you be—
PSSHT
You...!
Stay out of this, lowly ration!
SGRRRCH

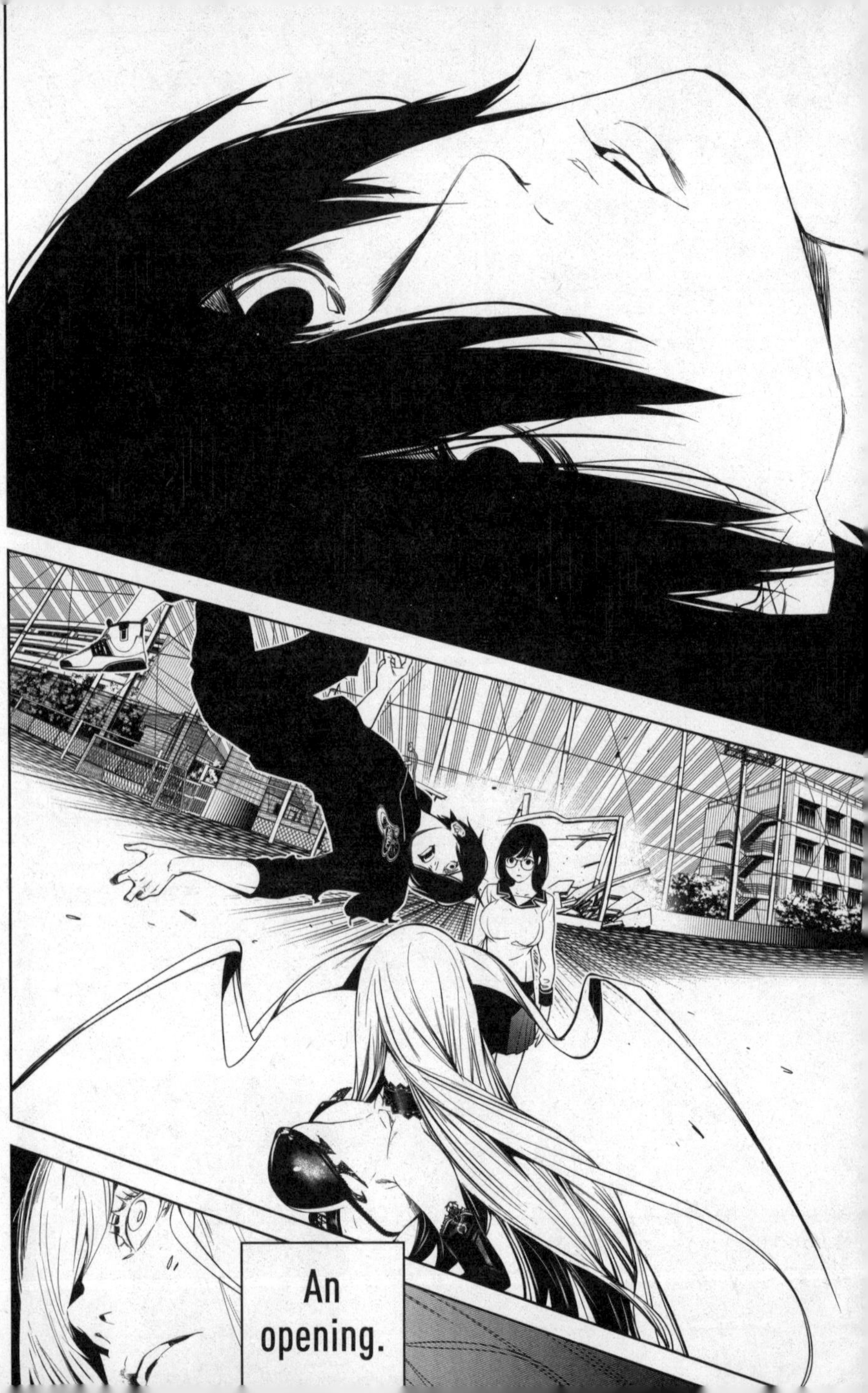
An opening.

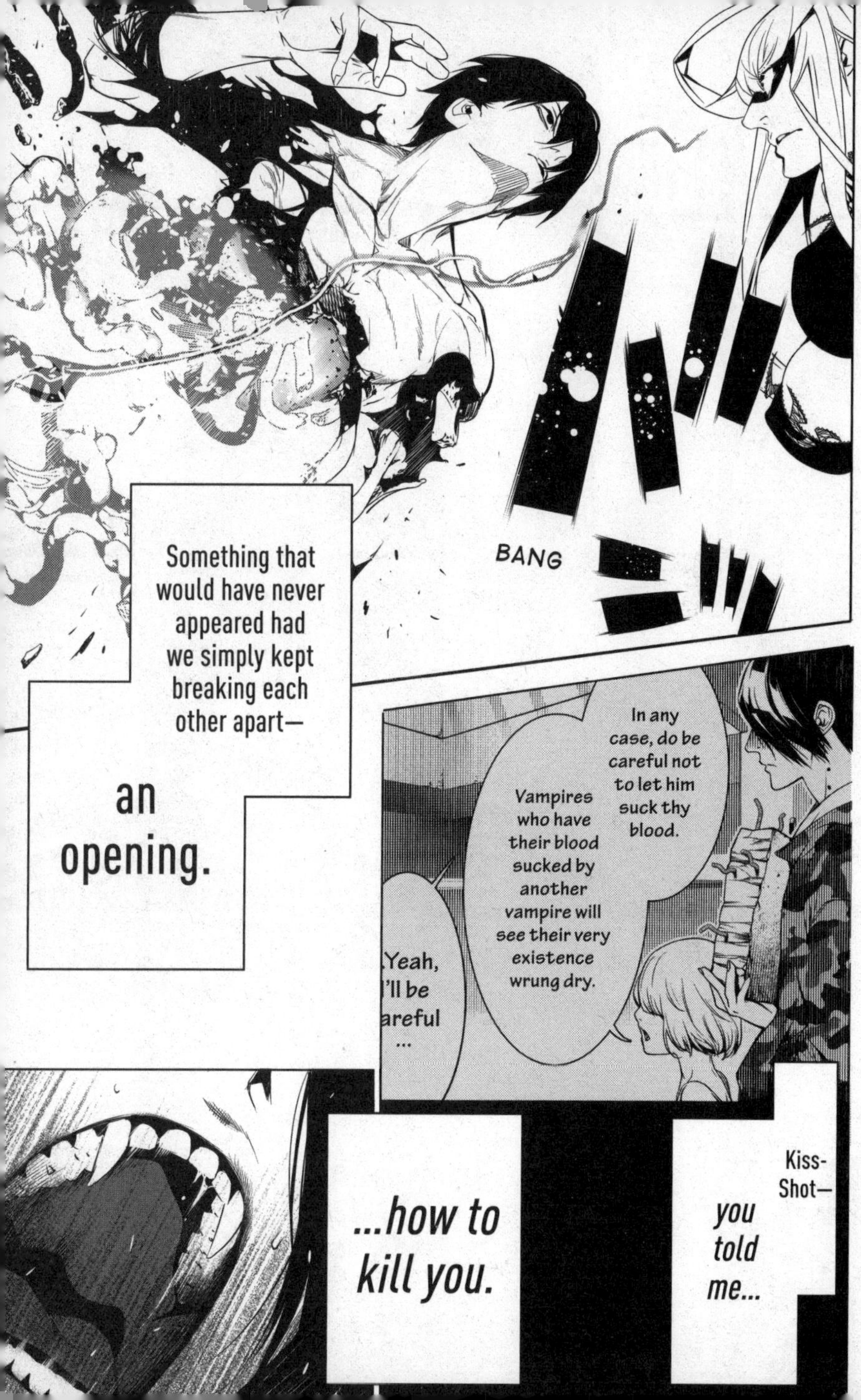
BANG
Something that would have never appeared had we simply kept breaking each other apart—
an opening.
In any case, do be careful not to let him suck thy blood.
Vampires who have their blood sucked by another vampire will see their very existence wrung dry.
Yeah, 'll be areful ...
Kiss-Shot—
you told me...
...how to kill you.

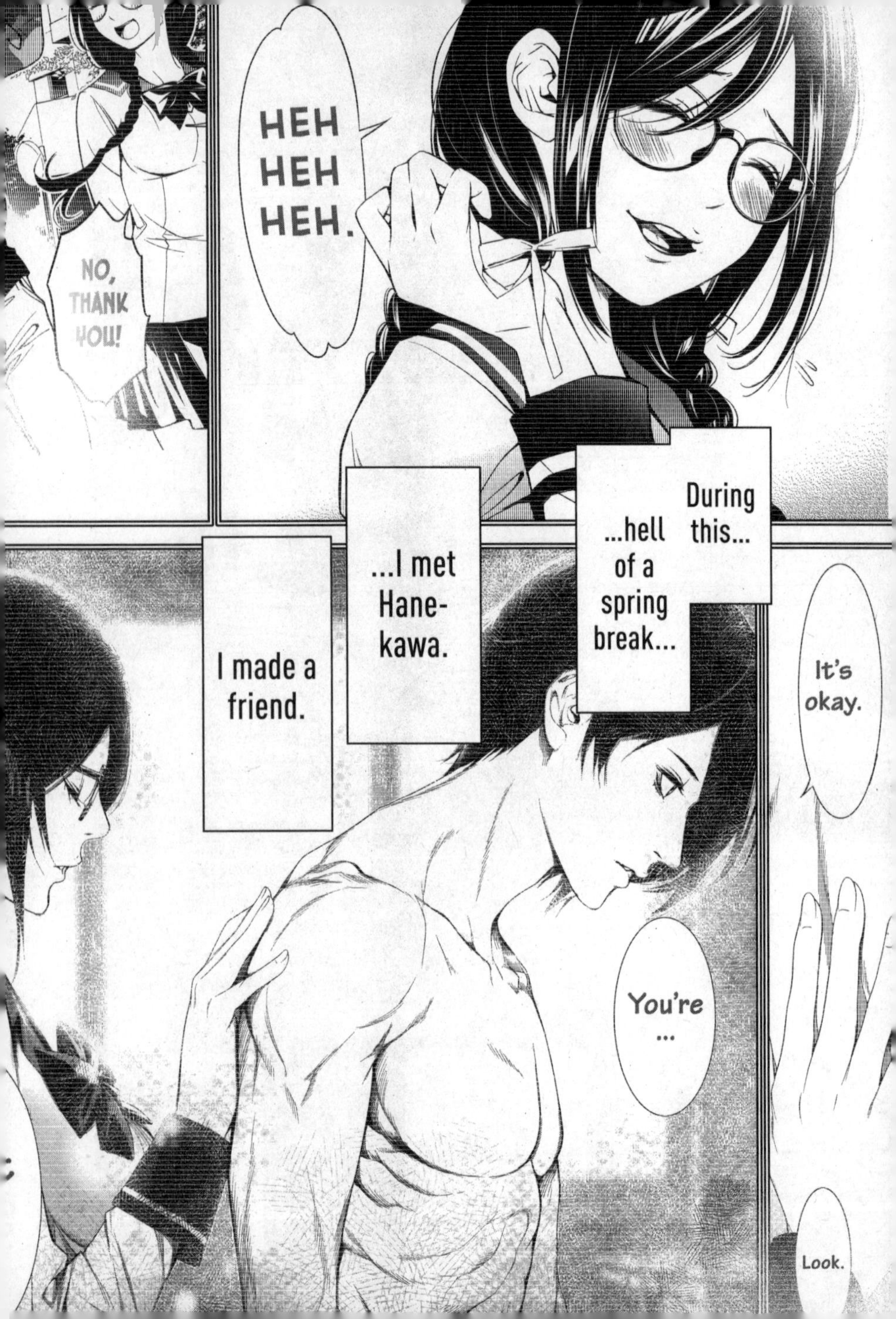
HEH HEH HEH.
NO, THANK YOU!
During this...
...hell of a spring break...
...I met Hane-kawa.
I made a friend.
It's okay.
You're ...
Look.

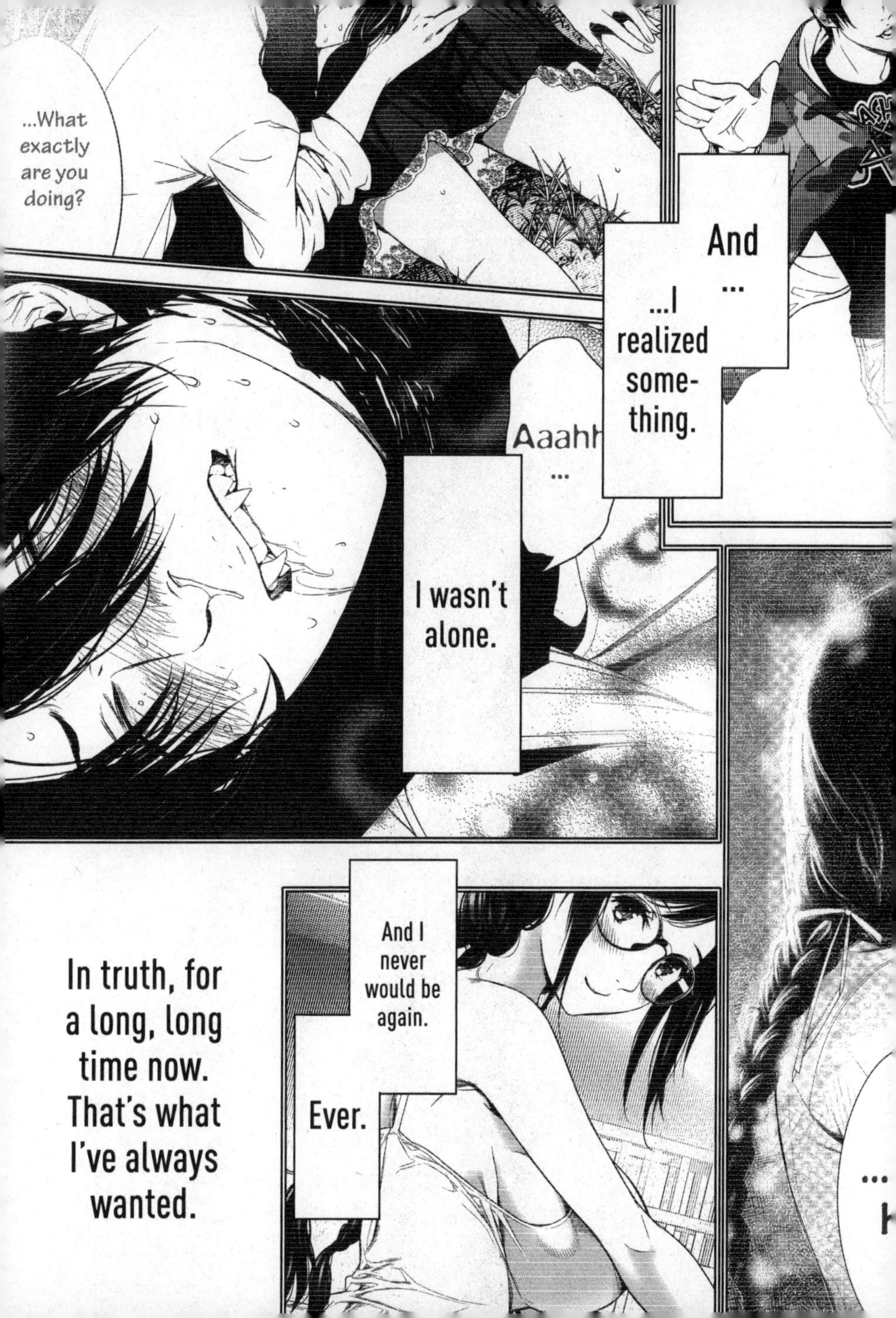
And ...
...I realized some-thing.
...What exactly are you doing?
...
Aaahh ...
I wasn't alone.
And I never would be again.
Ever.
In truth, for a long, long time now. That's what I've always wanted.

Which is why
to you I say...

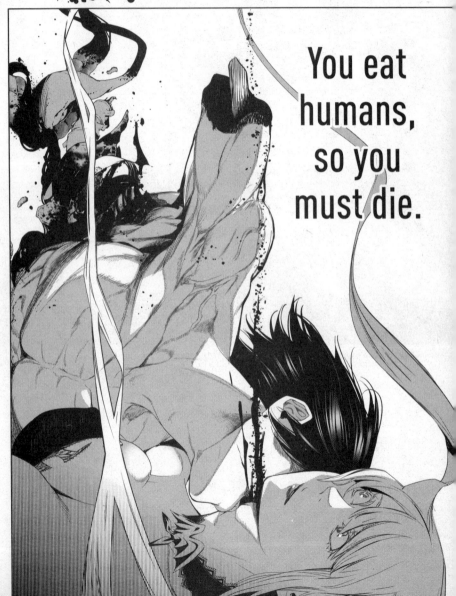

You eat
humans,
so you
must die.

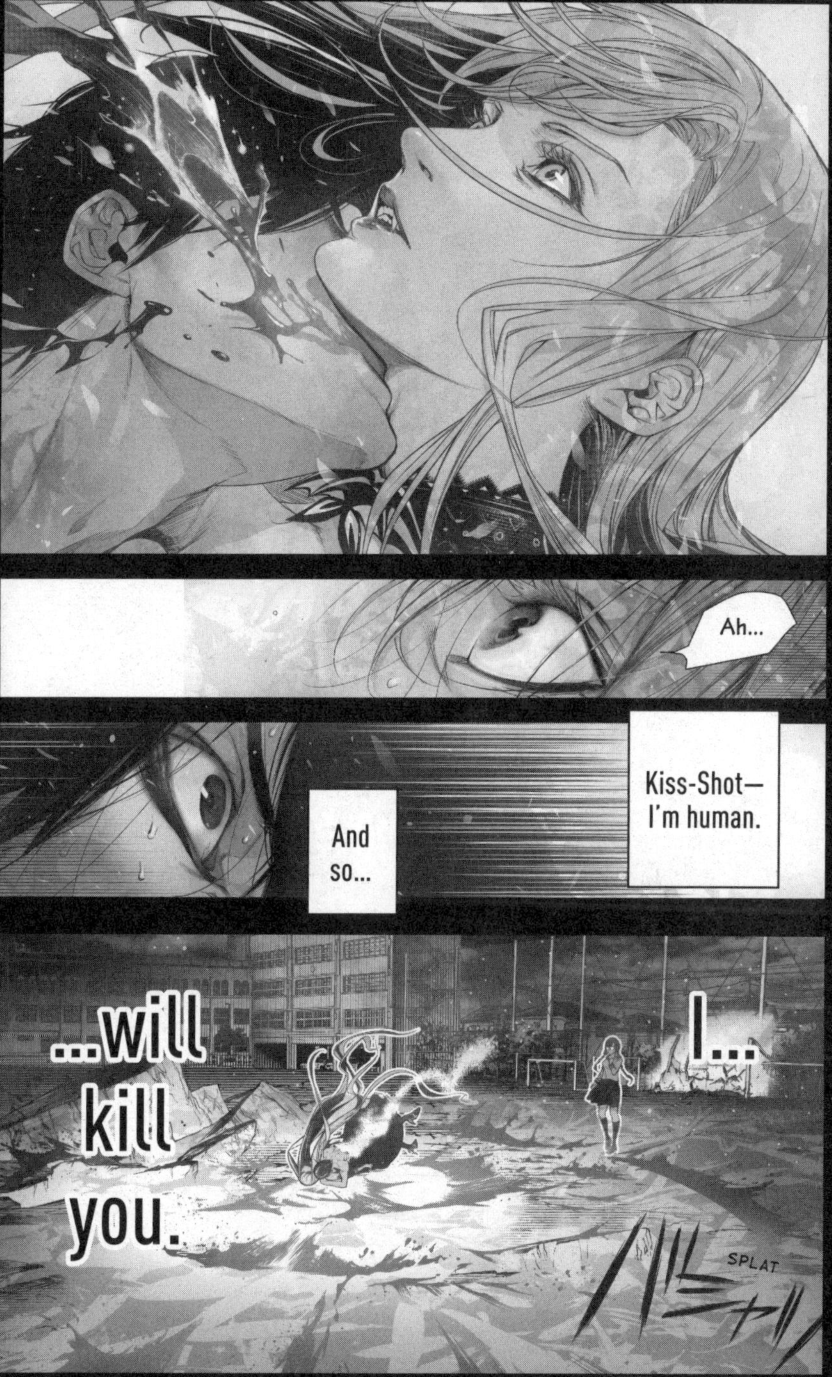
Ah...
Kiss-Shot— I'm human.
And so...
I...
...will kill you.
SPLAT

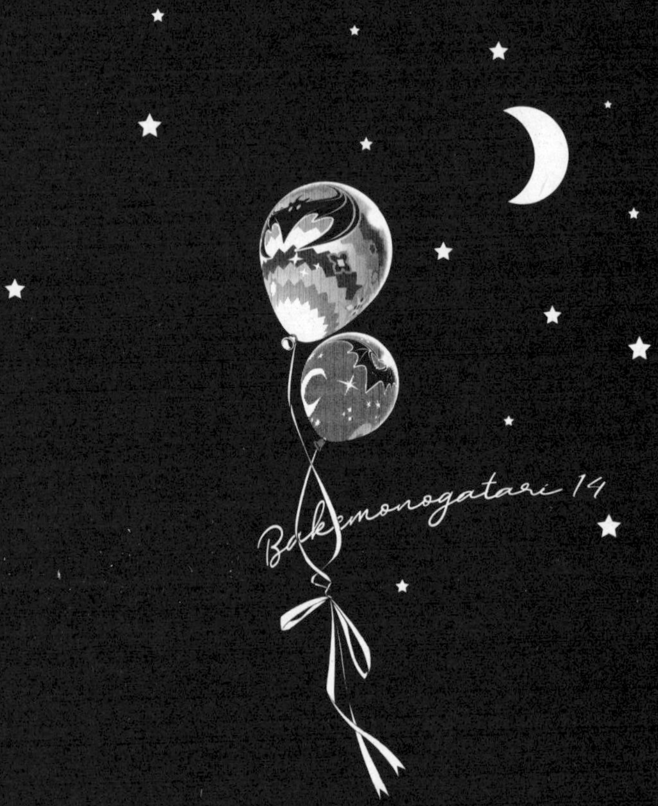
Bakemonogatari 14

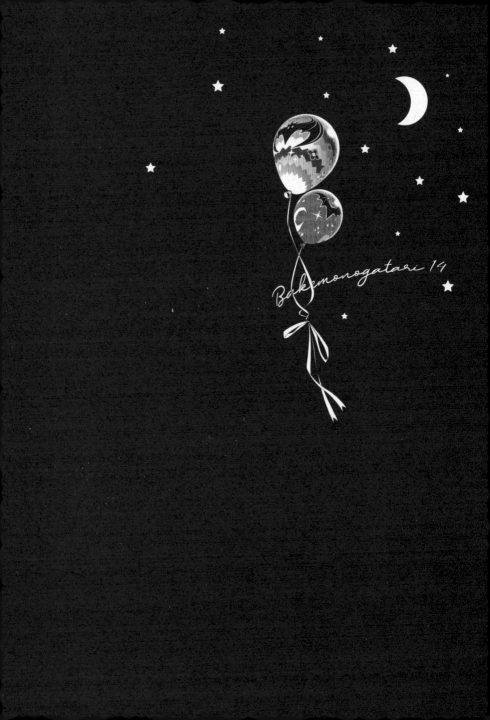

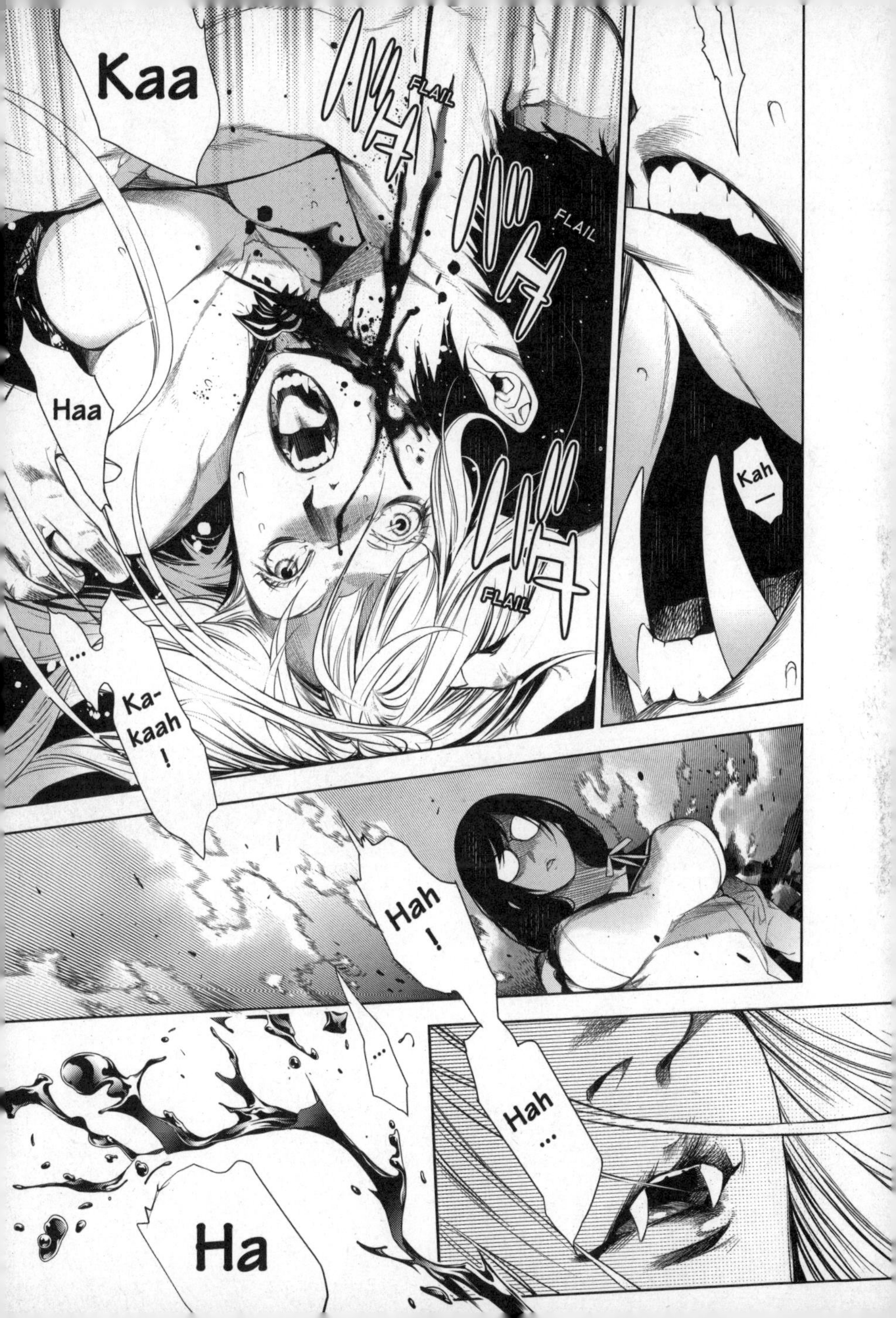

Kah —
FLAIL
Kaa
FLAIL
Haa
FLAIL
...
Ka-kaah!
Hah!
Hah ...
...
Ha

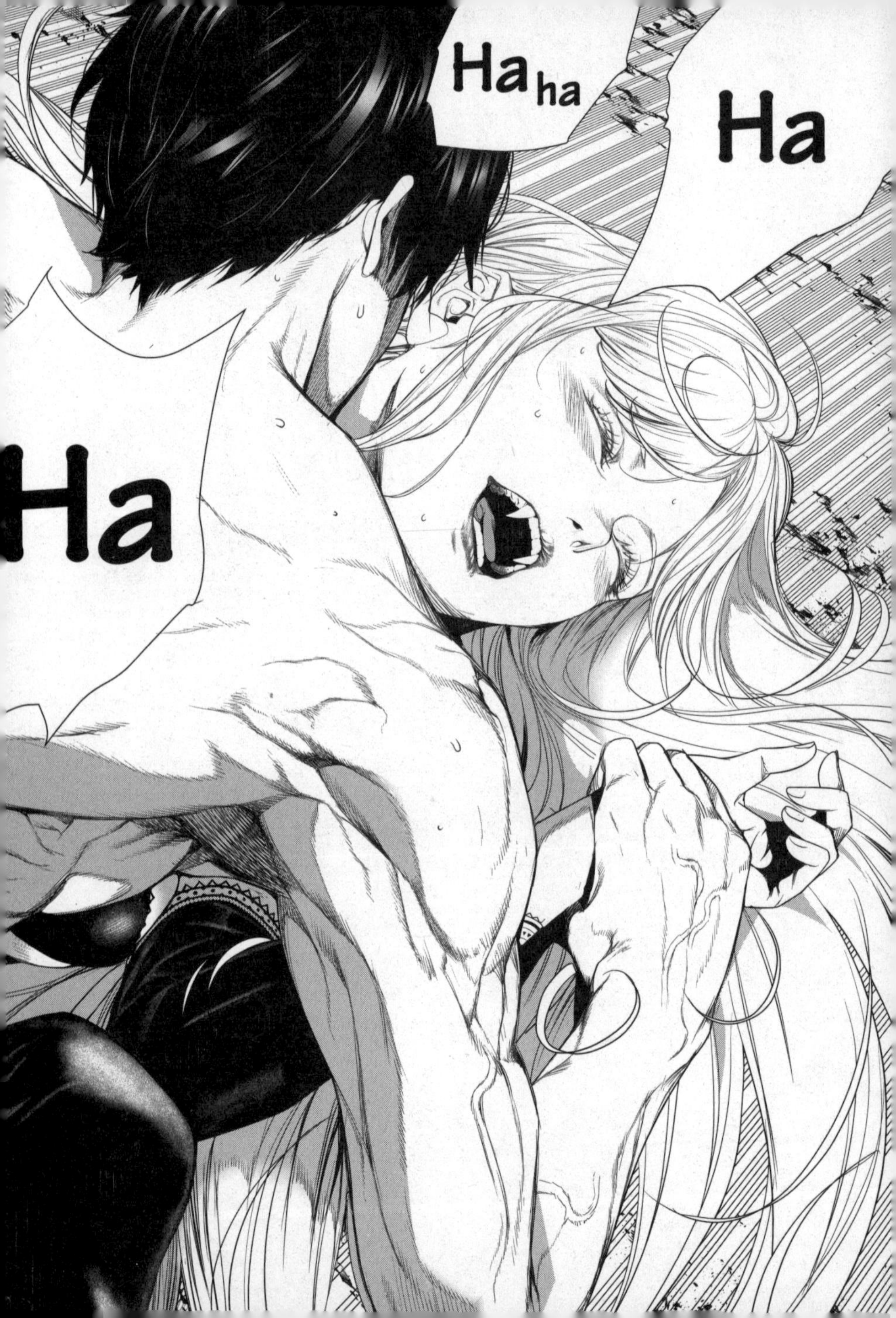
Ha
Ha ha
Ha

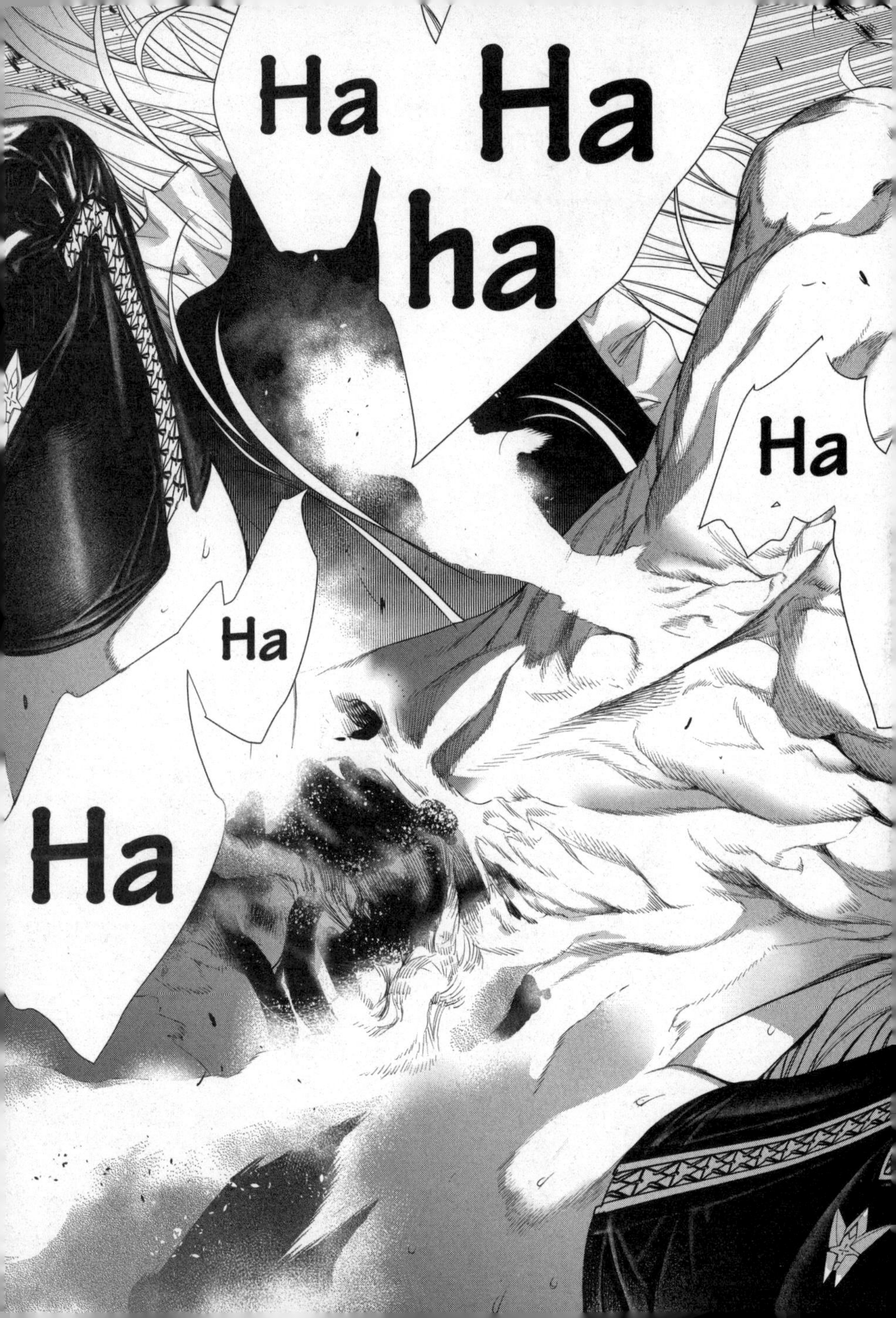
Ha Ha ha
Ha
Ha
Ha

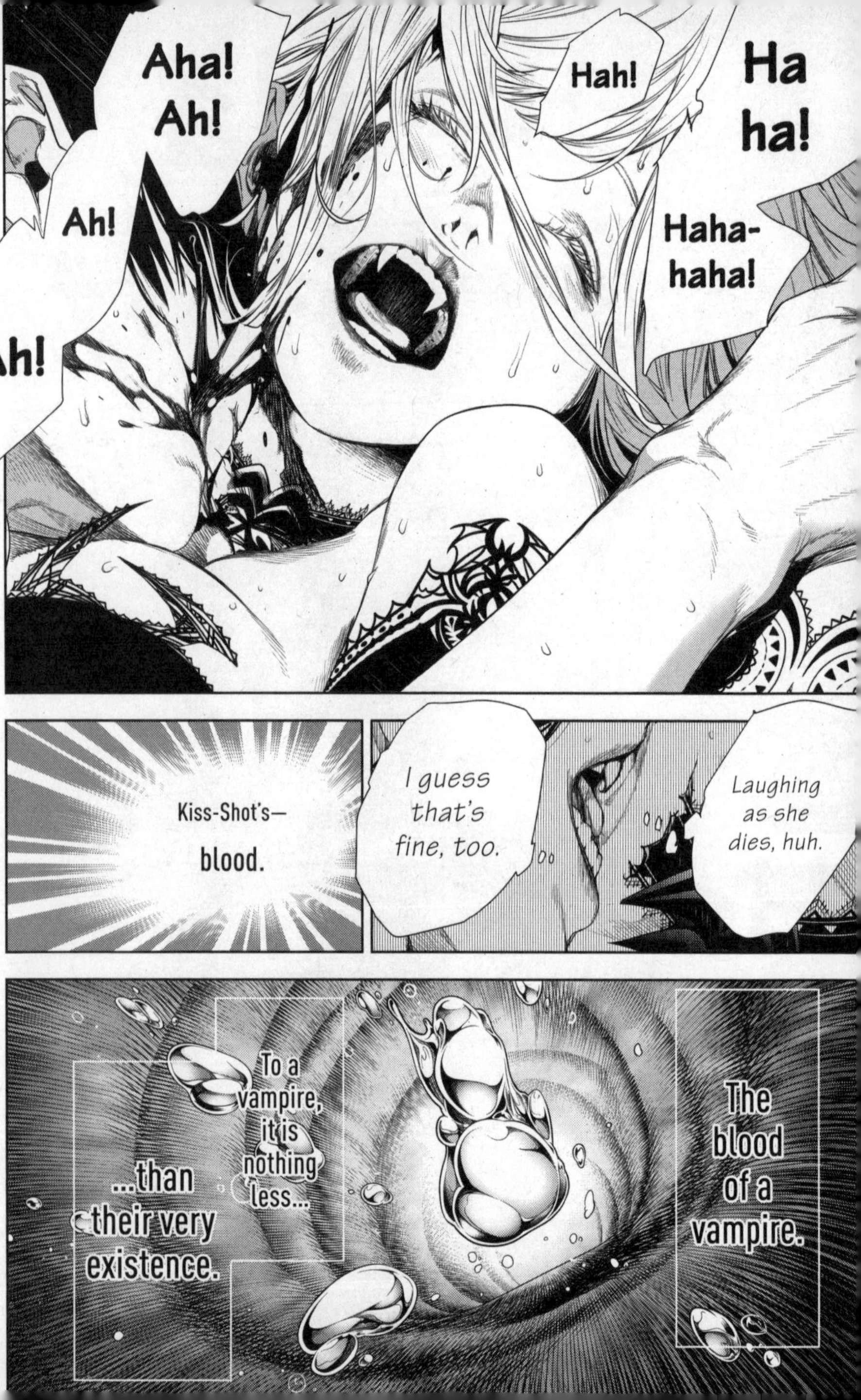
Ha ha!
Hah!
Aha! Ah!
Haha-haha!
Ah!
Ah!
Laughing as she dies, huh.
I guess that's fine, too.
Kiss-Shot's—
blood.
The blood of a vampire.
To a vampire, it is nothing less...
...than their very existence.

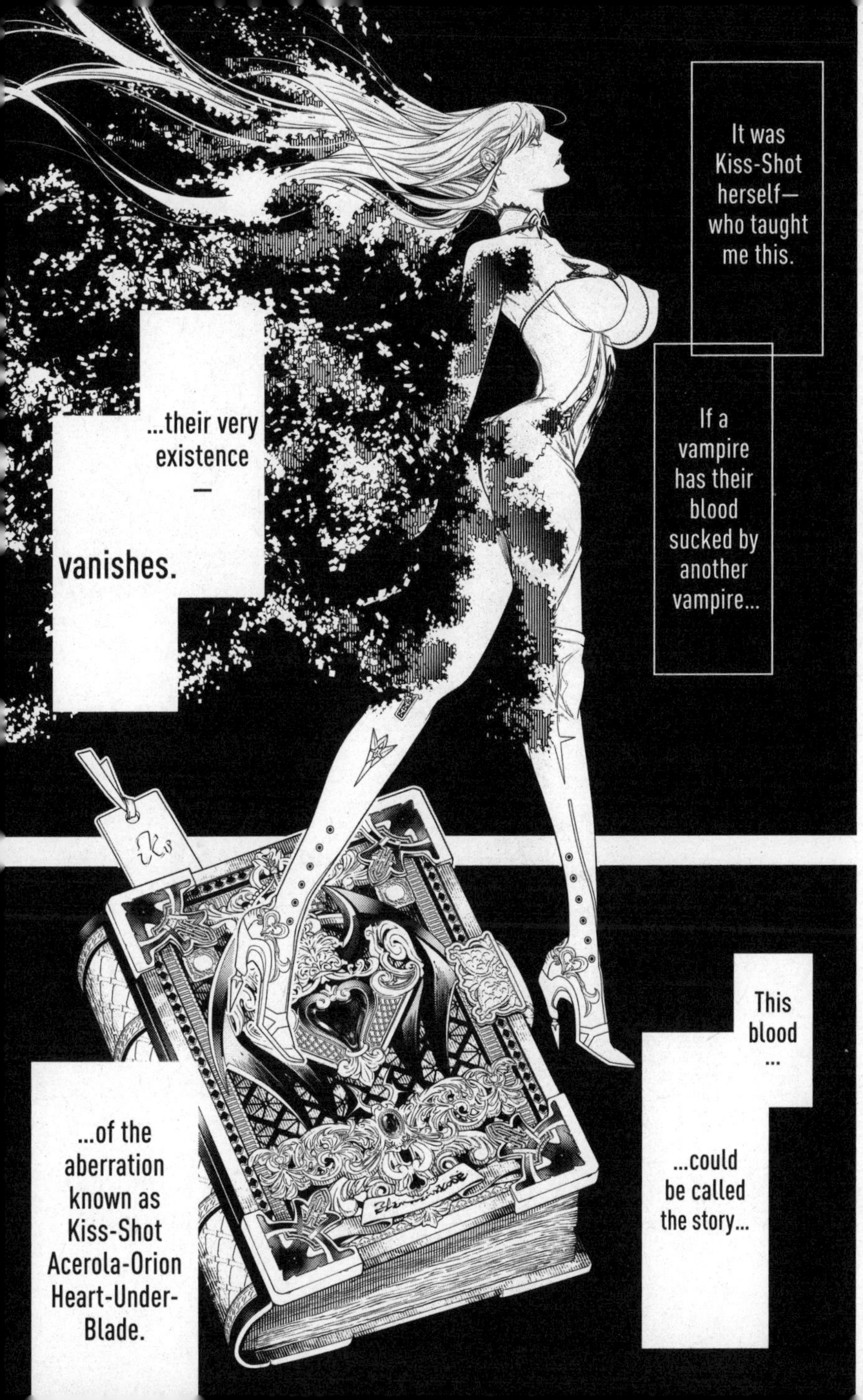

It was Kiss-Shot herself— who taught me this.
If a vampire has their blood sucked by another vampire...
...their very existence
—
vanishes.
This blood ...
...could be called the story...
...of the aberration known as Kiss-Shot Acerola-Orion Heart-Under-Blade.

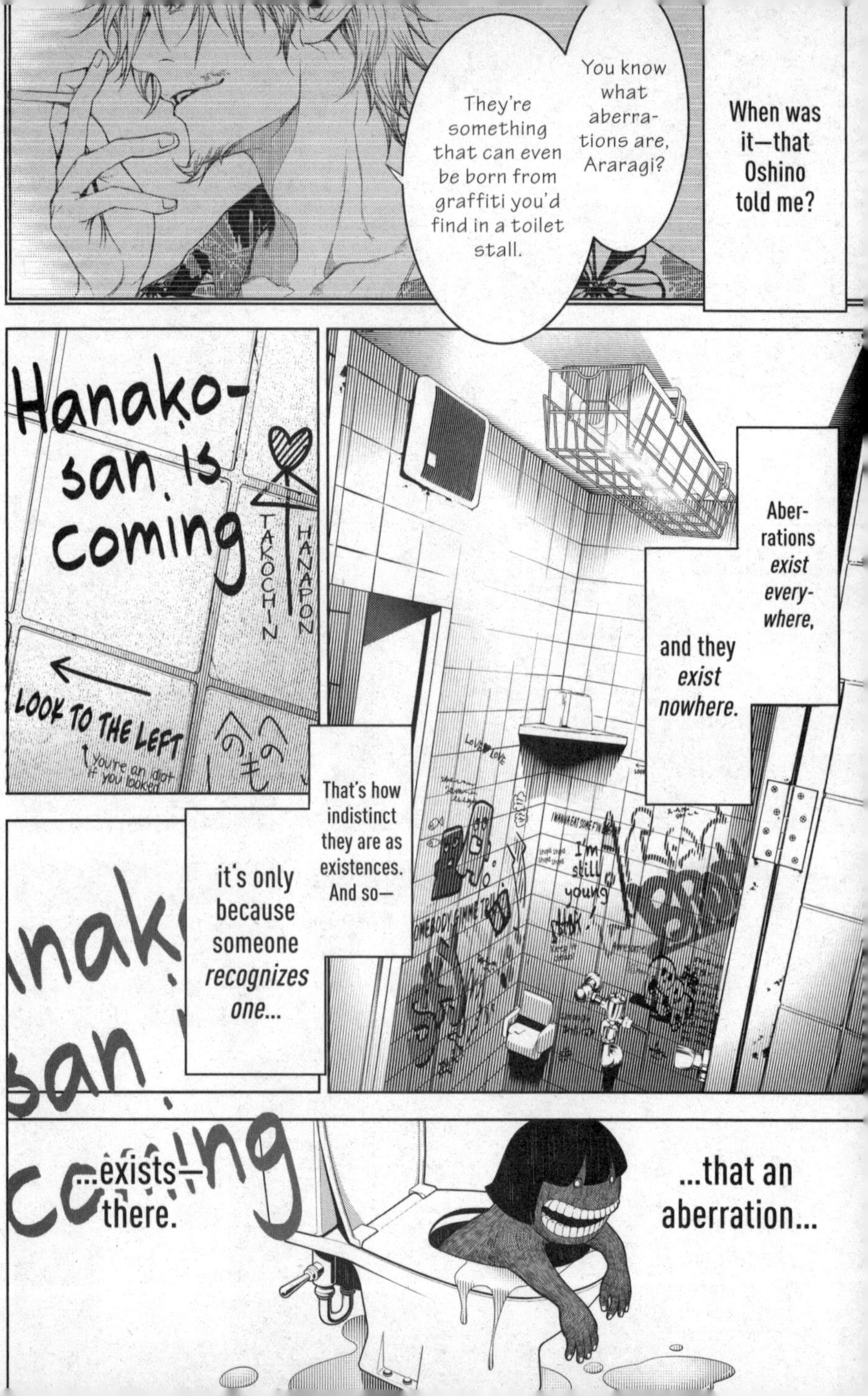
When was it—that Oshino told me?
You know what aberrations are, Araragi?
They're something that can even be born from graffiti you'd find in a toilet stall.
Aberrations exist everywhere,
and they exist nowhere.
I'm still young
That's how indistinct they are as existences. And so—
Hanako-san is coming
HANAPON
TAKOCHIN
LOOK TO THE LEFT
You're an idiot if you looked
it's only because someone recognizes one...
...that an aberration...
...exists—there.

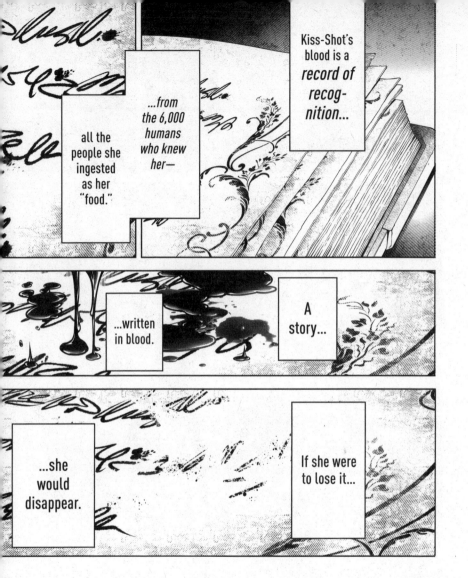

Kiss-Shot's blood is a *record of recognition...*
...from the 6,000 humans who knew her—
all the people she ingested as her "food."
A story...
...written in blood.
If she were to lose it...
...she would disappear.

It would be as if...

...she never even existed in the first place.

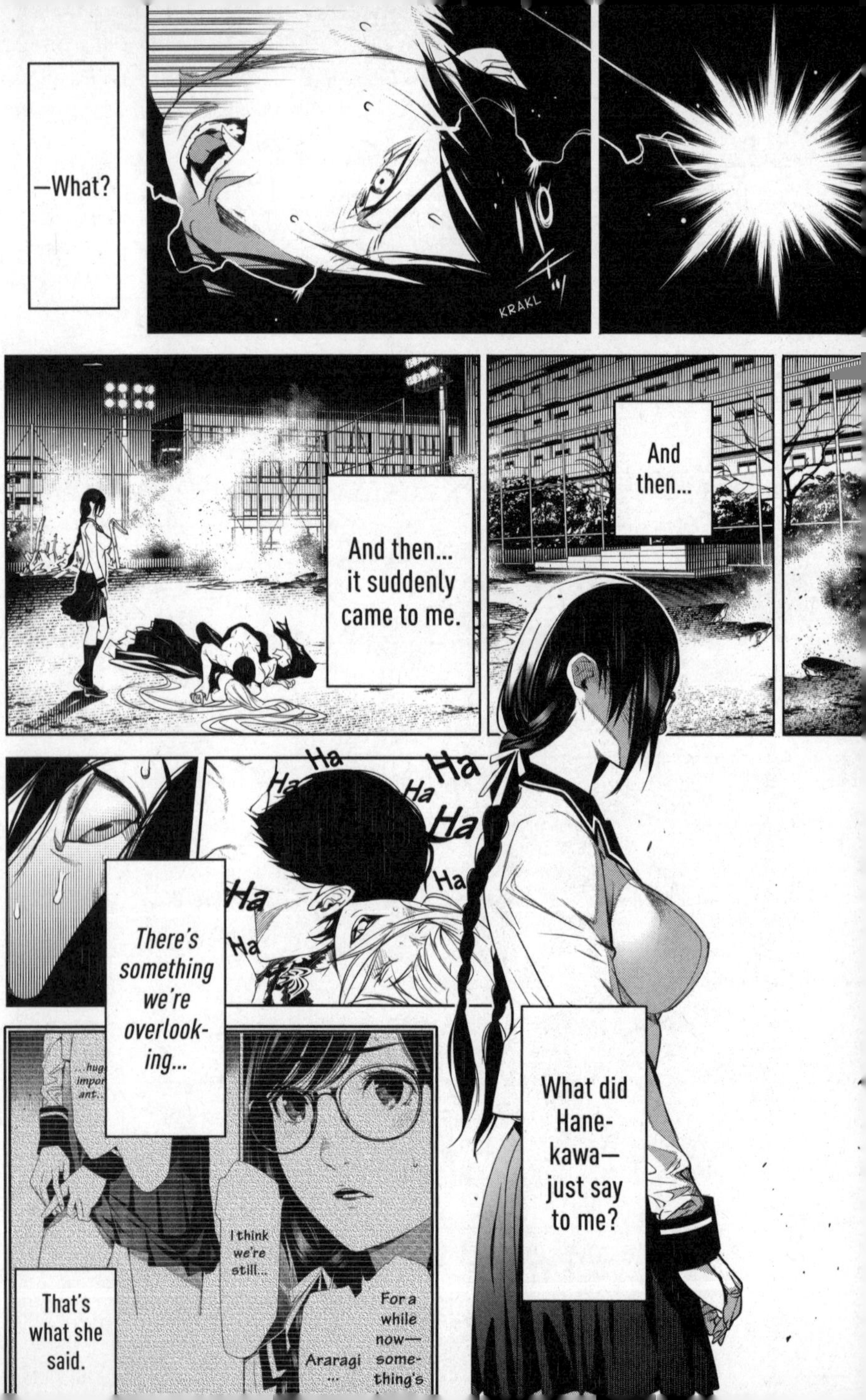
KRAKL
—What?
And then...
And then... it suddenly came to me.
What did Hane-kawa—just say to me?
Ha Ha Ha Ha Ha Ha Ha Ha
There's something we're overlook-ing...
For a while now—some-thing's
I think we're still...
Araragi...
That's what she said.

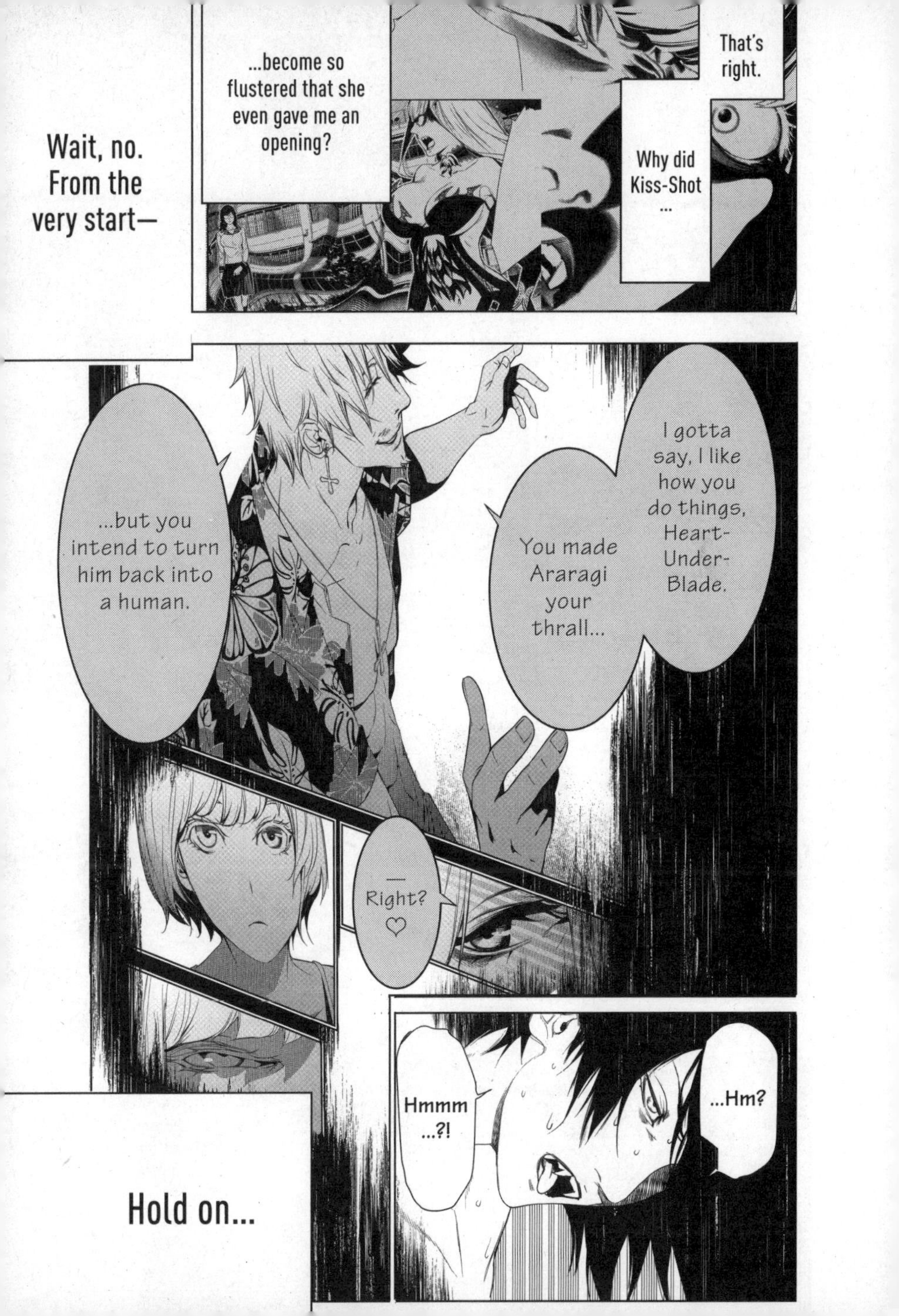
That's right.
Why did Kiss-Shot ...
...become so flustered that she even gave me an opening?
Wait, no. From the very start—
I gotta say, I like how you do things, Heart-Under-Blade.
You made Araragi your thrall...
...but you intend to turn him back into a human.
—Right? ♡
...Hm?
Hmmm ...?!
Hold on...

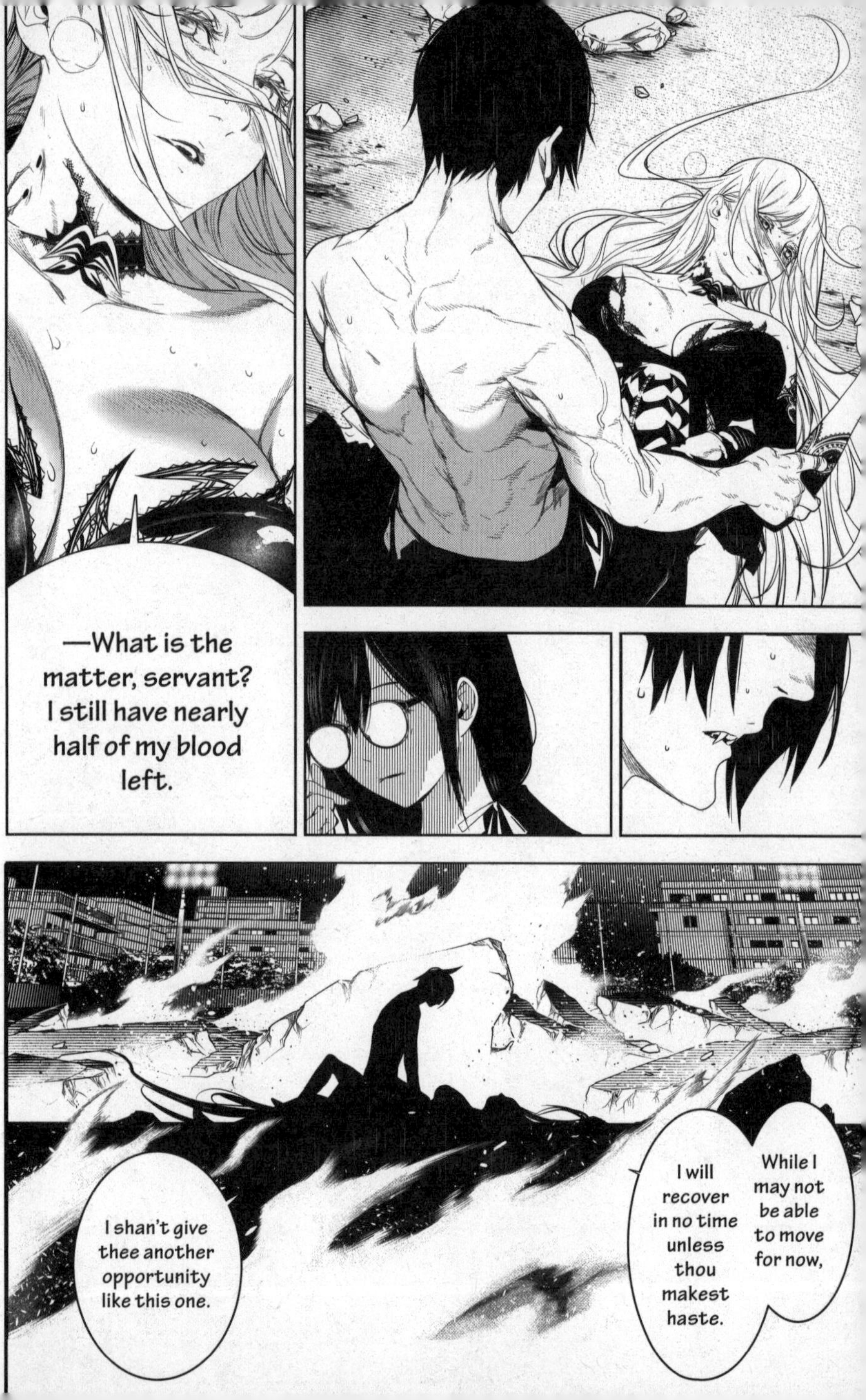
—What is the matter, servant? I still have nearly half of my blood left.
While I may not be able to move for now,
I will recover in no time unless thou makest haste.
I shan't give thee another opportunity like this one.

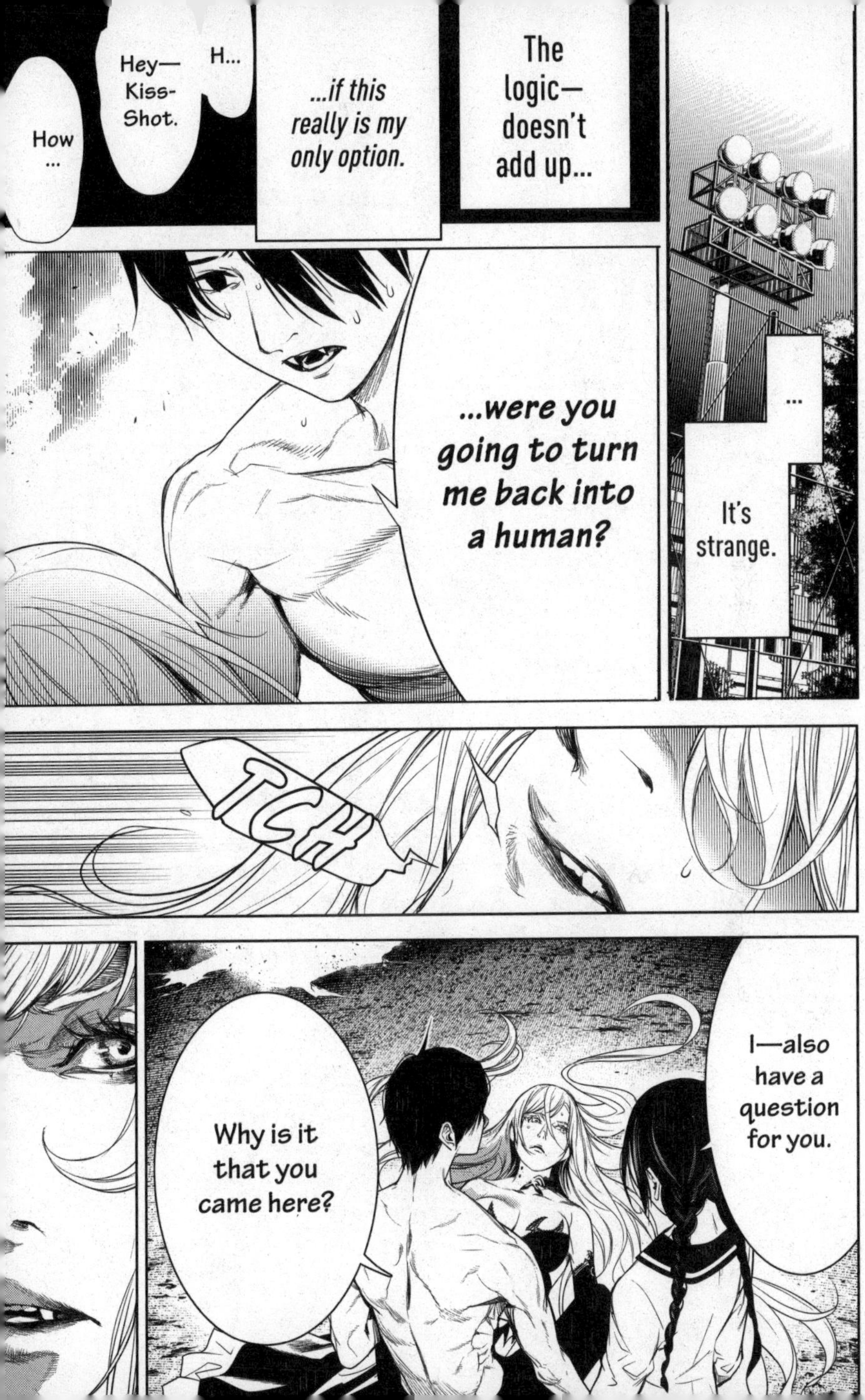
...
It's strange.
The logic—doesn't add up...
...if this really is my only option.
H...
Hey—Kiss-Shot.
How ...
...were you going to turn me back into a human?
TCH
I—also have a question for you.
Why is it that you came here?

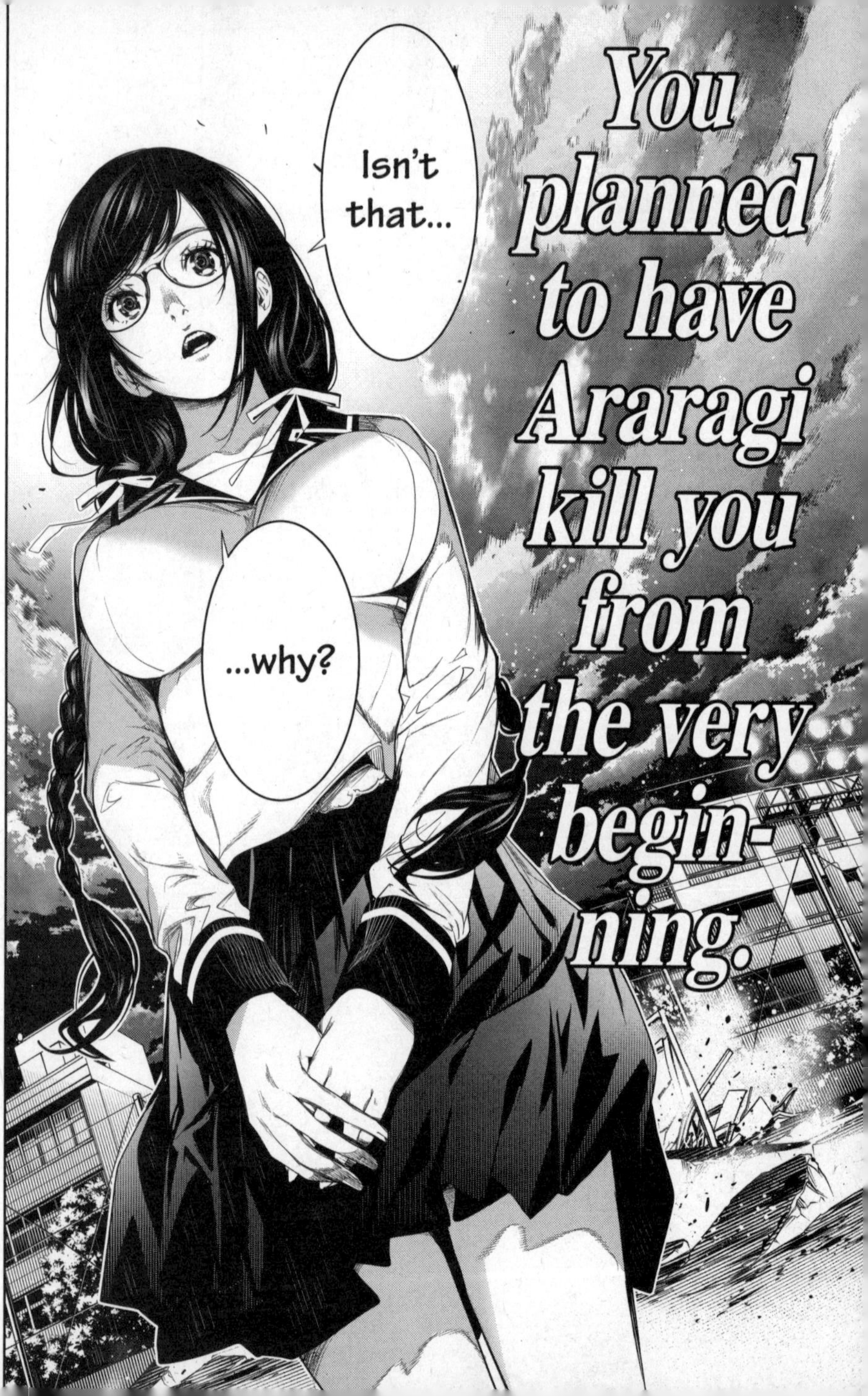
You planned to have Araragi kill you from the very begin-ning.
Isn't that...
...why?

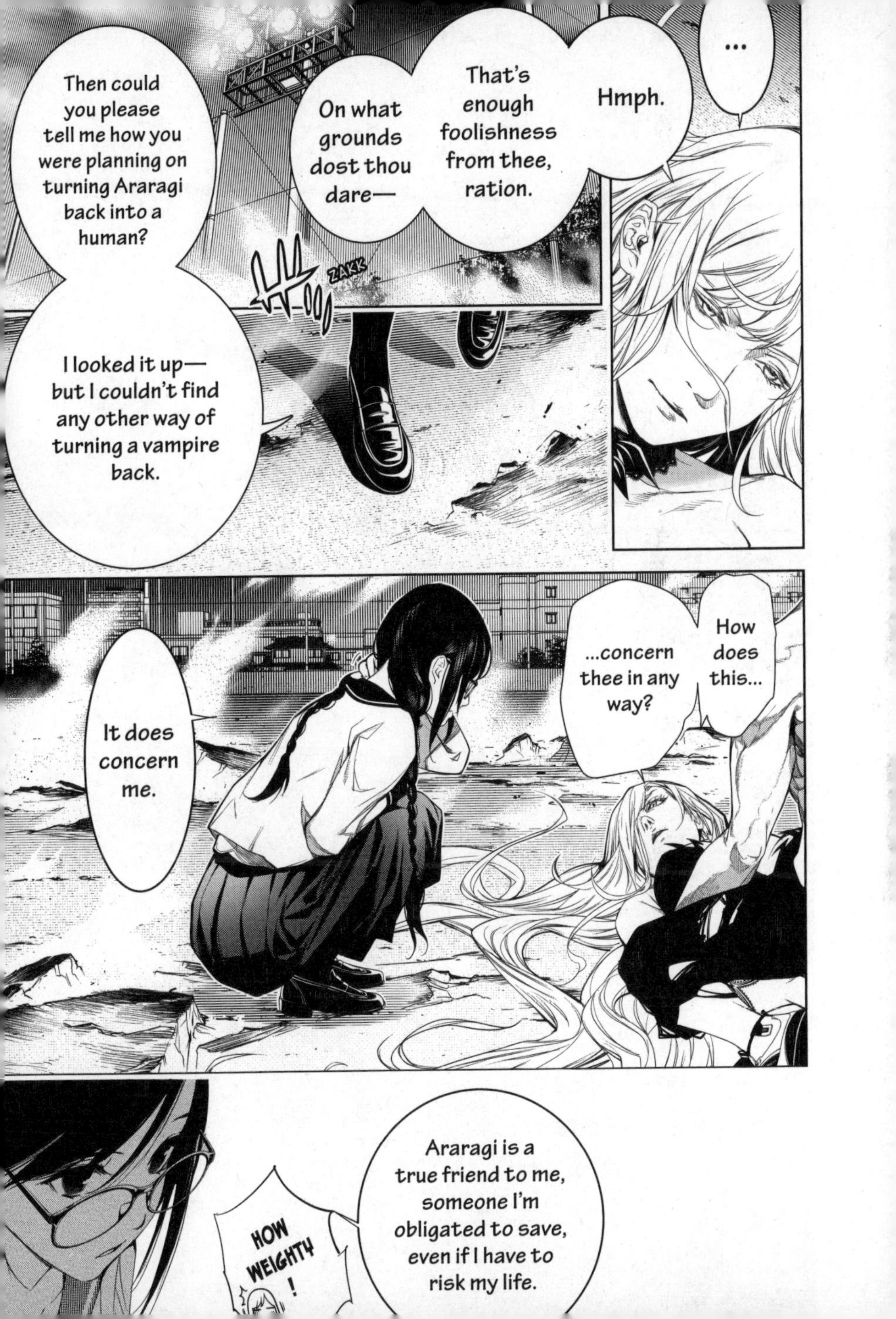
...
Hmph.
That's enough foolishness from thee, ration.
On what grounds dost thou dare—
Then could you please tell me how you were planning on turning Araragi back into a human?
ZAKK
I looked it up— but I couldn't find any other way of turning a vampire back.
How does this...
...concern thee in any way?
It does concern me.
Araragi is a true friend to me, someone I'm obligated to save, even if I have to risk my life.
HOW WEIGHTY!

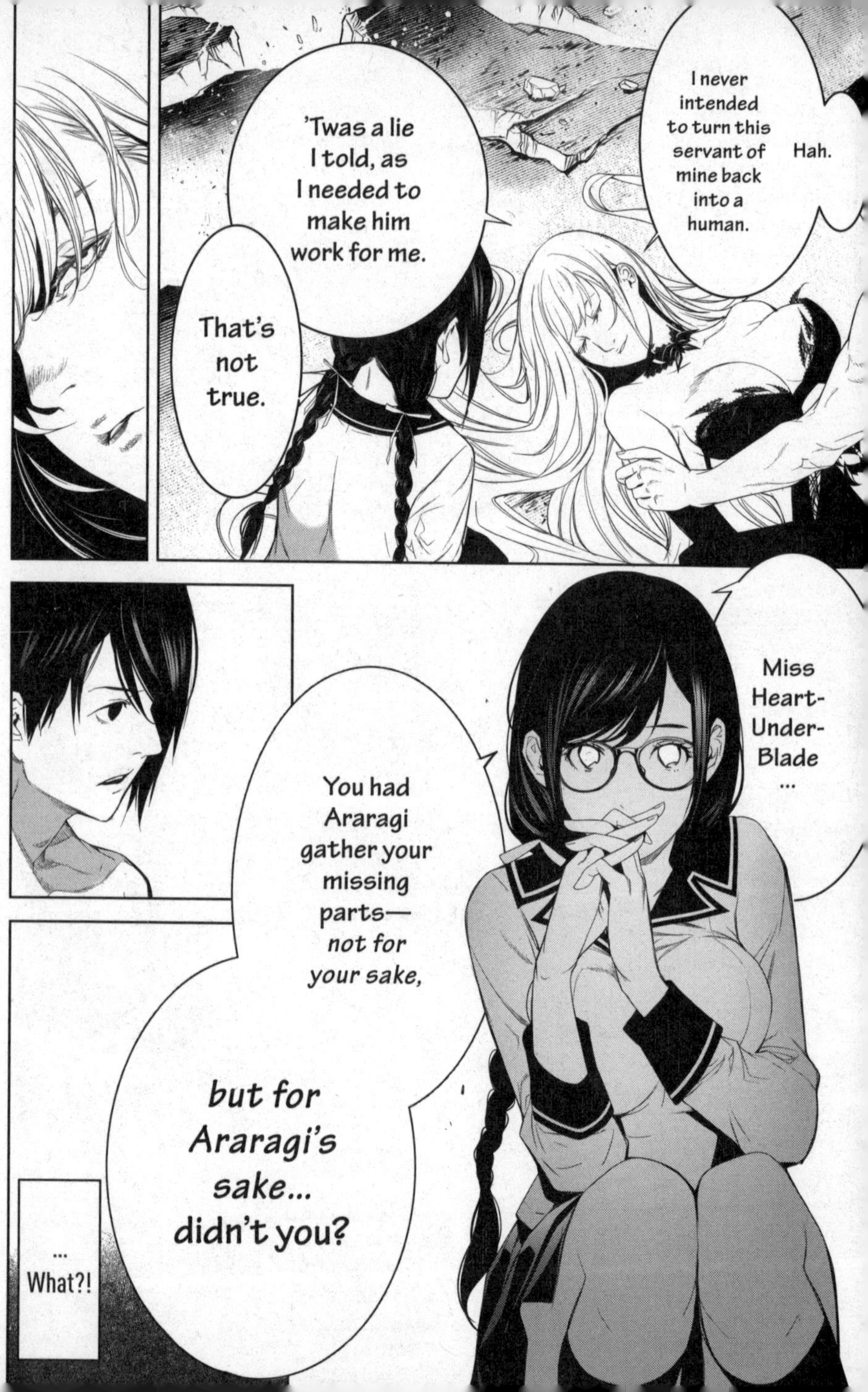
Hah.
I never intended to turn this servant of mine back into a human.
'Twas a lie I told, as I needed to make him work for me.
That's not true.
Miss Heart-Under-Blade...
You had Araragi gather your missing parts—*not for your sake,*
but for Araragi's sake... didn't you?
... What?!

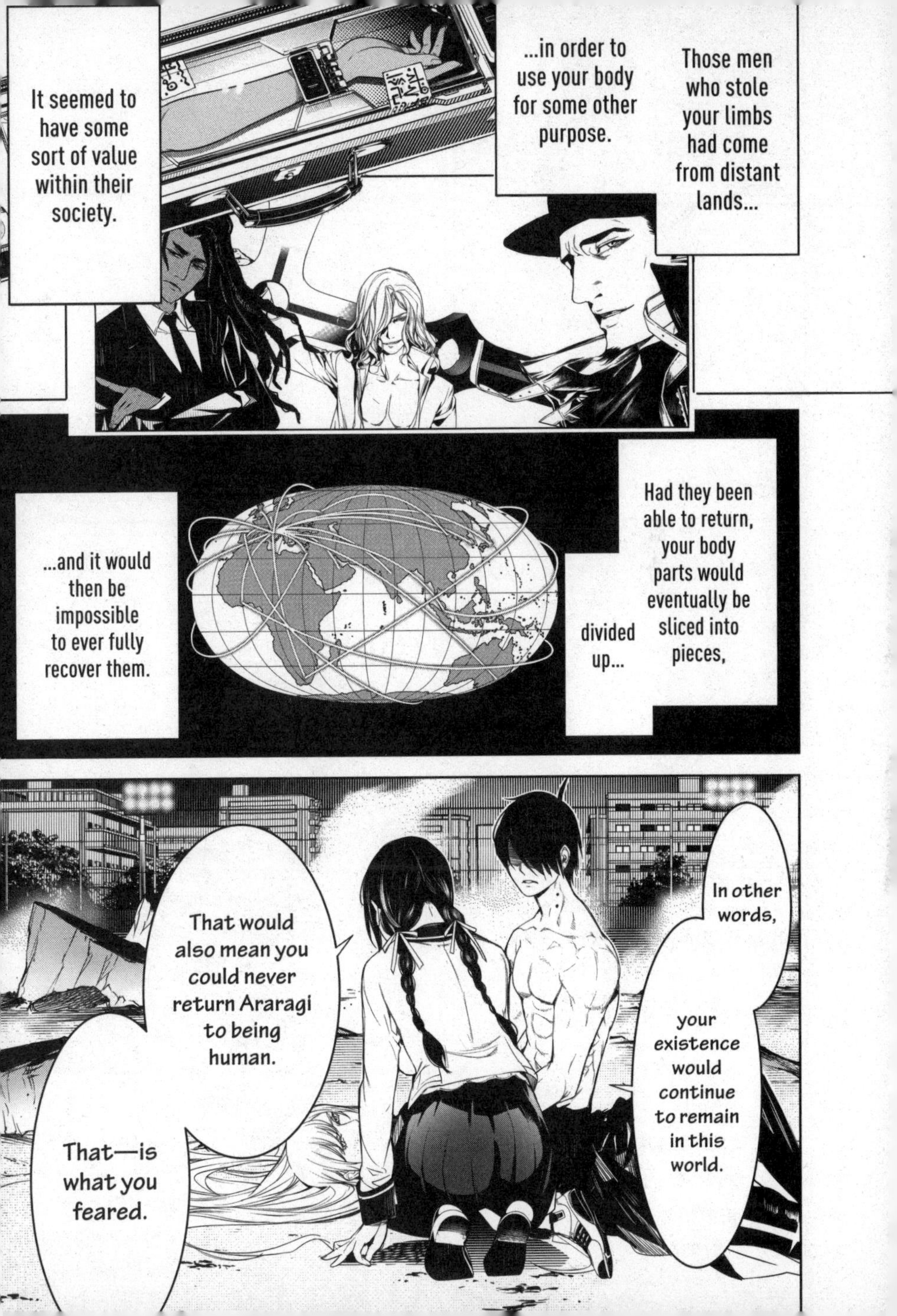
Those men who stole your limbs had come from distant lands...
...in order to use your body for some other purpose.
It seemed to have some sort of value within their society.
Had they been able to return, your body parts would eventually be sliced into pieces,
divided up...
...and it would then be impossible to ever fully recover them.
In other words,
your existence would continue to remain in this world.
That would also mean you could never return Araragi to being human.
That—is what you feared.

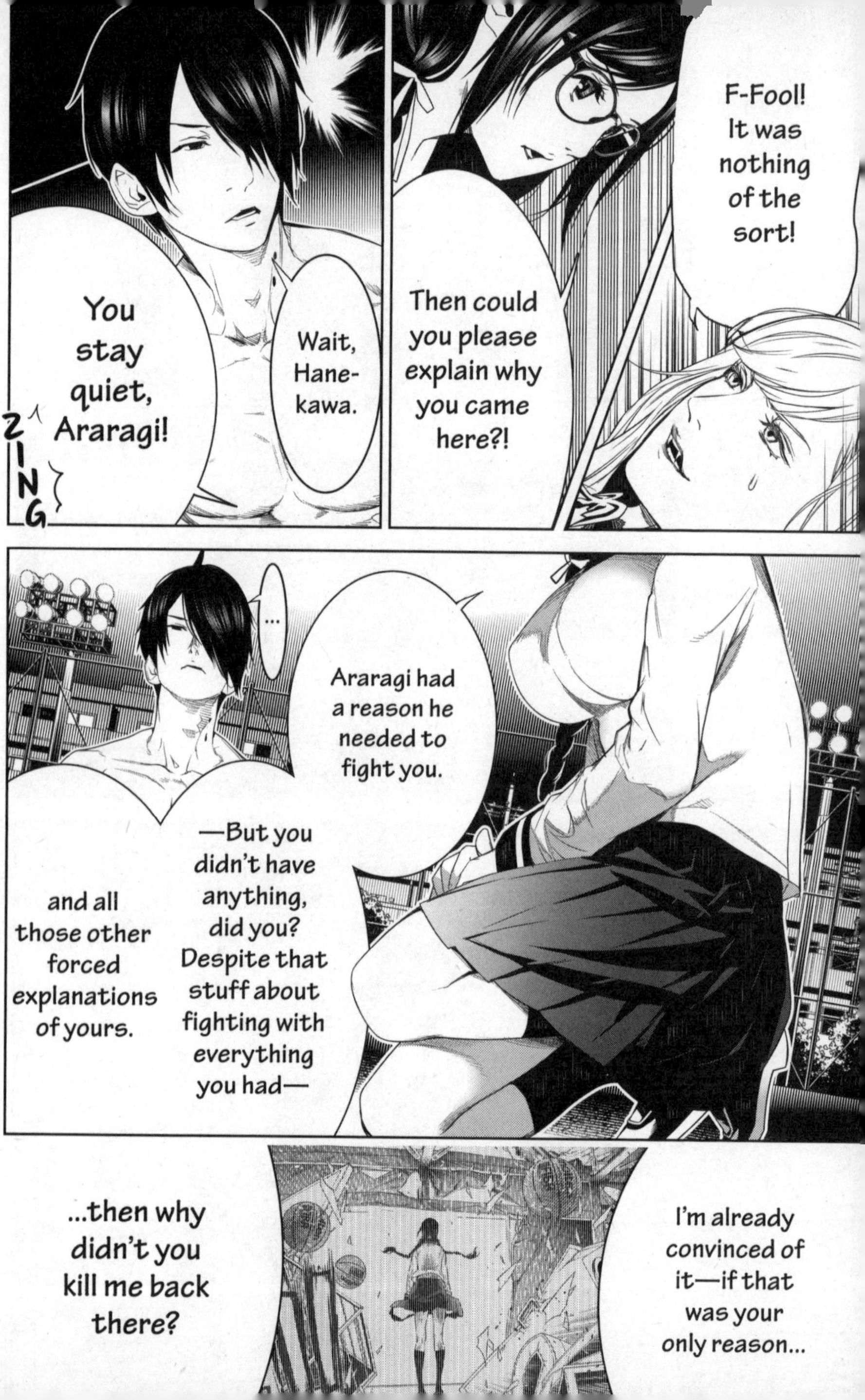
F-Fool! It was nothing of the sort!
Then could you please explain why you came here?!
Wait, Hane-kawa.
You stay quiet, Araragi!
ZING
Araragi had a reason he needed to fight you.
...
—But you didn't have anything, did you? Despite that stuff about fighting with everything you had—
and all those other forced explanations of yours.
I'm already convinced of it—if that was your only reason...
...then why didn't you kill me back there?

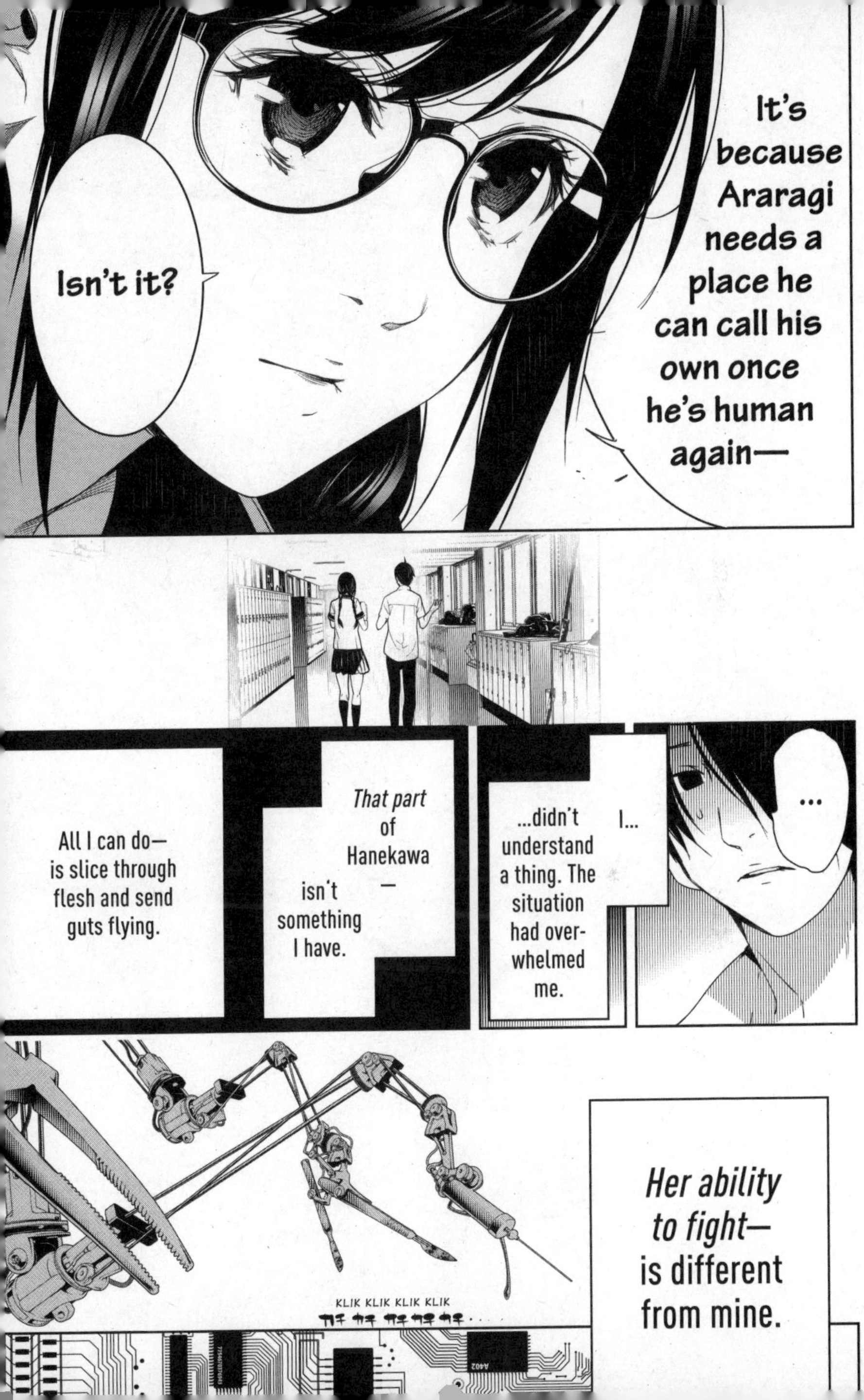
It's because Araragi needs a place he can call his own once he's human again—
Isn't it?
...
I...
...didn't understand a thing. The situation had over-whelmed me.
That part of Hanekawa — isn't something I have.
All I can do— is slice through flesh and send guts flying.
Her ability to fight— is different from mine.
KLIK KLIK KLIK KLIK

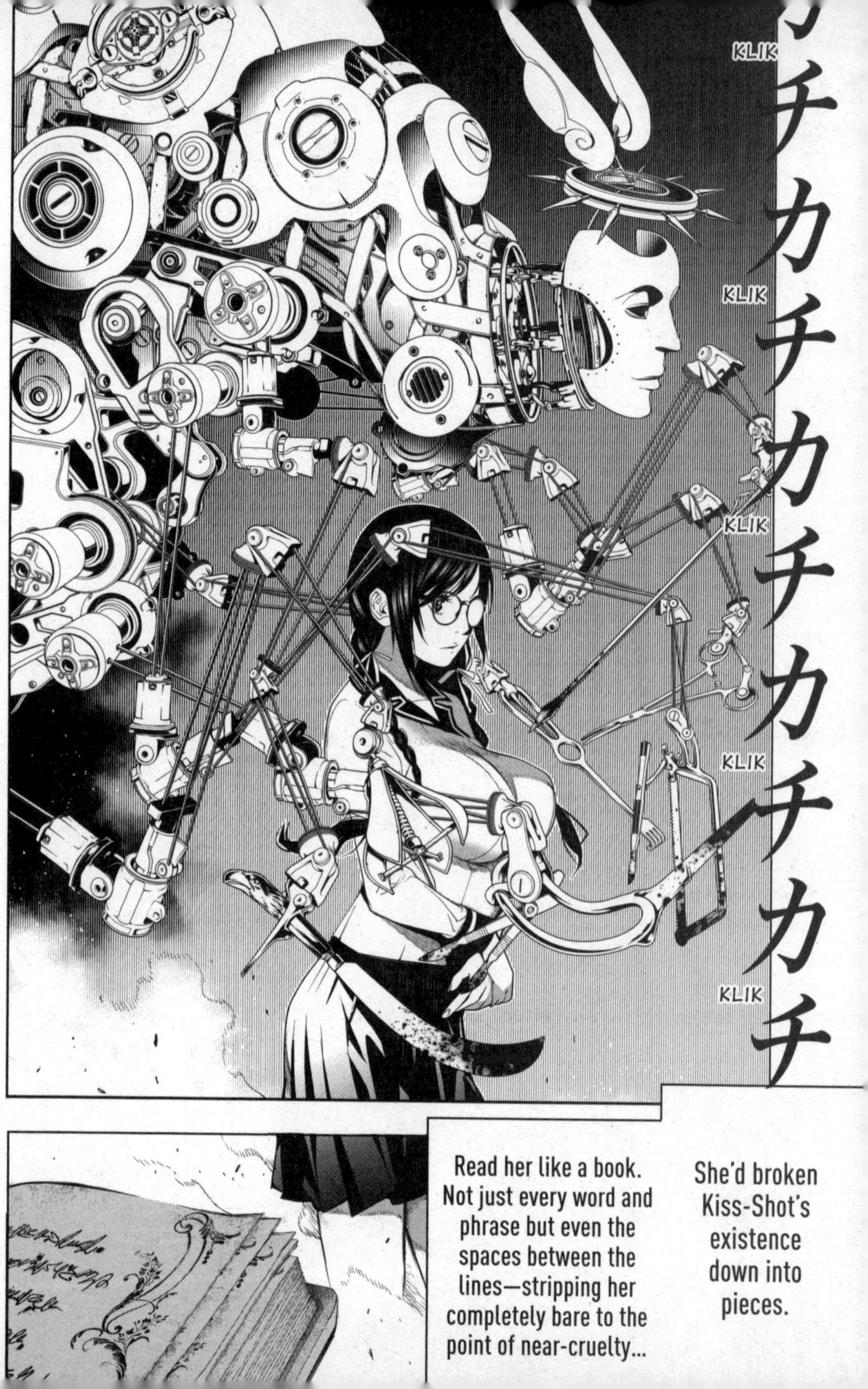
KLIK
KLIK
KLIK
KLIK
KLIK
チカチカチカチカチ
She'd broken Kiss-Shot's existence down into pieces.
Read her like a book. Not just every word and phrase but even the spaces between the lines—stripping her completely bare to the point of near-cruelty...

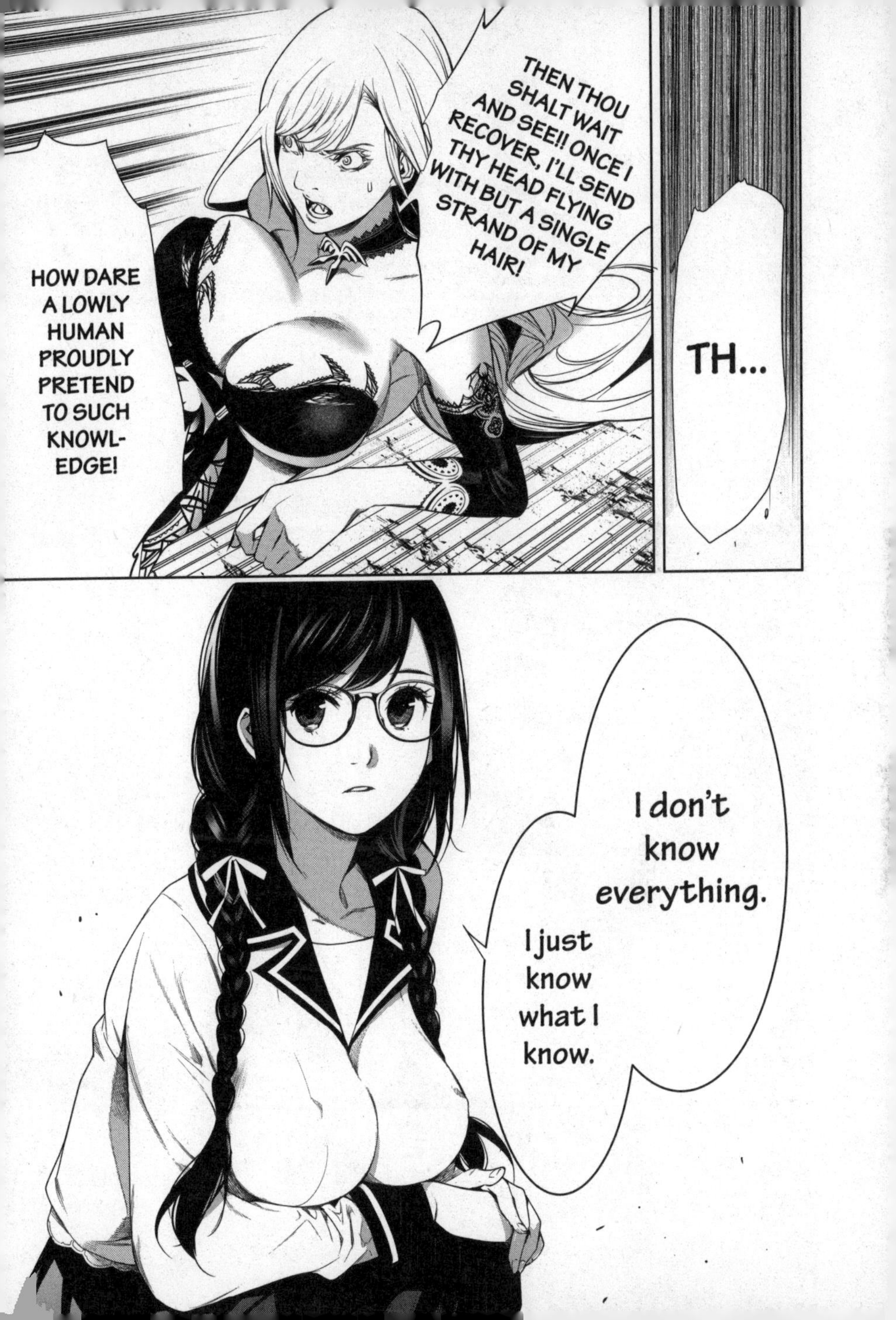
TH...
THEN THOU SHALT WAIT AND SEE!! ONCE I RECOVER, I'LL SEND THY HEAD FLYING WITH BUT A SINGLE STRAND OF MY HAIR!
HOW DARE A LOWLY HUMAN PROUDLY PRETEND TO SUCH KNOWL-EDGE!
I don't know everything.
I just know what I know.

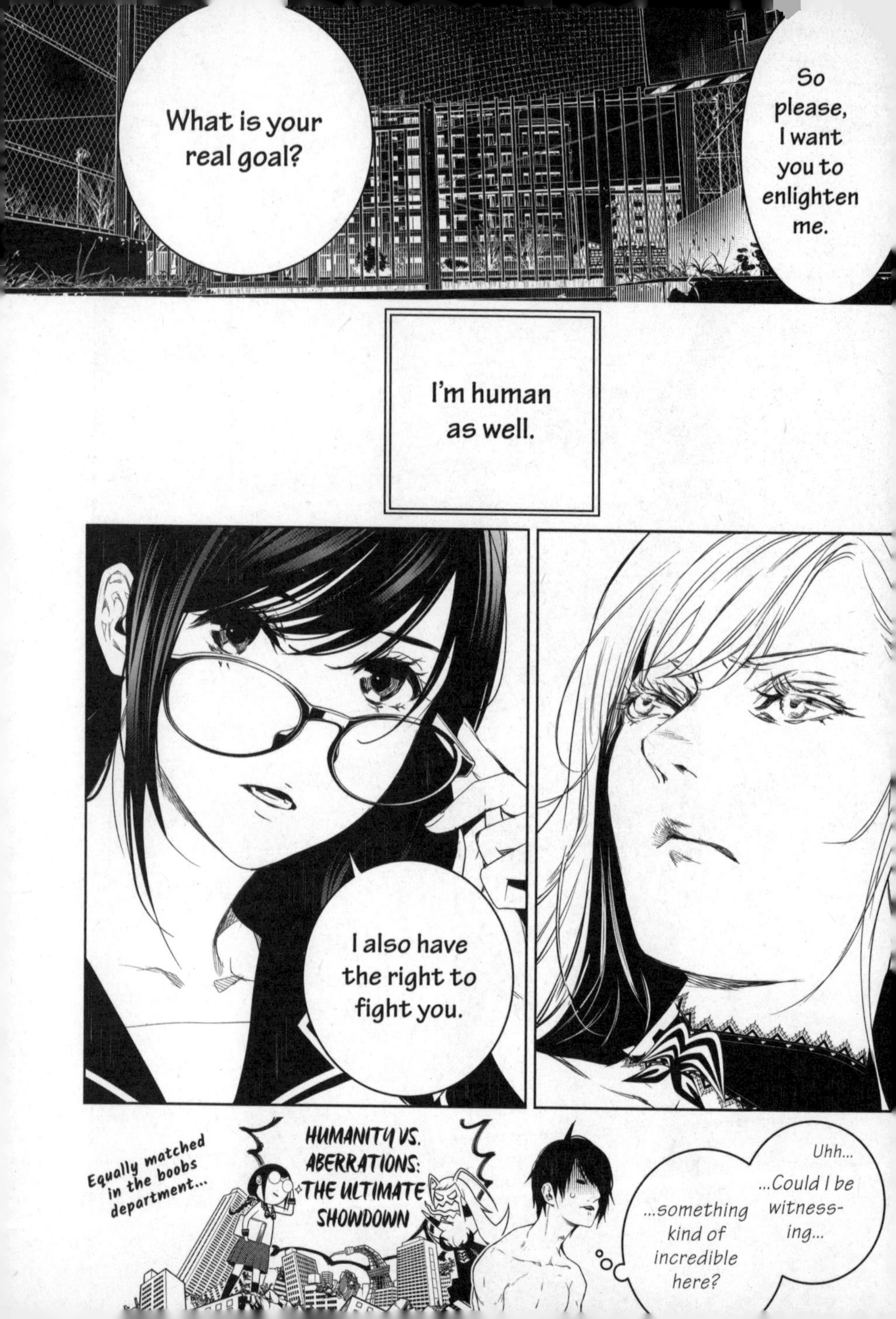
So please, I want you to enlighten me.
What is your real goal?
I'm human as well.
I also have the right to fight you.
Uhh... ...Could I be witness-ing...
...something kind of incredible here?
HUMANITY VS. ABERRATIONS: THE ULTIMATE SHOWDOWN
Equally matched in the boobs department...

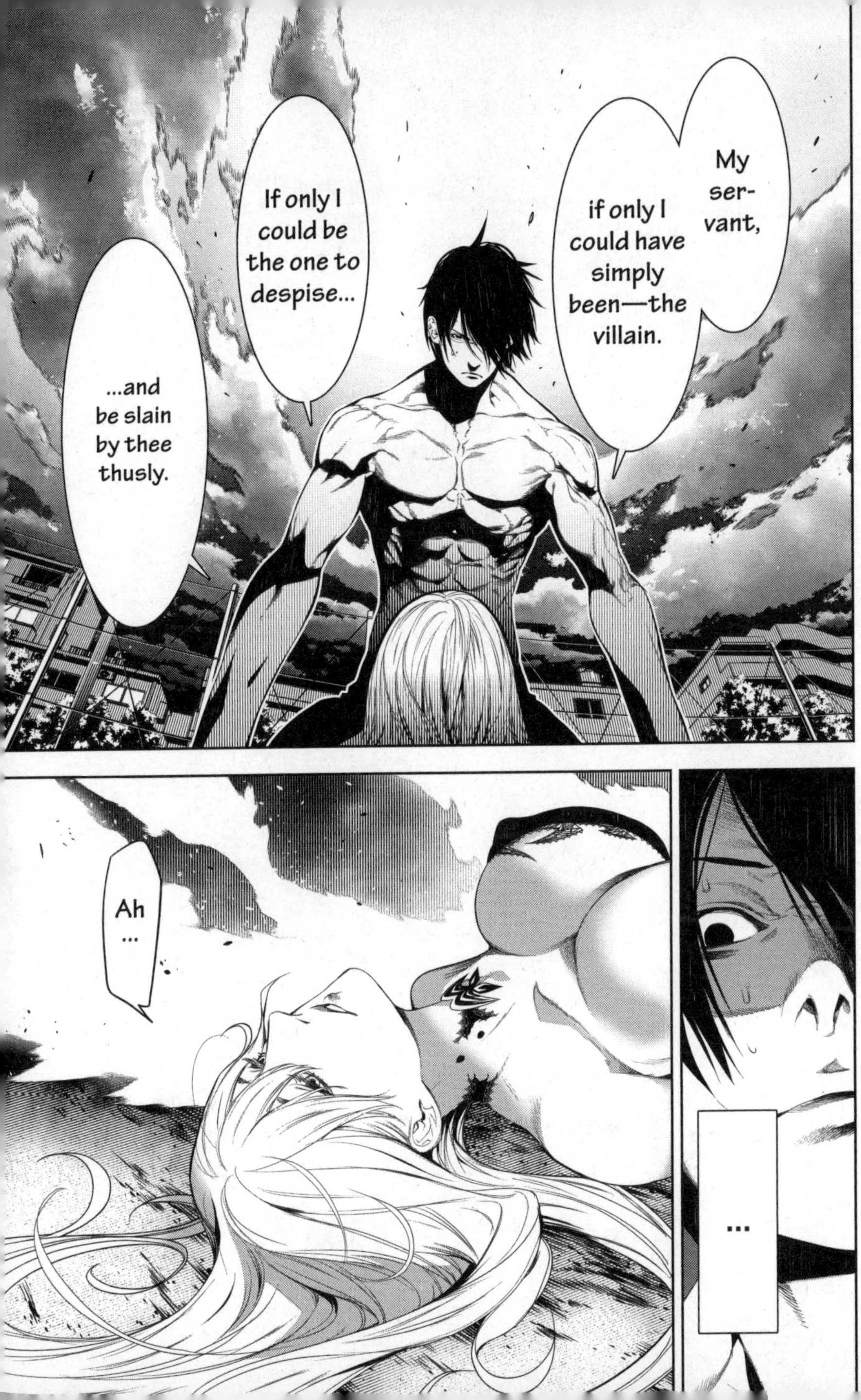
My ser-vant,
if only I could have simply been—the villain.
If only I could be the one to despise...
...and be slain by thee thusly.
...
Ah ...

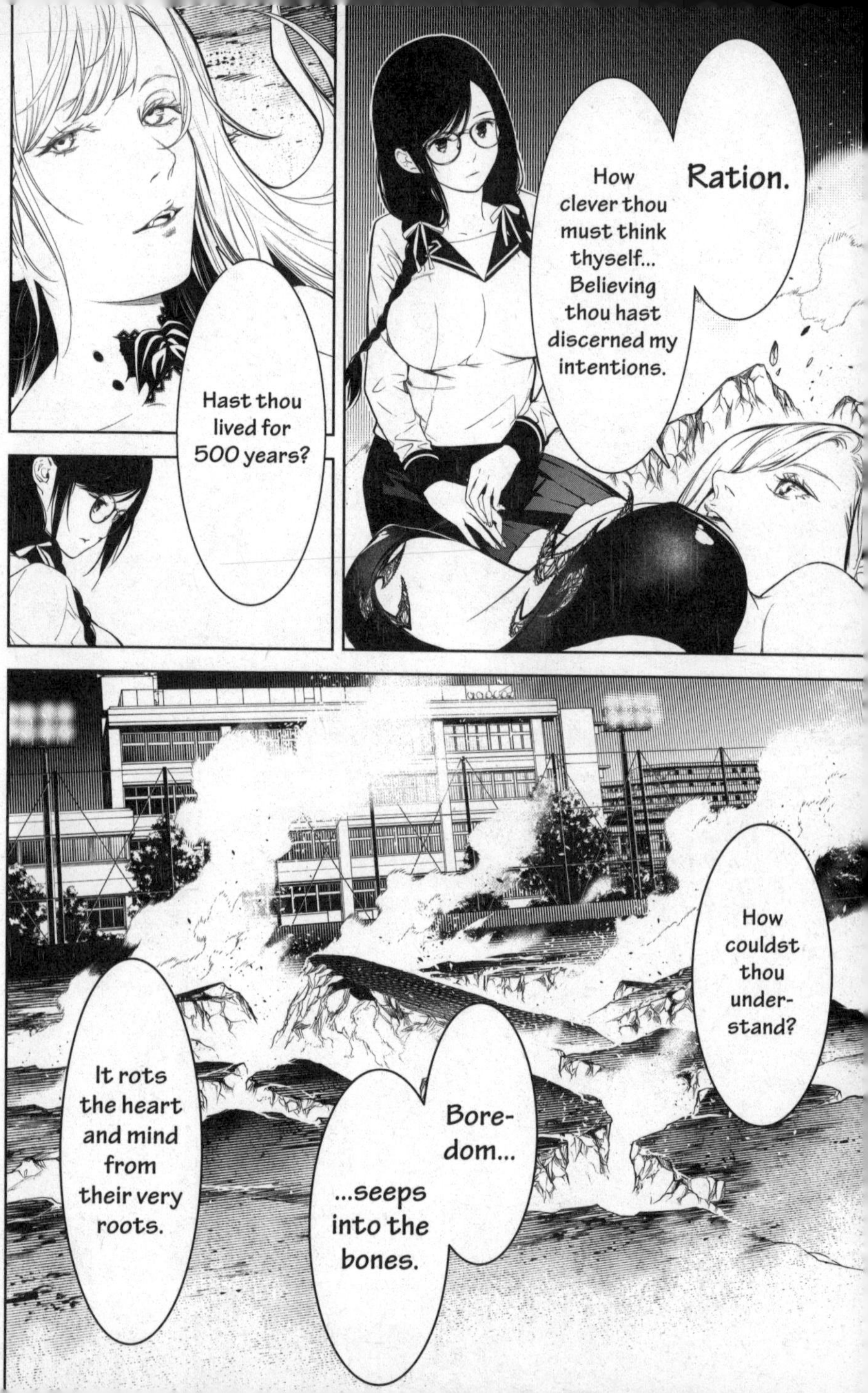
Ration.
How clever thou must think thyself... Believing thou hast discerned my intentions.
Hast thou lived for 500 years?
How couldst thou under-stand?
Bore-dom...
...seeps into the bones.
It rots the heart and mind from their very roots.

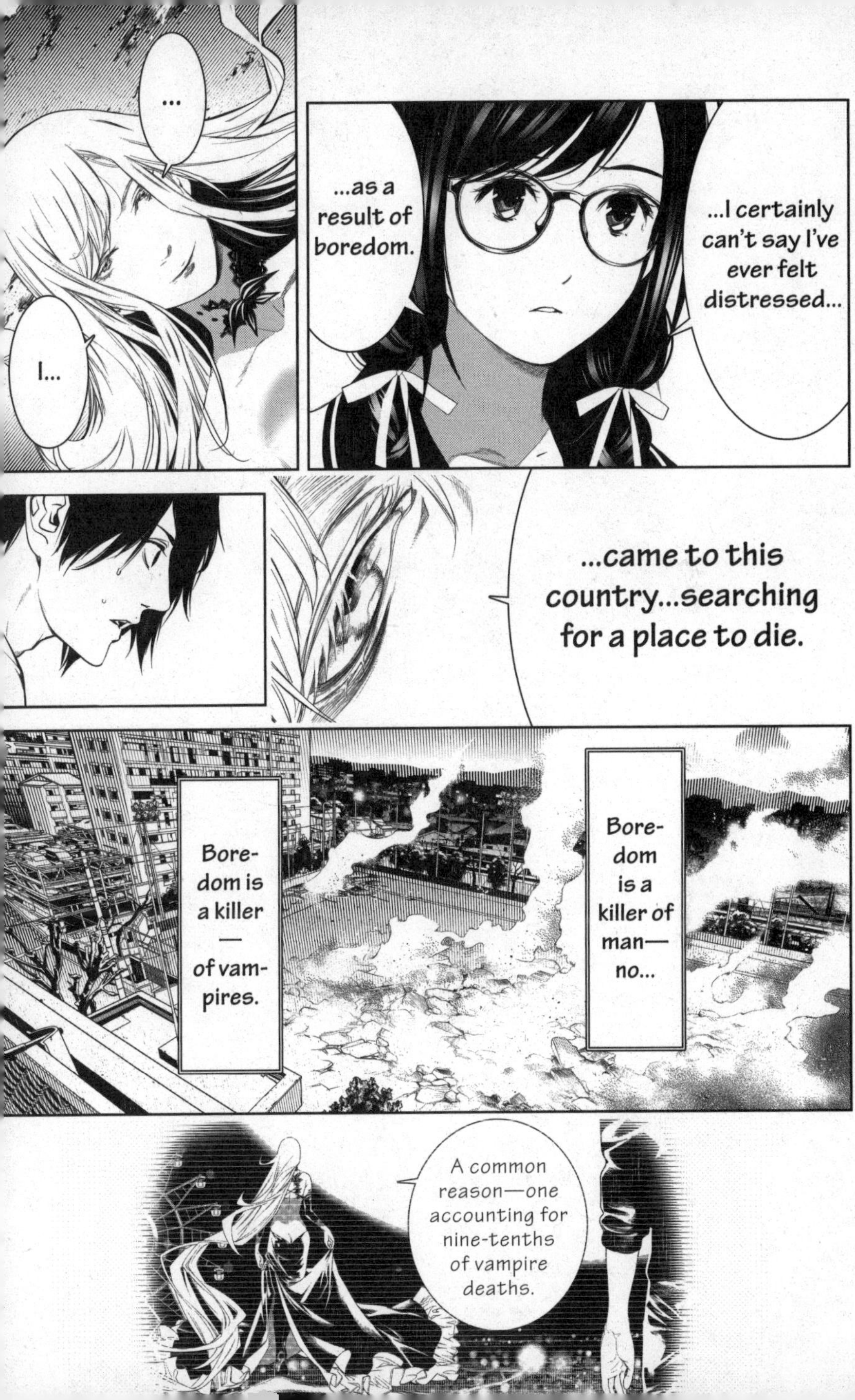
...I certainly can't say I've ever felt distressed...
...as a result of boredom.
...
I...
...came to this country...searching for a place to die.
Bore-dom is a killer of man—no...
Bore-dom is a killer—of vam-pires.
A common reason—one accounting for nine-tenths of vampire deaths.

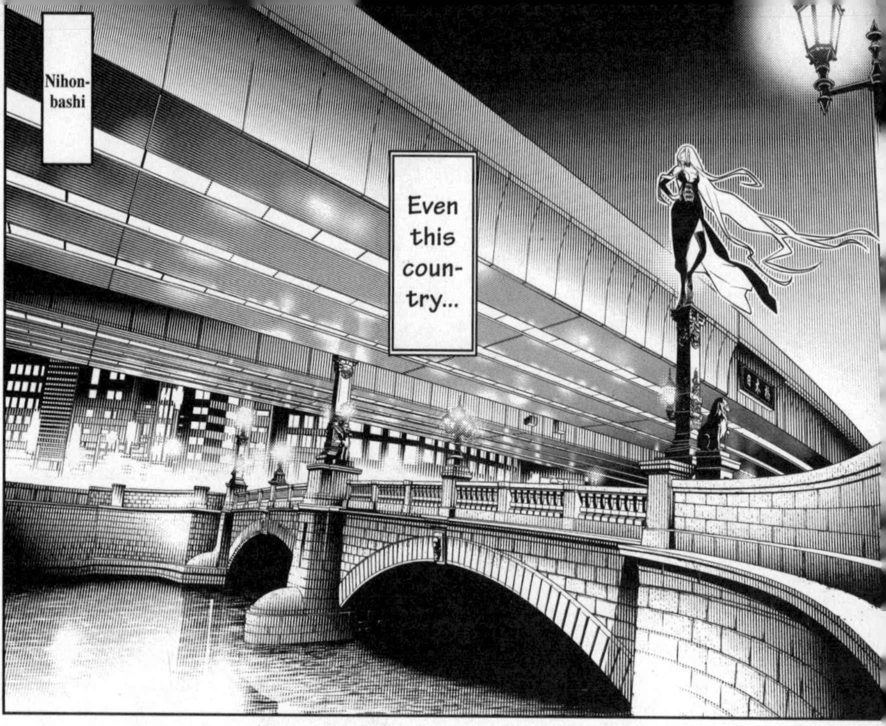
Nihon-
bashi
Even this coun-
try...

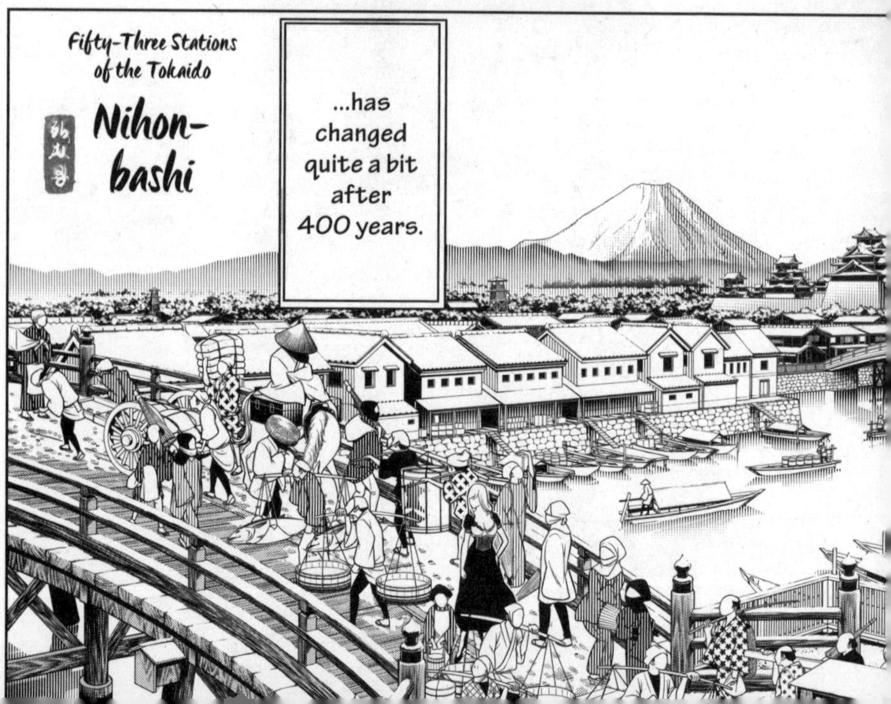
...has changed quite a bit after 400 years.
Fifty-Three Stations
of the Tokaido
Nihon-
bashi

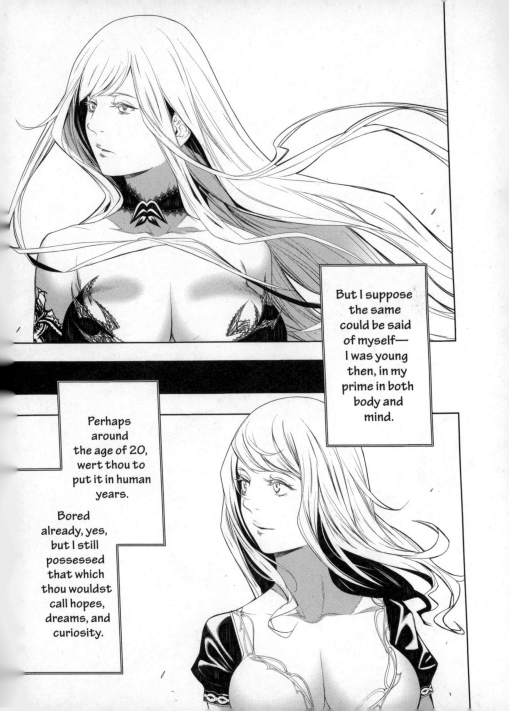

But I suppose the same could be said of myself—I was young then, in my prime in both body and mind.

Perhaps around the age of 20, wert thou to put it in human years.

Bored already, yes, but I still possessed that which thou wouldst call hopes, dreams, and curiosity.

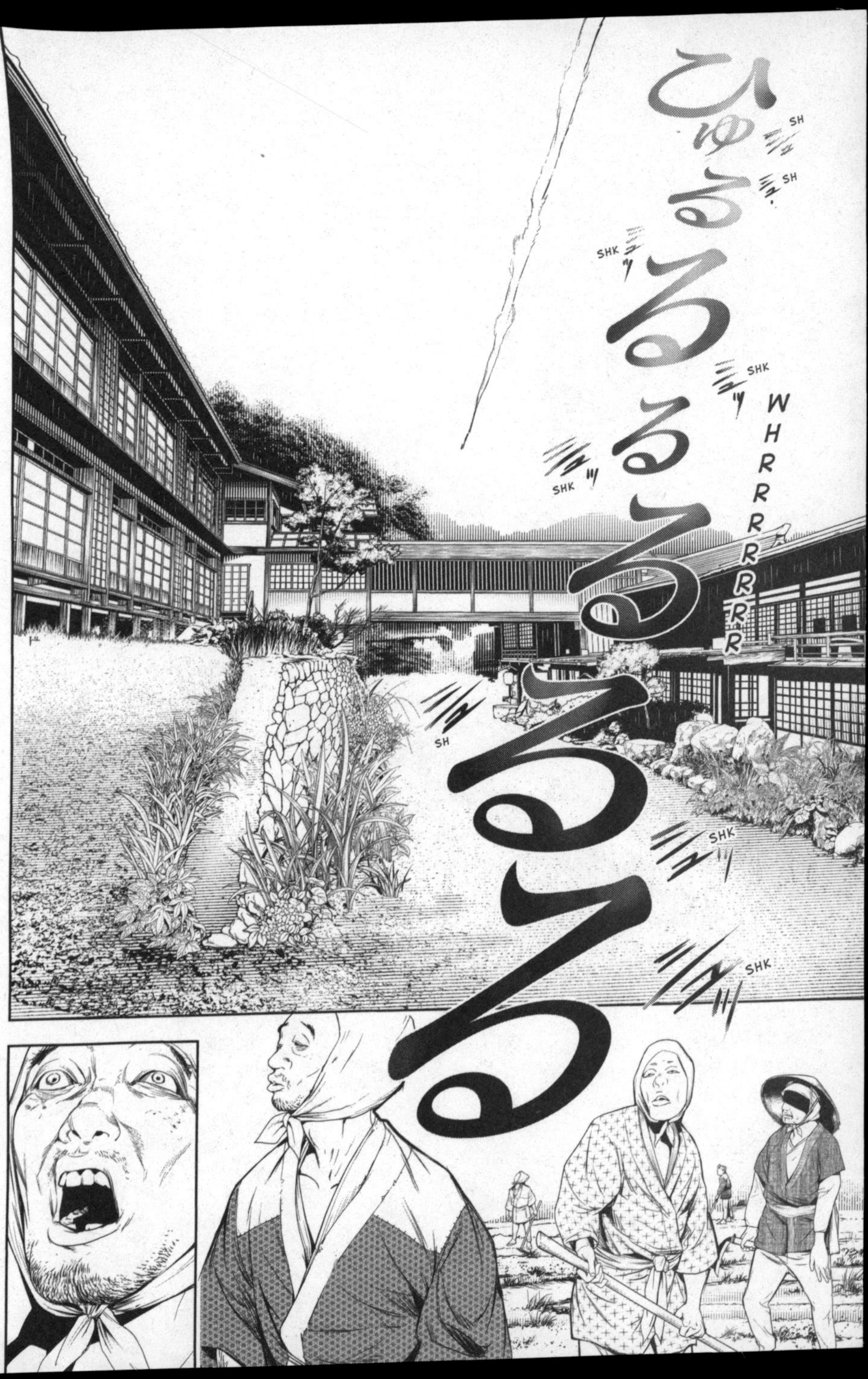

ひゅるるるるるる
WHRRRRRR
SH
SH
SHK
SHK
SHK
SH
SHK
SHK

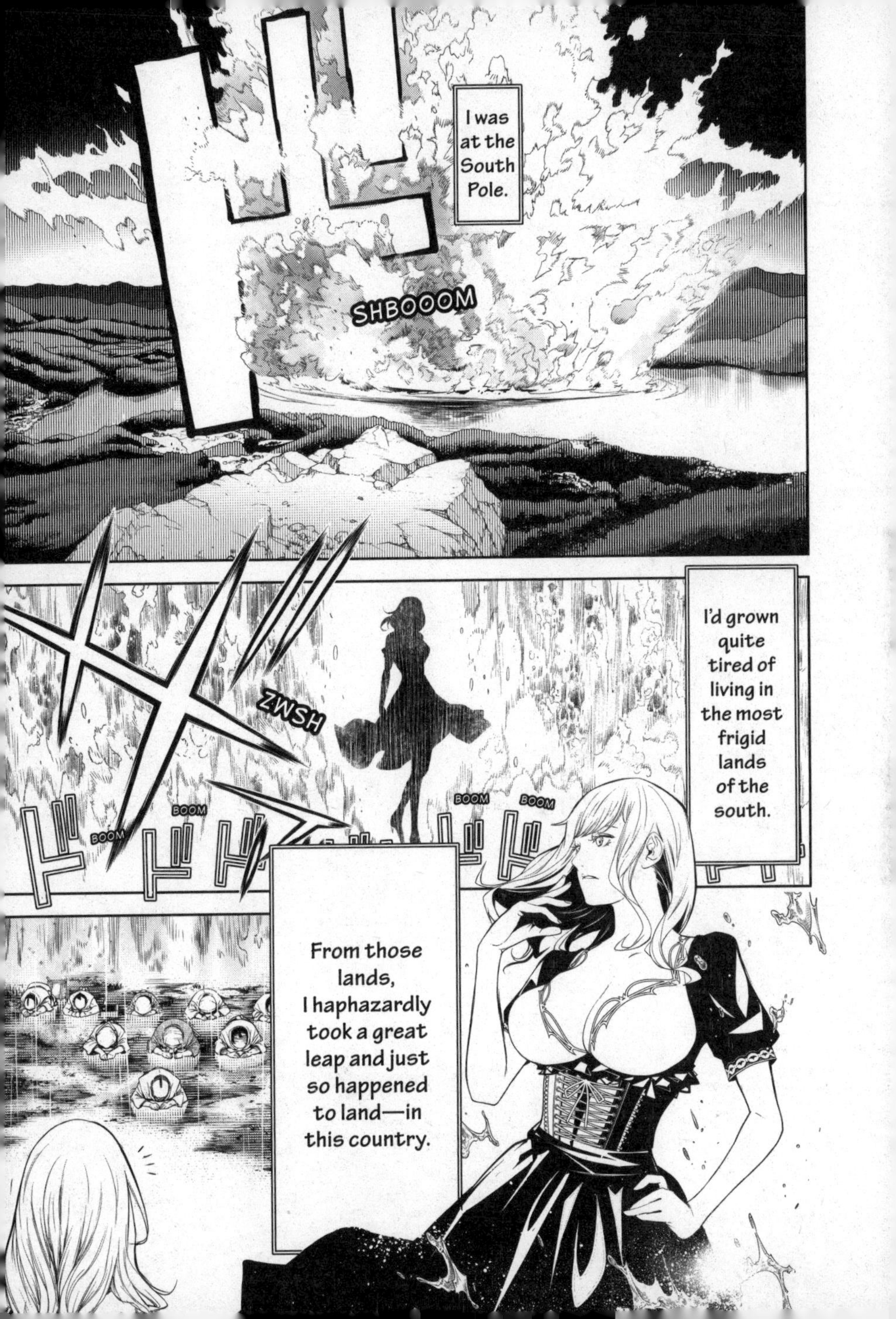
I was at the South Pole.
SHBOOOM
I'd grown quite tired of living in the most frigid lands of the south.
ZWSH
BOOM
BOOM
BOOM
BOOM
From those lands, I haphazardly took a great leap and just so happened to land—in this country.

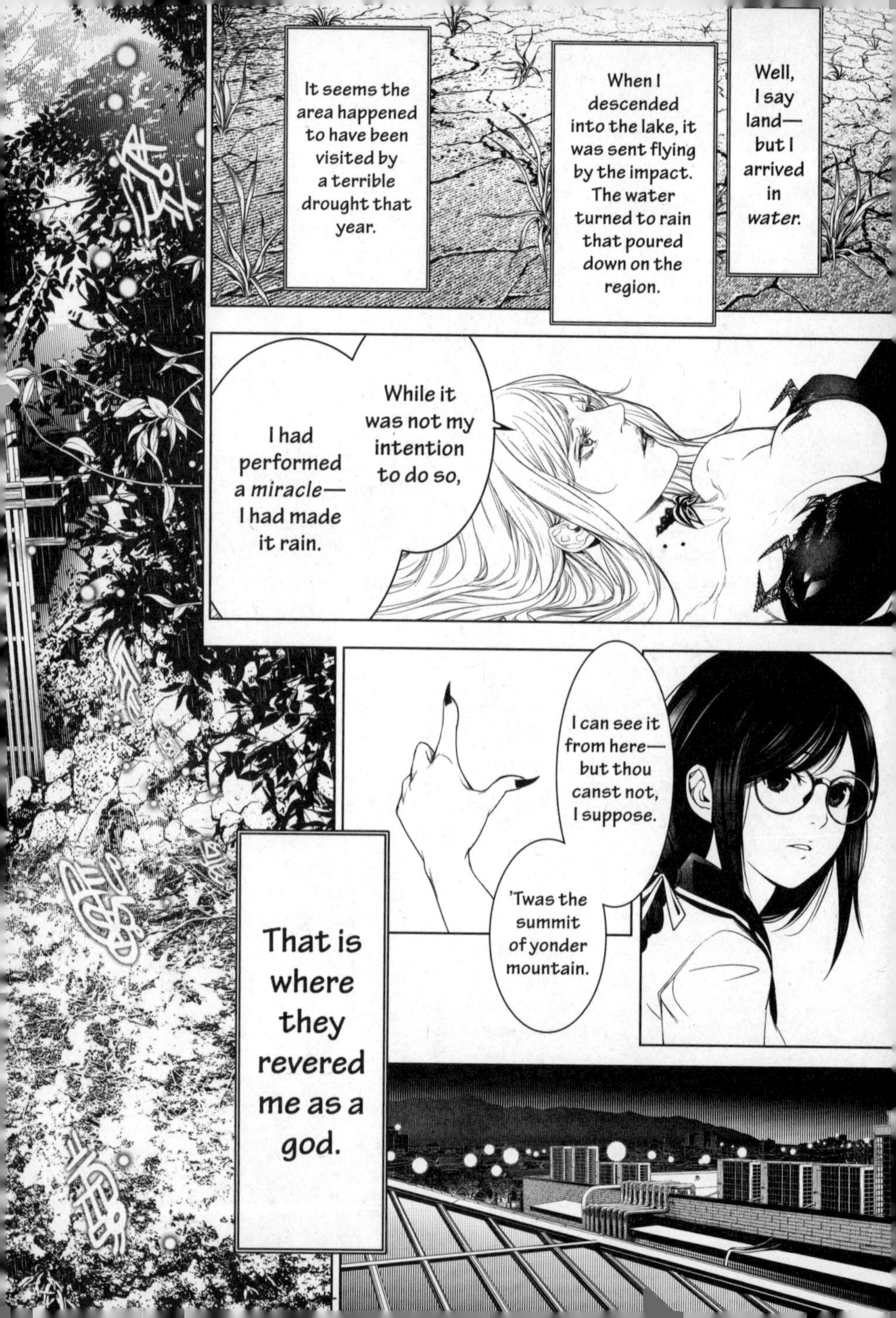
Well, I say land— but I arrived in *water.*
When I descended into the lake, it was sent flying by the impact. The water turned to rain that poured down on the region.
It seems the area happened to have been visited by a terrible drought that year.
While it was not my intention to do so,
I had performed a *miracle*— I had made it rain.
I can see it from here— but thou canst not, I suppose.
'Twas the summit of yonder mountain.
That is where they revered me as a god.

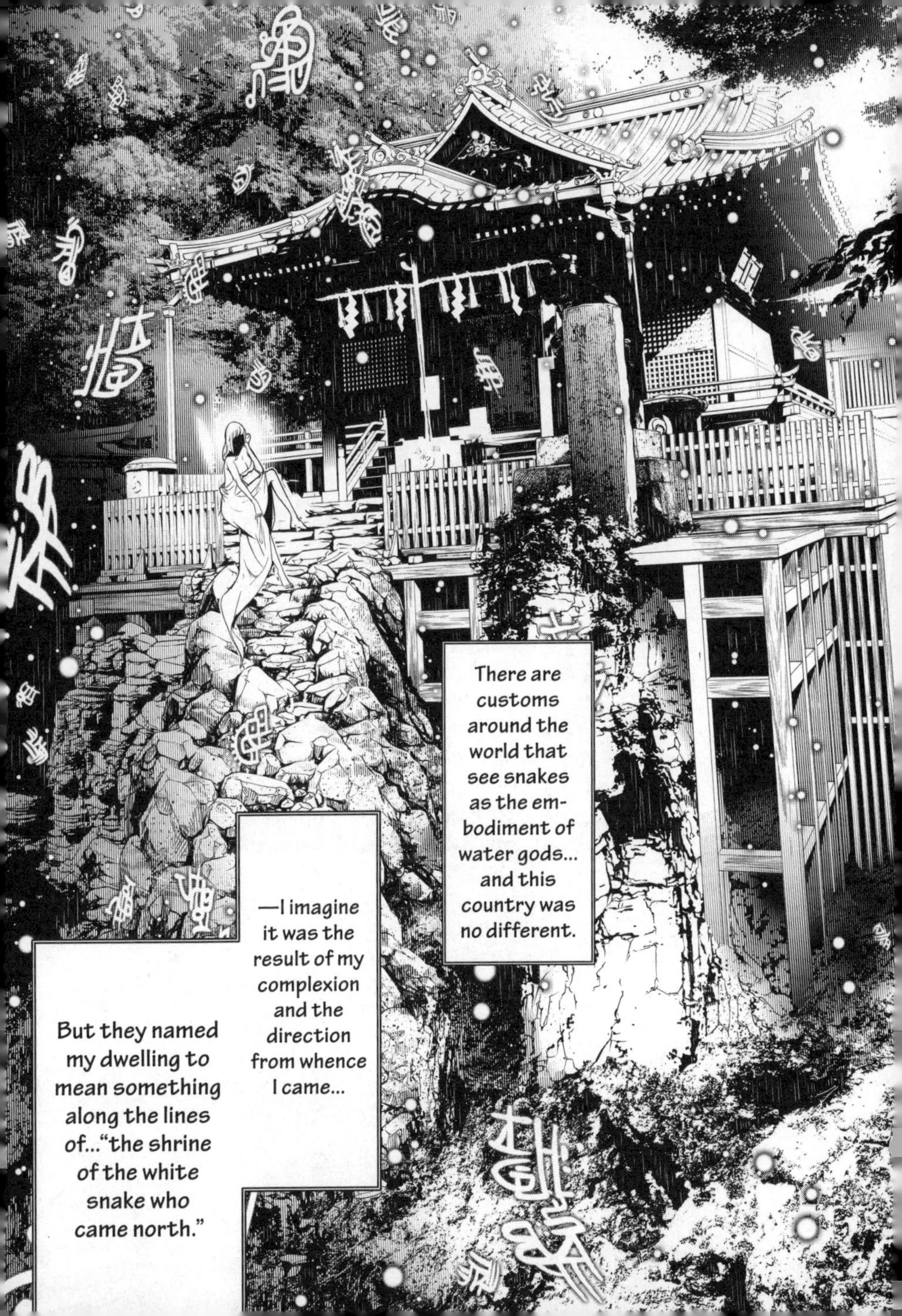
There are customs around the world that see snakes as the em-bodiment of water gods... and this country was no different.
—I imagine it was the result of my complexion and the direction from whence I came...
But they named my dwelling to mean something along the lines of..."the shrine of the white snake who came north."

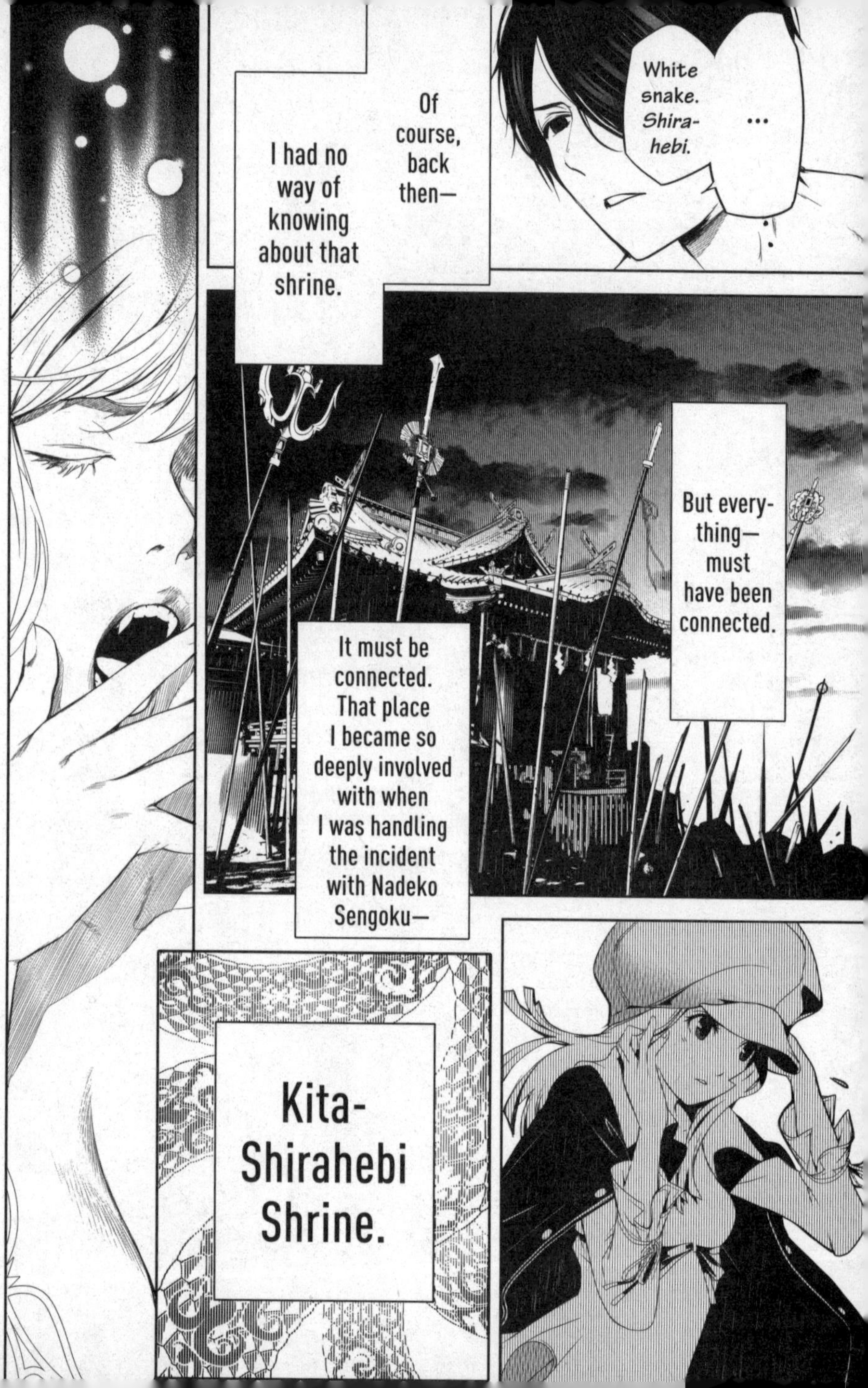
White snake. Shira-hebi.
...
Of course, back then—
I had no way of knowing about that shrine.
But every-thing—must have been connected.
It must be connected. That place I became so deeply involved with when I was handling the incident with Nadeko Sengoku—
Kita-Shirahebi Shrine.

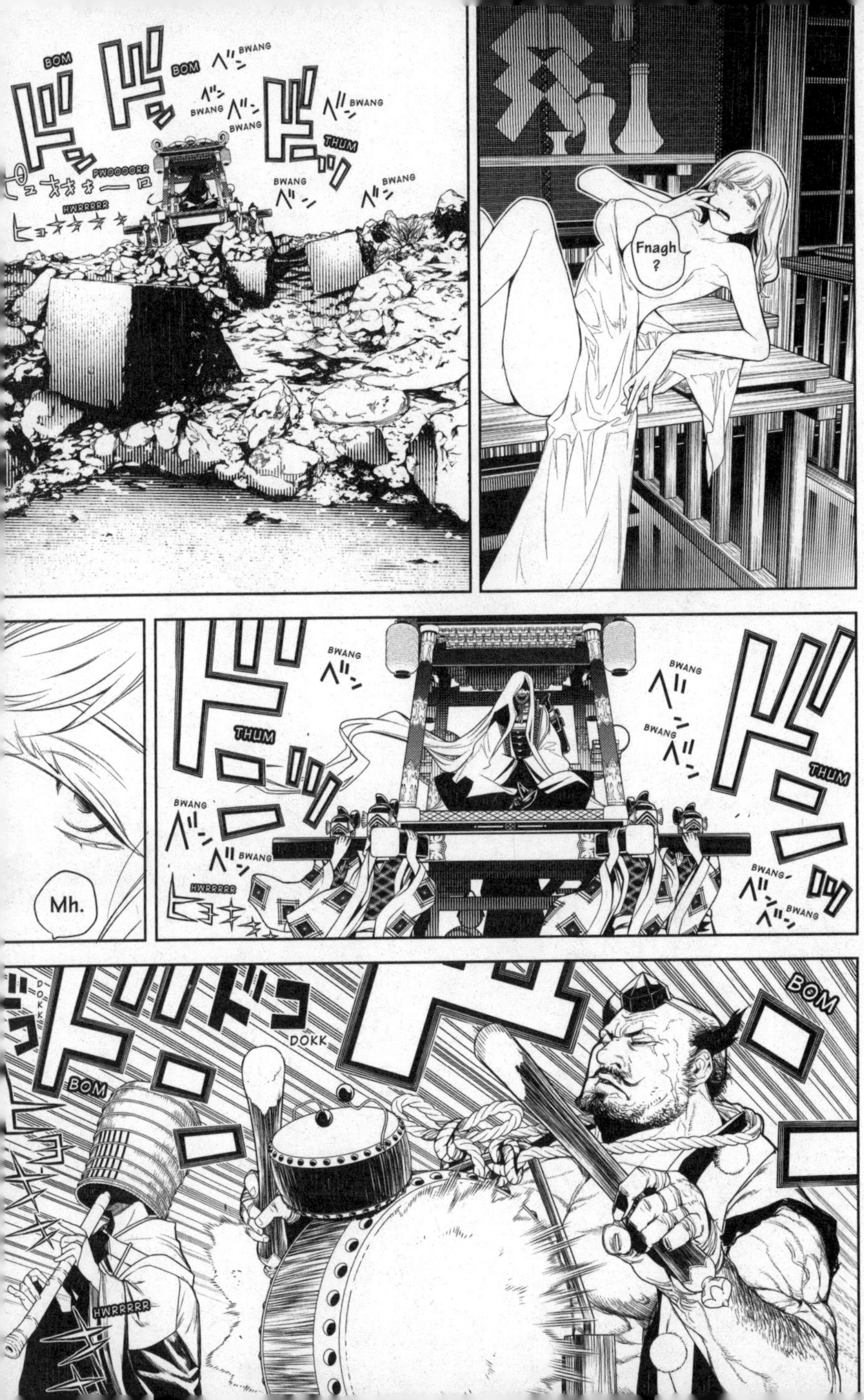
Fnagh?
BOM
BOM
BWANG
BWANG
BWANG
BWANG
BWANG
THUM
PWOOOORR
HWRRRRR
BWANG
BWANG
BWANG
BWANG
BWANG
THUM
BWANG
BWANG
BWANG
THUM
BWANG
BWANG
HWRRRRR
Mh.
BOM
DOKK
DOKK
BOM
HWRRRRR

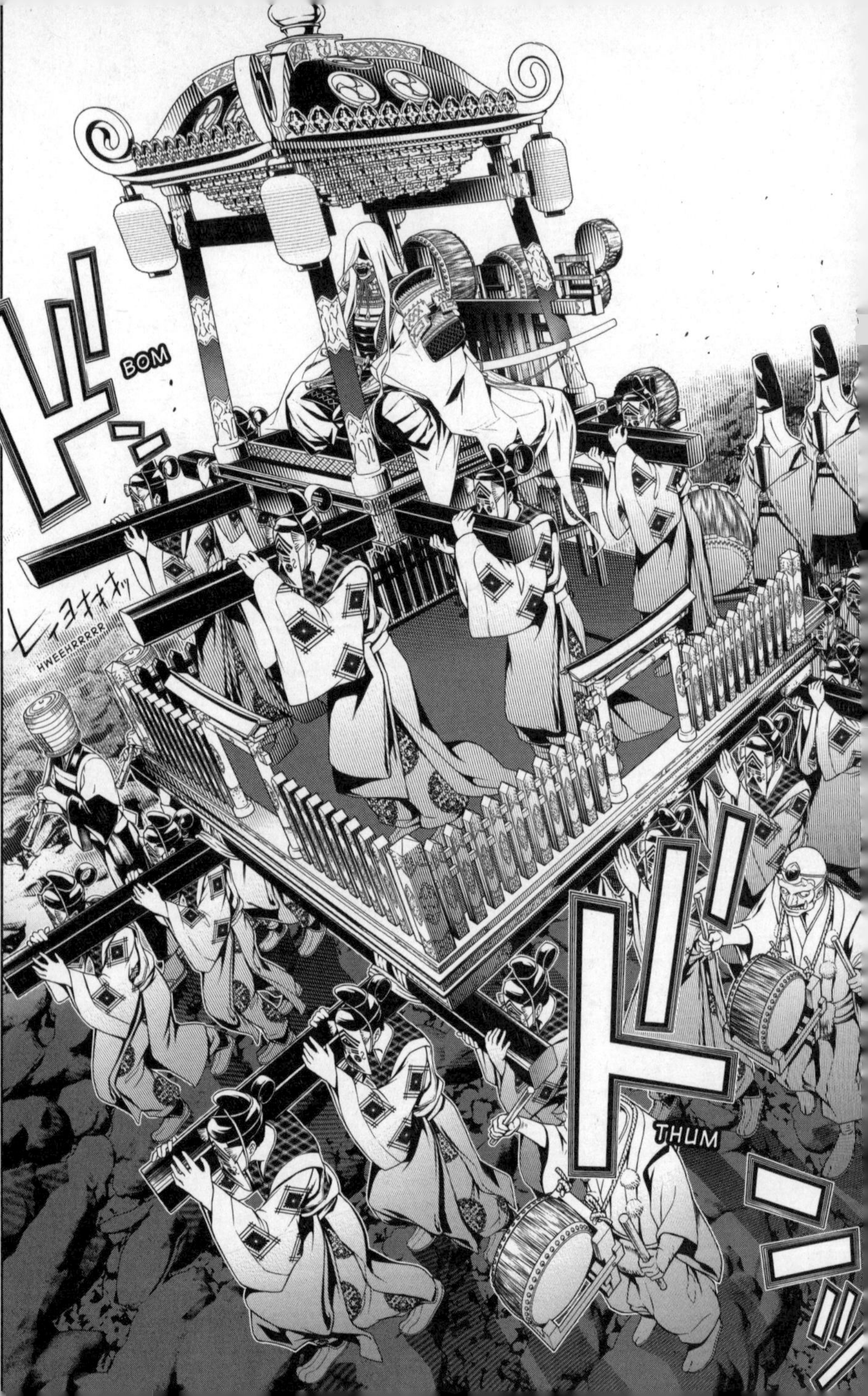
BOM
HWEEHRRRRR
THUM

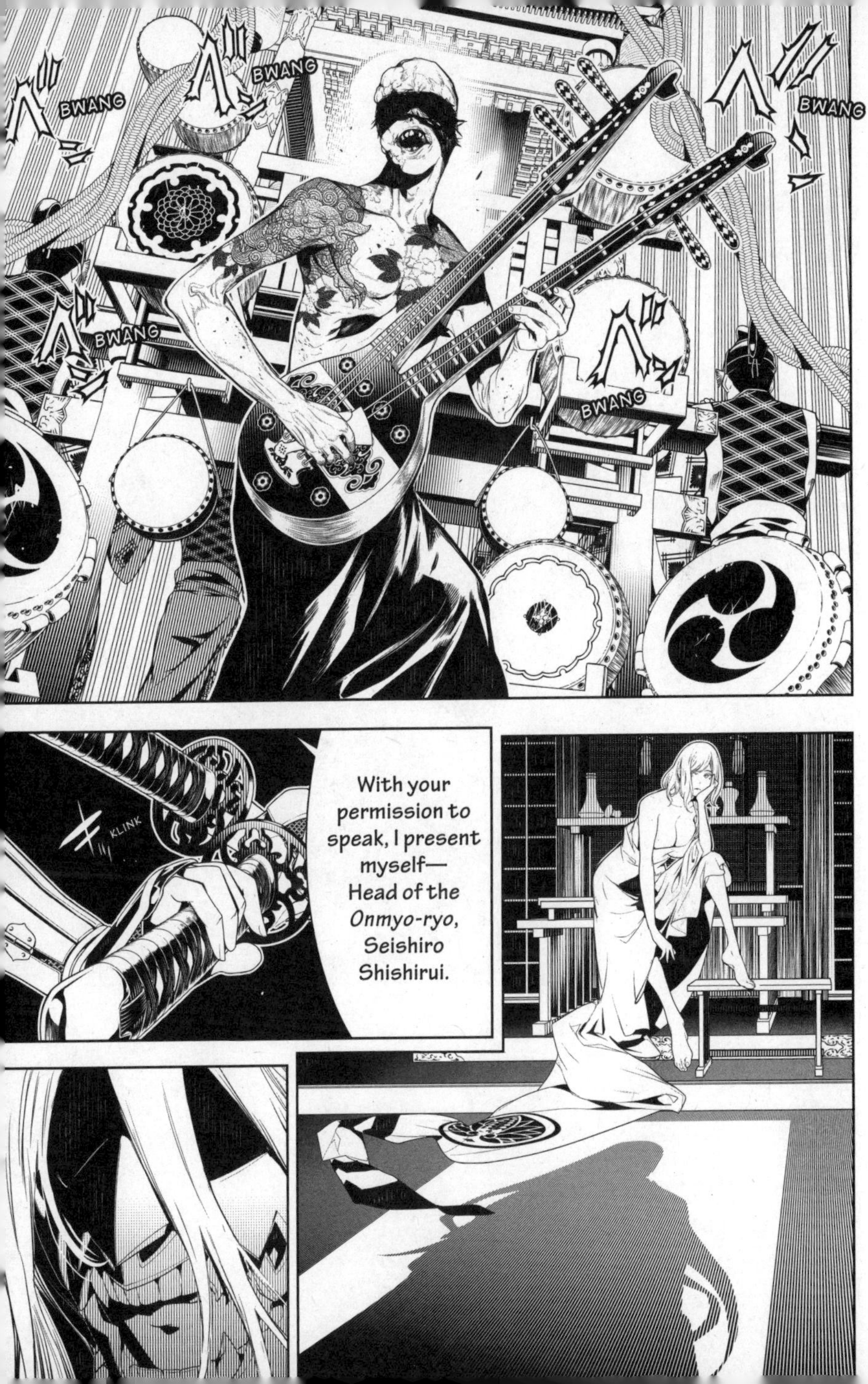
BWANG
BWANG
BWANG
BWANG
BWANG
With your permission to speak, I present myself—Head of the *Onmyo-ryo*, Seishiro Shishirui.
KLINK

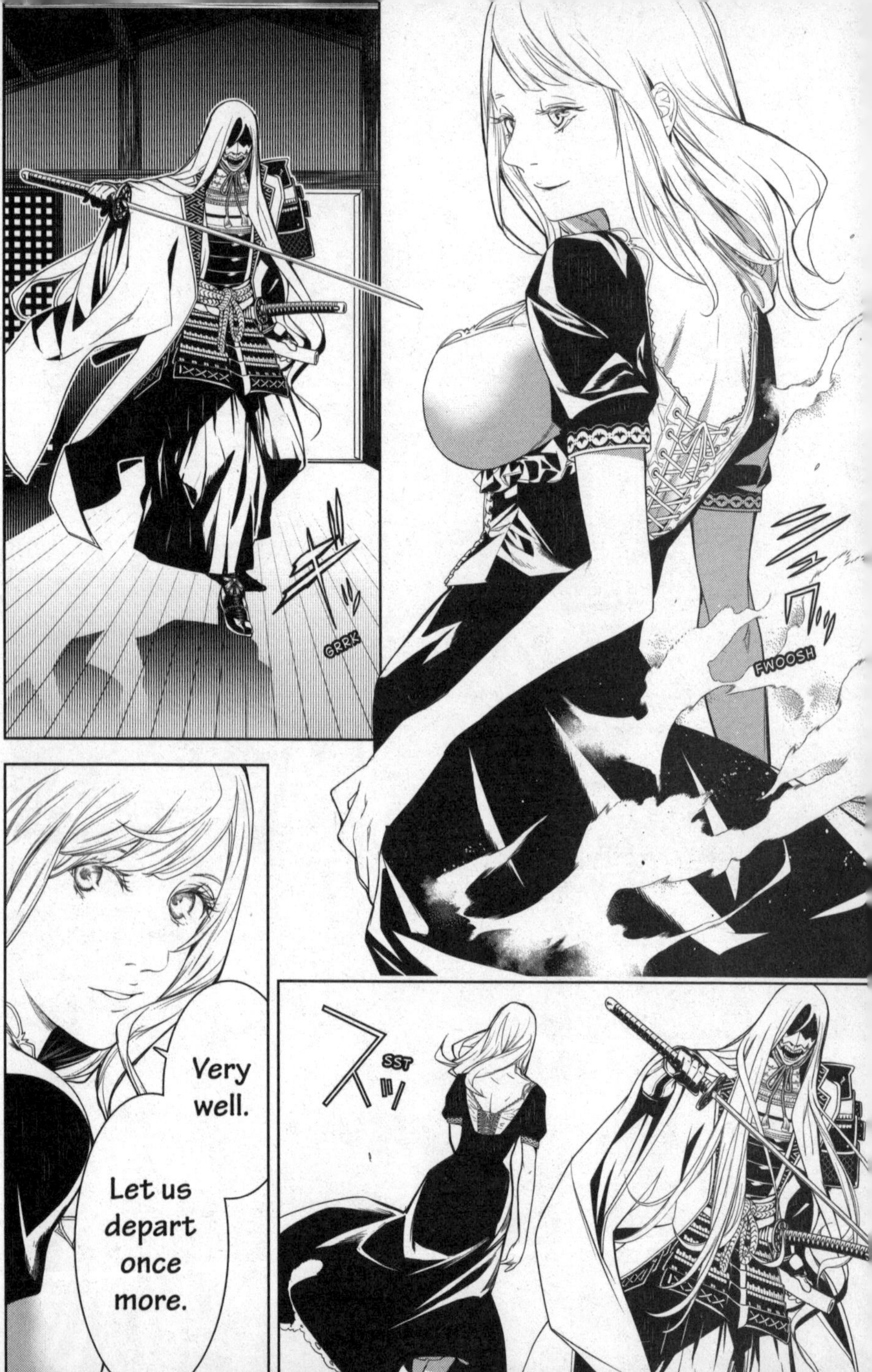
FWOOSH
GRRK
SST
Very well.
Let us depart once more.

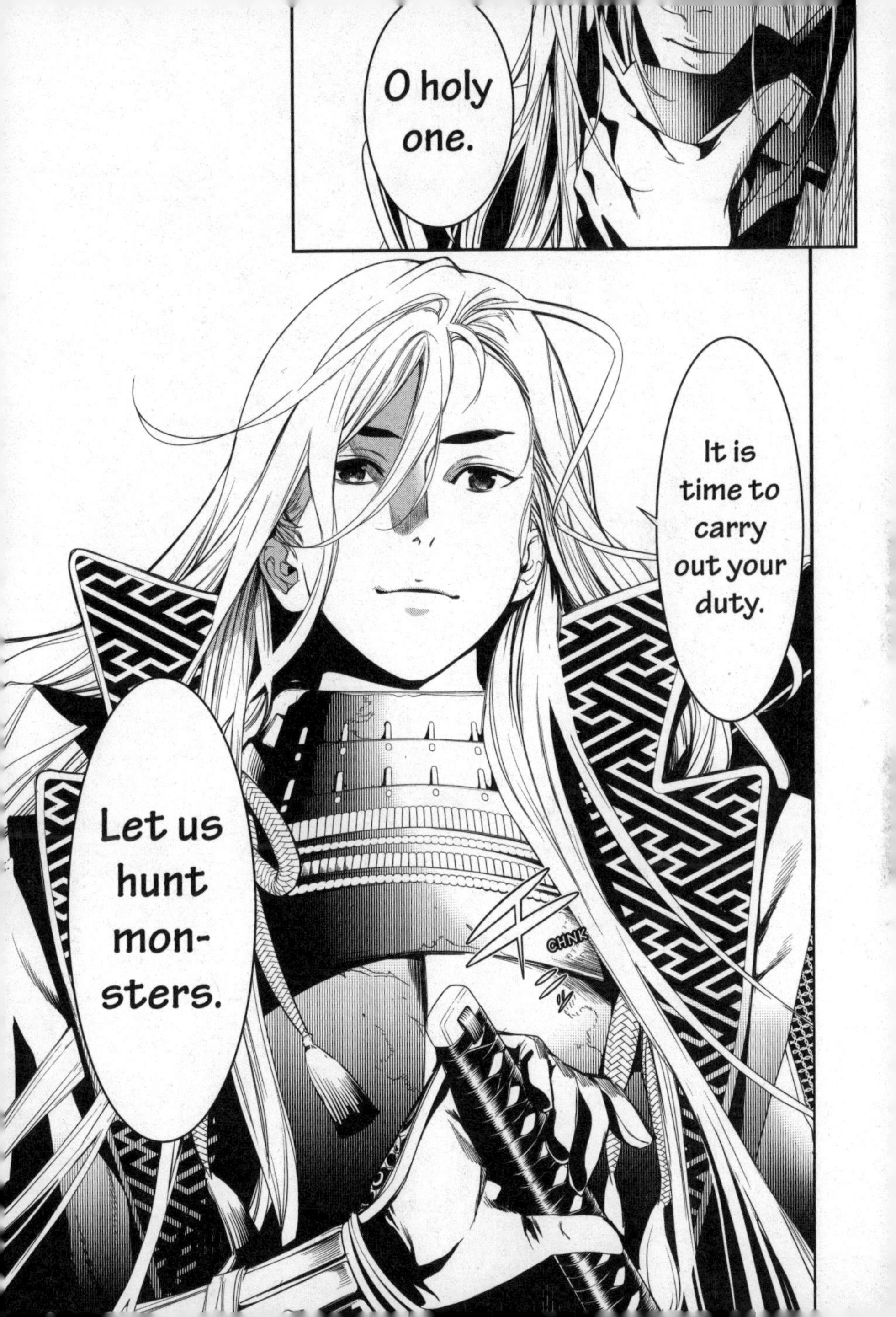
O holy one.
It is time to carry out your duty.
Let us hunt mon-sters.
CHNK

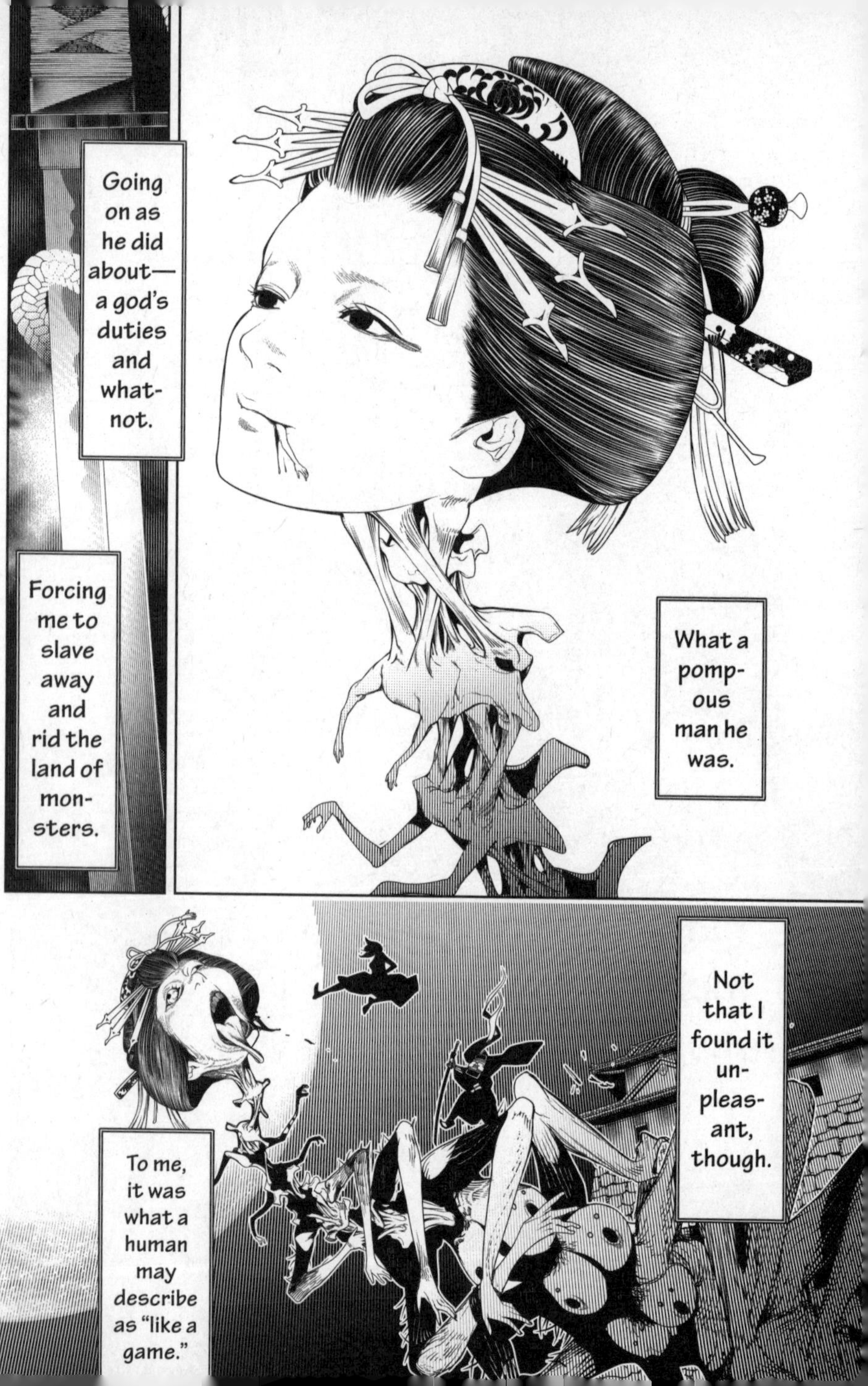
What a pompous man he was.
Going on as he did about—a god's duties and what-not.
Forcing me to slave away and rid the land of monsters.
Not that I found it unpleasant, though.
To me, it was what a human may describe as "like a game."

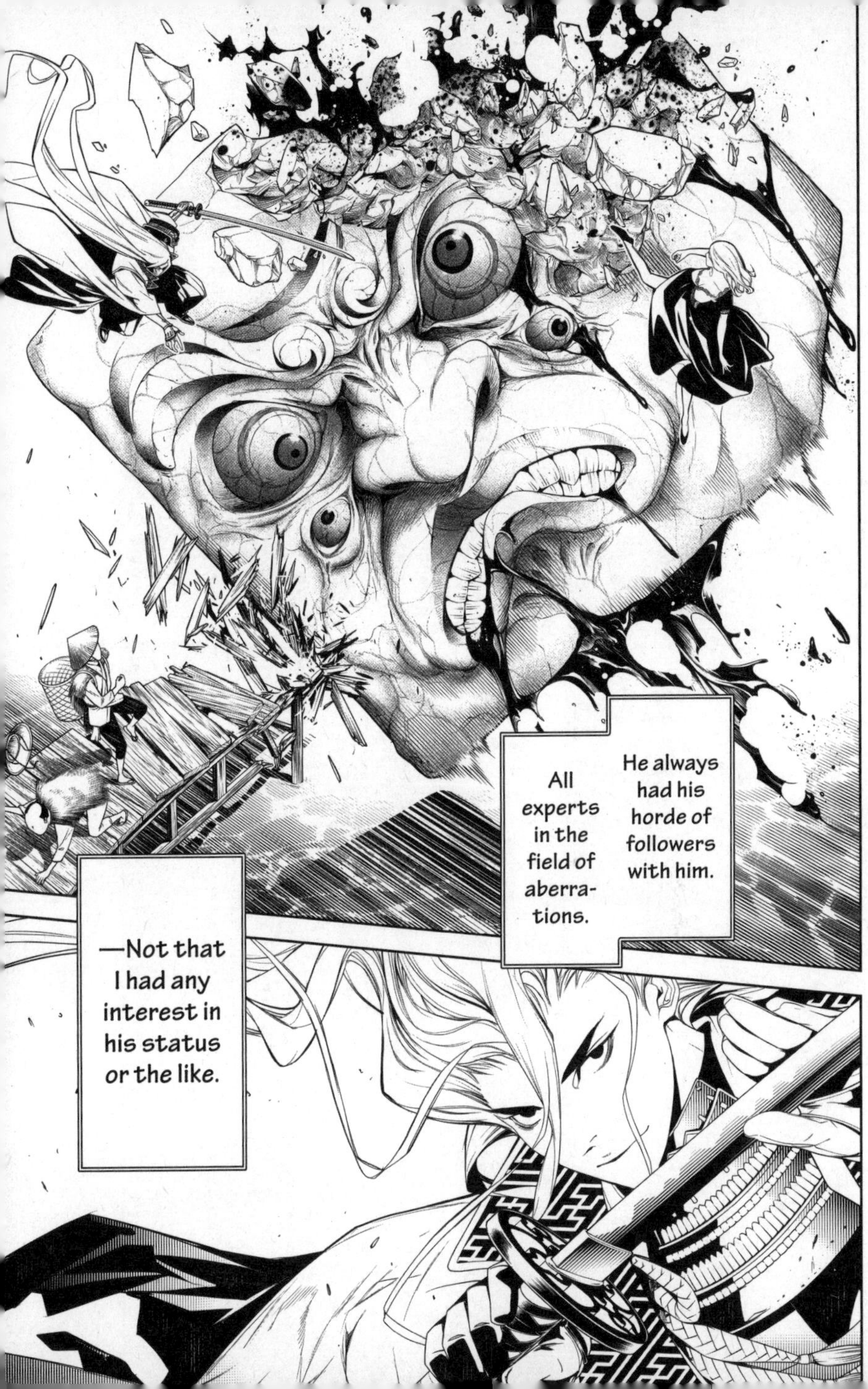
He always had his horde of followers with him.
All experts in the field of aberrations.
—Not that I had any interest in his status or the like.

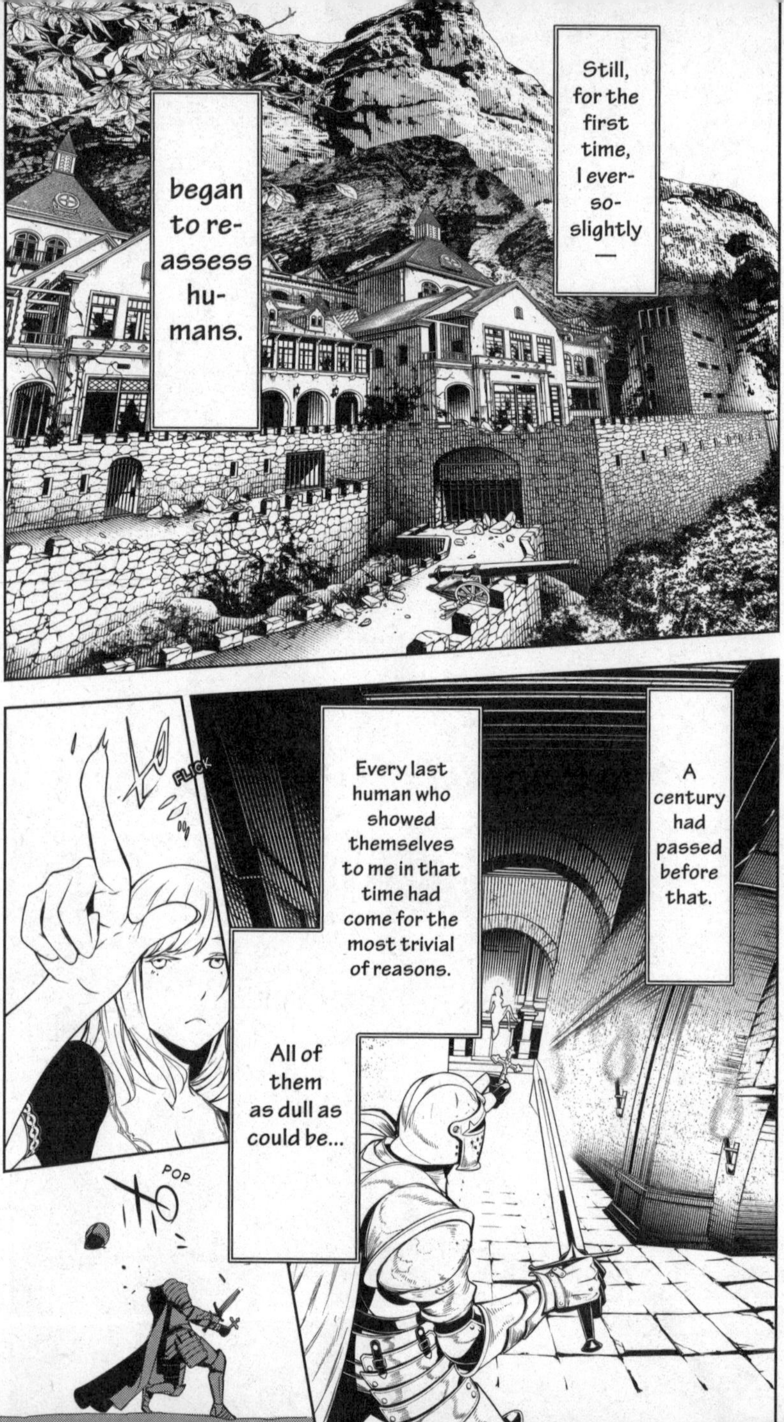

Still, for the first time, I ever-so-slightly—
began to re-assess hu-mans.
A century had passed before that.
Every last human who showed themselves to me in that time had come for the most trivial of reasons.
All of them as dull as could be...
FLICK
POP

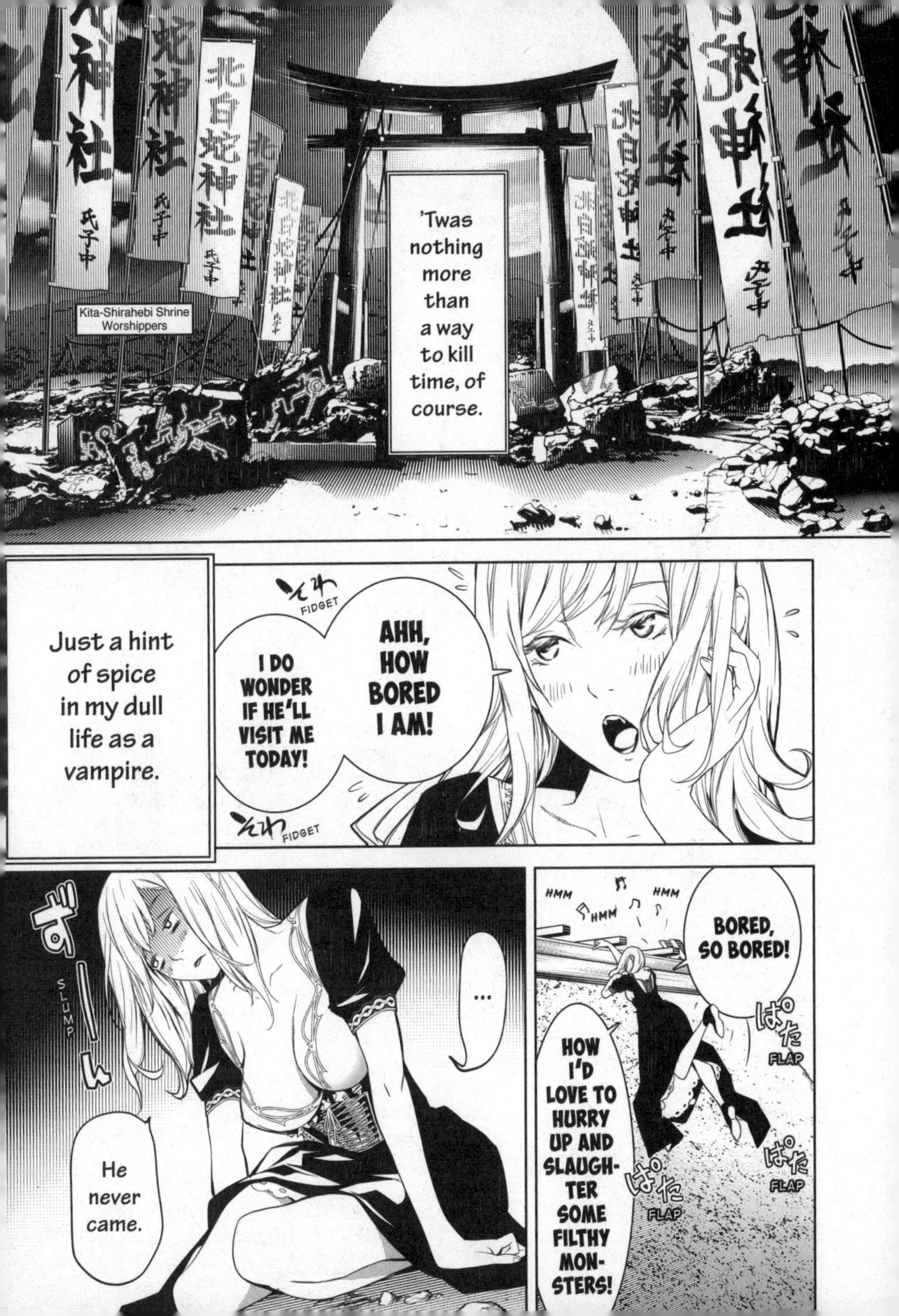
'Twas nothing more than a way to kill time, of course.
Kita-Shirahebi Shrine Worshippers
FIDGET
AHH, HOW BORED I AM!
I DO WONDER IF HE'LL VISIT ME TODAY!
FIDGET
Just a hint of spice in my dull life as a vampire.
HMM HMM HMM HMM
BORED, SO BORED!
FLAP
HOW I'D LOVE TO HURRY UP AND SLAUGHTER SOME FILTHY MONSTERS!
FLAP
FLAP
SLUMP
...
He never came.

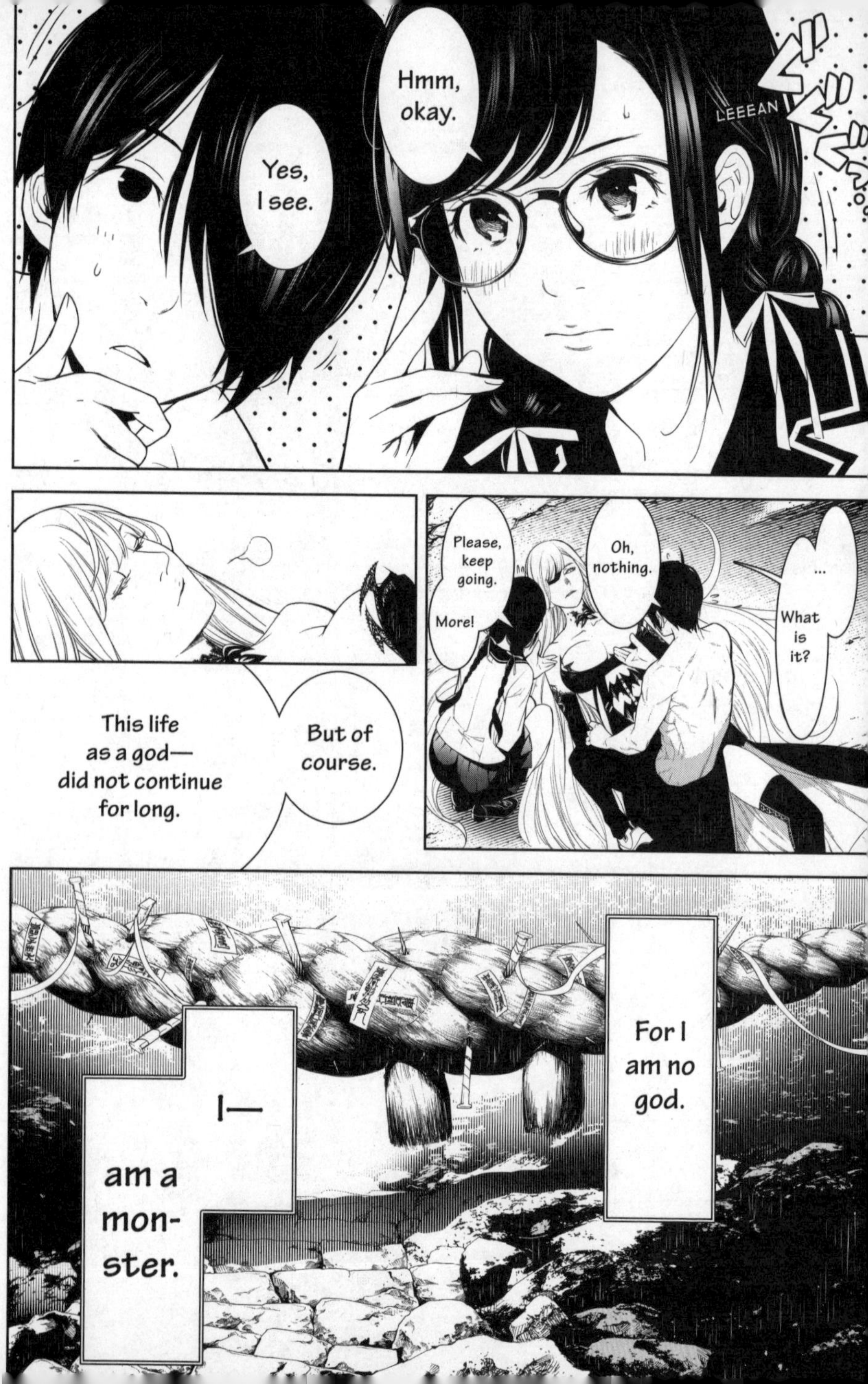
LEEEAN
Hmm, okay.
Yes, I see.
... What is it?
Oh, nothing.
Please, keep going.
More!
But of course.
This life as a god—did not continue for long.
For I am no god.
I—
am a monster.

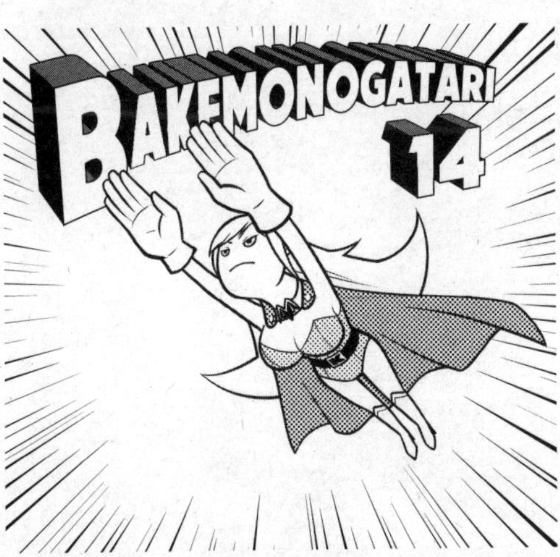
BAKEMONOGATARI
14

14

BakeMonogaTari

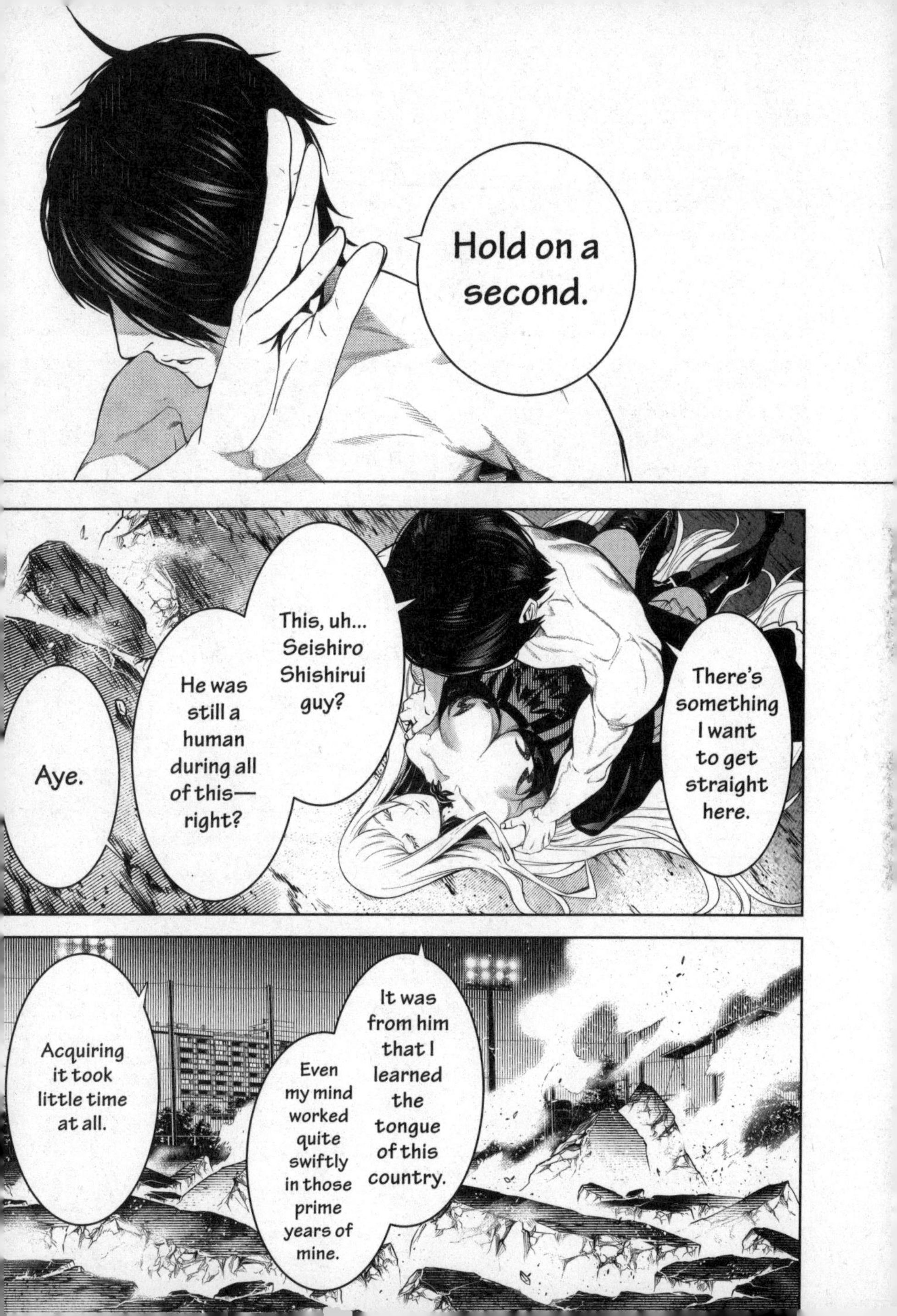
Hold on a second.
There's something I want to get straight here.
This, uh... Seishiro Shishirui guy?
He was still a human during all of this—right?
Aye.
It was from him that I learned the tongue of this country.
Even my mind worked quite swiftly in those prime years of mine.
Acquiring it took little time at all.

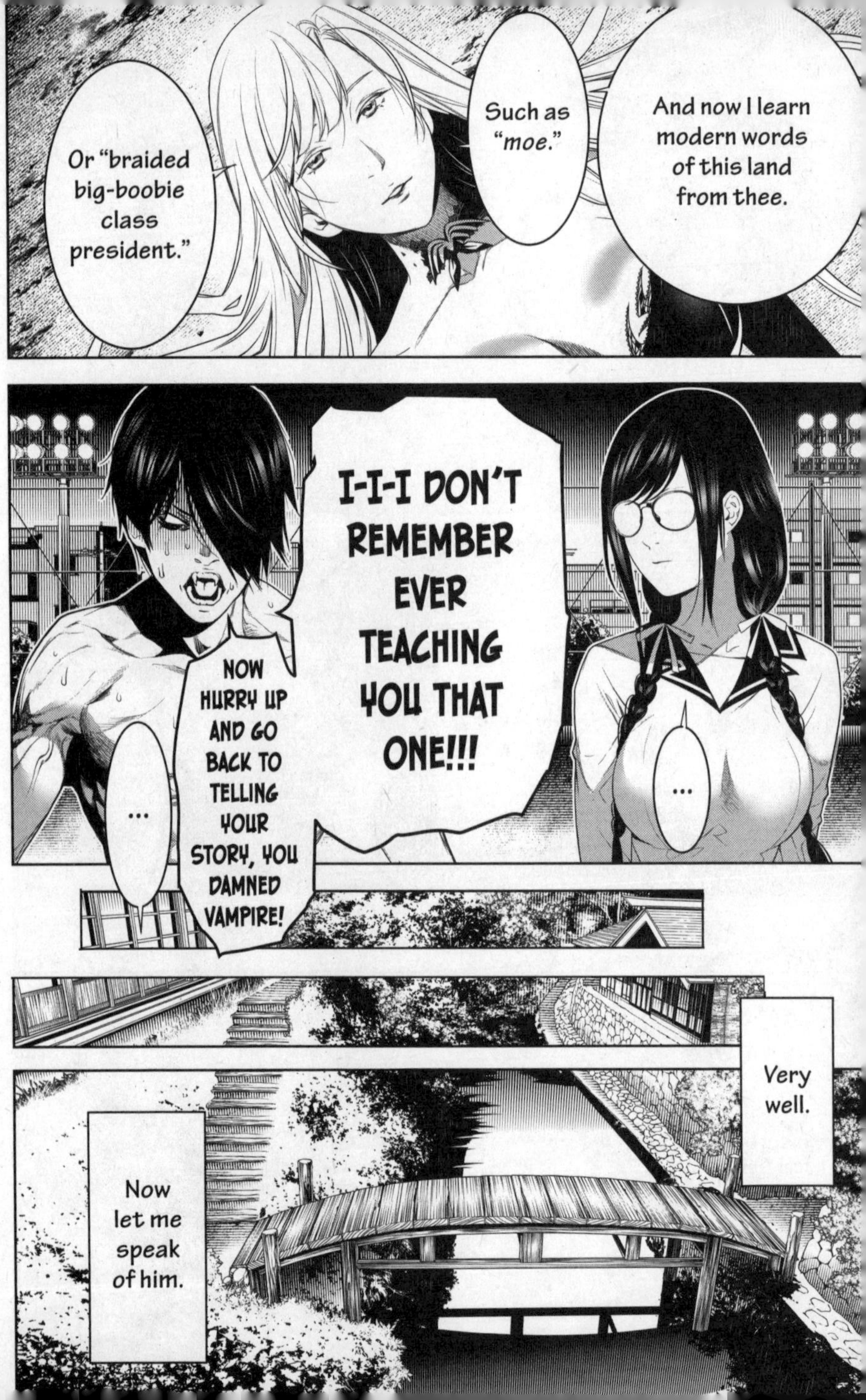

And now I learn modern words of this land from thee.
Such as "moe."
Or "braided big-boobie class president."
...
I-I-I DON'T REMEMBER EVER TEACHING YOU THAT ONE!!!
NOW HURRY UP AND GO BACK TO TELLING YOUR STORY, YOU DAMNED VAMPIRE!
...
Very well.
Now let me speak of him.

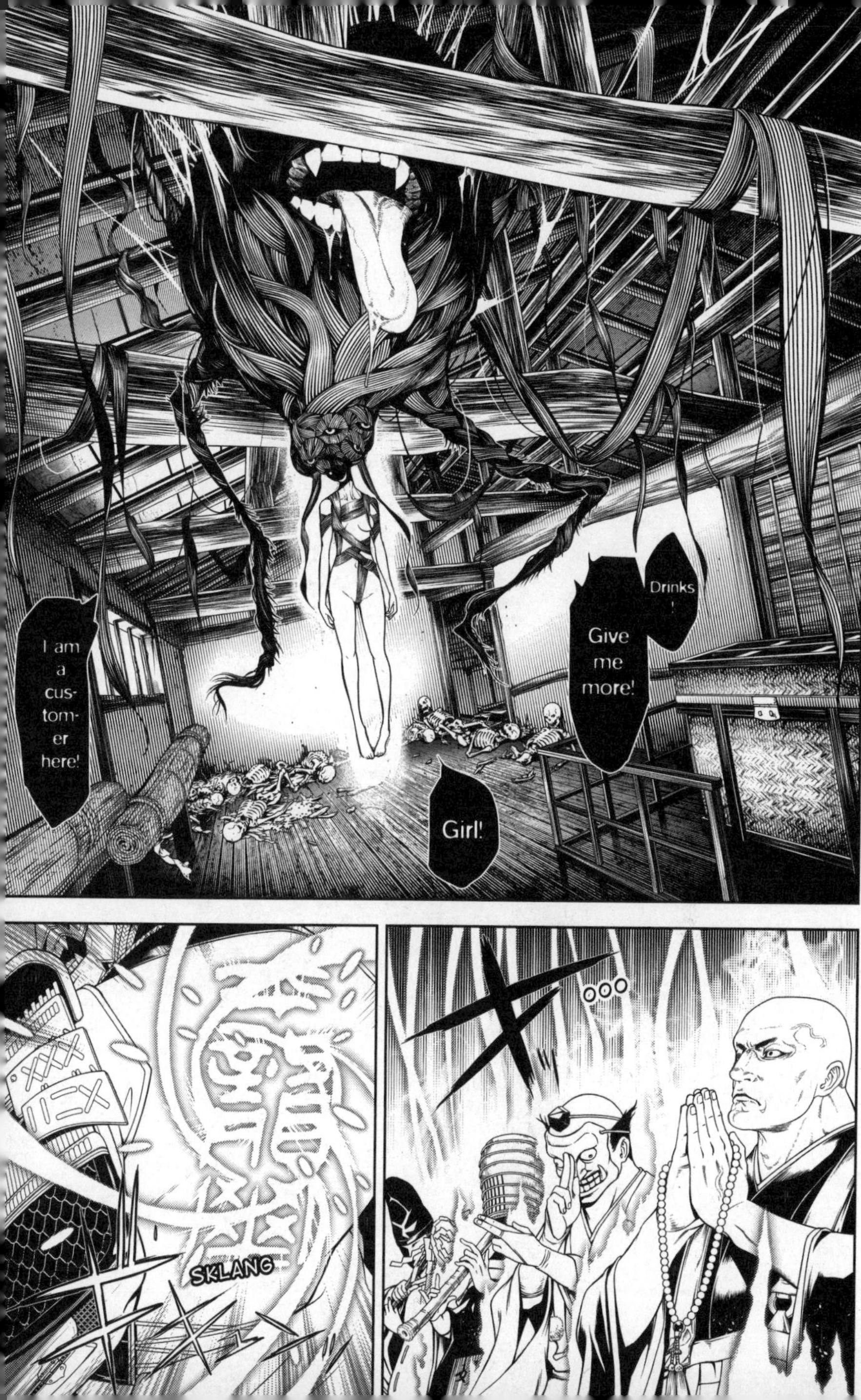
Drinks!
Give me more!
Girl!
I am a customer here!
ooo
SKLANG

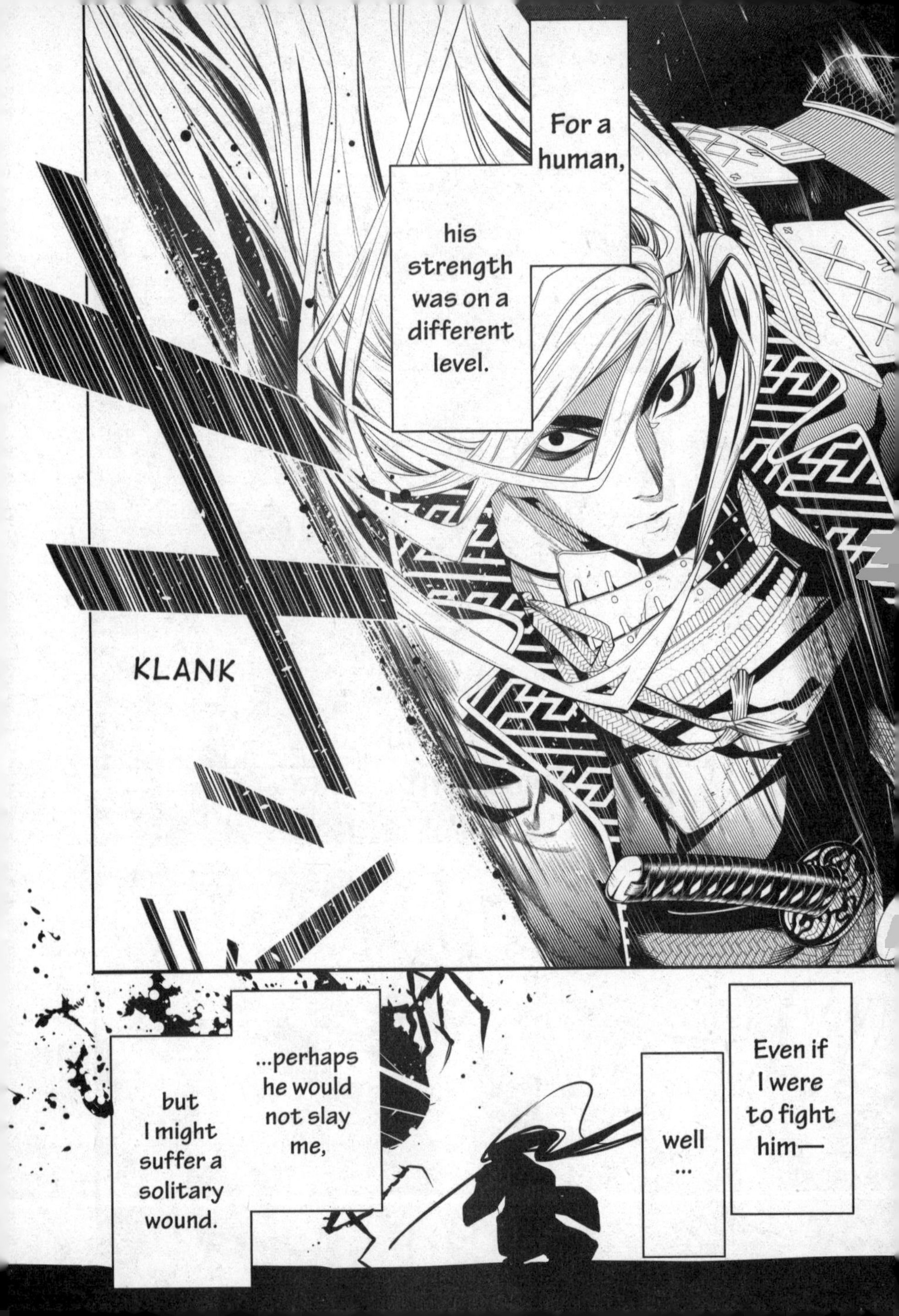
For a human,
his strength was on a different level.
KLANK
Even if I were to fight him—
well ...
...perhaps he would not slay me,
but I might suffer a solitary wound.

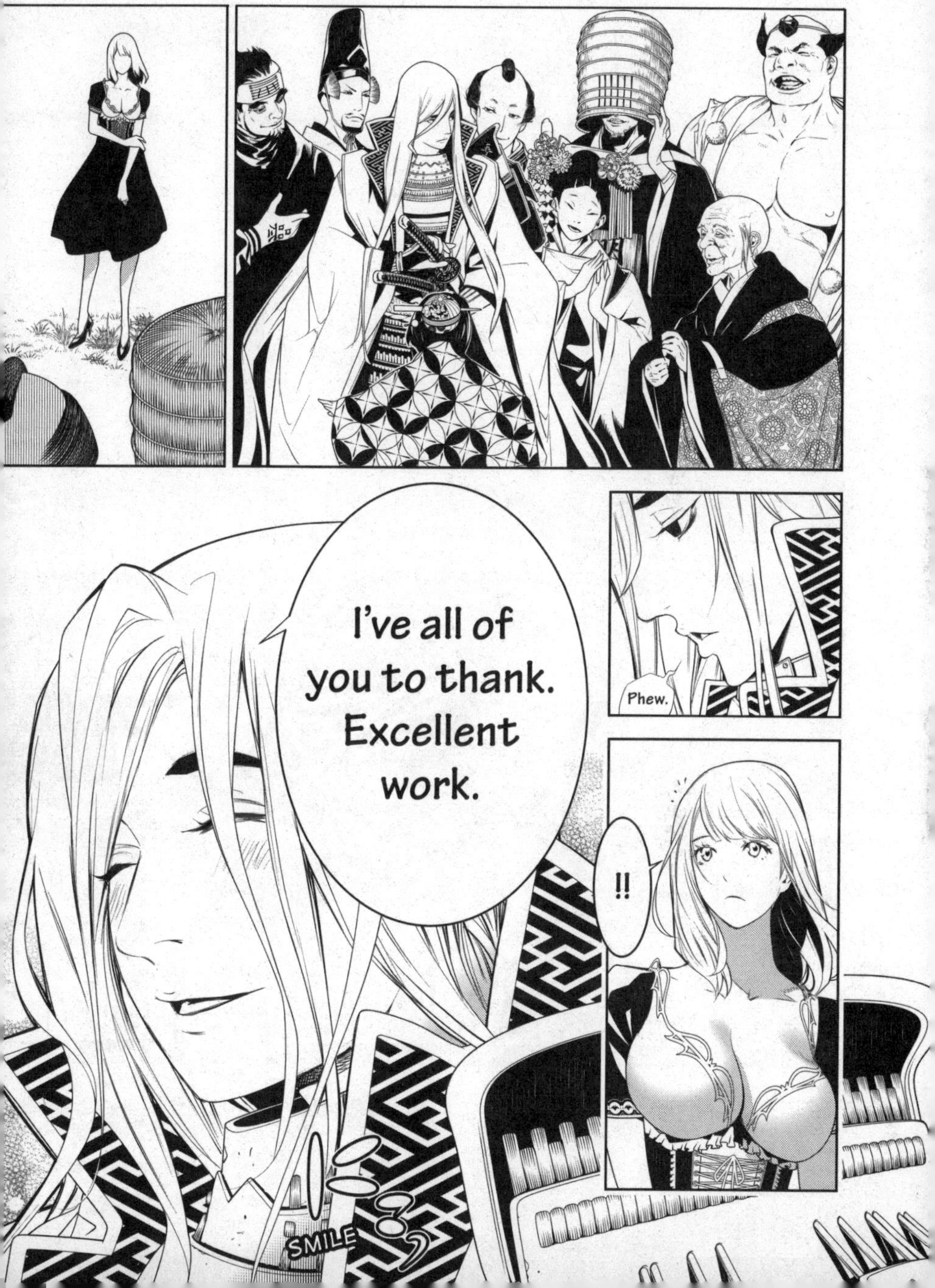
Phew.
!!
I've all of you to thank. Excellent work.
SMILE

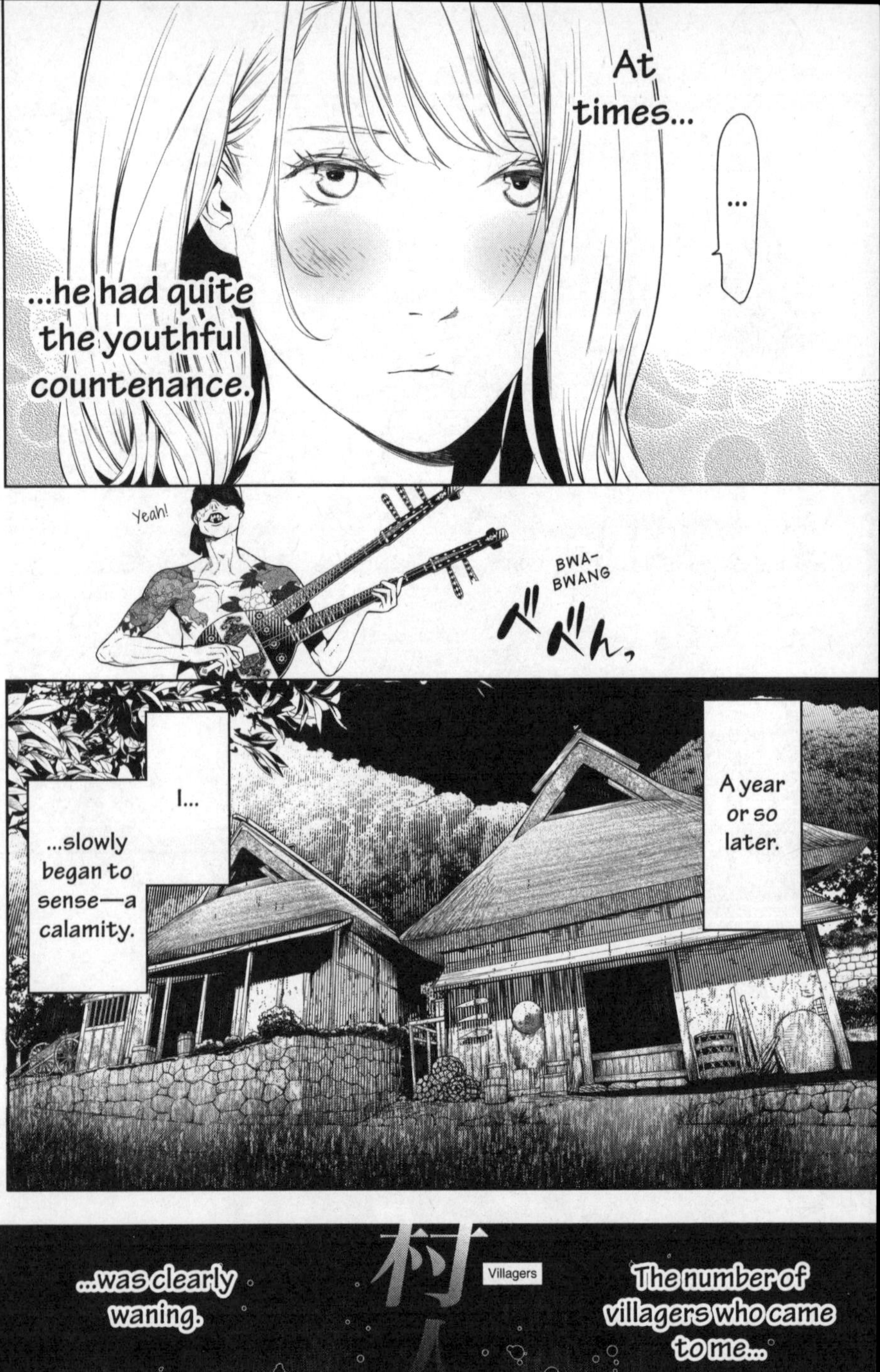
At times...
...
...he had quite the youthful countenance.
Yeah!
BWA-BWANG
べべん
A year or so later.
I...
...slowly began to sense—a calamity.
The number of villagers who came to me...
村
Villagers
...was clearly waning.

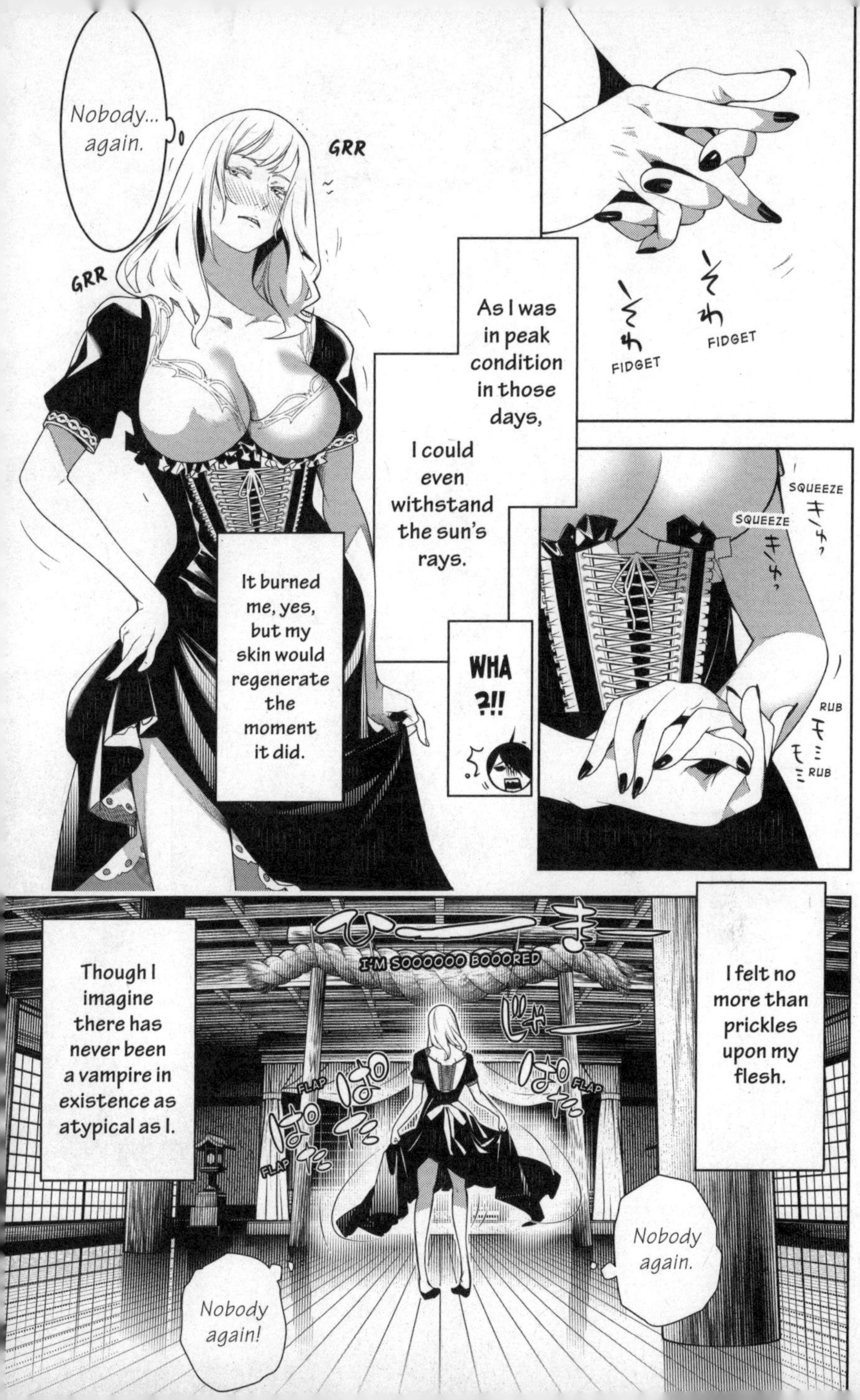
FIDGET
FIDGET
As I was in peak condition in those days,
SQUEEZE
SQUEEZE
RUB
RUB
WHA ?!!
I could even withstand the sun's rays.
Nobody... again.
GRR
GRR
It burned me, yes, but my skin would regenerate the moment it did.
I felt no more than prickles upon my flesh.
I'M SOOOOOO BOOORED
Nobody again.
FLAP
FLAP
FLAP
FLAP
Though I imagine there has never been a vampire in existence as atypical as I.
Nobody again!

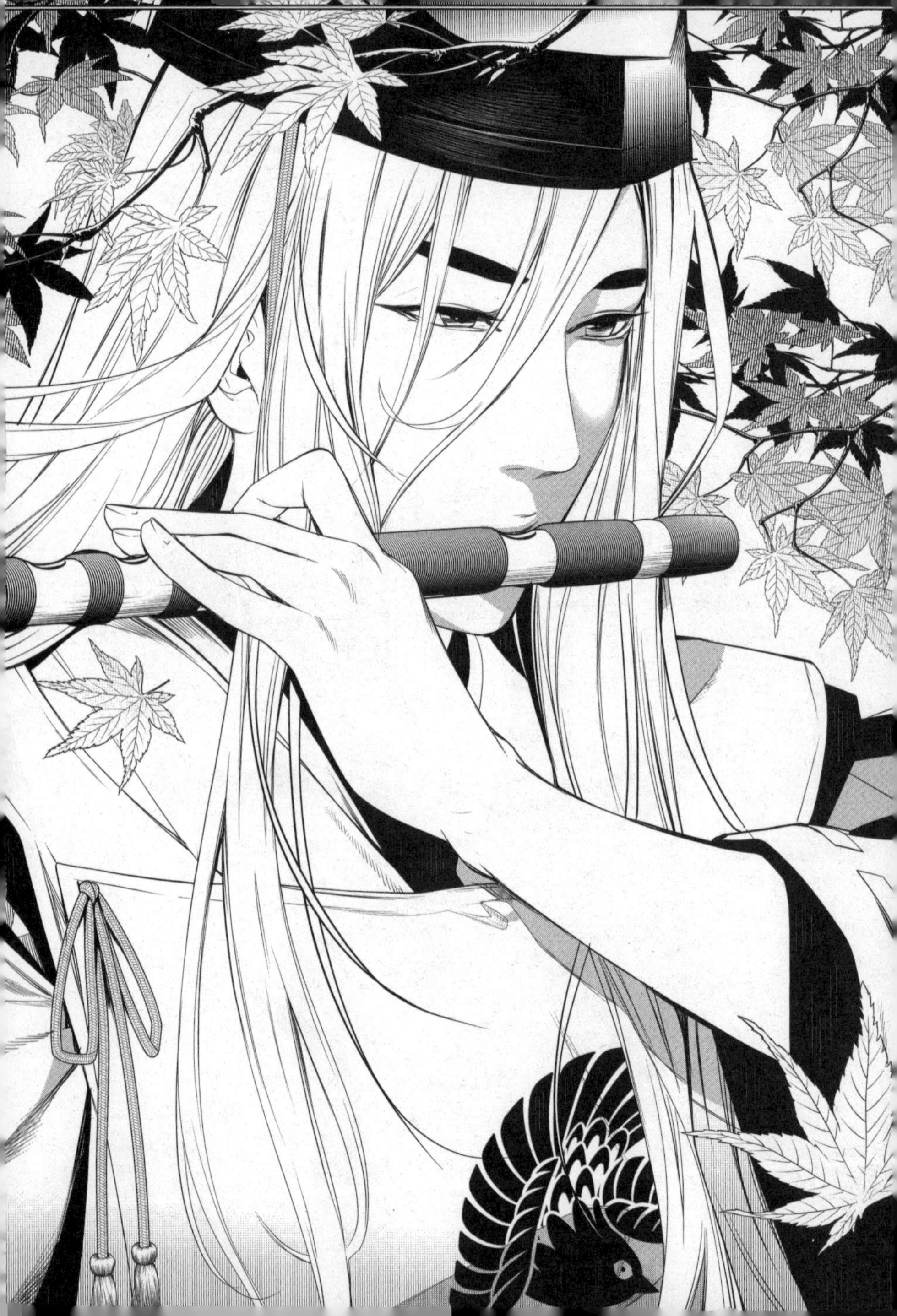

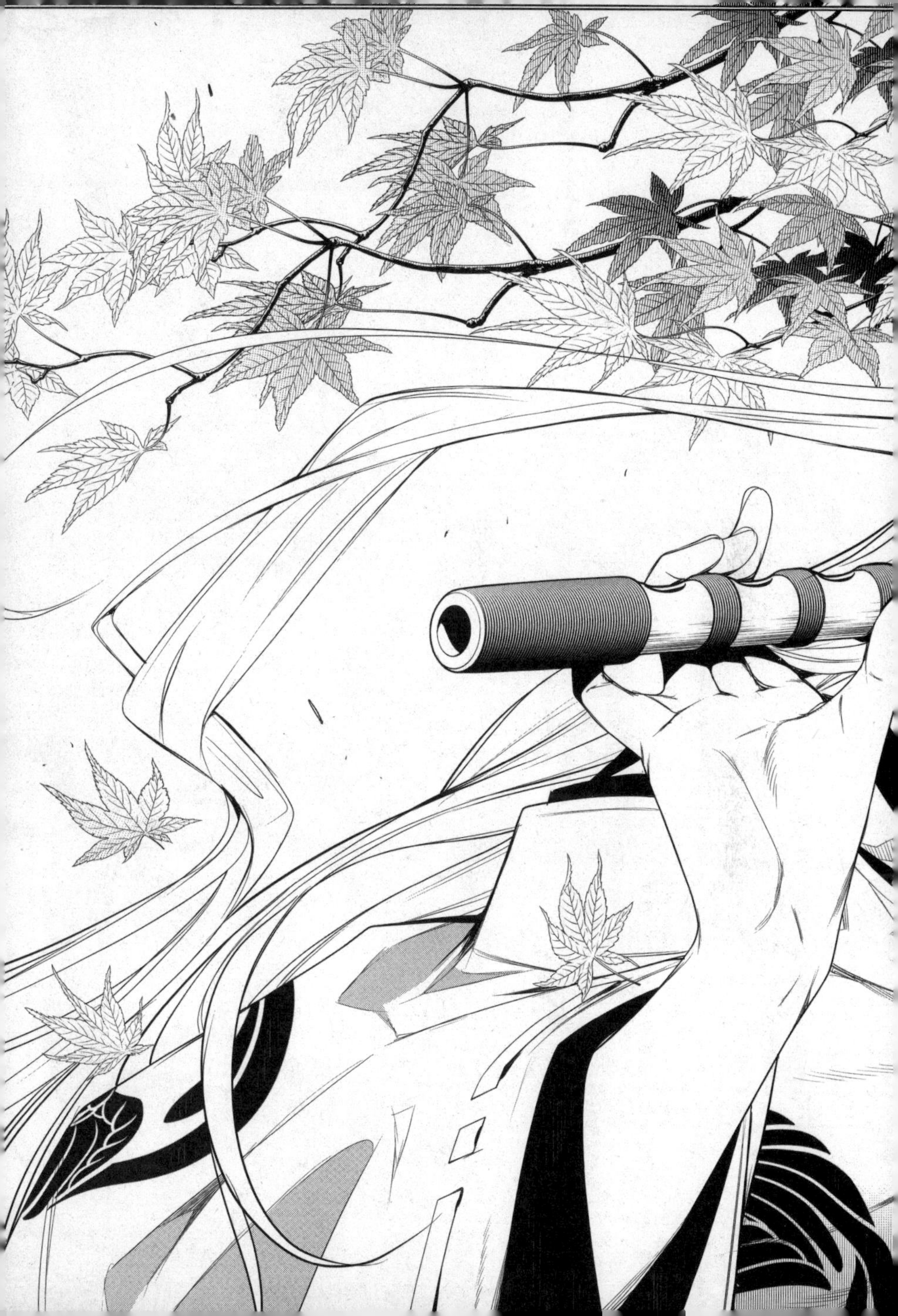

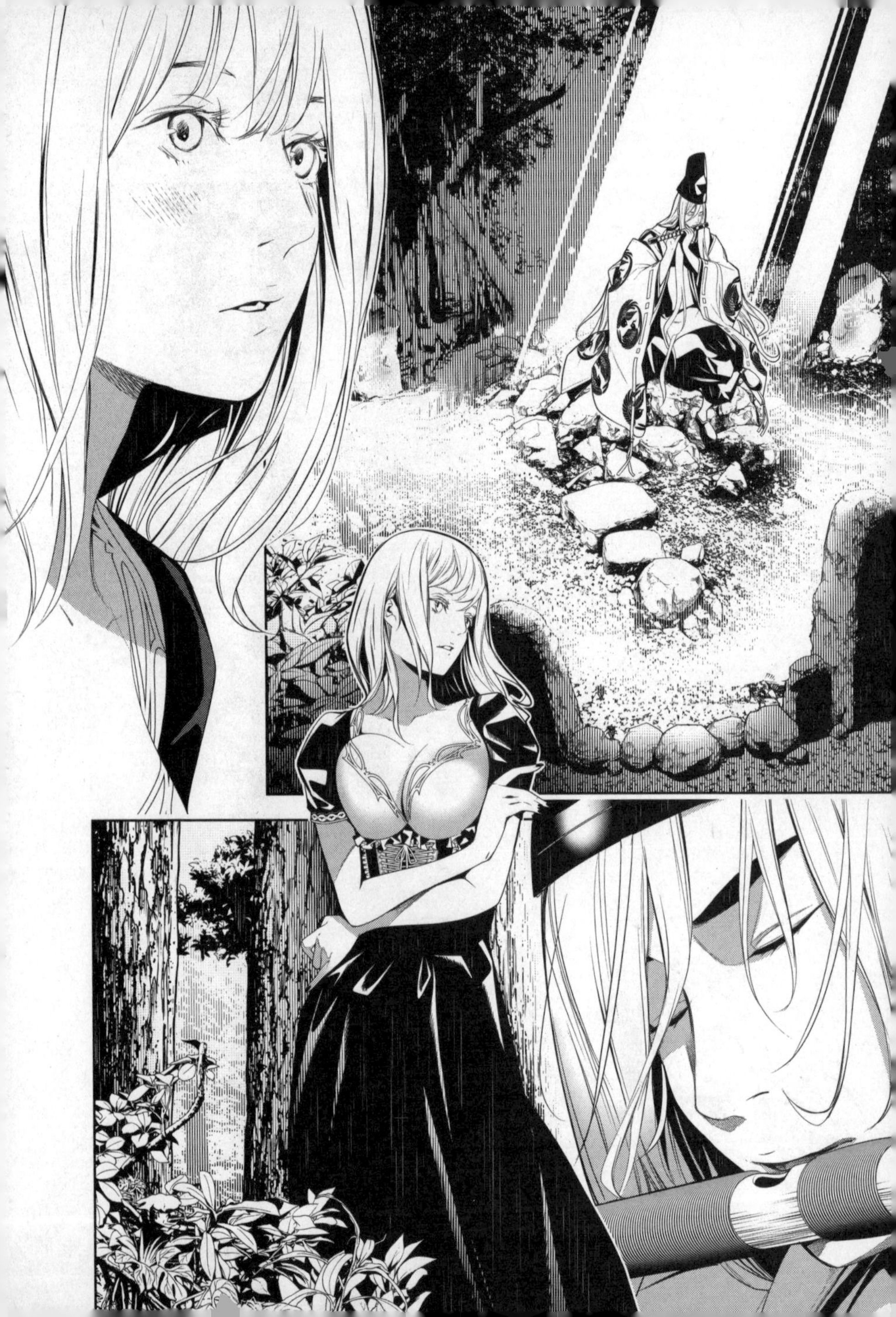

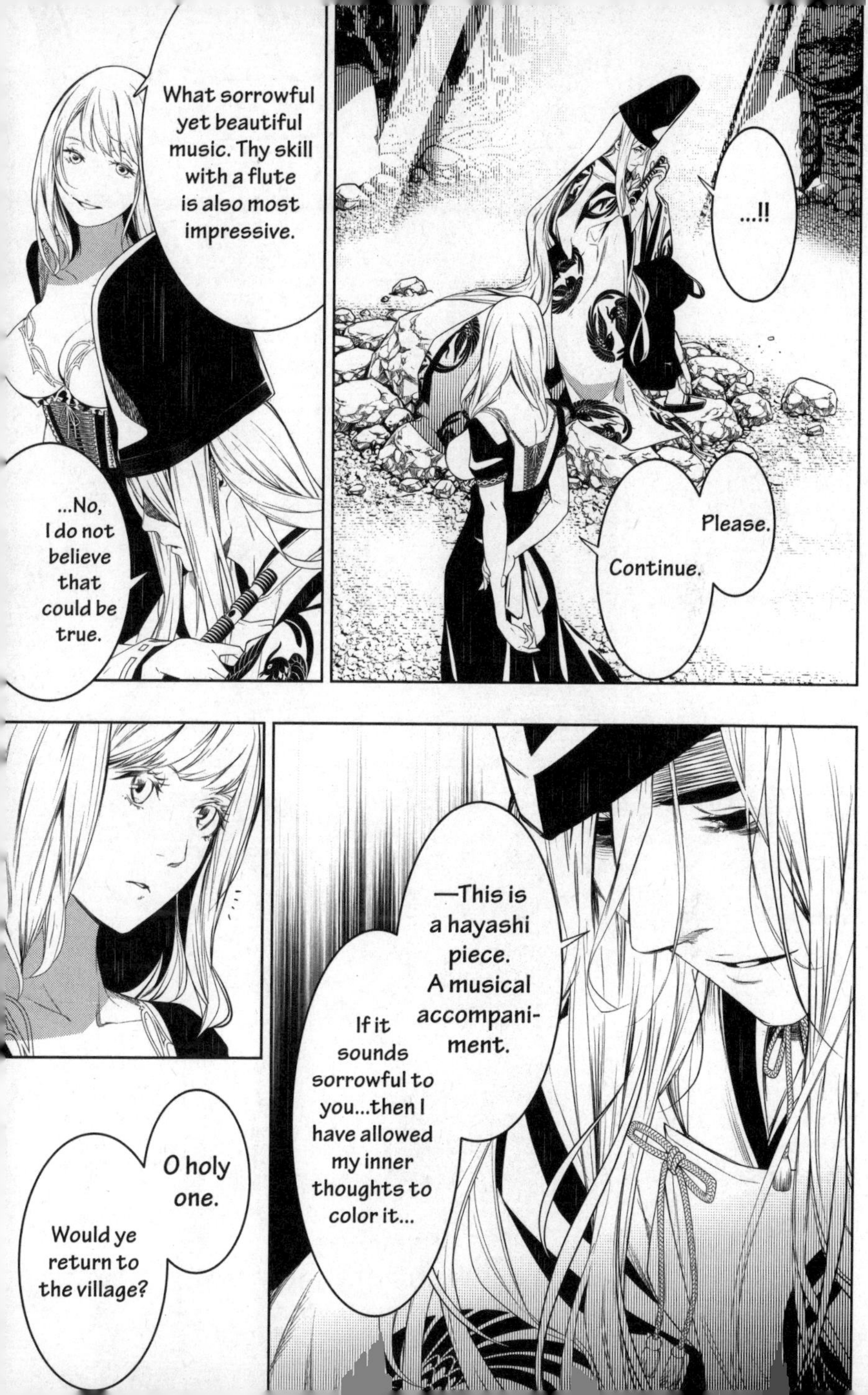
...!!
Please.
Continue.
What sorrowful yet beautiful music. Thy skill with a flute is also most impressive.
...No, I do not believe that could be true.
—This is a hayashi piece. A musical accompani-ment.
If it sounds sorrowful to you...then I have allowed my inner thoughts to color it...
O holy one.
Would ye return to the village?

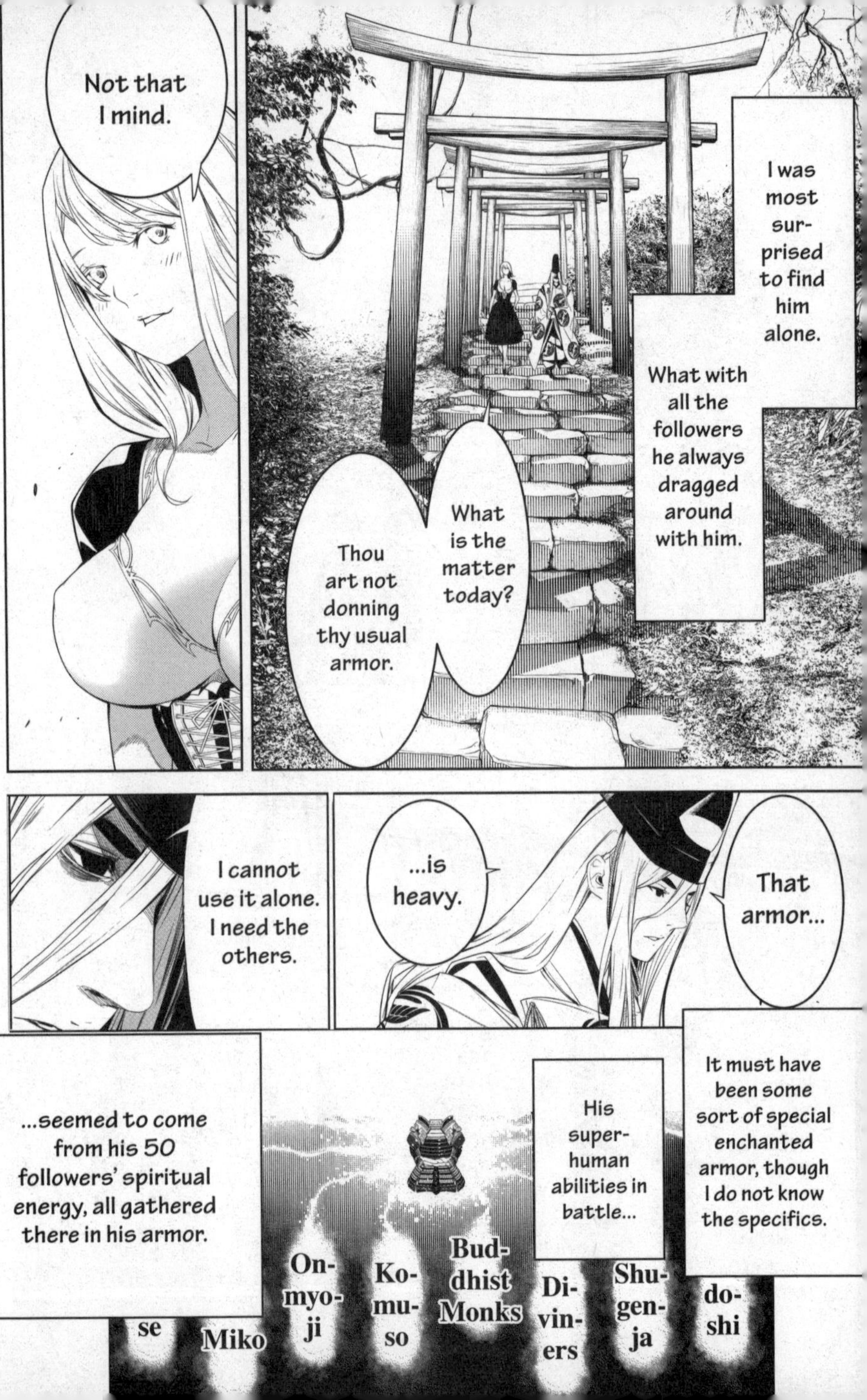

I was most surprised to find him alone.
What with all the followers he always dragged around with him.
What is the matter today?
Thou art not donning thy usual armor.
Not that I mind.
That armor...
...is heavy.
I cannot use it alone. I need the others.
It must have been some sort of special enchanted armor, though I do not know the specifics.
His superhuman abilities in battle...
...seemed to come from his 50 followers' spiritual energy, all gathered there in his armor.
doshi
Shugenja
Diviners
Buddhist Monks
Komuso
Onmyoji
Miko
se

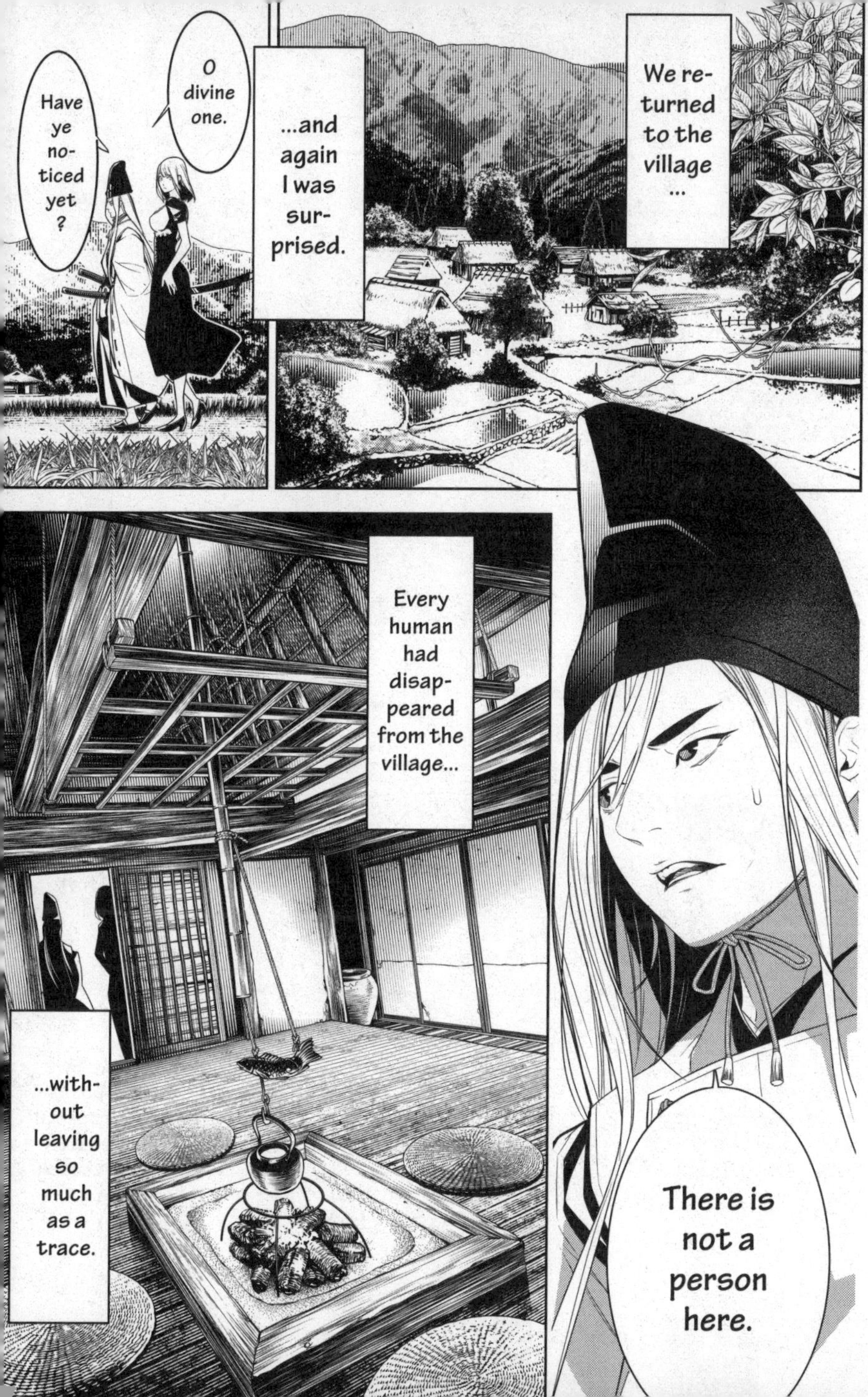
We re-turned to the village...
...and again I was sur-prised.
O divine one.
Have ye no-ticed yet?
There is not a person here.
Every human had disap-peared from the village...
...with-out leaving so much as a trace.

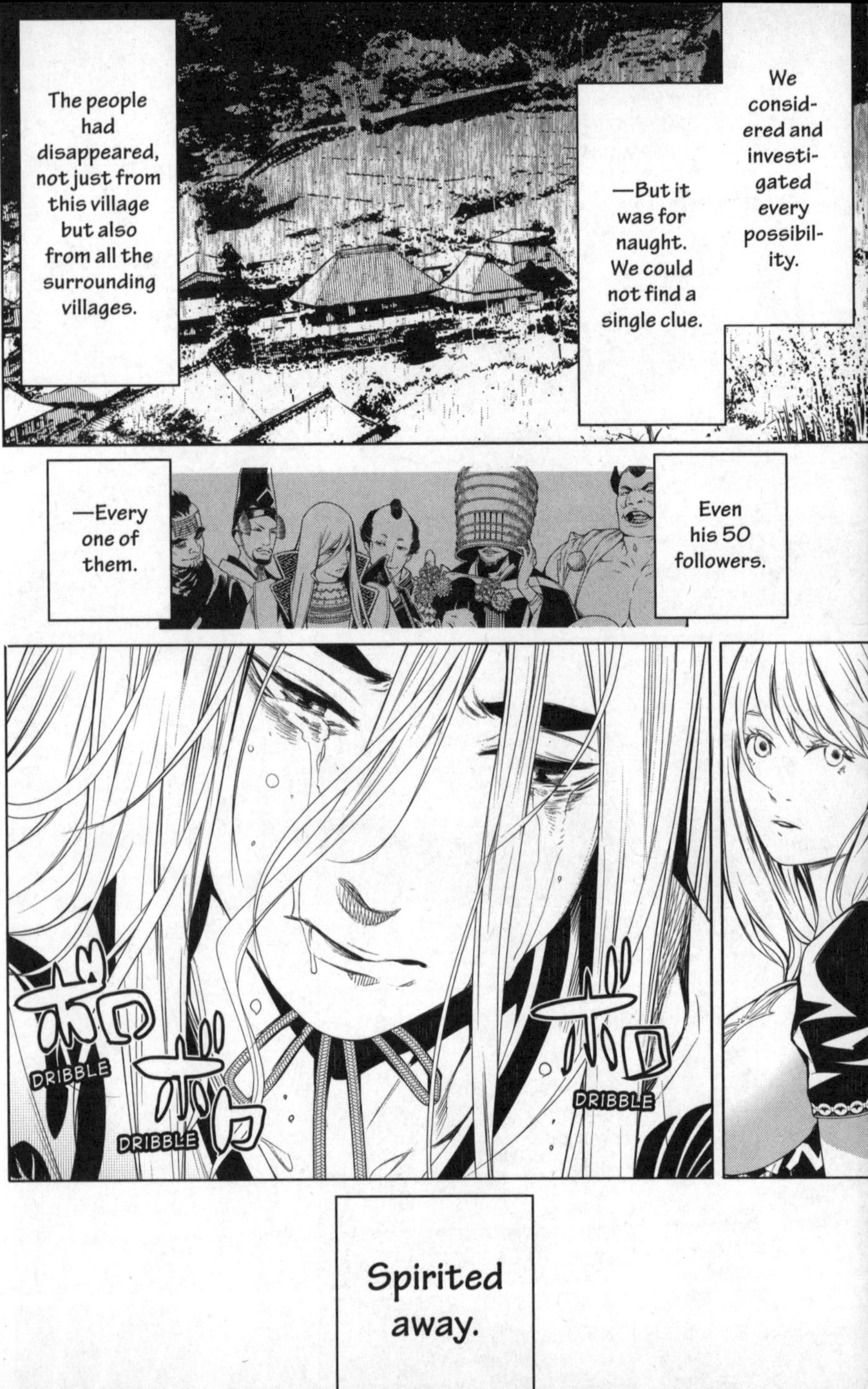
We considered and investigated every possibility.
—But it was for naught. We could not find a single clue.
The people had disappeared, not just from this village but also from all the surrounding villages.
Even his 50 followers.
—Every one of them.
DRIBBLE
DRIBBLE
DRIBBLE
Spirited away.

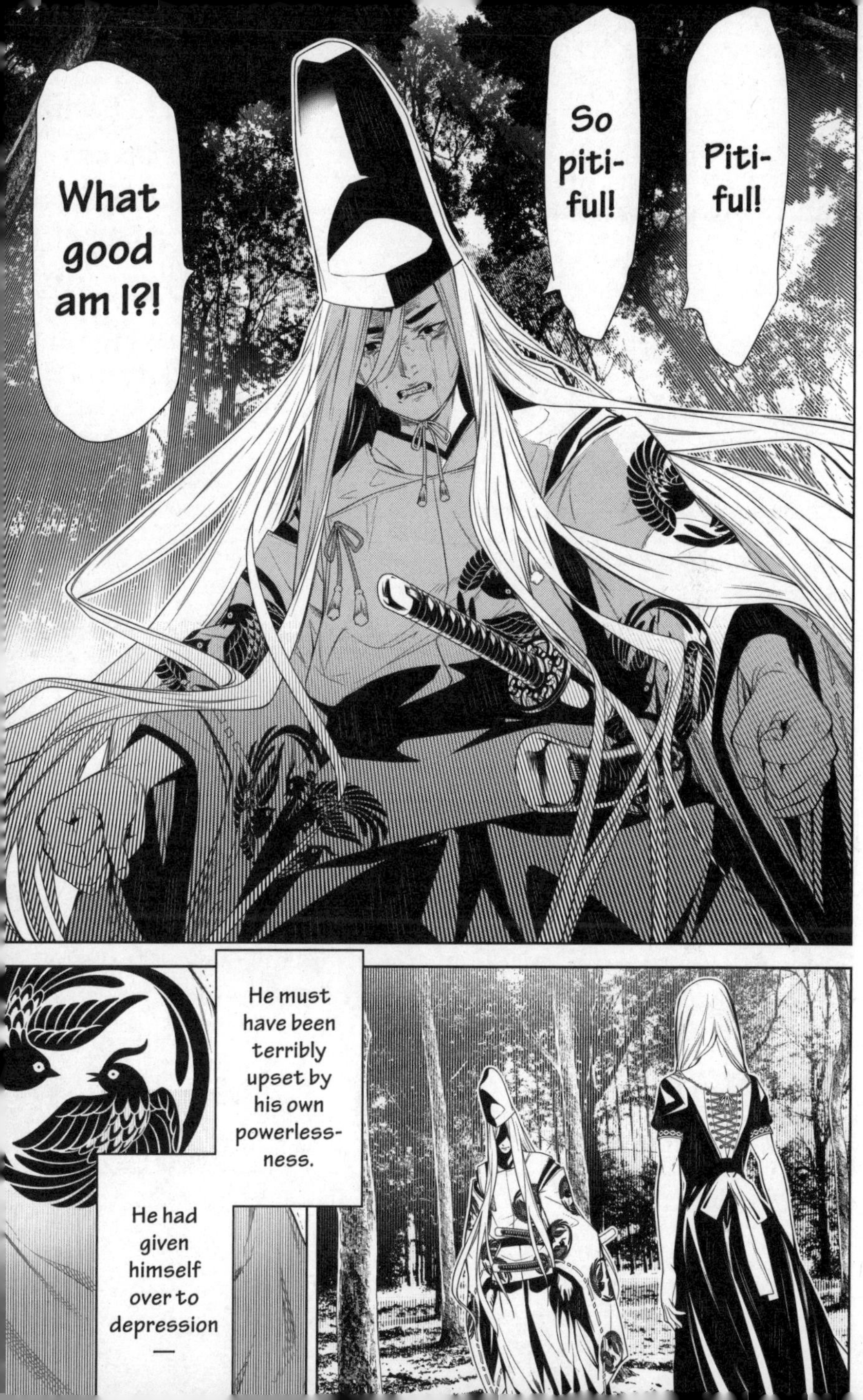

Piti-ful!
So piti-ful!
What good am I?!
He must have been terribly upset by his own powerless-ness.
He had given himself over to depression —

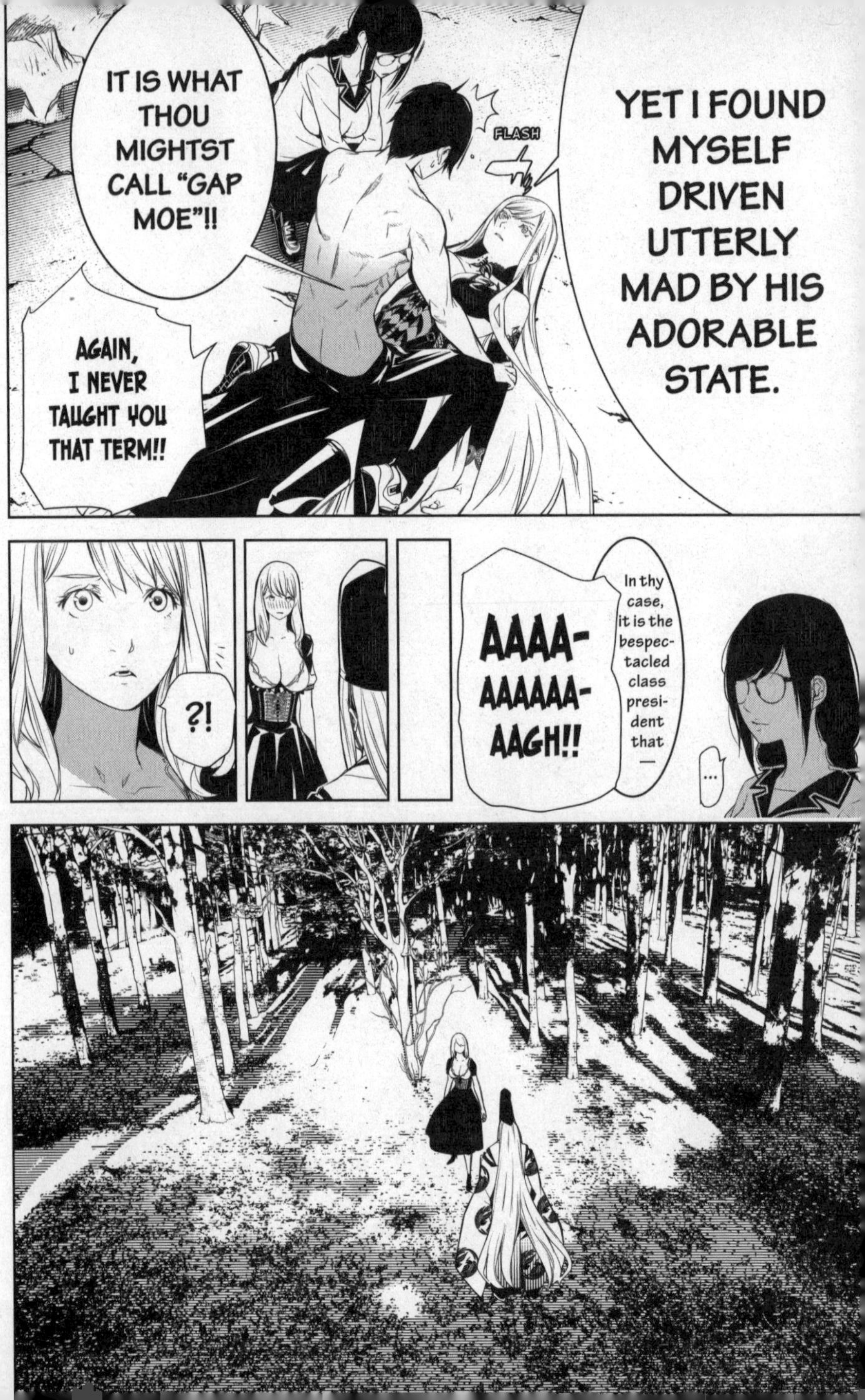
YET I FOUND MYSELF DRIVEN UTTERLY MAD BY HIS ADORABLE STATE.
FLASH
IT IS WHAT THOU MIGHTST CALL "GAP MOE"!!
AGAIN, I NEVER TAUGHT YOU THAT TERM!!
...
In thy case, it is the bespectacled class president that—
AAAA-AAAAAA-AAGH!!
?!

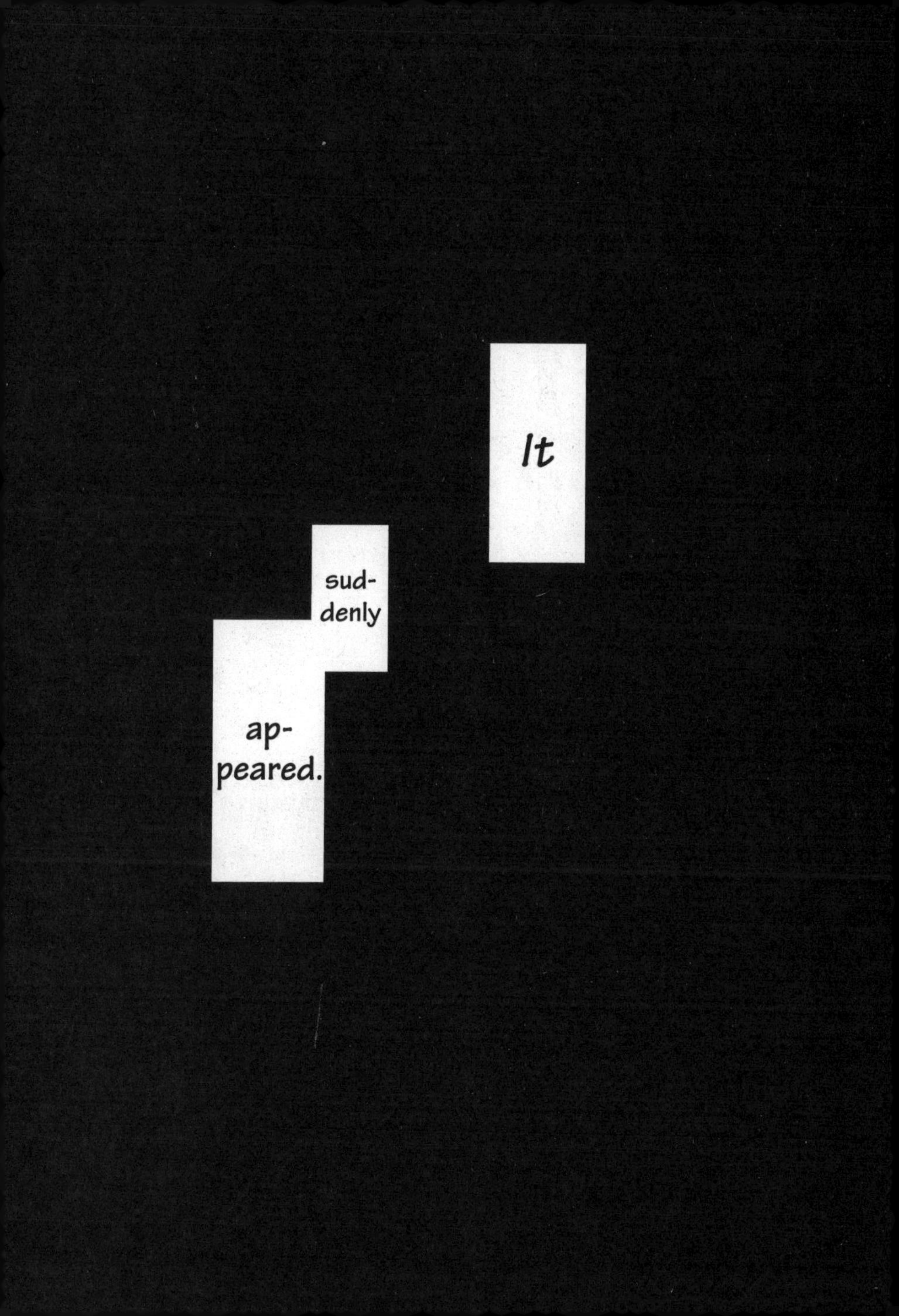
It
sud-
denly
ap-
peared.

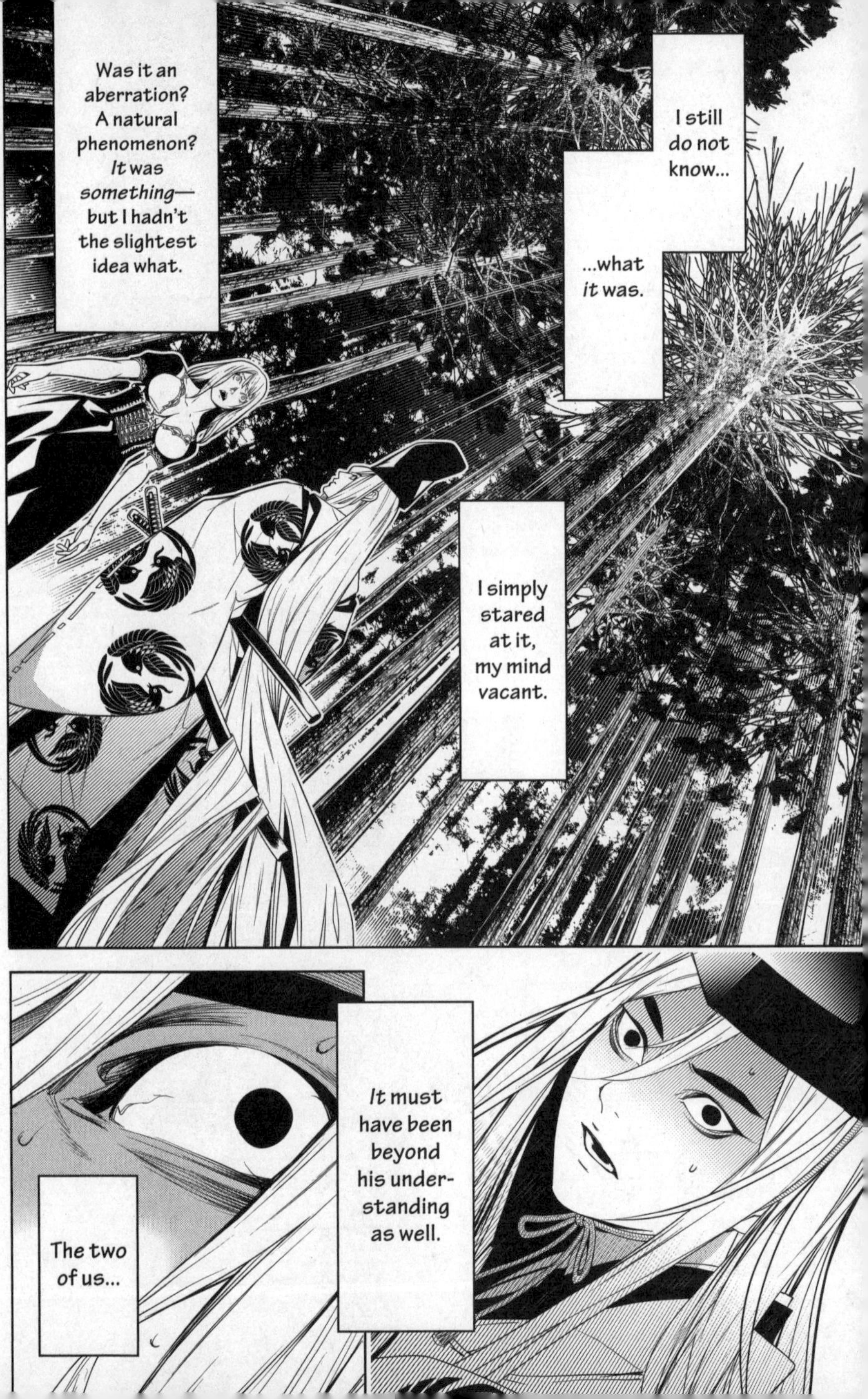
I still do not know...
...what *it* was.
Was it an aberration? A natural phenomenon? *It* was *something*—but I hadn't the slightest idea what.
I simply stared at it, my mind vacant.
It must have been beyond his under-standing as well.
The two of us...

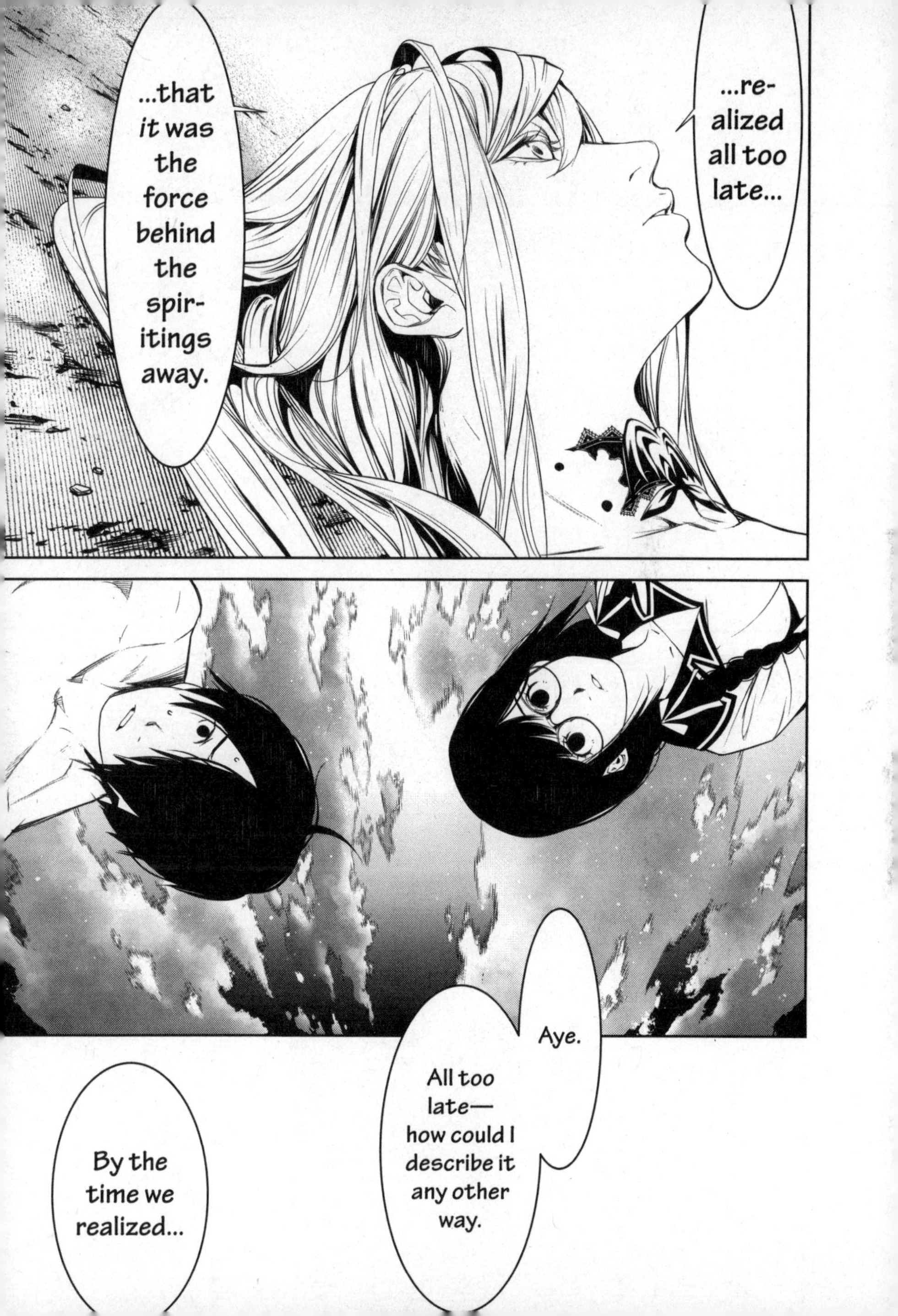
...re-alized all too late...
...that it was the force behind the spir-itings away.
Aye.
All too late—how could I describe it any other way.
By the time we realized...

...only a
quarter of
my body
remained.

As for
him...

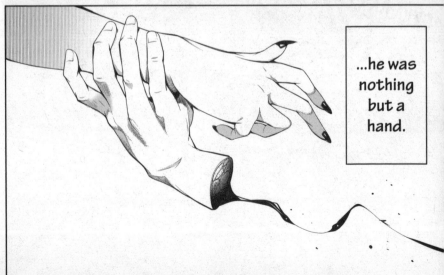

...he was
nothing
but a
hand.

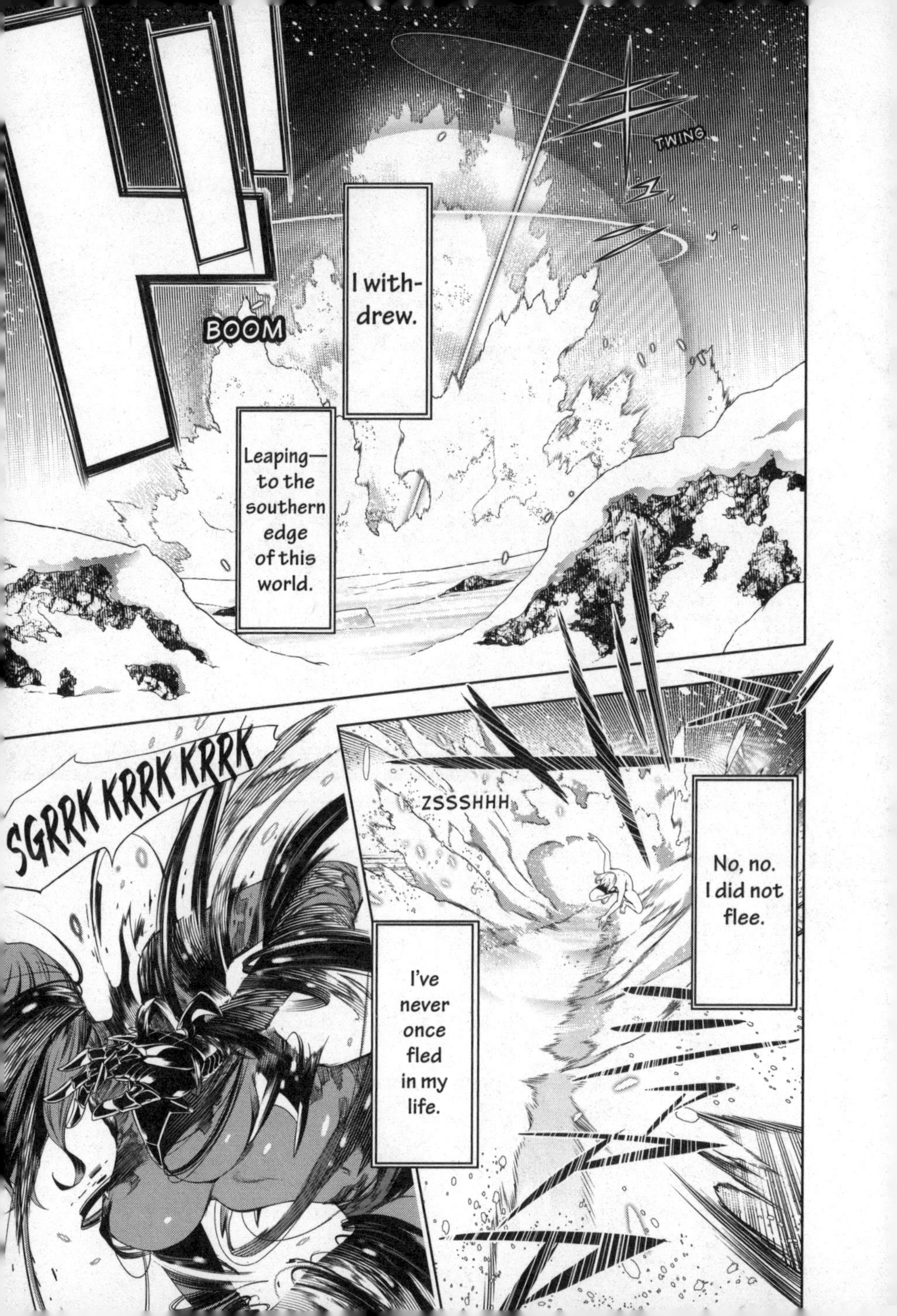
TWING
I with-drew.
BOOM
Leaping—to the southern edge of this world.
No, no. I did not flee.
ZSSSHHH
I've never once fled in my life.
SGRRK KRRK KRRK

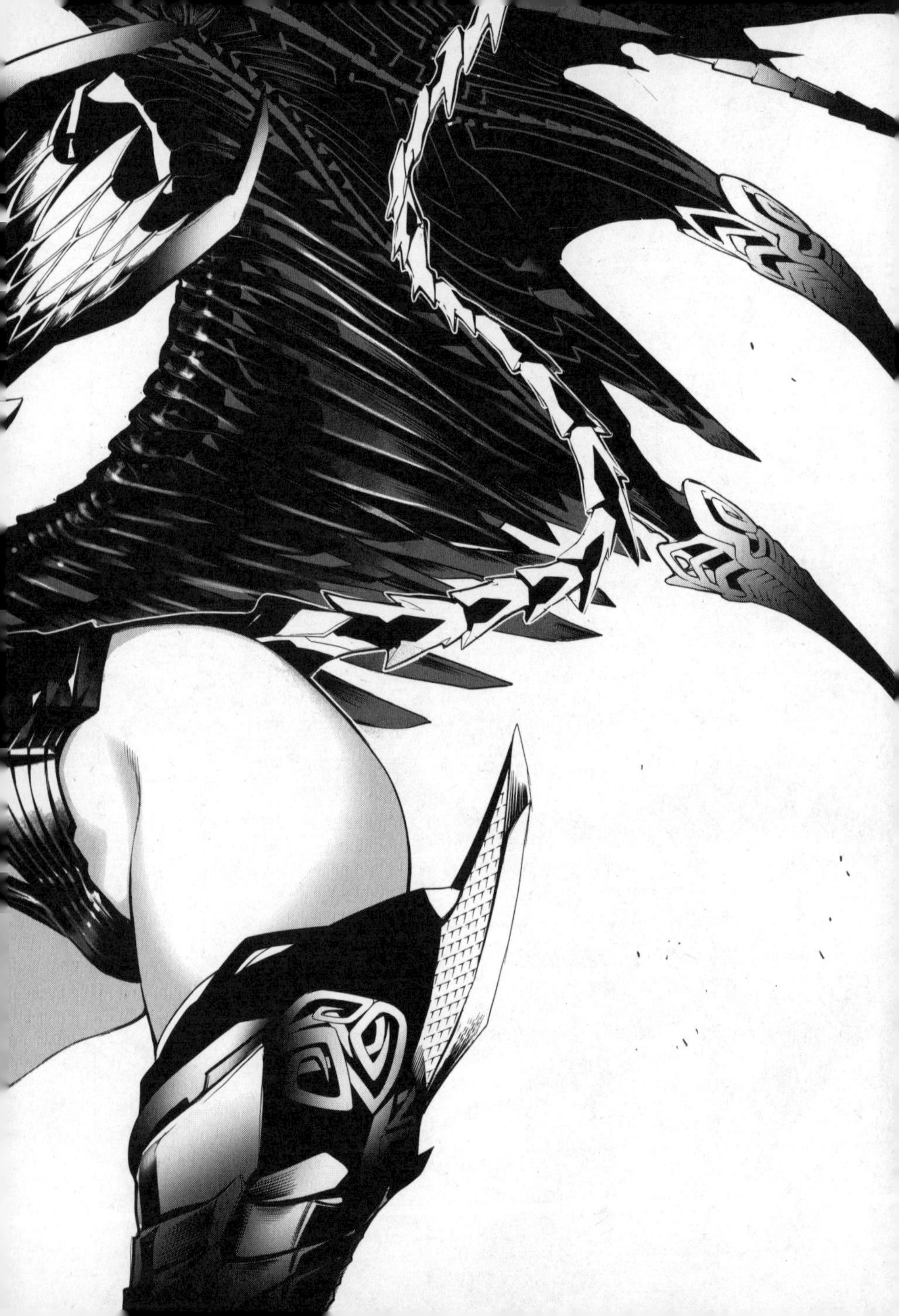

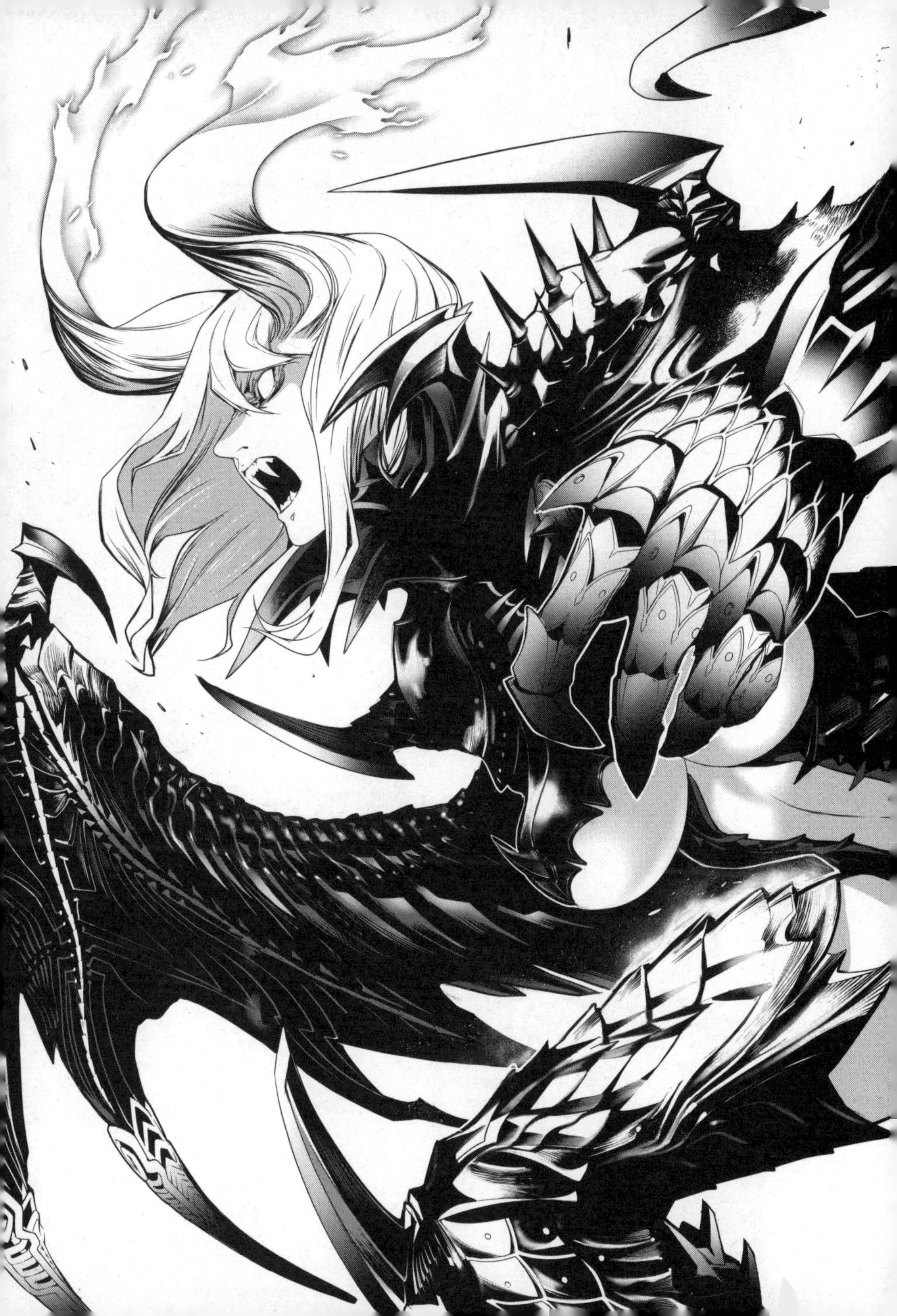

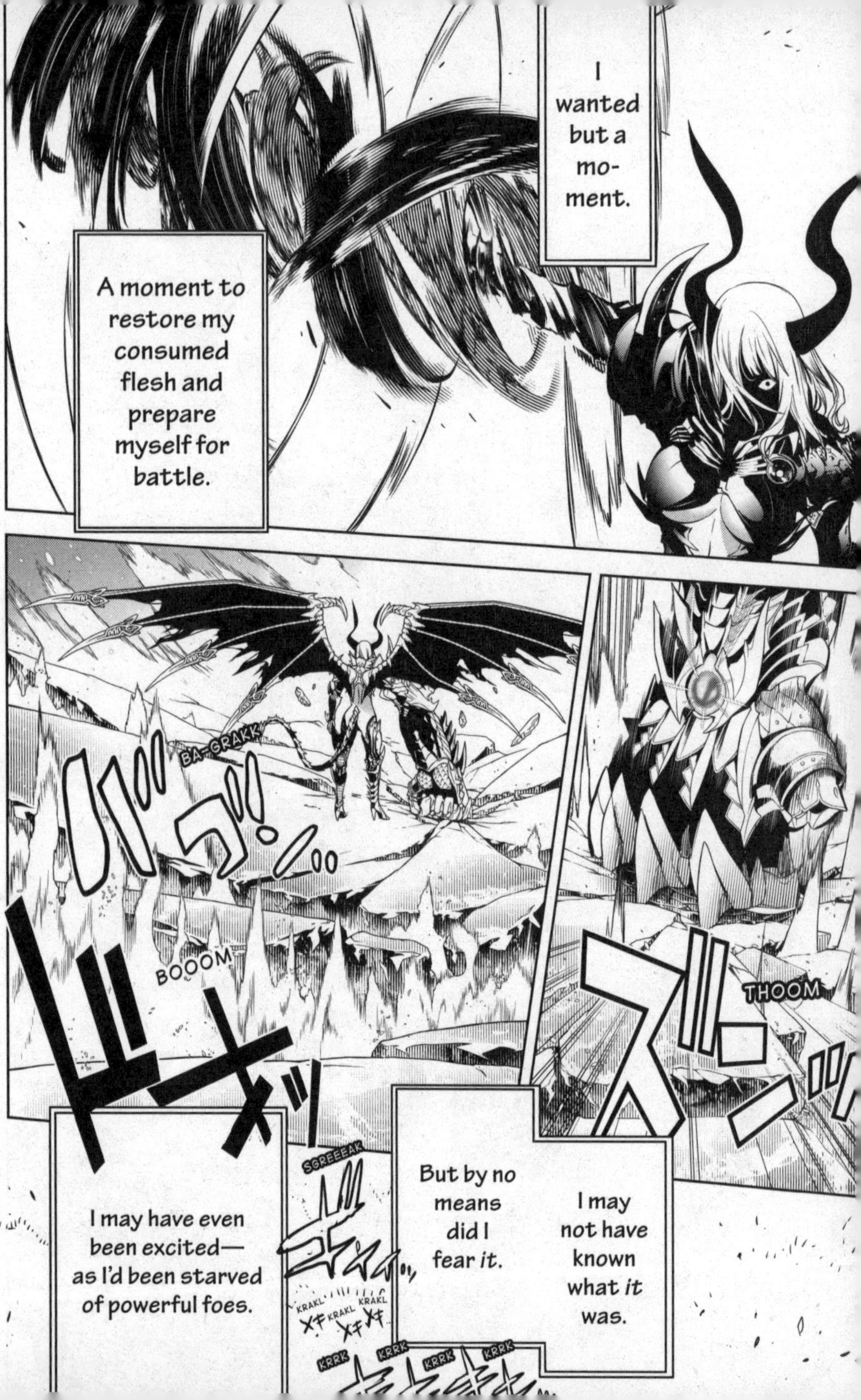
I wanted but a moment.
A moment to restore my consumed flesh and prepare myself for battle.
THOOM
BA-GRAKK
BOOOM
I may not have known what *it* was.
But by no means did I fear *it*.
SCREEEAK
I may have even been excited—as I'd been starved of powerful foes.
KRAKL KRAKL KRAKL
KRRK KRRK KRRK KRRK

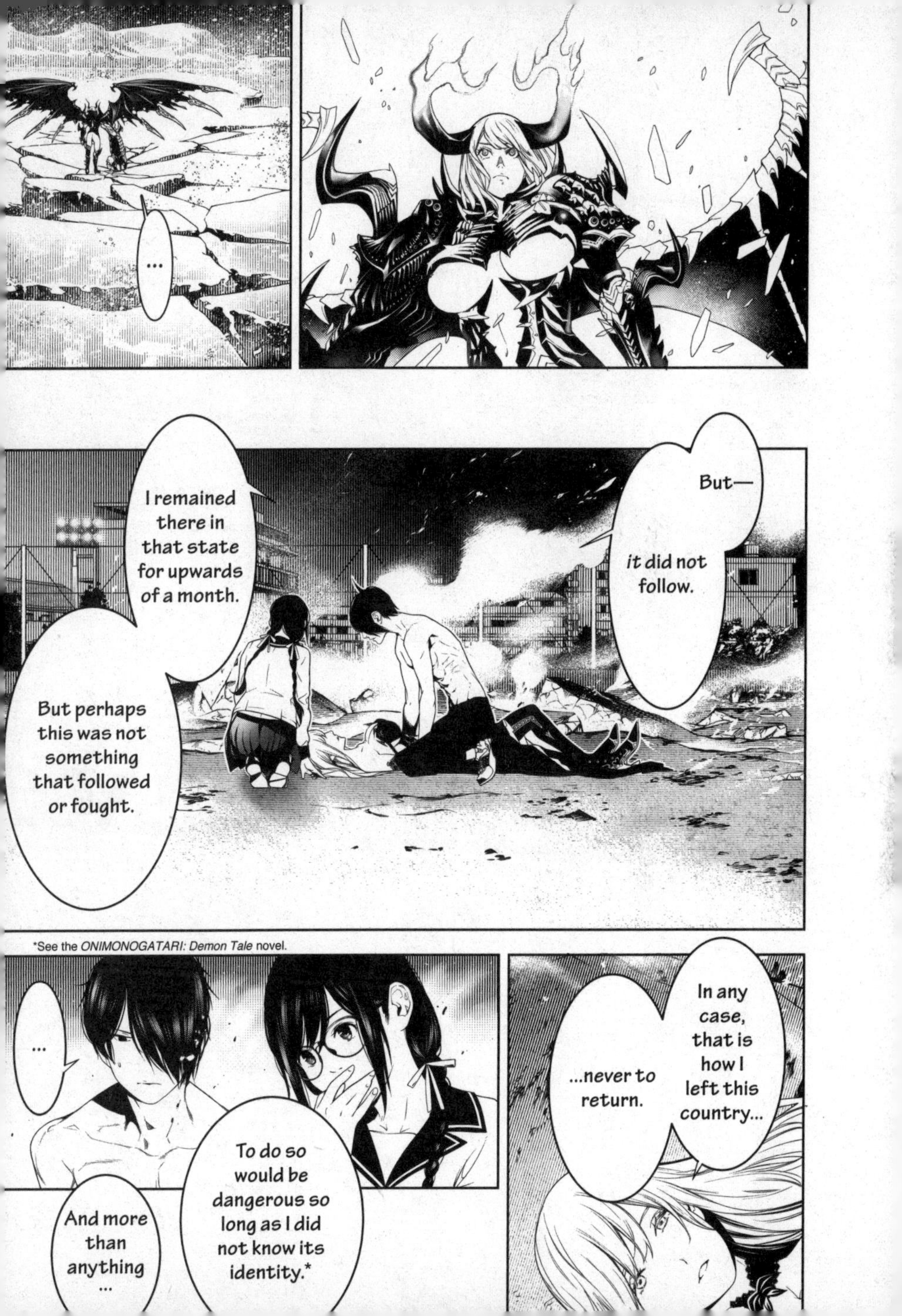
...
But—
it did not follow.
I remained there in that state for upwards of a month.
But perhaps this was not something that followed or fought.
In any case, that is how I left this country...
...never to return.
...
To do so would be dangerous so long as I did not know its identity.*
And more than anything ...

*See the *ONIMONOGATARI: Demon Tale* novel.

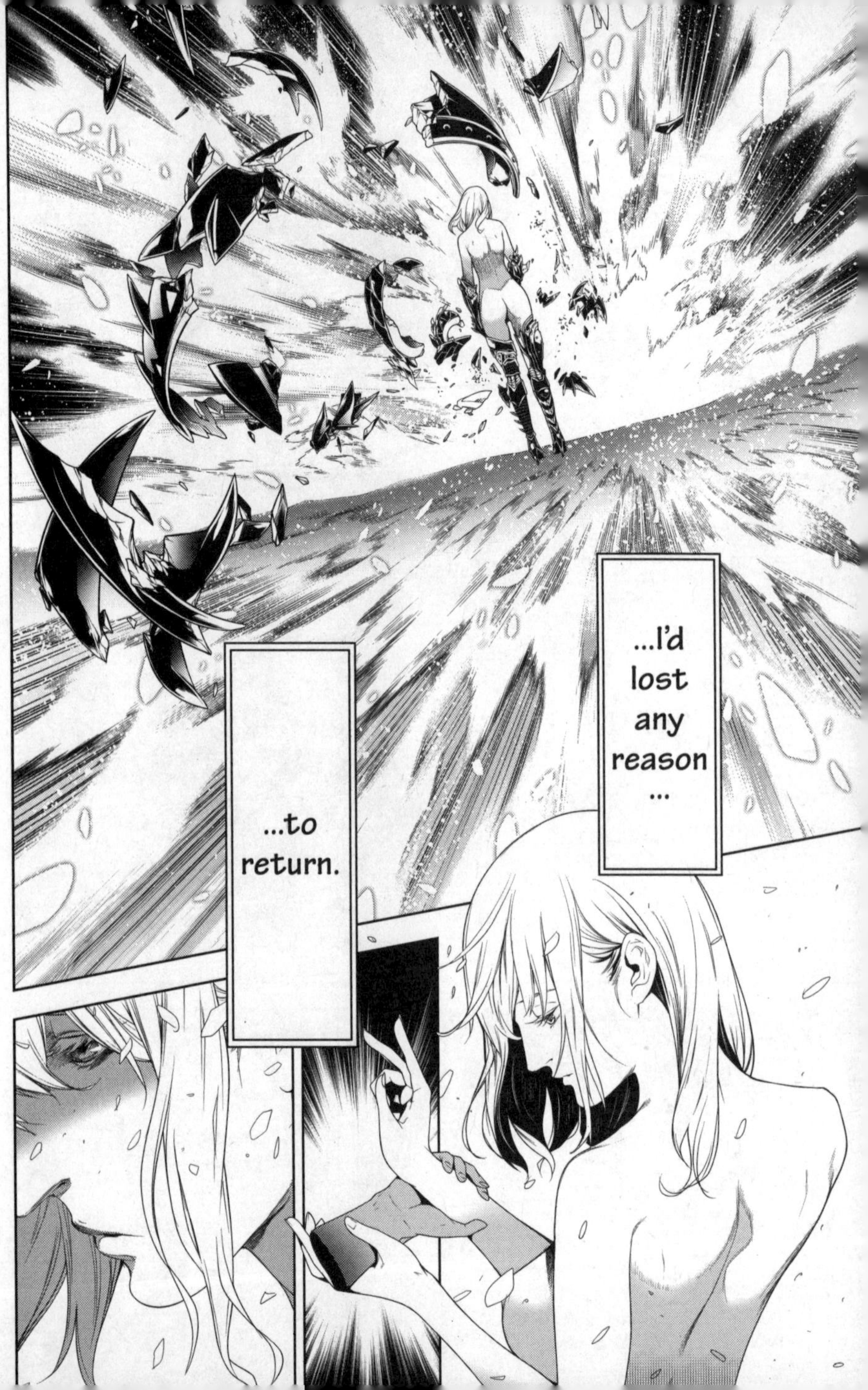
...I'd lost any reason ...
...to return.

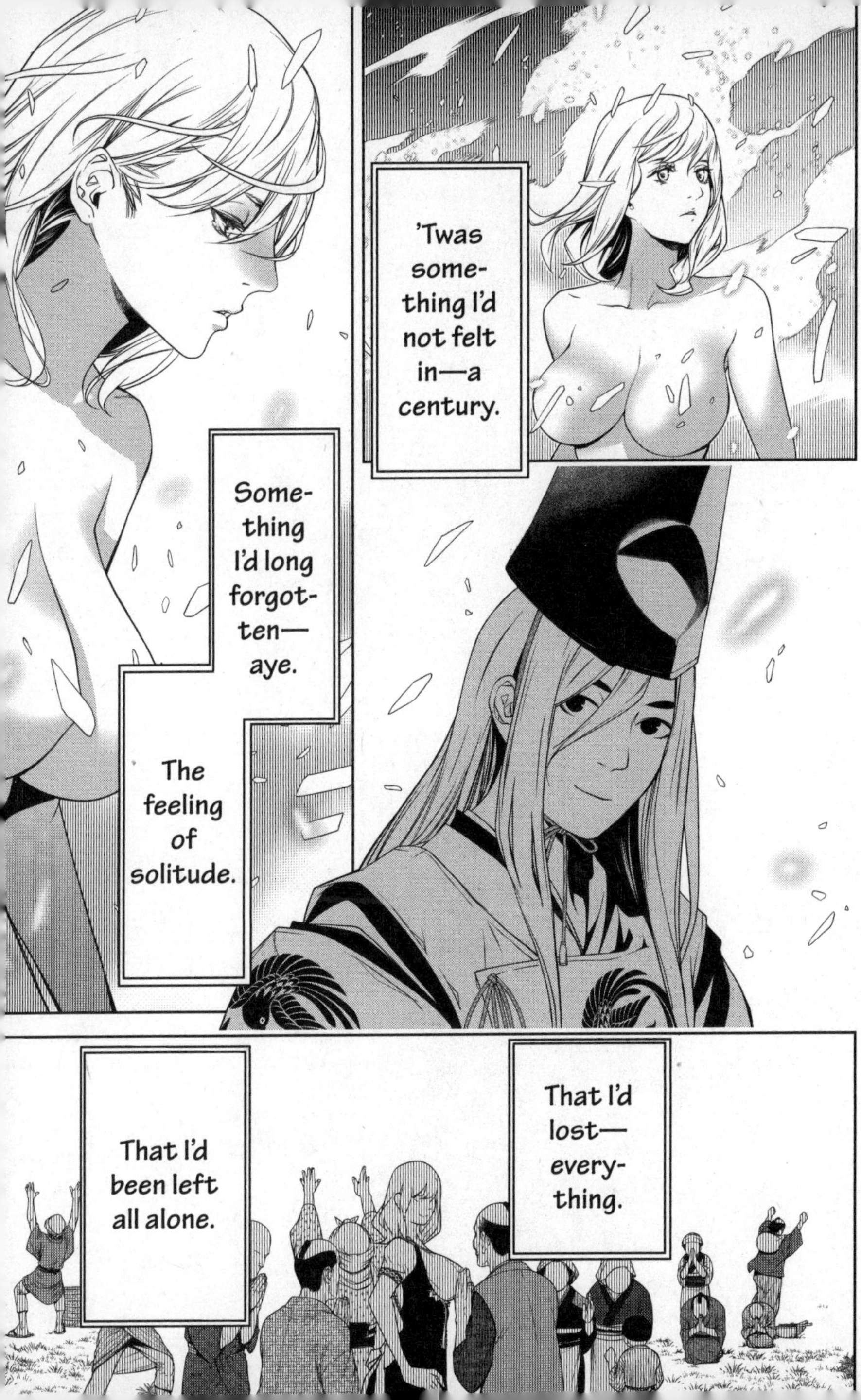
'Twas something I'd not felt in—a century.
Something I'd long forgotten—aye.
The feeling of solitude.
That I'd lost—everything.
That I'd been left all alone.

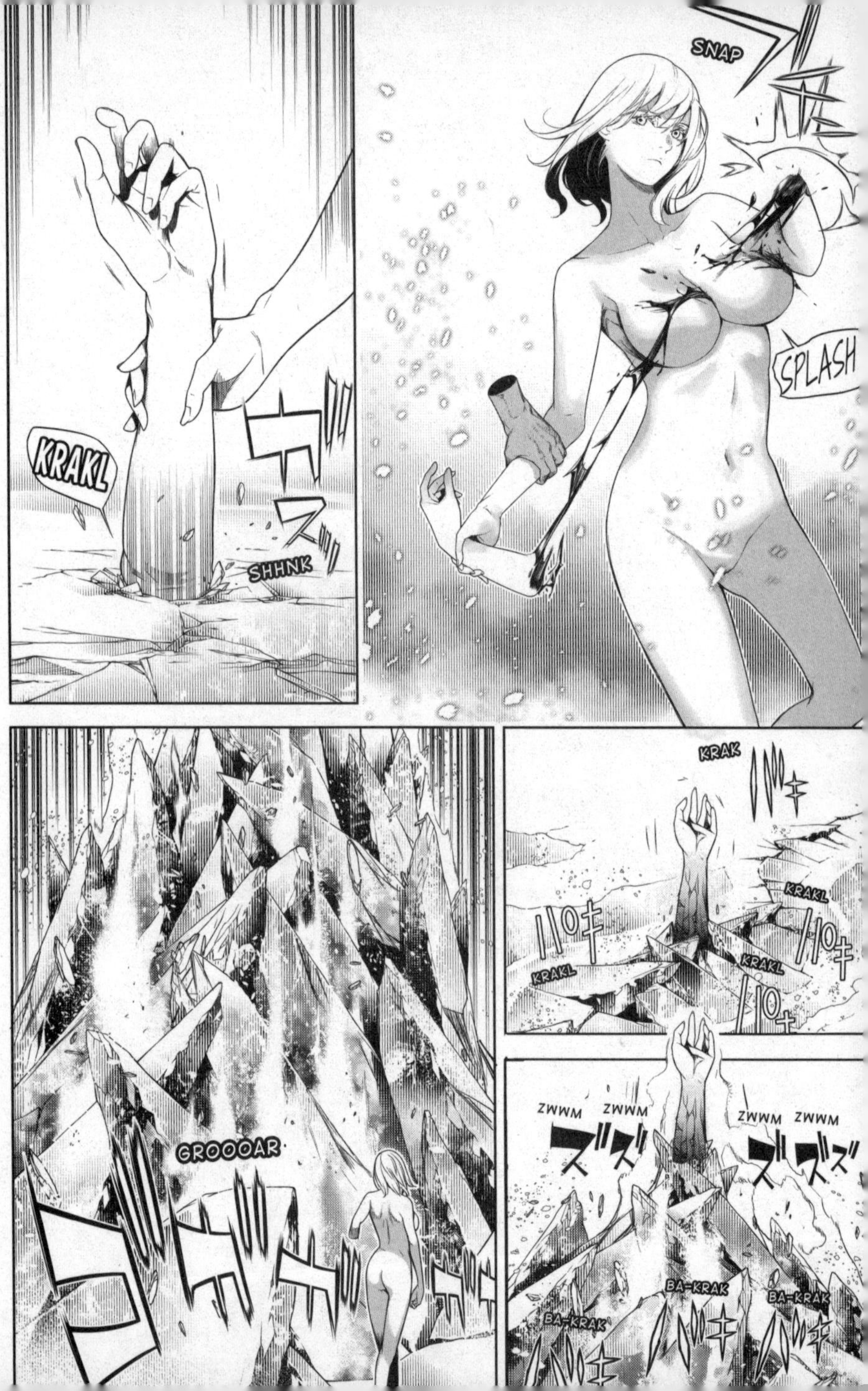
SNAP
SPLASH
KRAKL
SHHNK
KRAK
KRAKL
KRAKL
KRAKL
ZWWM ZWWM
ZWWM ZWWM
BA-KRAK
BA-KRAK
BA-KRAK
GROOOAR

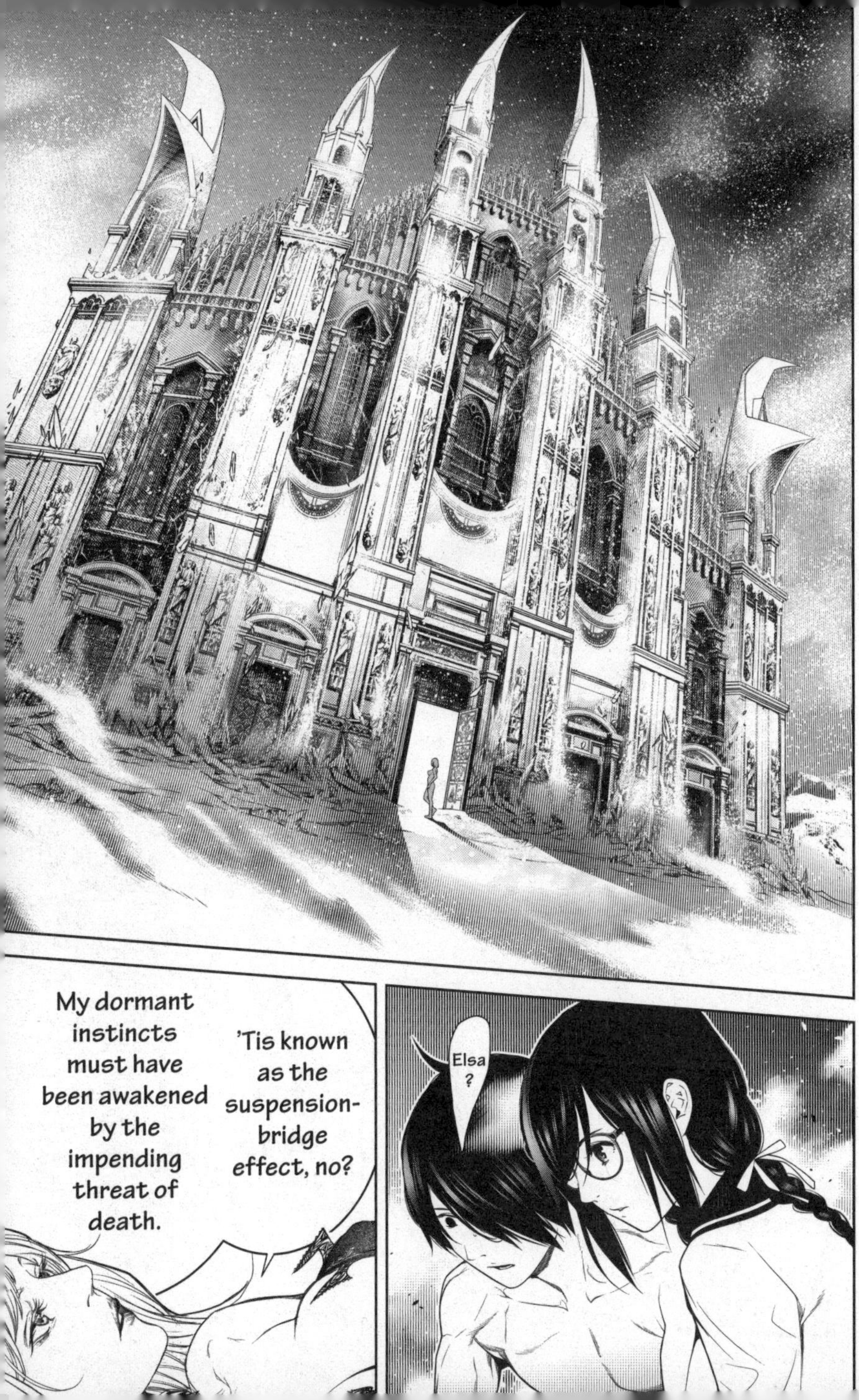
Elsa?
'Tis known as the suspension-bridge effect, no?
My dormant instincts must have been awakened by the impending threat of death.

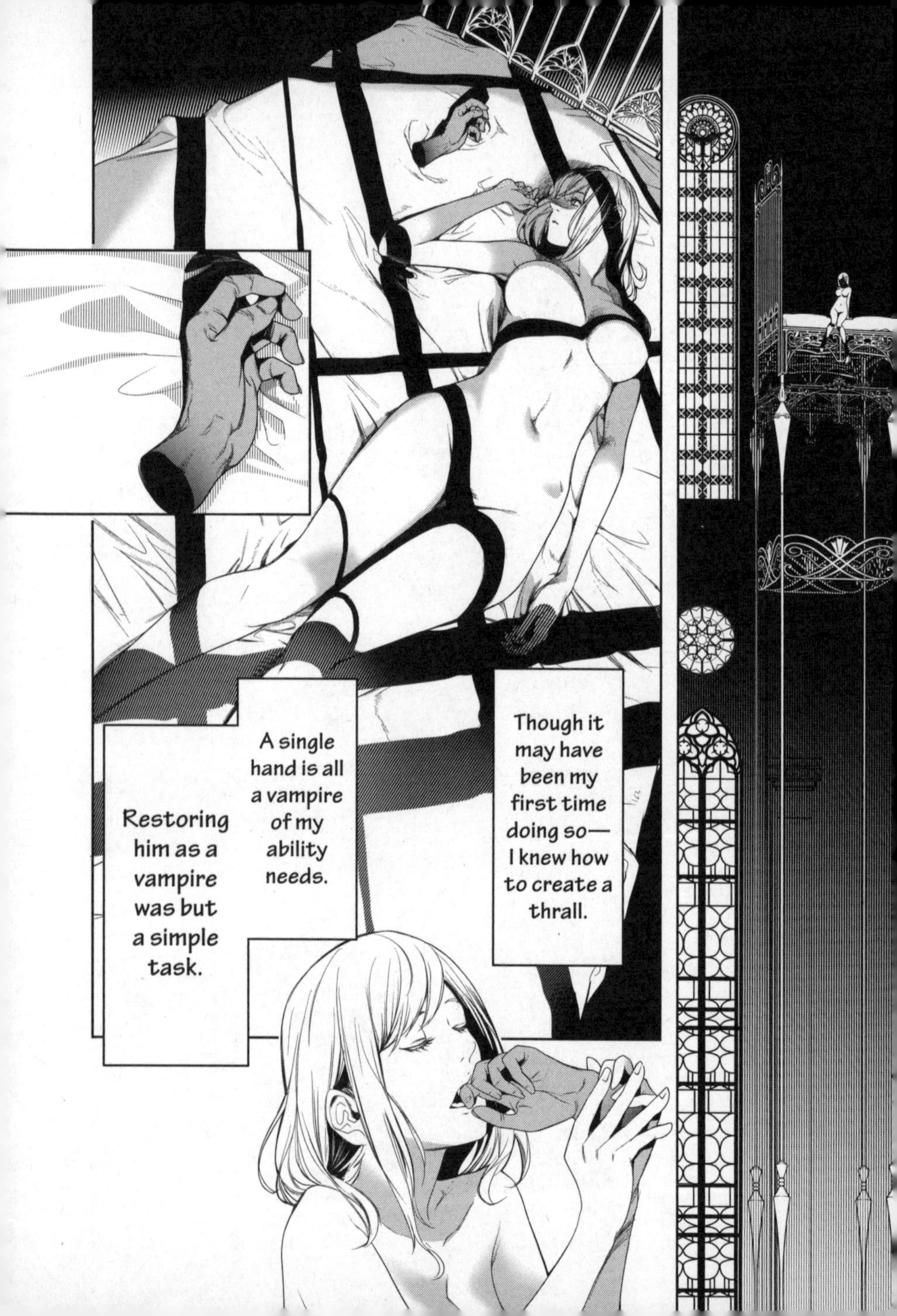
Though it may have been my first time doing so— I knew how to create a thrall.
A single hand is all a vampire of my ability needs.
Restoring him as a vampire was but a simple task.

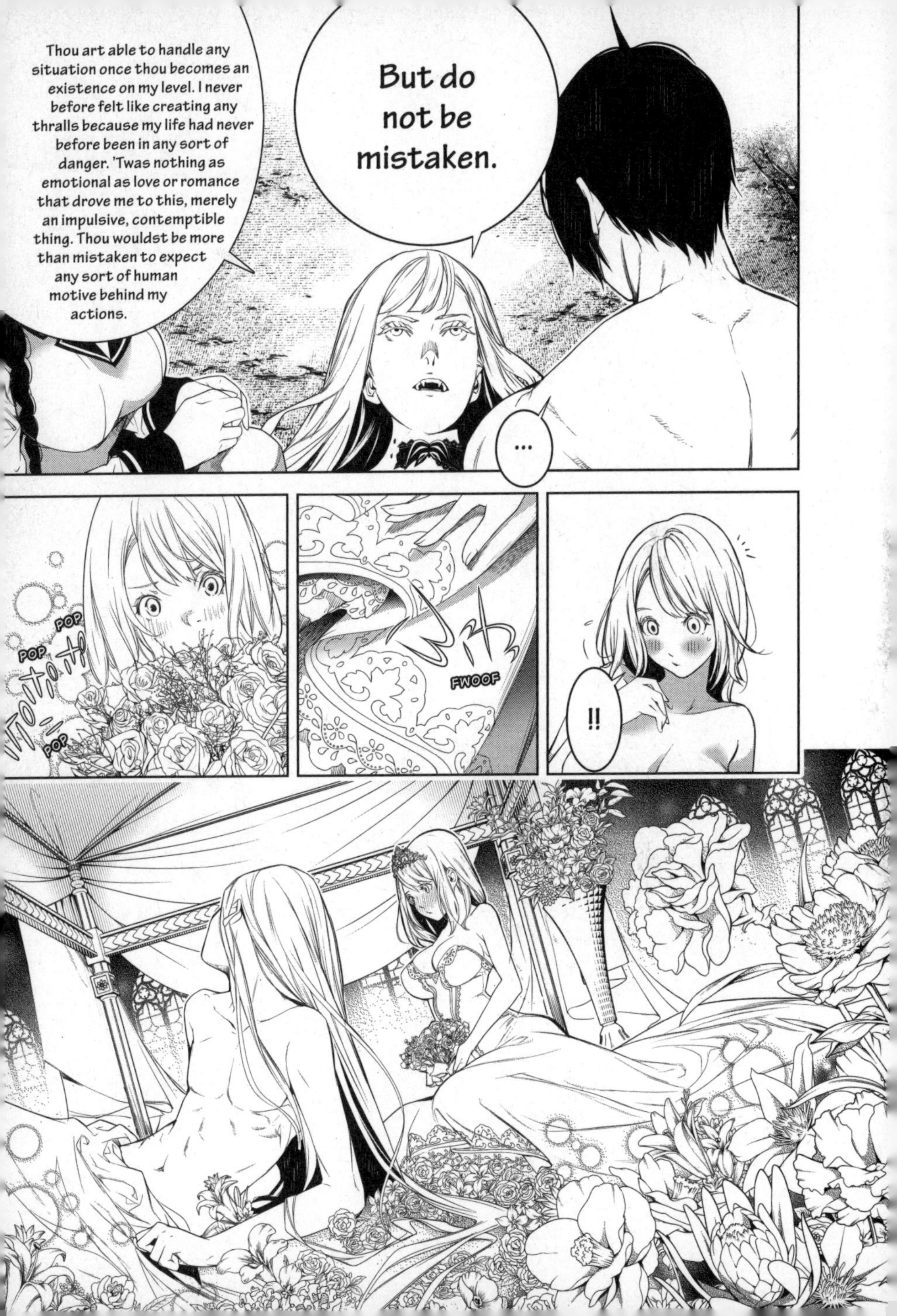
But do not be mistaken.
Thou art able to handle any situation once thou becomes an existence on my level. I never before felt like creating any thralls because my life had never before been in any sort of danger. 'Twas nothing as emotional as love or romance that drove me to this, merely an impulsive, contemptible thing. Thou wouldst be more than mistaken to expect any sort of human motive behind my actions.
...
!!
FWOOF
POP
POP
POP

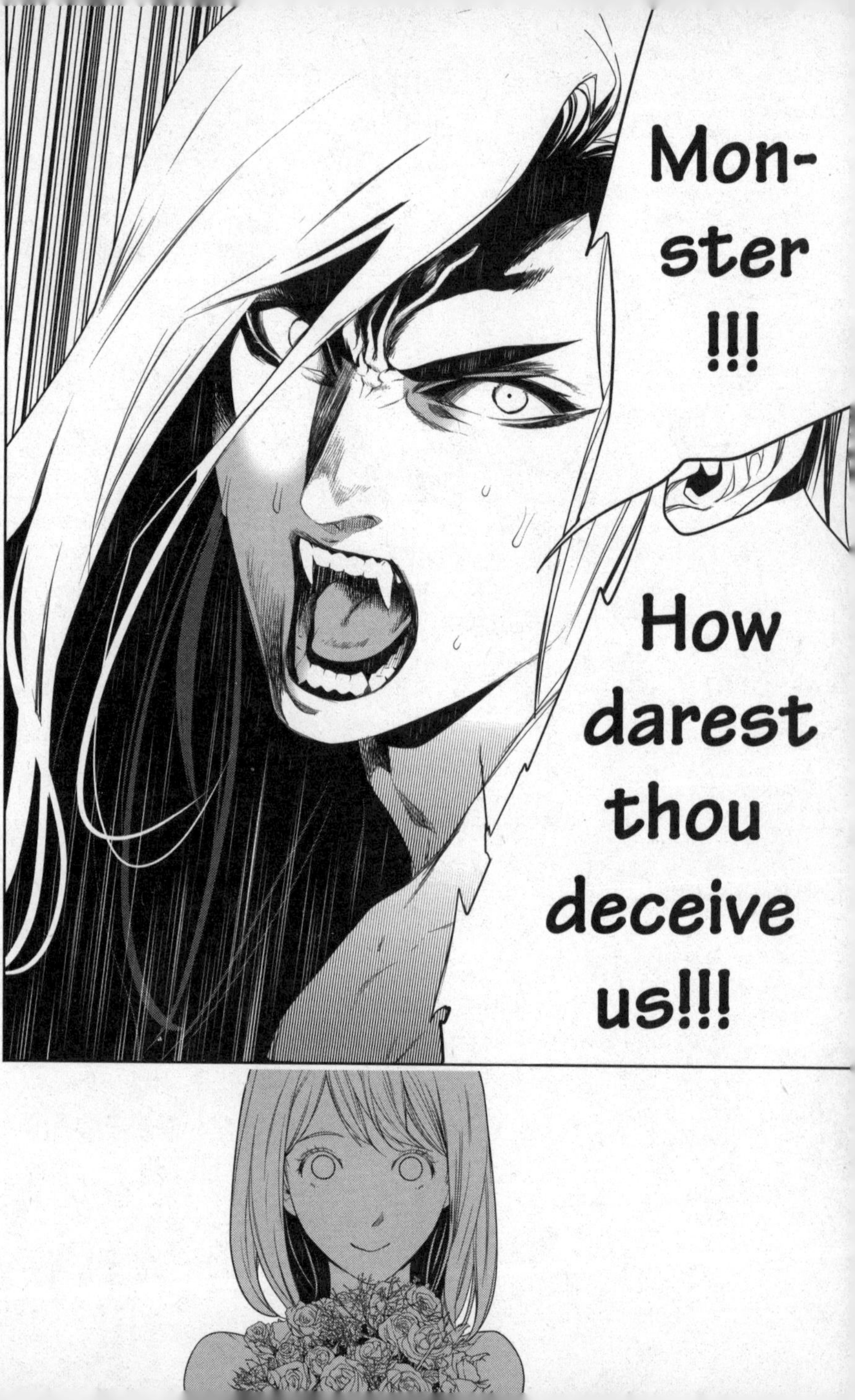
Mon-
ster
!!!
How
darest
thou
deceive
us!!!

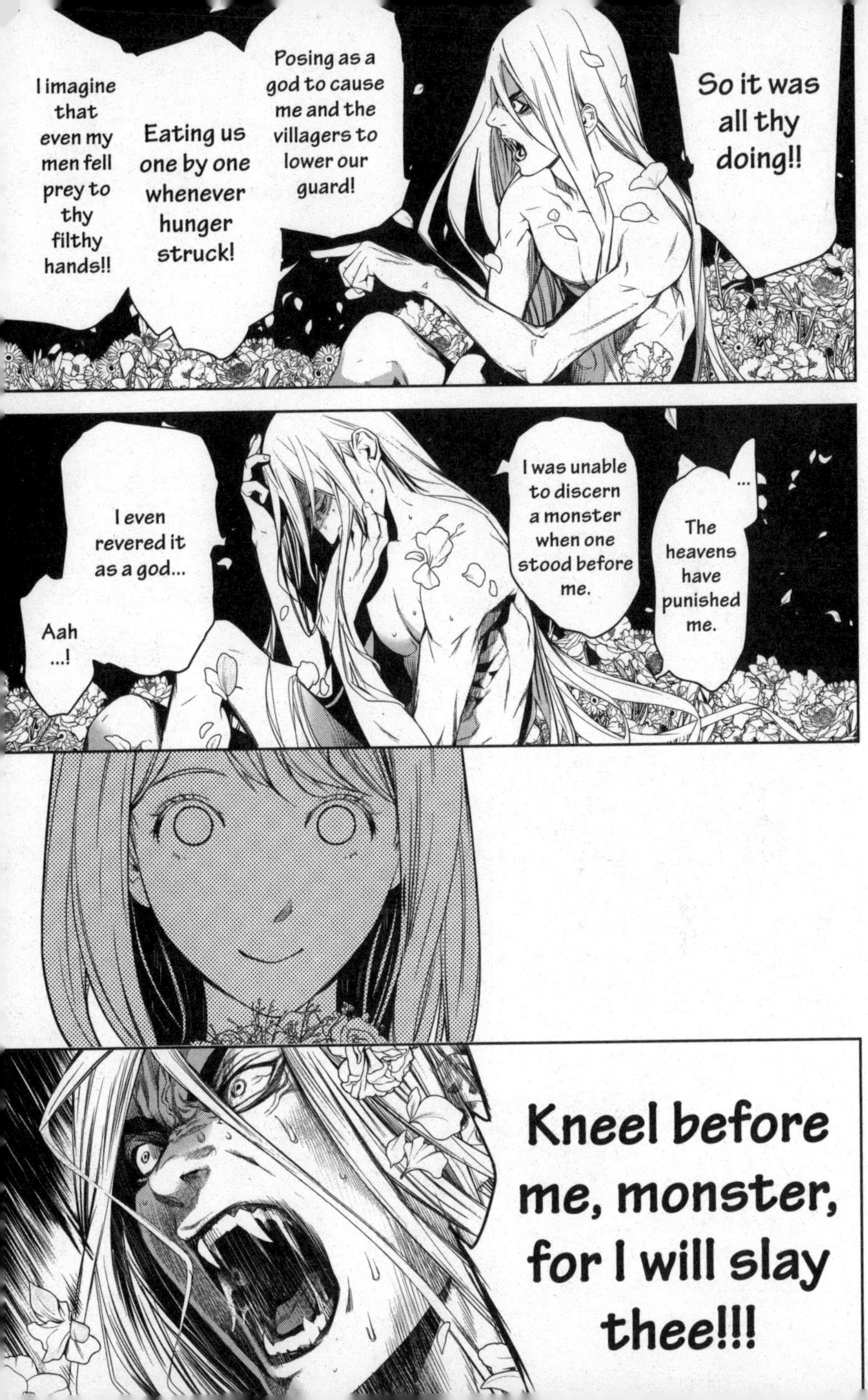
So it was all thy doing!!
Posing as a god to cause me and the villagers to lower our guard!
Eating us one by one whenever hunger struck!
I imagine that even my men fell prey to thy filthy hands!!
...
The heavens have punished me.
I was unable to discern a monster when one stood before me.
I even revered it as a god...
Aah ...!
Kneel before me, monster, for I will slay thee!!!

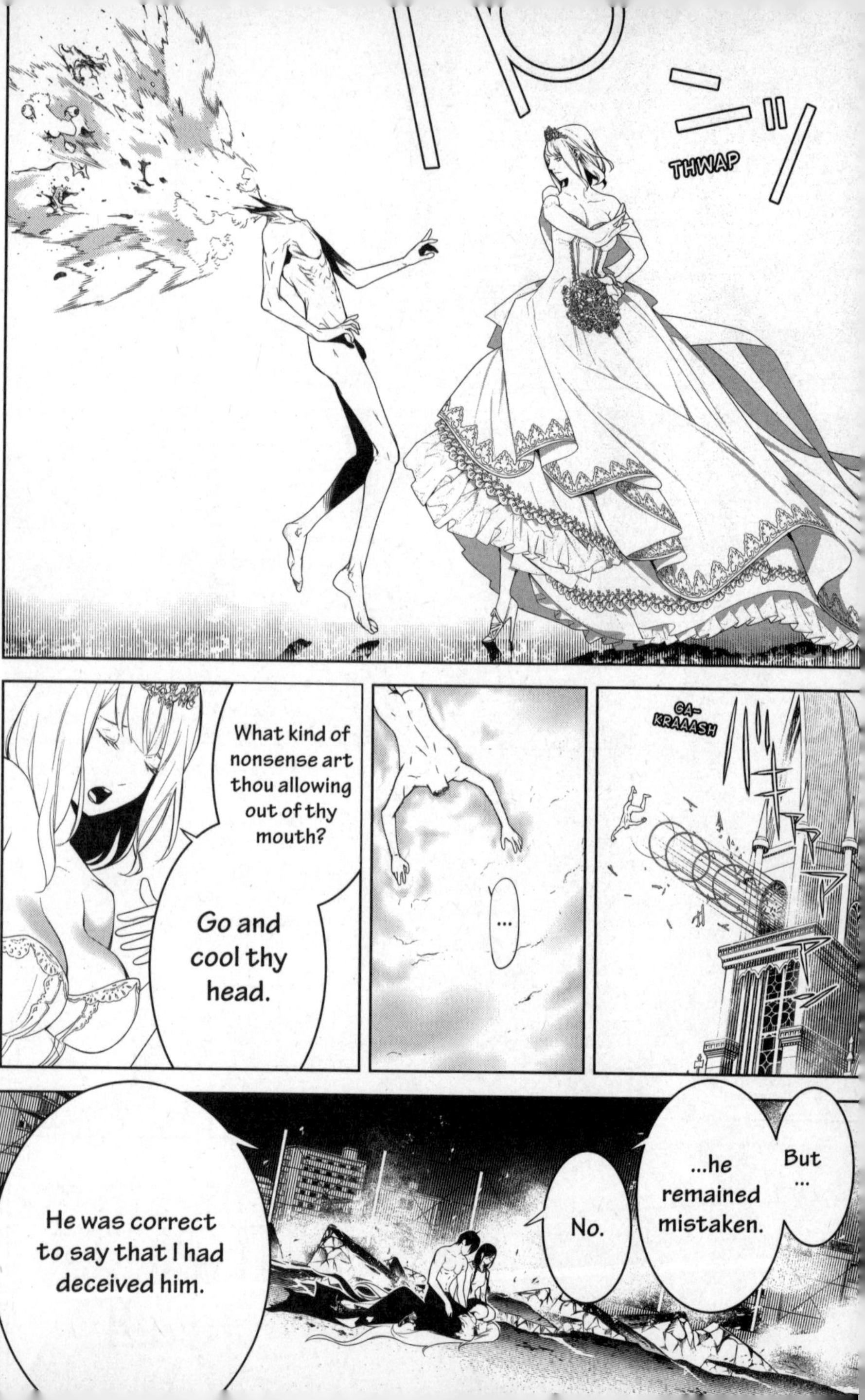
THWAP
GA-KRAAASH
...
What kind of nonsense art thou allowing out of thy mouth?
Go and cool thy head.
But ...
...he remained mistaken.
No.
He was correct to say that I had deceived him.

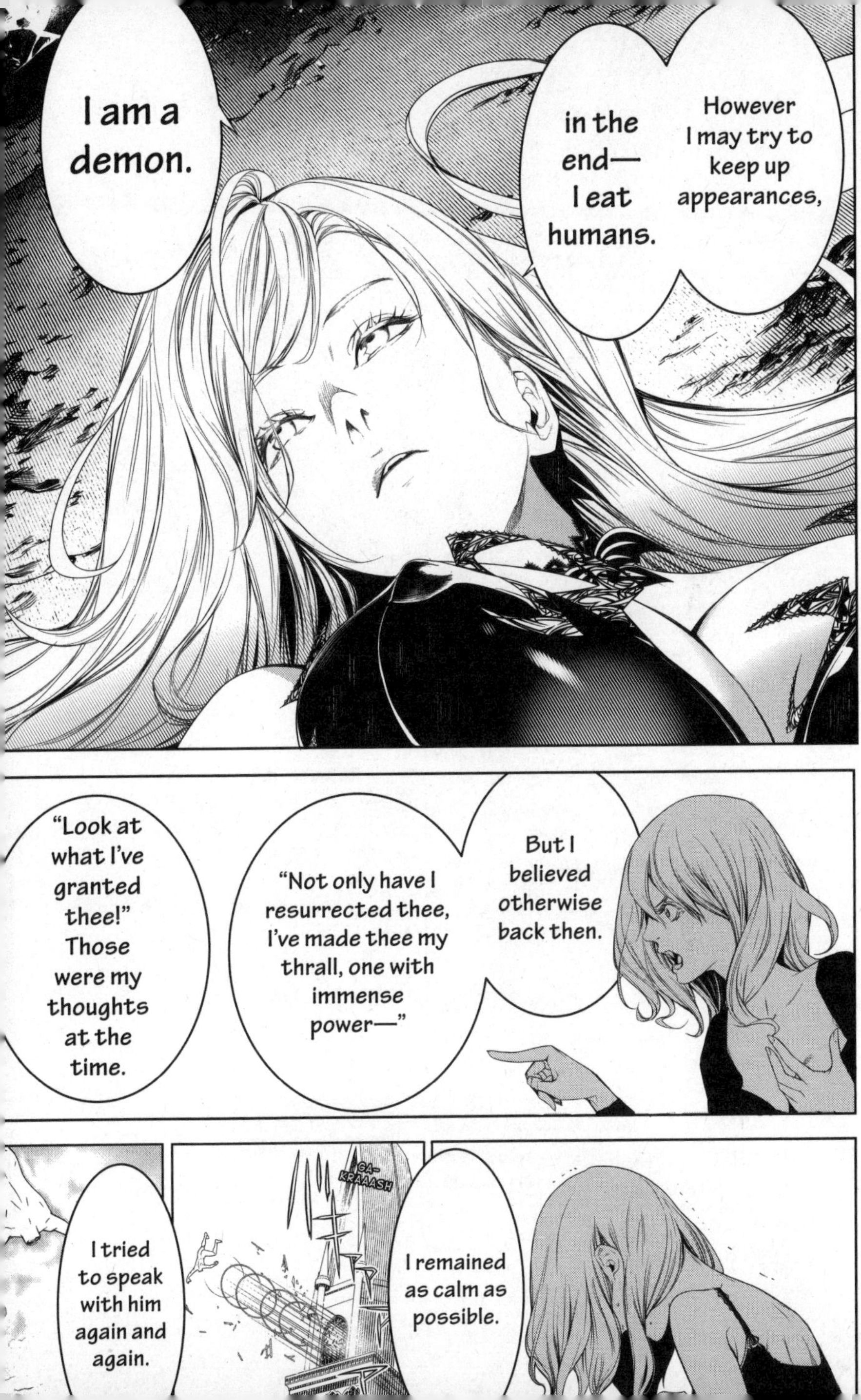
However I may try to keep up appearances,
in the end— I eat humans.
I am a demon.
But I believed otherwise back then.
“Not only have I resurrected thee, I’ve made thee my thrall, one with immense power—”
“Look at what I’ve granted thee!” Those were my thoughts at the time.
I remained as calm as possible.
GA-KRAAASH
I tried to speak with him again and again.

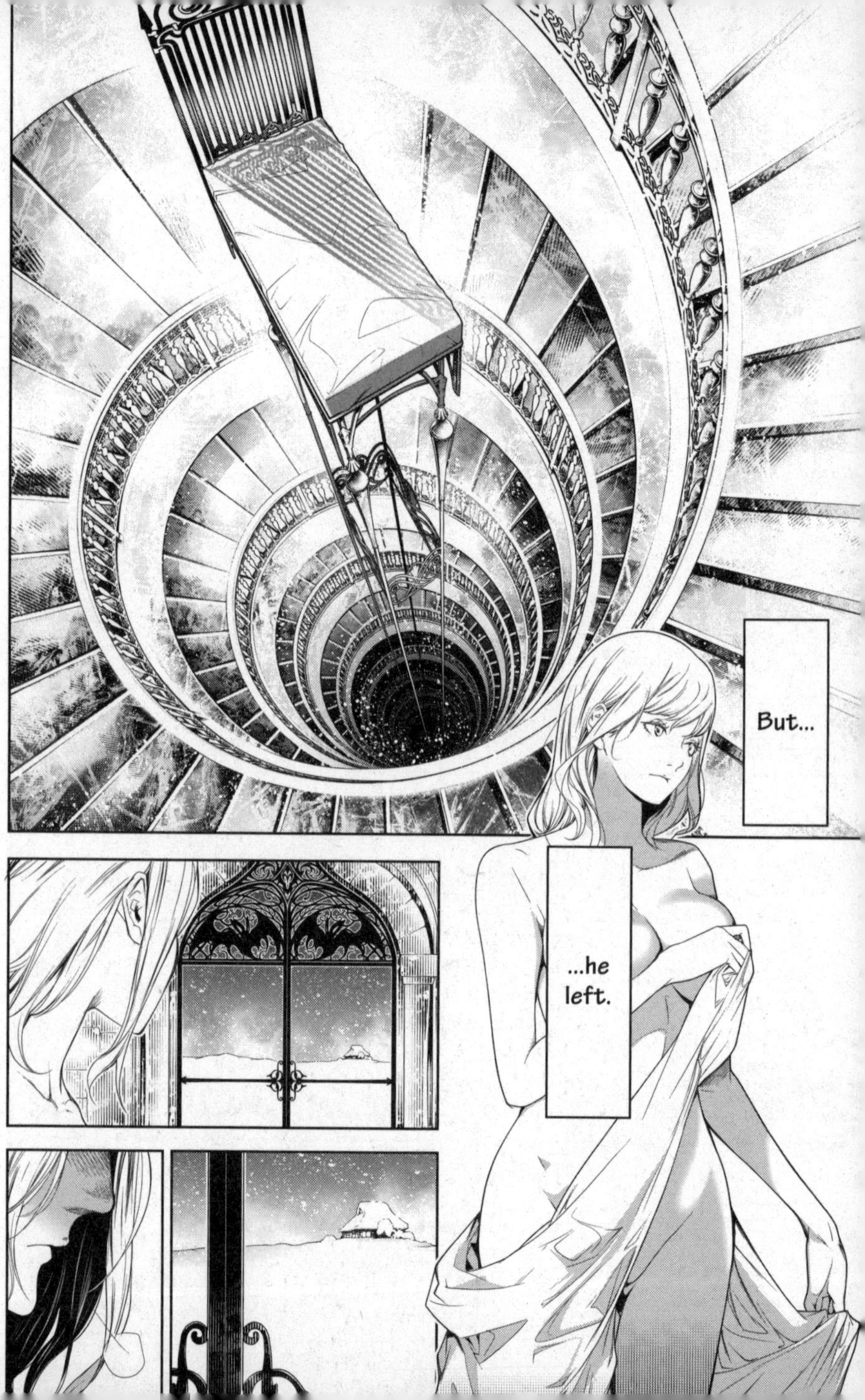
But...
...he left.

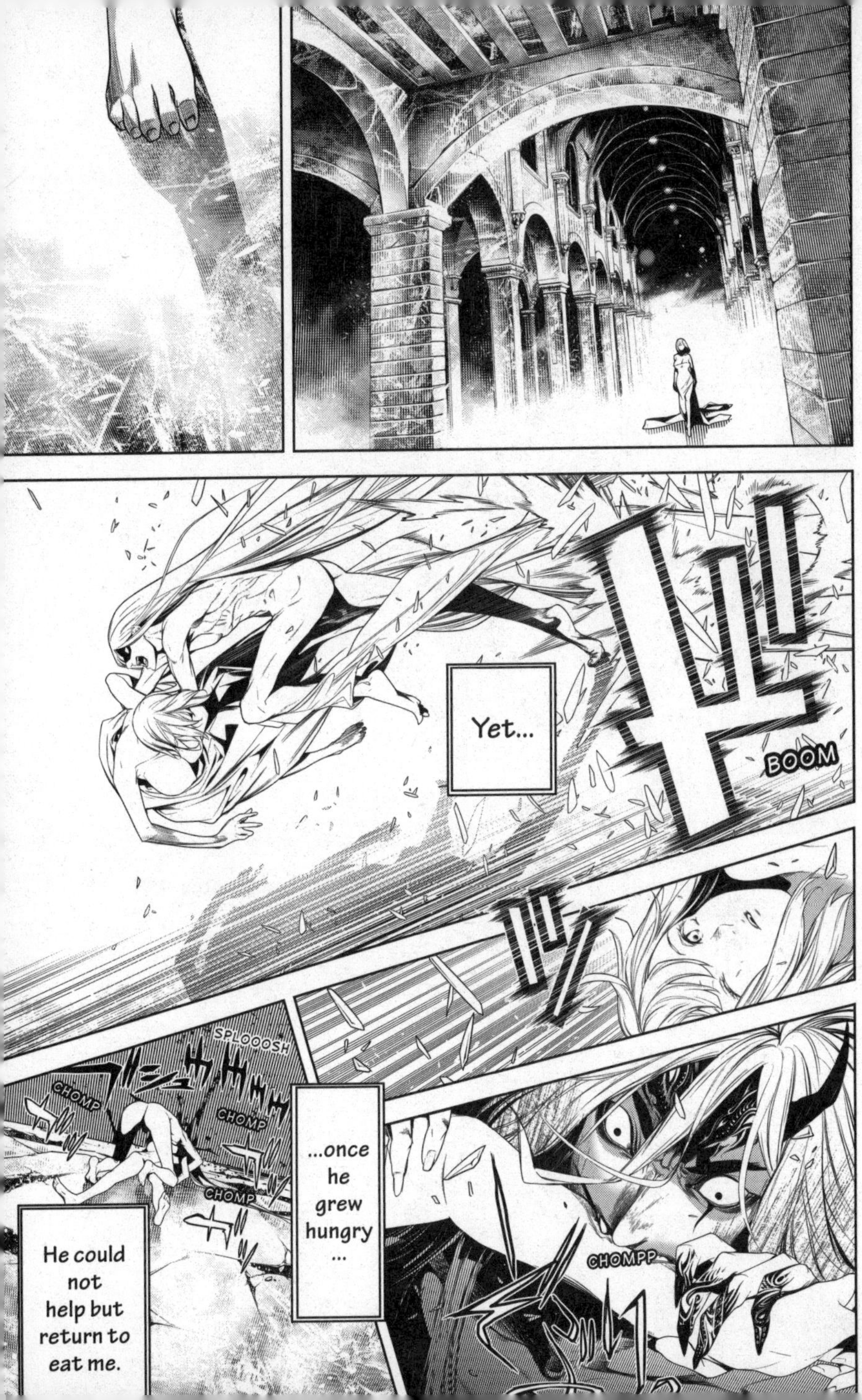
Yet...
BOOM
...once he grew hungry ...
CHOMPP
SPLOOOSH
CHOMP
CHOMP
CHOMP
He could not help but return to eat me.

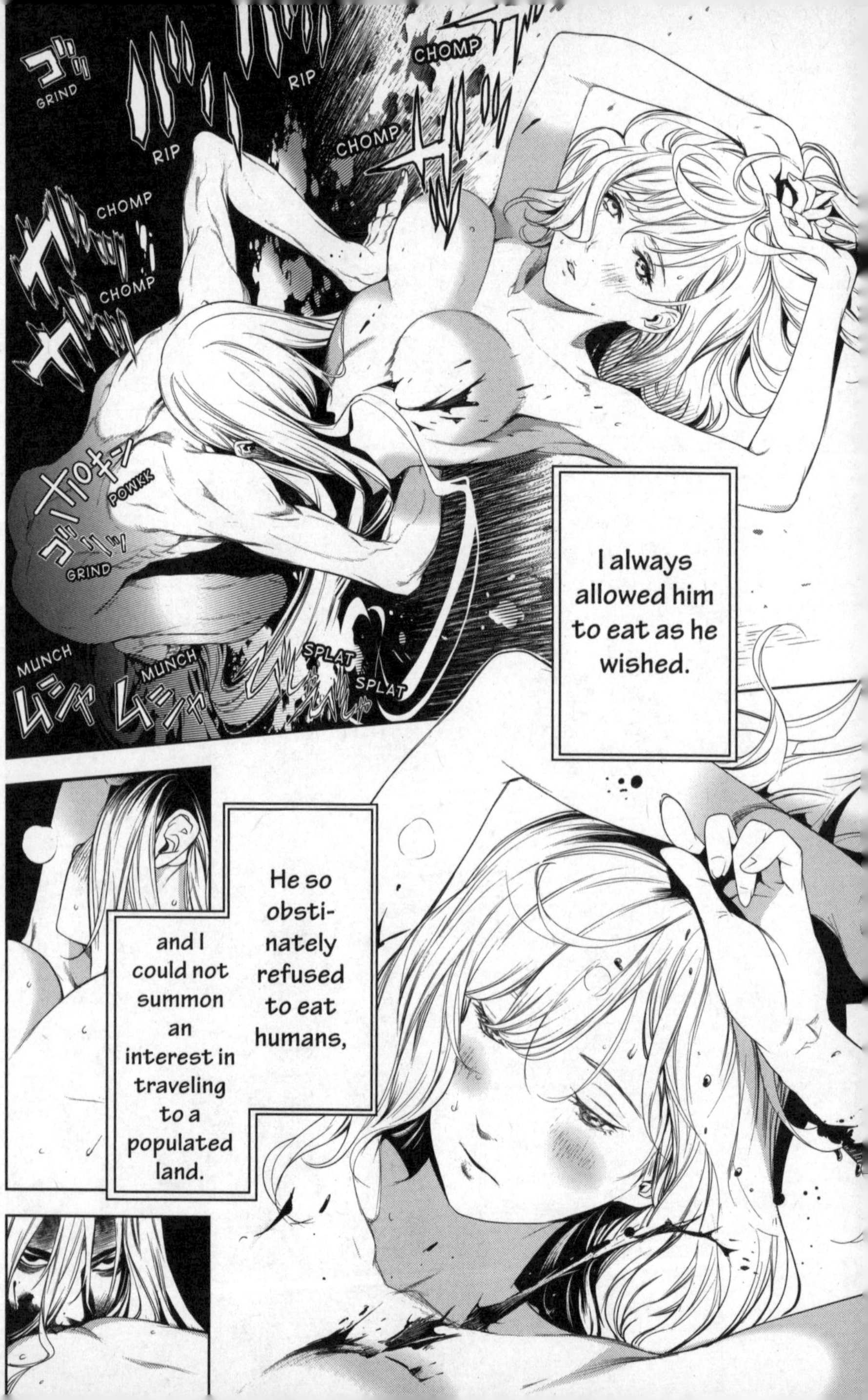
CHOMP
RIP
CHOMP
GRIND
RIP
CHOMP
CHOMP
I always allowed him to eat as he wished.
POWKK
GRIND
SPLAT
SPLAT
MUNCH
MUNCH
He so obstinately refused to eat humans,
and I could not summon an interest in traveling to a populated land.

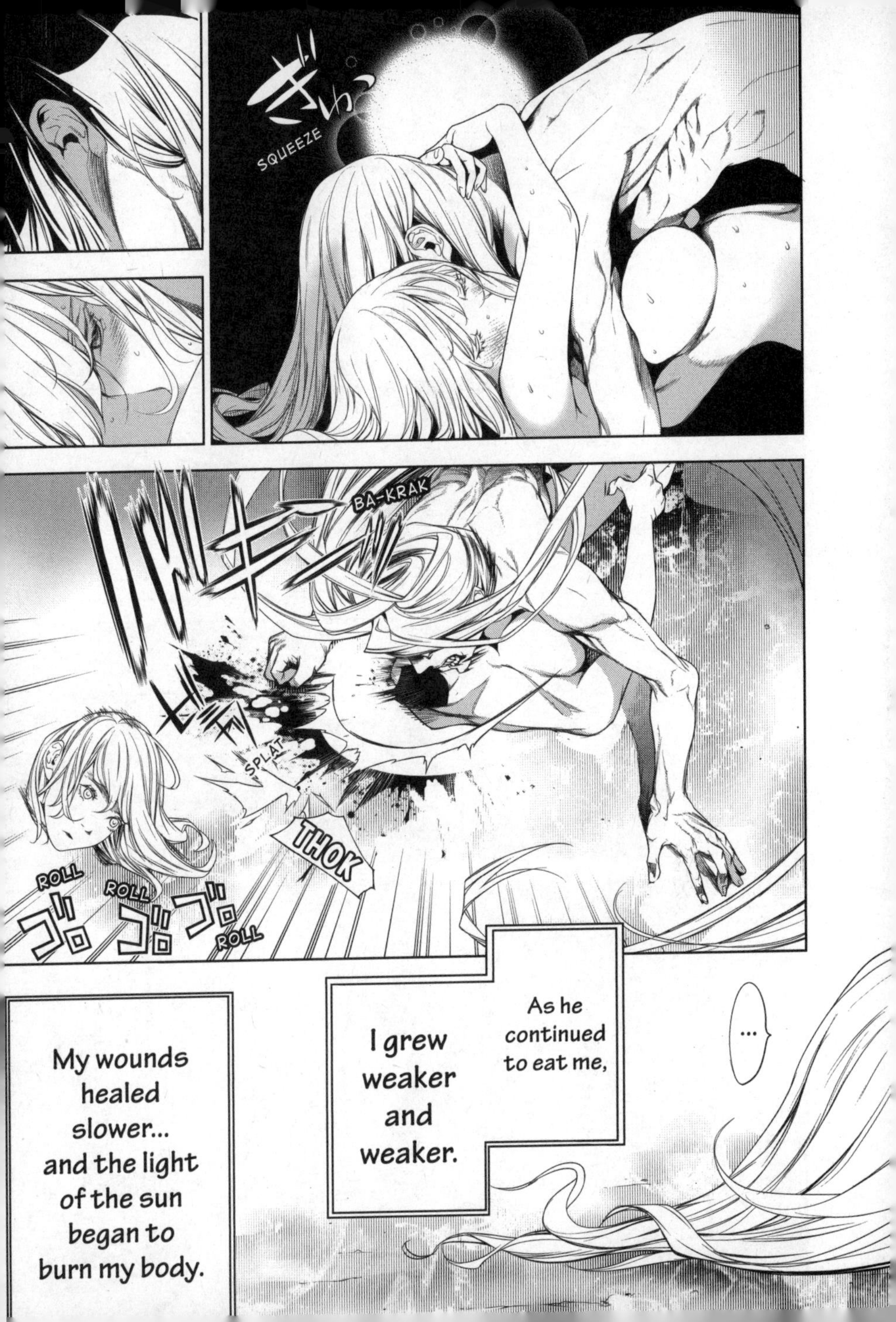
SQUEEZE
BA-KRAK
SPLAT
THOK
ROLL
ROLL
ROLL
...
As he continued to eat me,
I grew weaker and weaker.
My wounds healed slower... and the light of the sun began to burn my body.

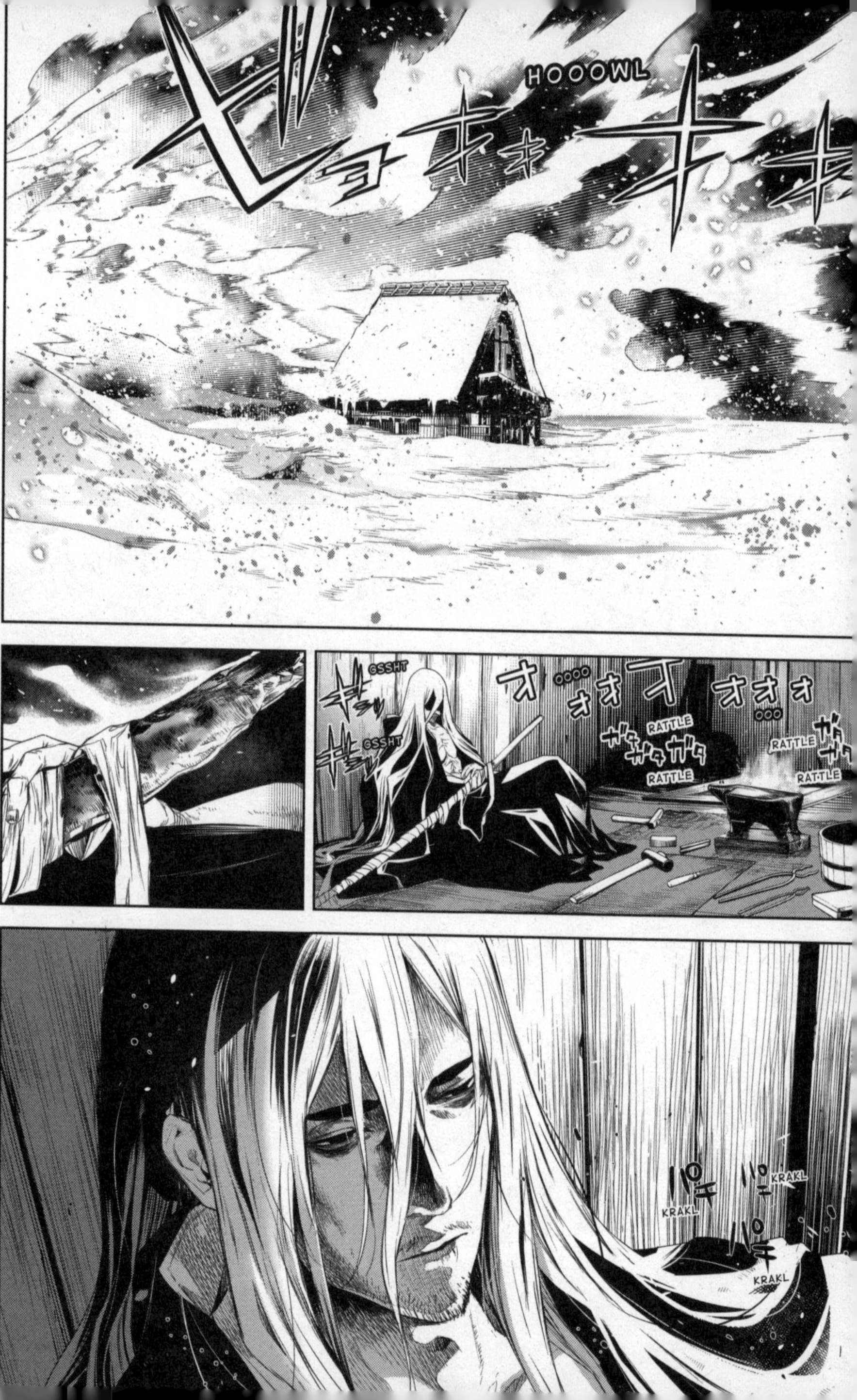
HOOOWL
RATTLE
RATTLE
RATTLE
RATTLE
GSSHT
GSSHT
KRAKL
KRAKL
KRAKL

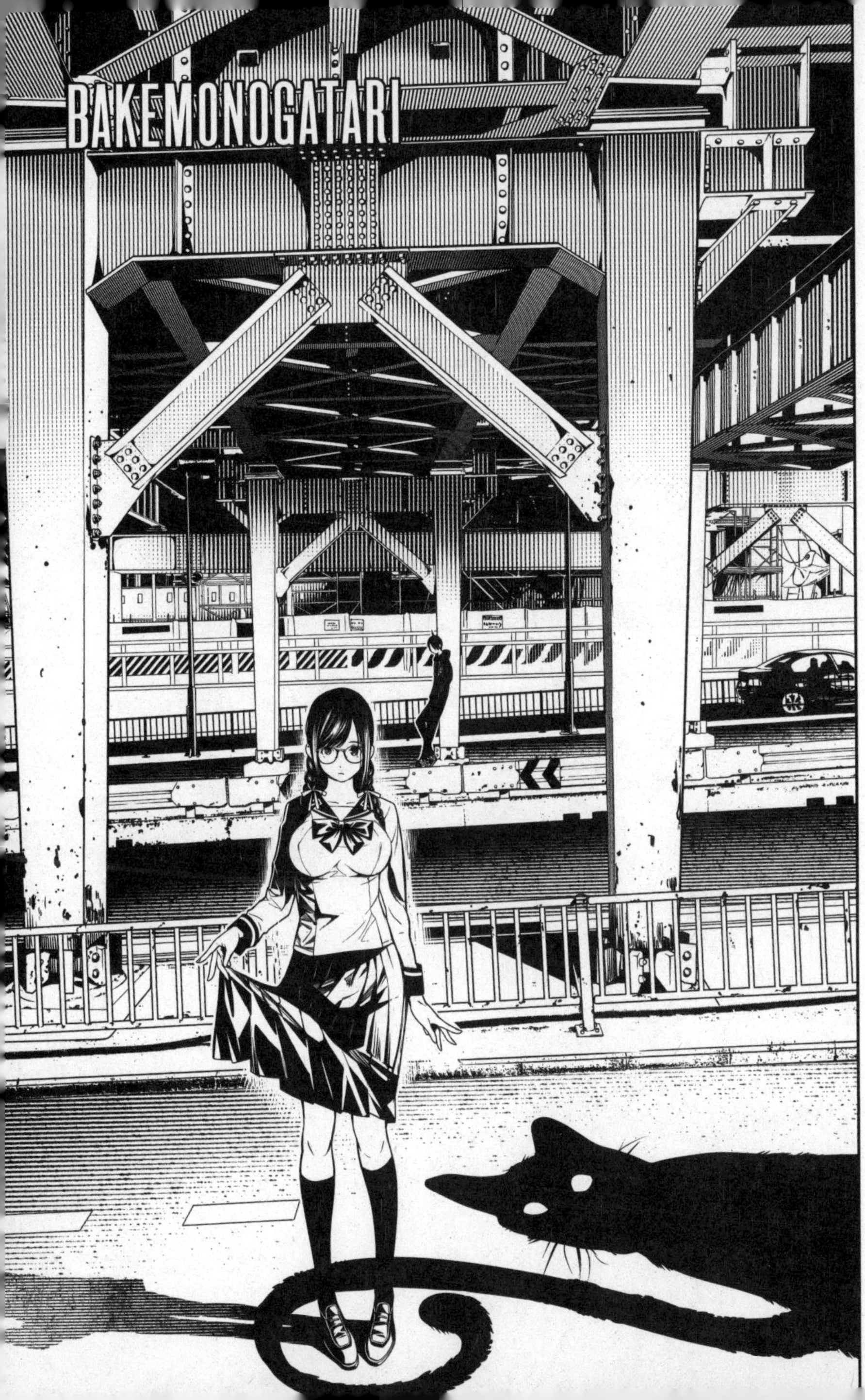
BAKEMONOGATARI

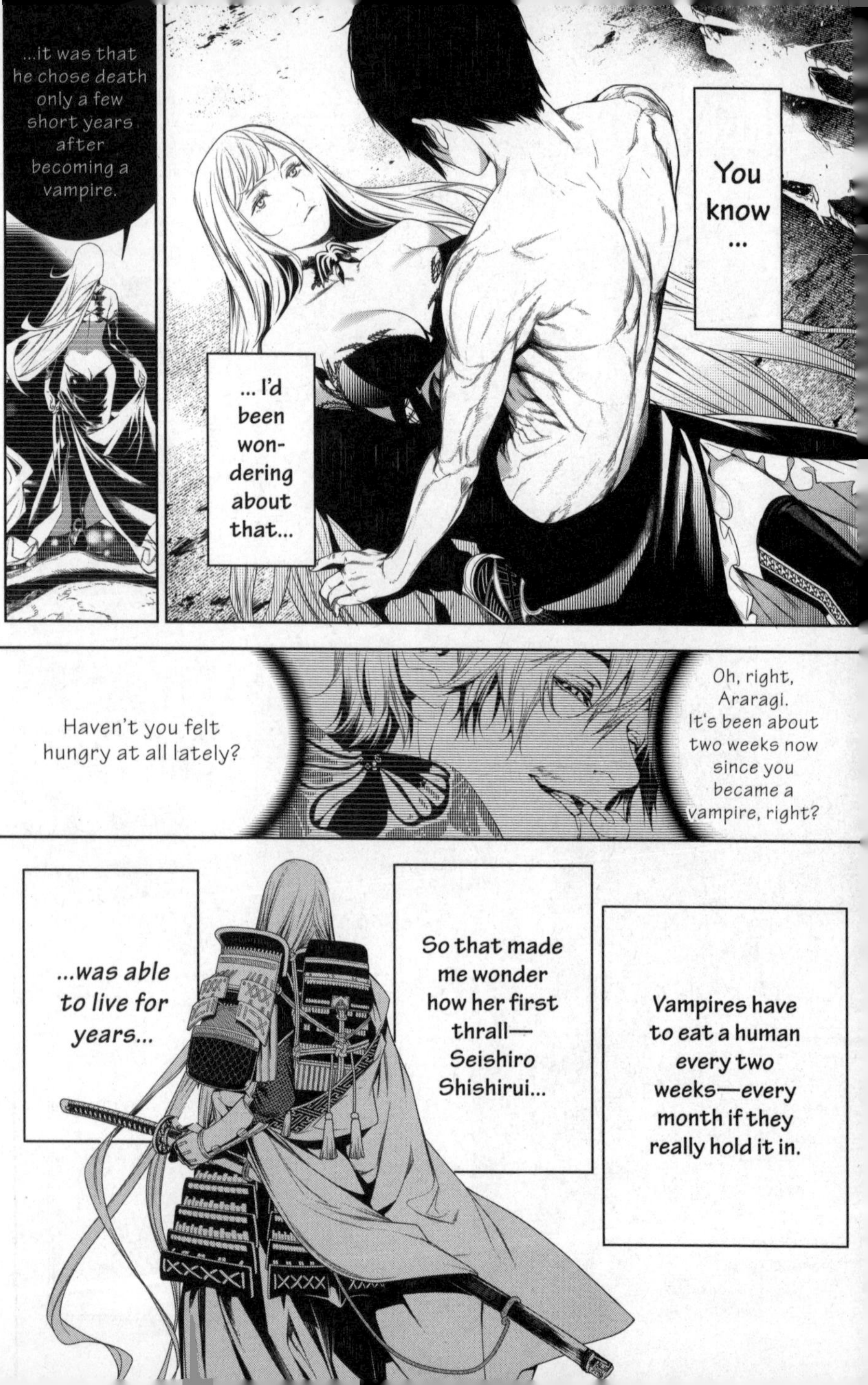
You know ...
... I'd been wondering about that...
...it was that he chose death only a few short years after becoming a vampire.
Oh, right, Araragi. It's been about two weeks now since you became a vampire, right?
Haven't you felt hungry at all lately?
Vampires have to eat a human every two weeks—every month if they really hold it in.
So that made me wonder how her first thrall—Seishiro Shishirui...
...was able to live for years...

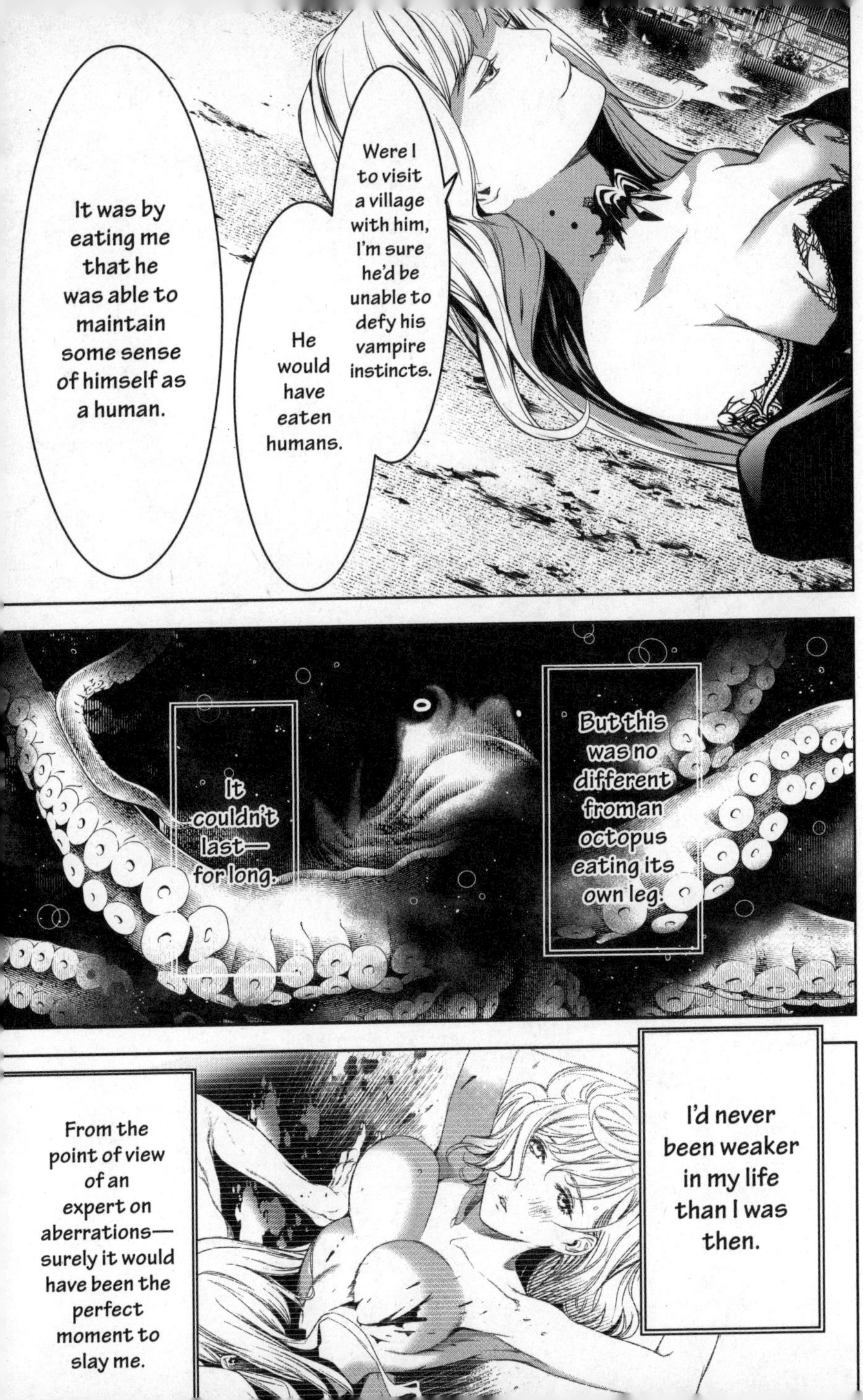
Were I to visit a village with him, I'm sure he'd be unable to defy his vampire instincts.
He would have eaten humans.
It was by eating me that he was able to maintain some sense of himself as a human.
But this was no different from an octopus eating its own leg.
It couldn't last—for long.
I'd never been weaker in my life than I was then.
From the point of view of an expert on aberrations—surely it would have been the perfect moment to slay me.

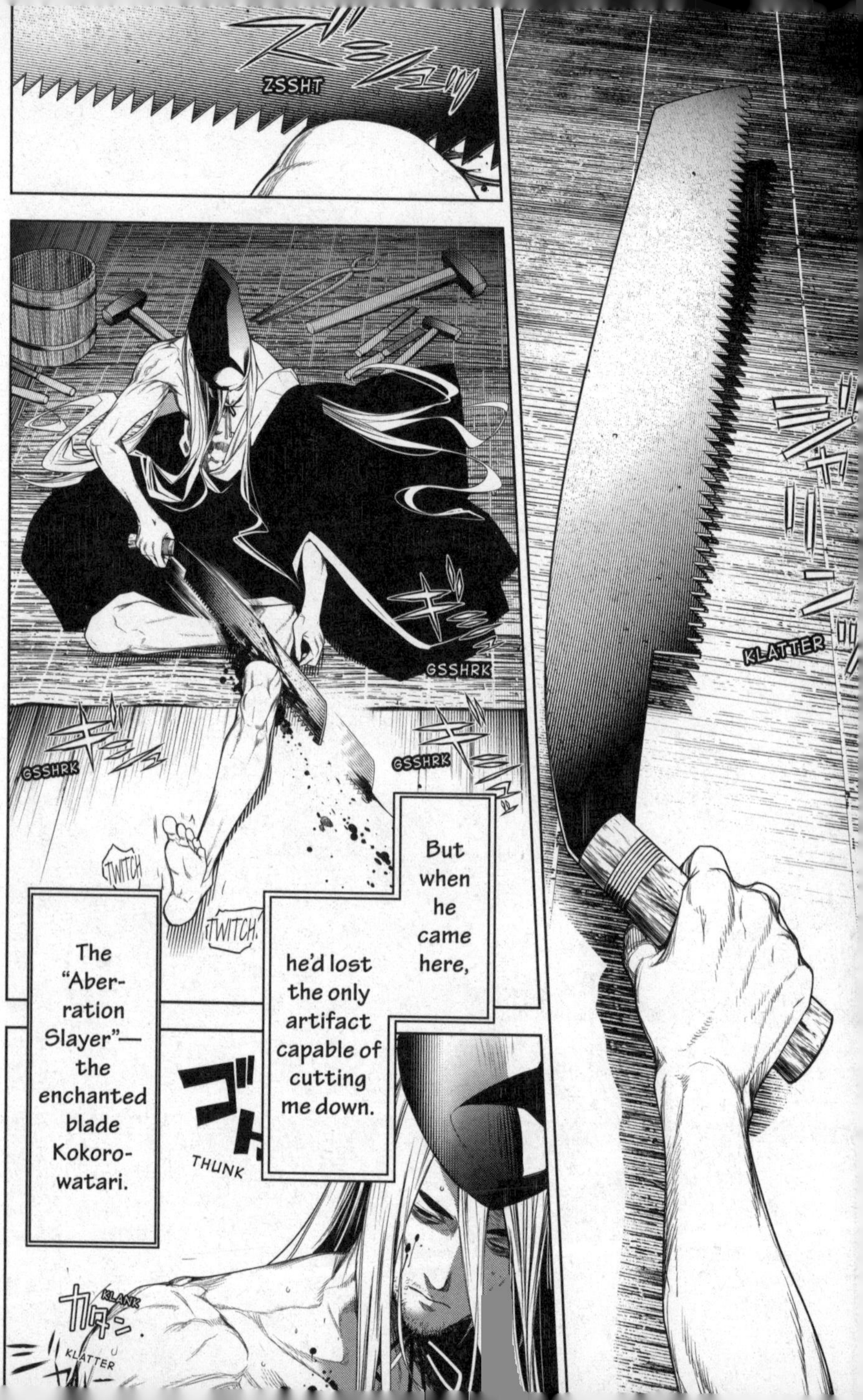
KLATTER
ZSSHT
GSSHRK
GSSHRK
GSSHRK
TWITCH
TWITCH
But when he came here, he'd lost the only artifact capable of cutting me down.
The "Aberration Slayer"—the enchanted blade Kokorowatari.
THUNK
KLANK
KLATTER

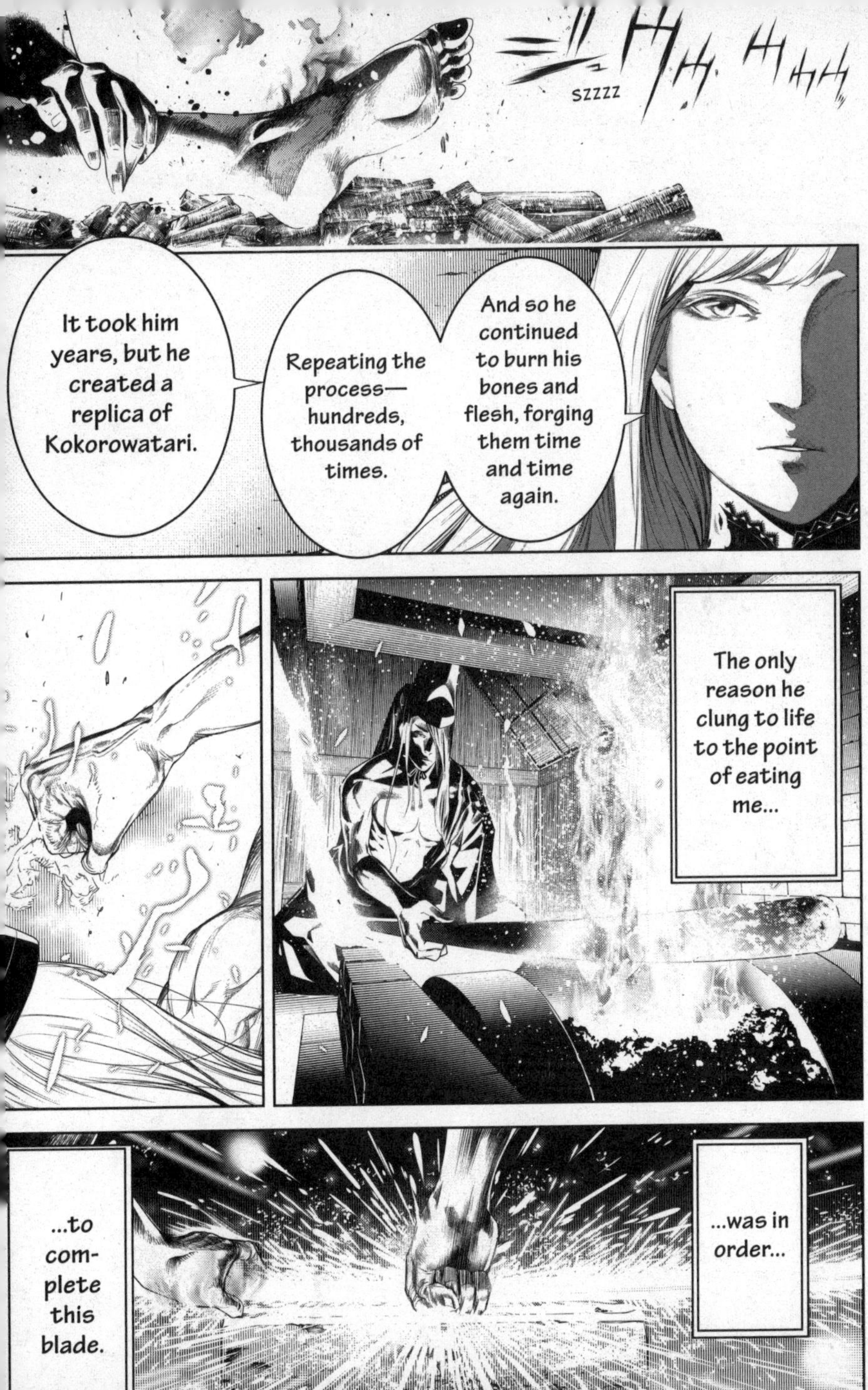
SZZZZ
And so he continued to burn his bones and flesh, forging them time and time again.
Repeating the process—hundreds, thousands of times.
It took him years, but he created a replica of Kokorowatari.
The only reason he clung to life to the point of eating me...
...was in order...
...to com-plete this blade.

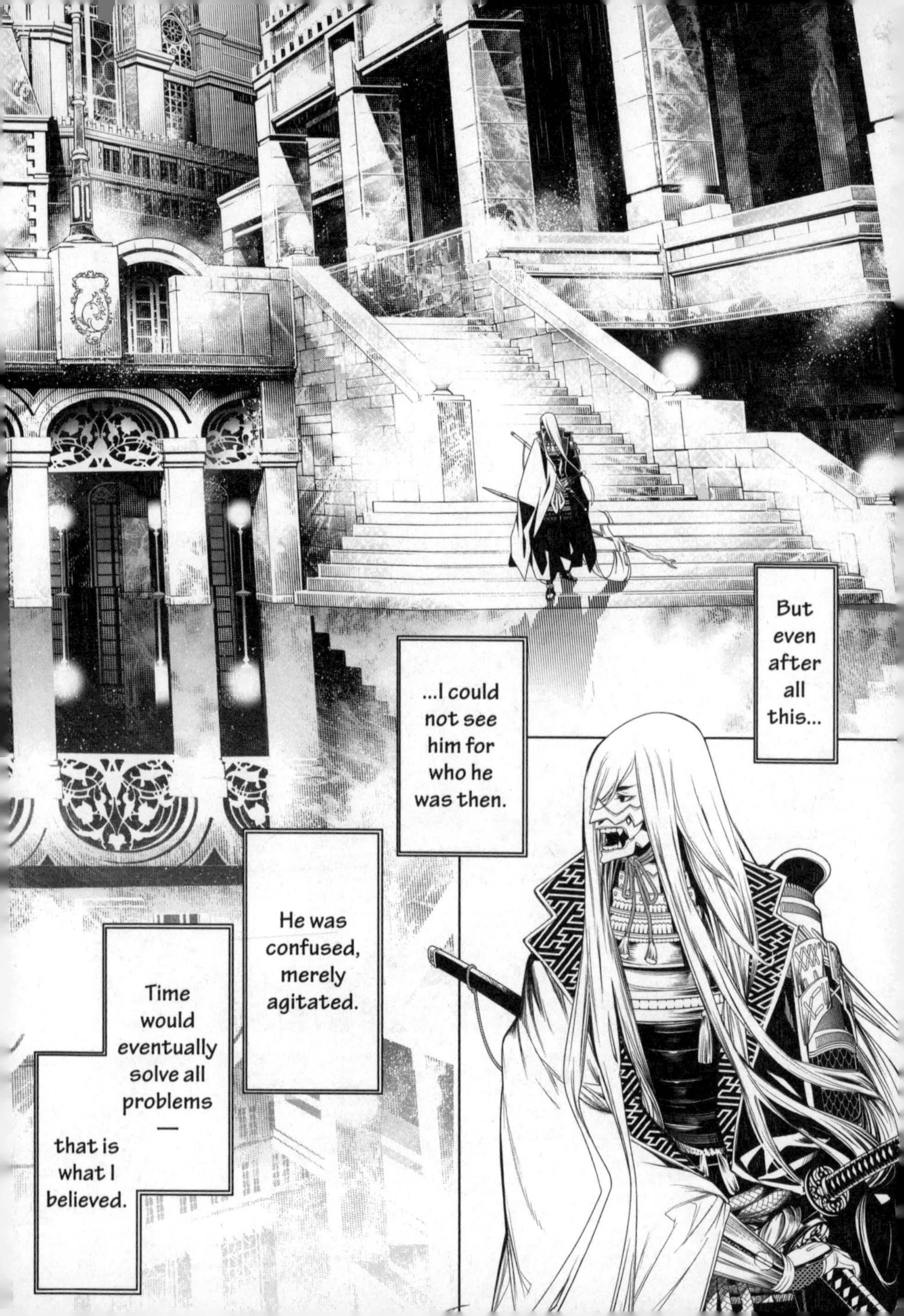
But even after all this...
...I could not see him for who he was then.
He was confused, merely agitated.
Time would eventually solve all problems — that is what I believed.

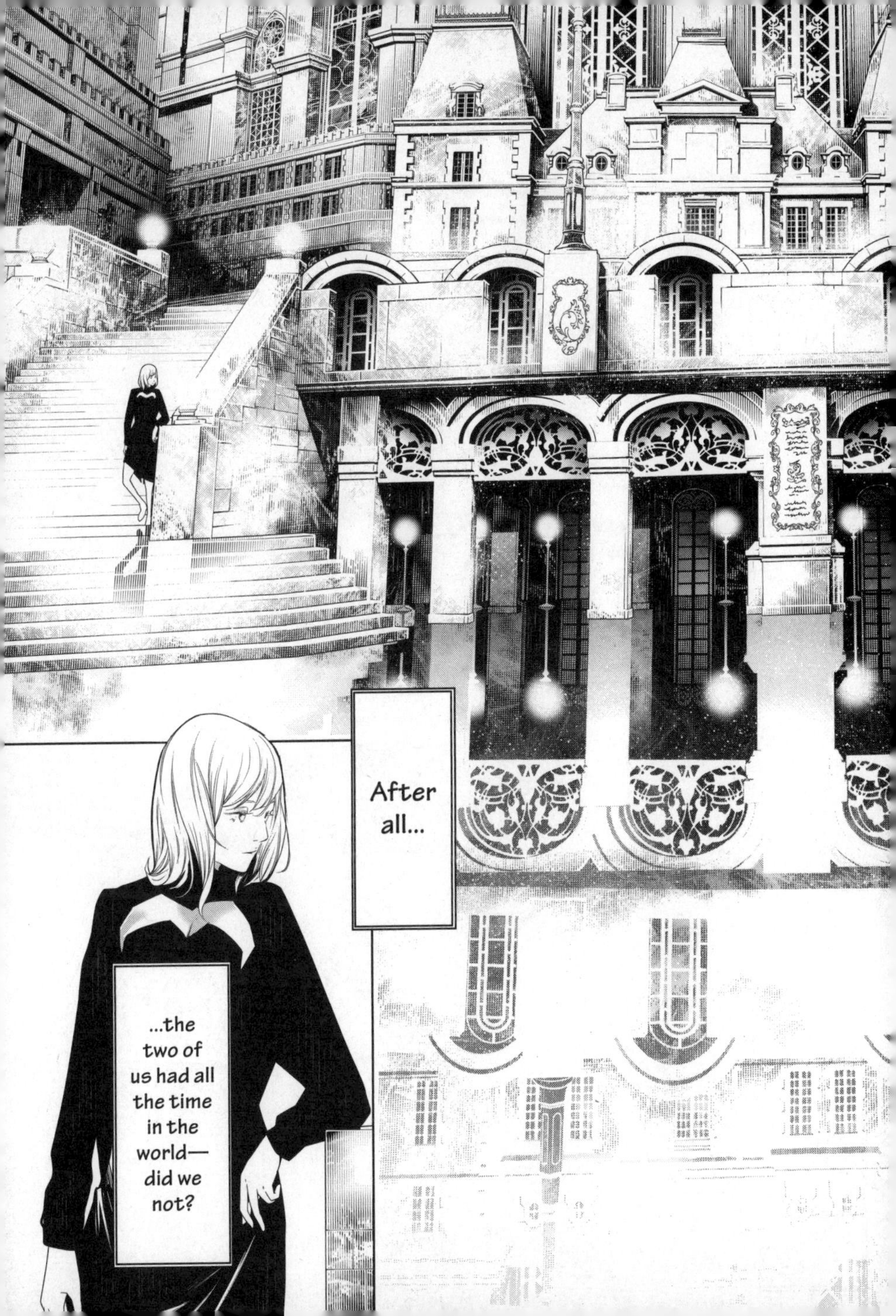
After all...
...the two of us had all the time in the world—did we not?

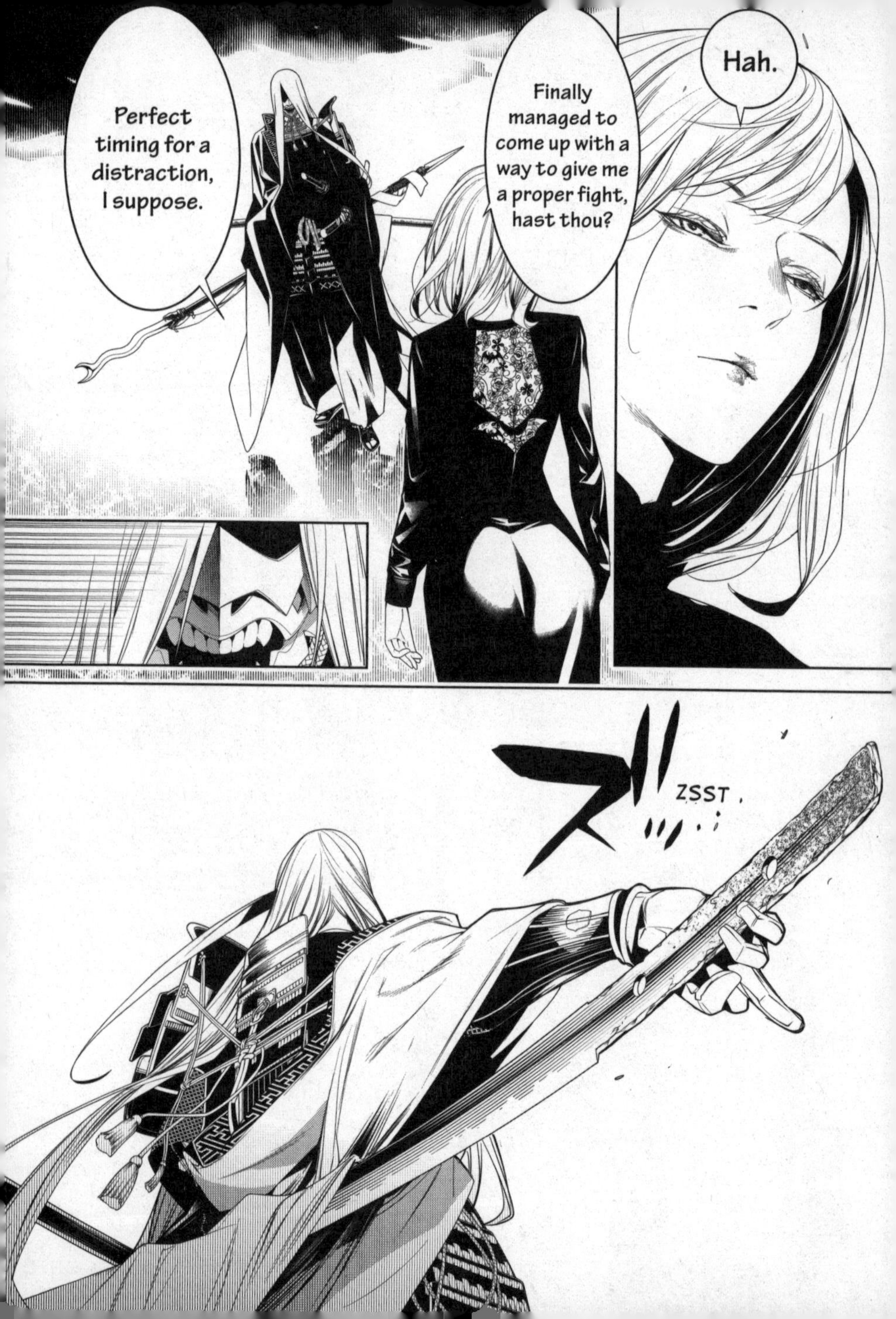
Hah.
Finally managed to come up with a way to give me a proper fight, hast thou?
Perfect timing for a distraction, I suppose.
ZSST

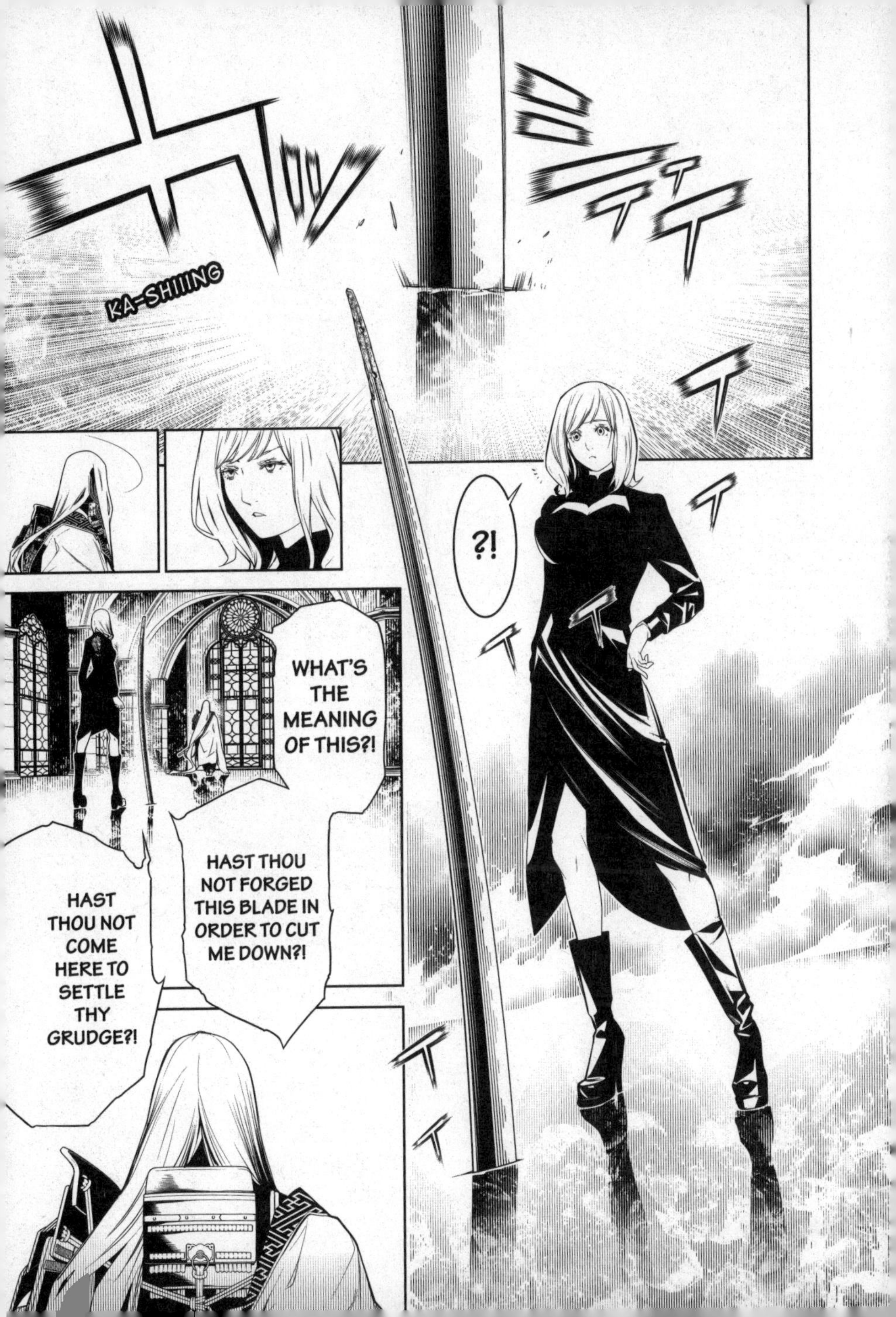
KA-SHIIING
?!
WHAT'S THE MEANING OF THIS?!
HAST THOU NOT FORGED THIS BLADE IN ORDER TO CUT ME DOWN?!
HAST THOU NOT COME HERE TO SETTLE THY GRUDGE?!

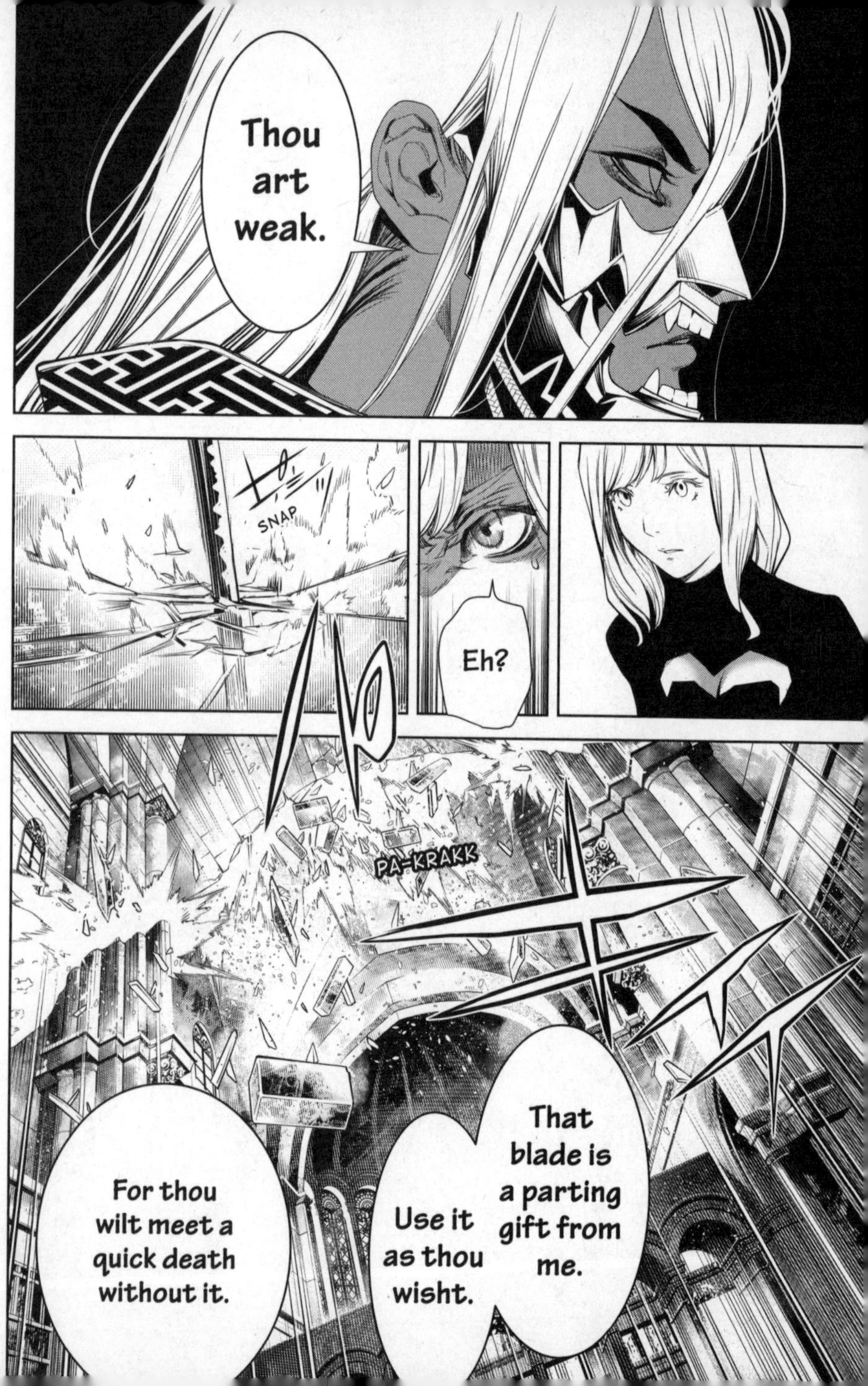
Thou art weak.
Eh?
SNAP
PA-KRAKK
That blade is a parting gift from me.
Use it as thou wisht.
For thou wilt meet a quick death without it.

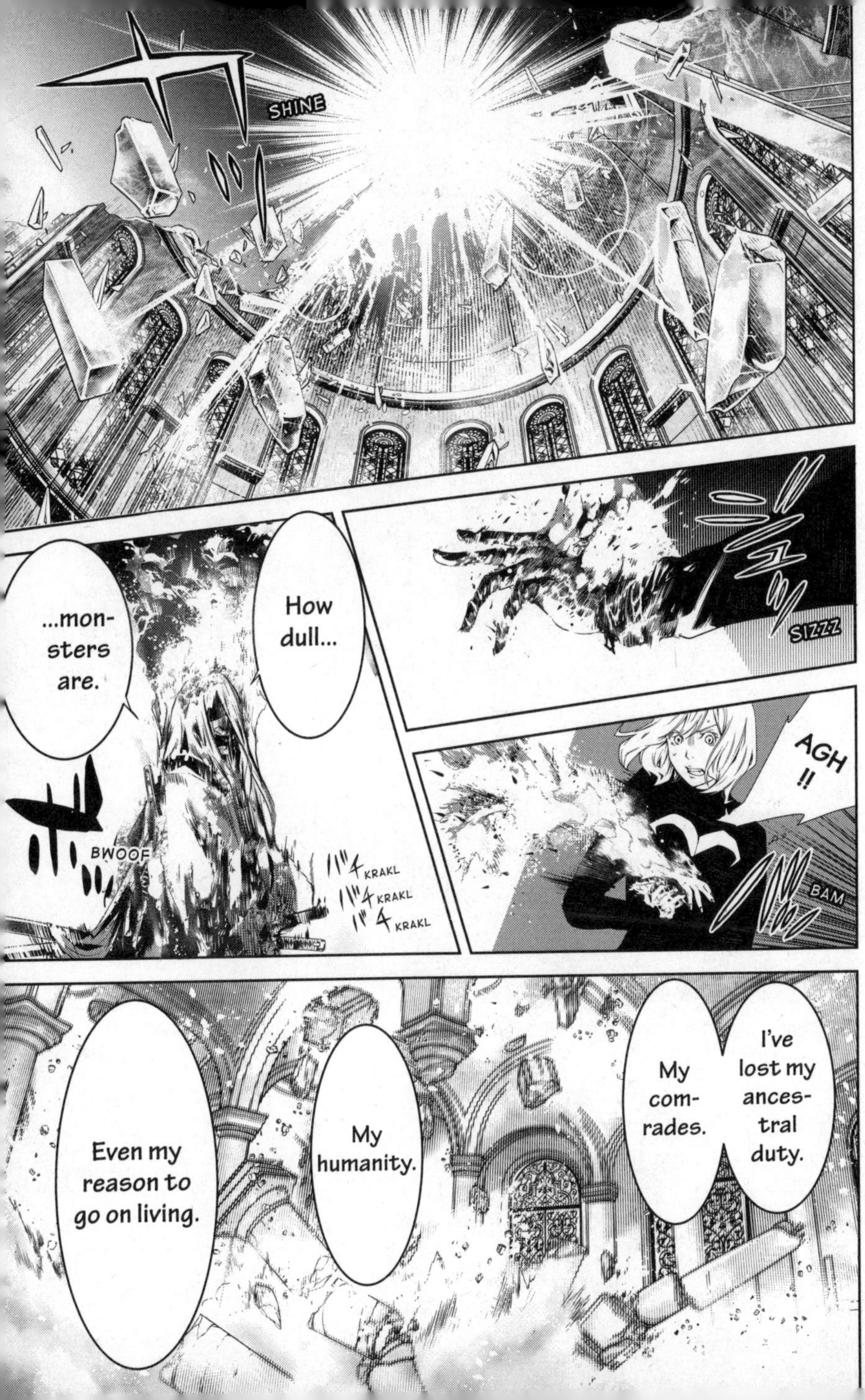
SHINE
SIZZZ
AGH!!
BAM
How dull...
...monsters are.
BWOOF
KRAKL
KRAKL
KRAKL
I've lost my ancestral duty.
My comrades.
My humanity.
Even my reason to go on living.

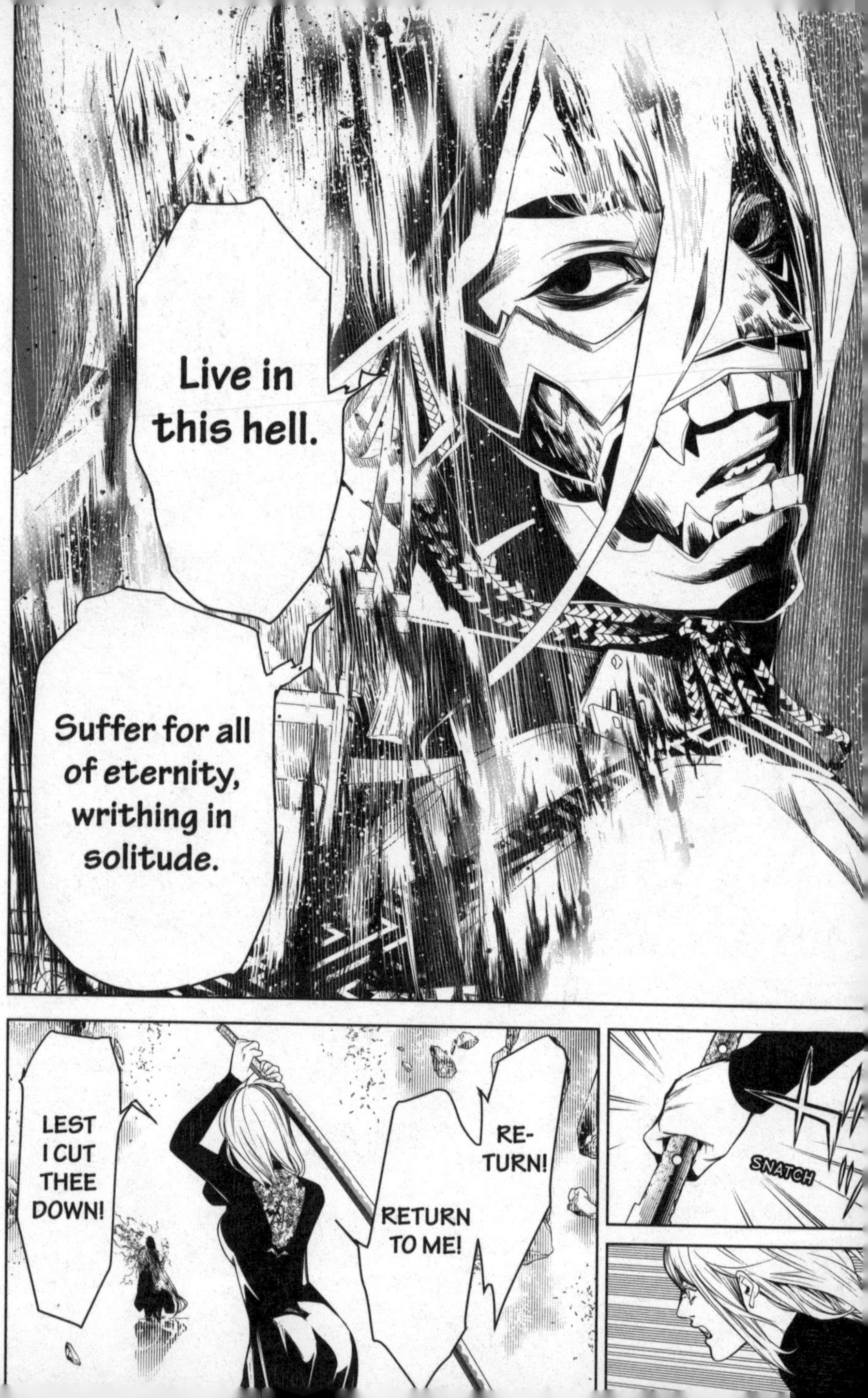
Live in this hell.
Suffer for all of eternity, writhing in solitude.
SNATCH
RE-TURN!
RETURN TO ME!
LEST I CUT THEE DOWN!

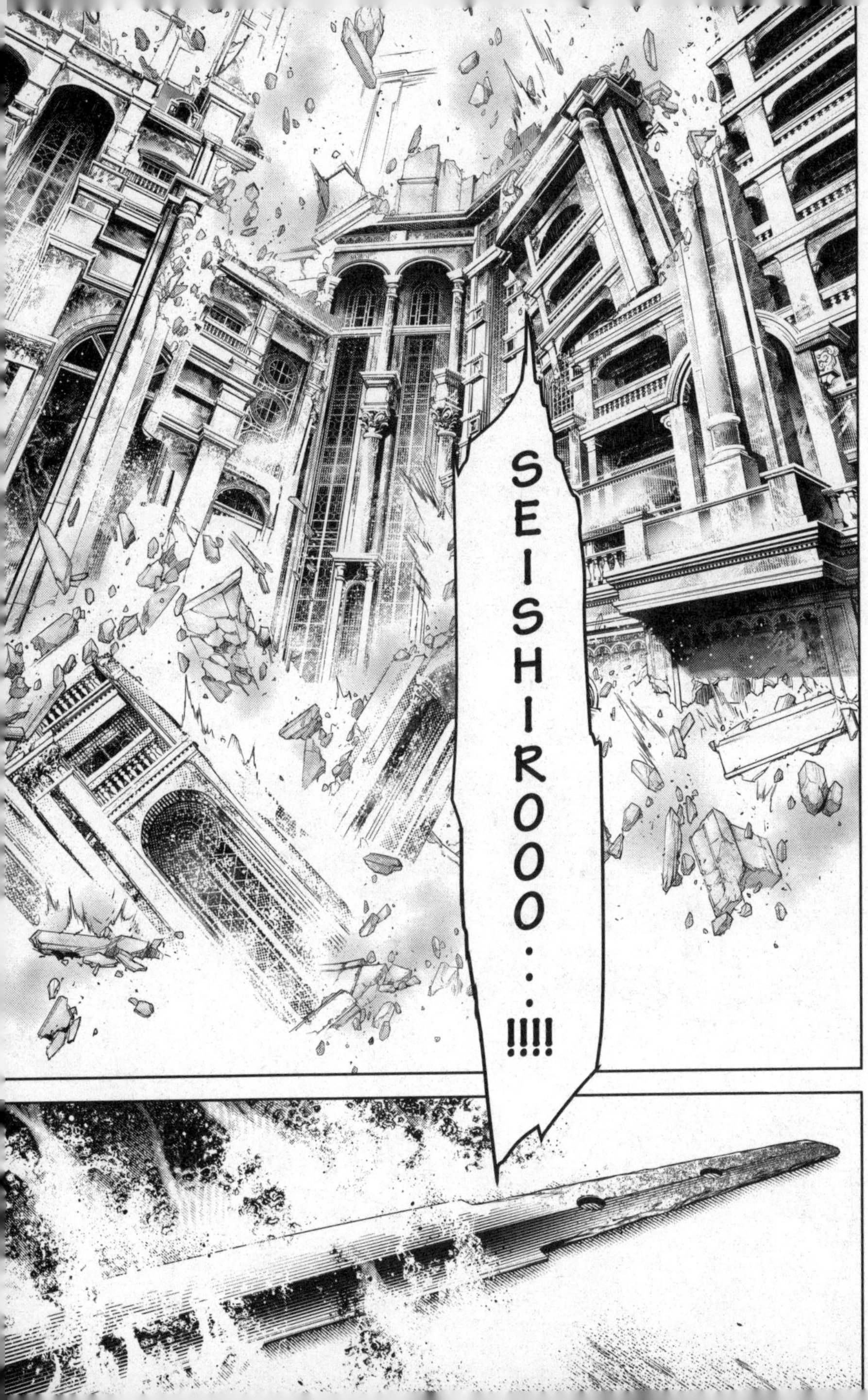
SEISHIROOO...!!!!

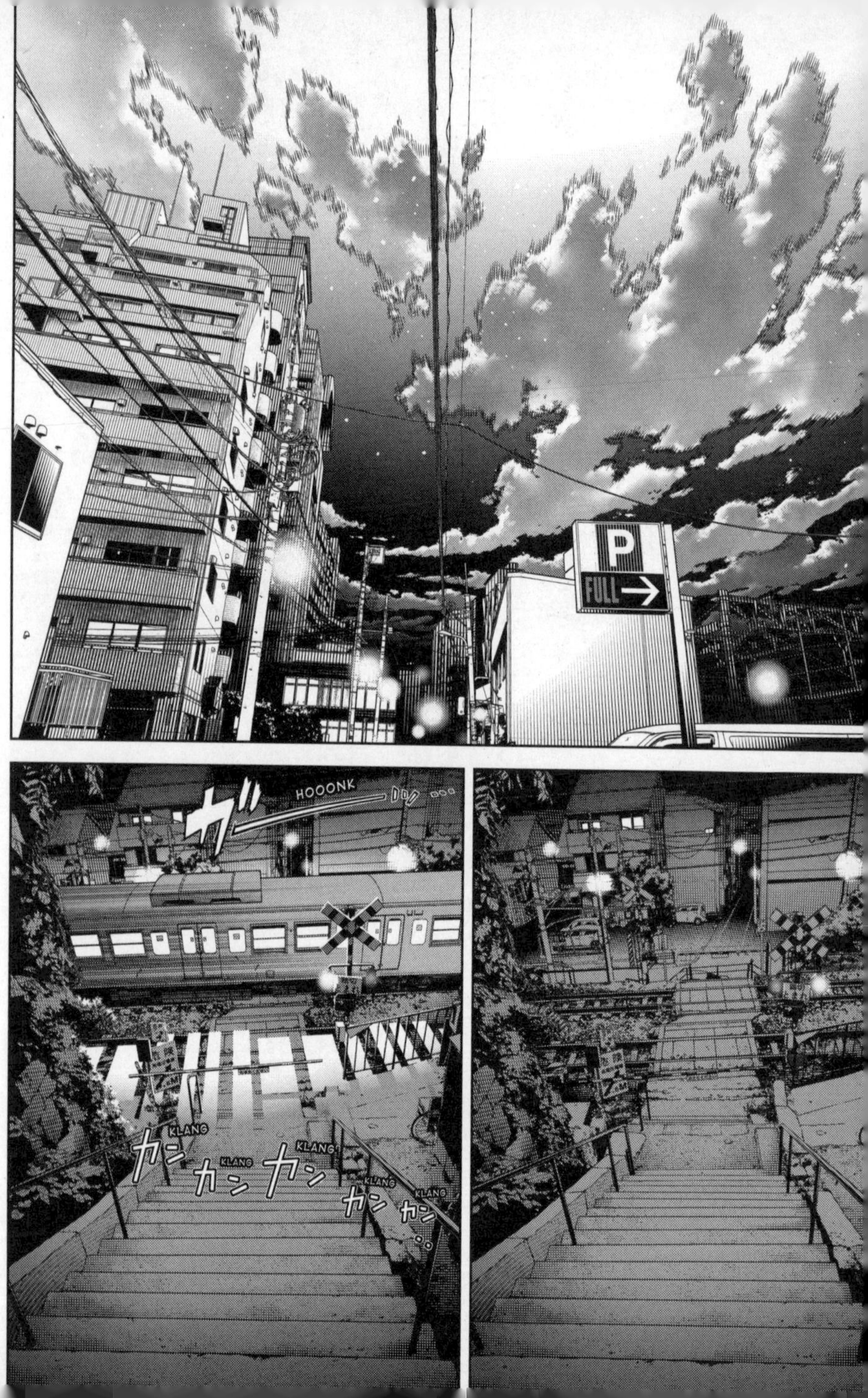
P
FULL →
ヴ
HOOONK
カン
KLANG
カン
KLANG
カン
KLANG
カン
KLANG
カン
KLANG

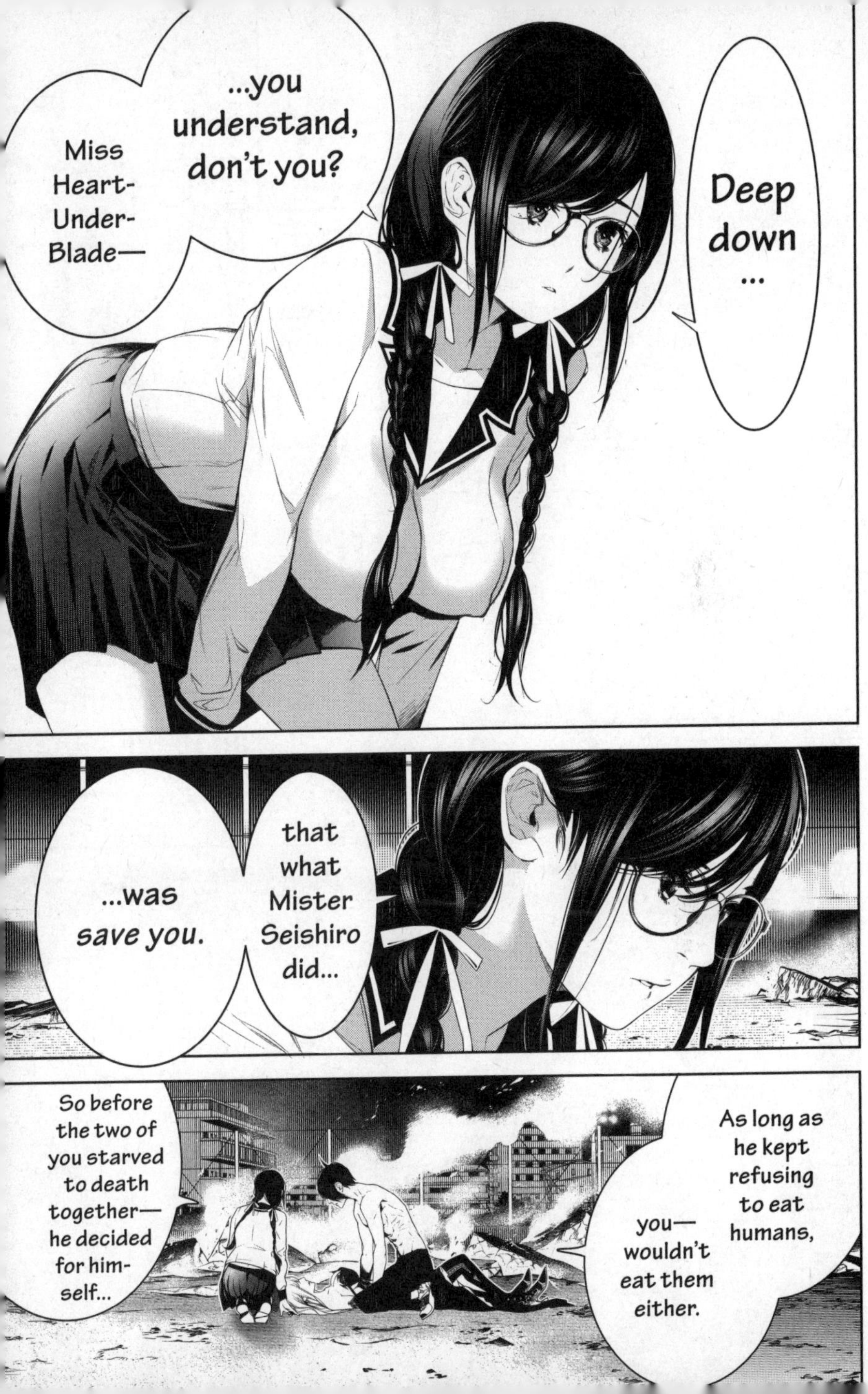
Deep down ...
...you understand, don't you?
Miss Heart-Under-Blade—
that what Mister Seishiro did...
...was save you.
As long as he kept refusing to eat humans,
you—wouldn't eat them either.
So before the two of you starved to death together—he decided for himself...

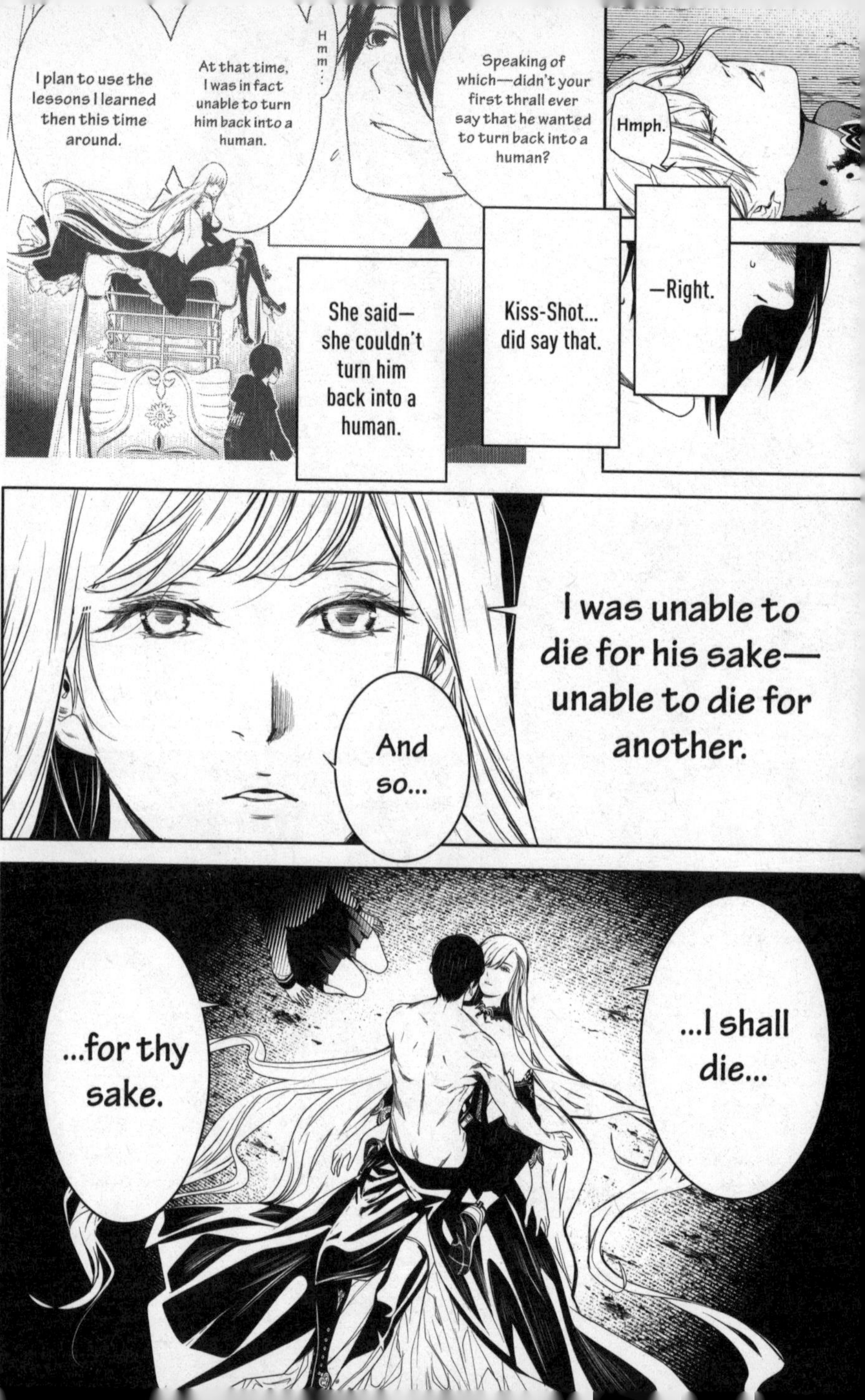
Hmph.
—Right.
Speaking of which—didn't your first thrall ever say that he wanted to turn back into a human?
Hmm...
At that time, I was in fact unable to turn him back into a human.
I plan to use the lessons I learned then this time around.
Kiss-Shot... did say that.
She said— she couldn't turn him back into a human.
I was unable to die for his sake— unable to die for another.
And so...
...I shall die...
...for thy sake.

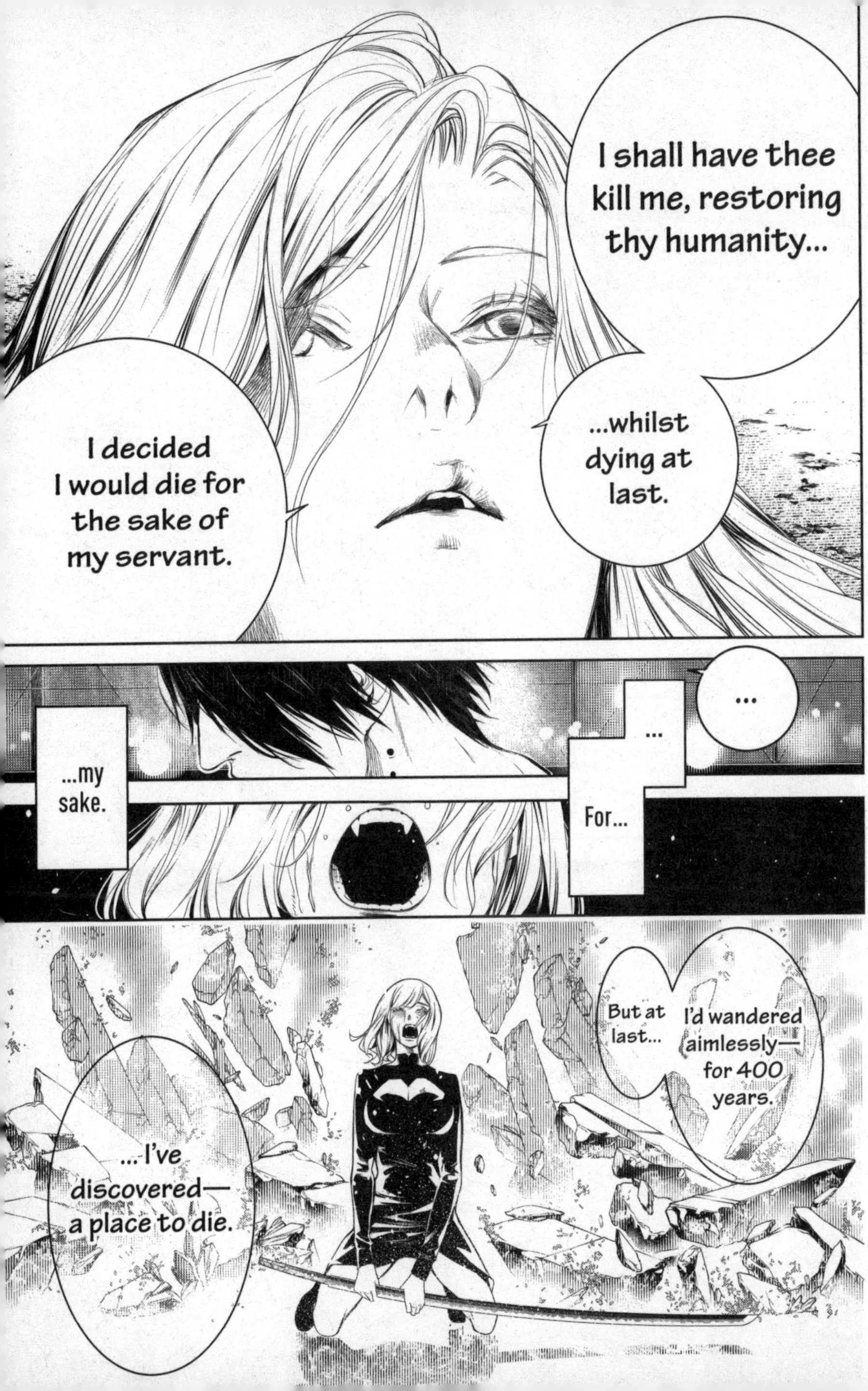
I shall have thee kill me, restoring thy humanity...
...whilst dying at last.
I decided I would die for the sake of my servant.
...
...
For...
...my sake.
I'd wandered aimlessly— for 400 years.
But at last...
...I've discovered— a place to die.

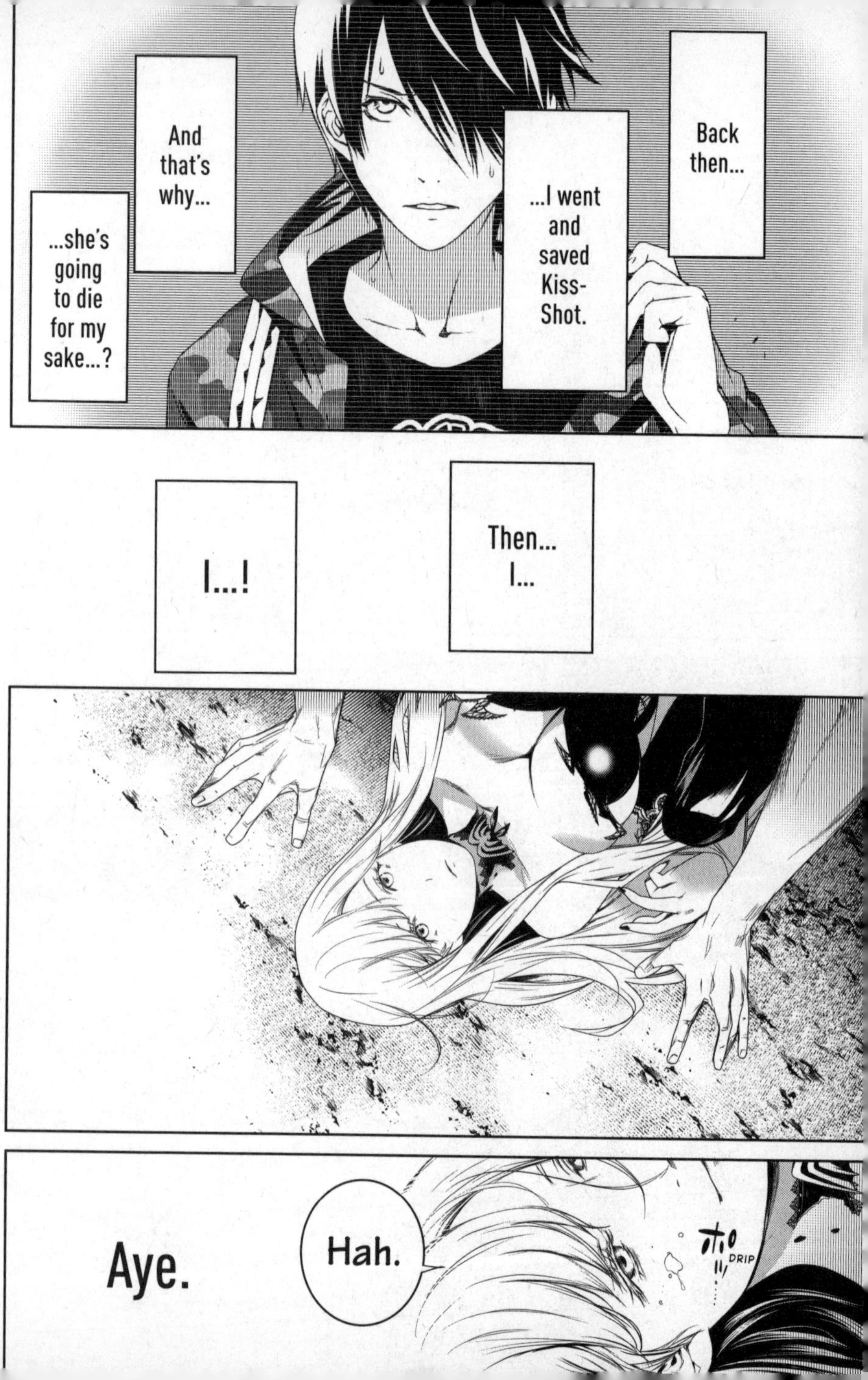
Back then...
...I went and saved Kiss-Shot.
And that's why...
...she's going to die for my sake...?
Then... I...
I...!
DRIP
Hah.
Aye.

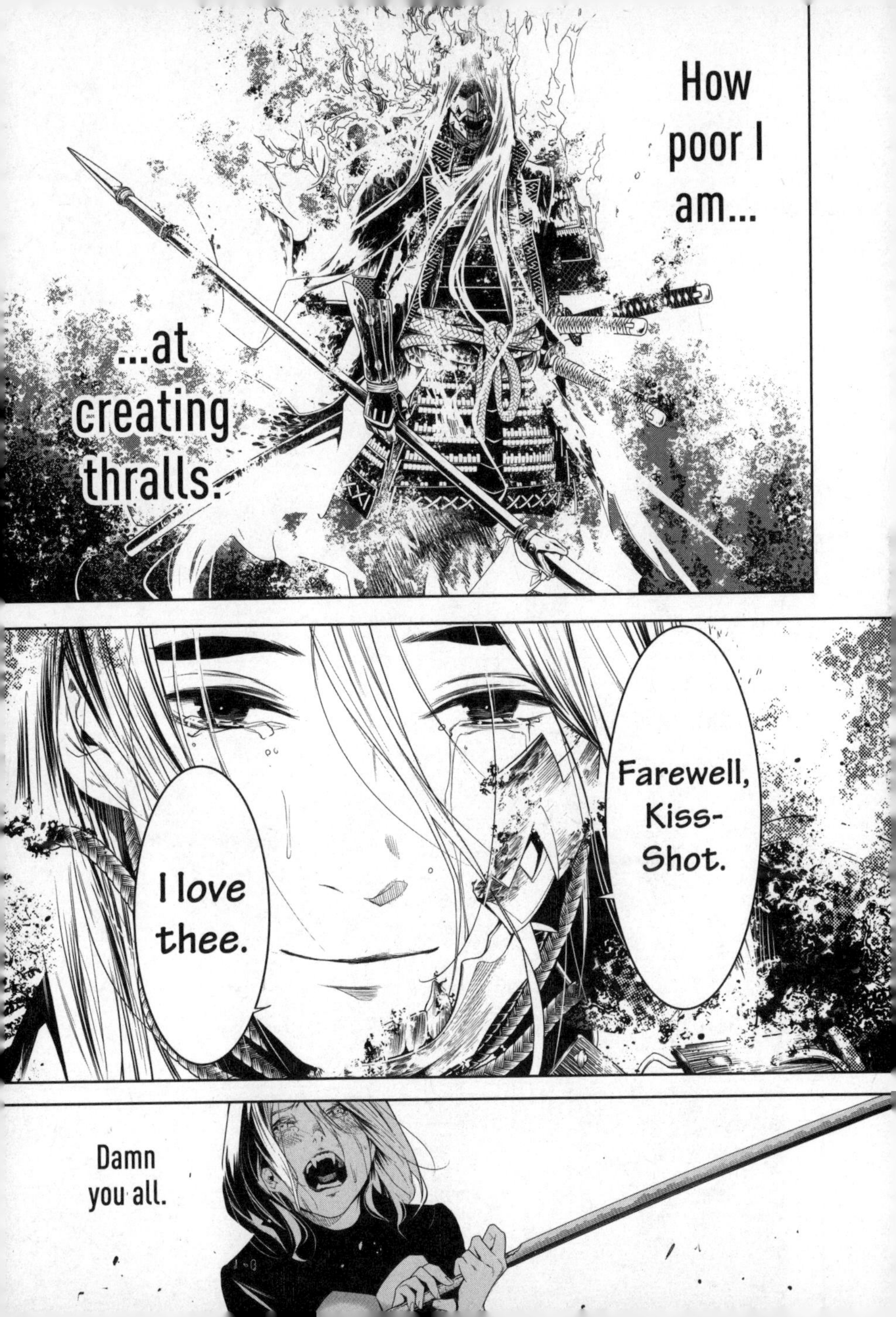
How poor I am...
...at creating thralls.
Farewell, Kiss-Shot.
I love thee.
Damn you all.

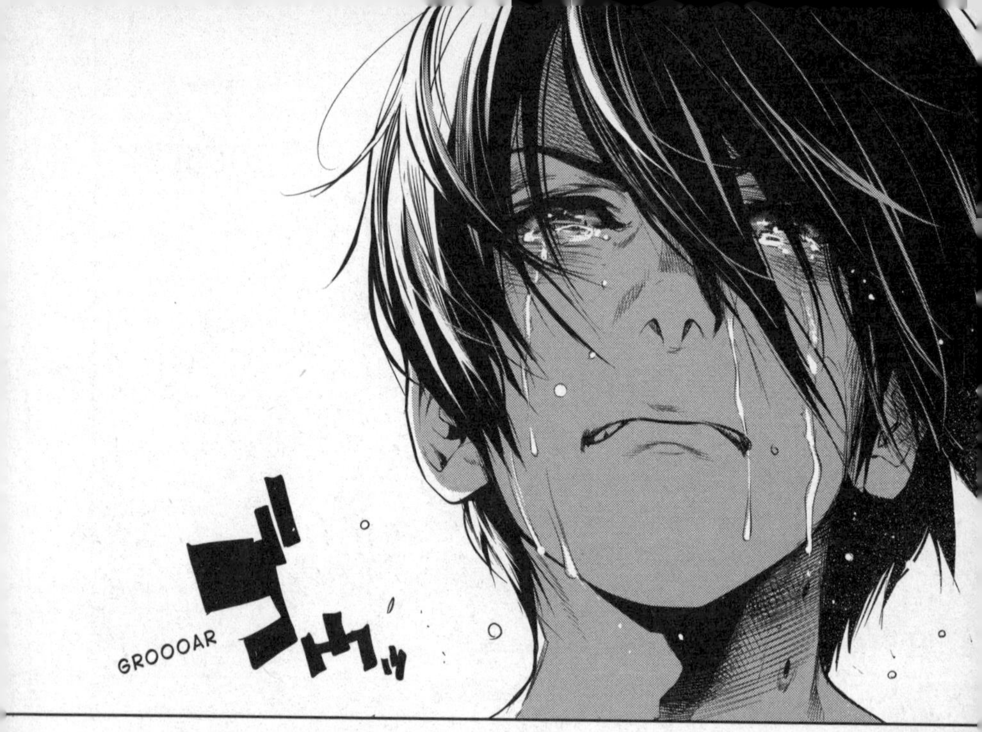
GROOOAR

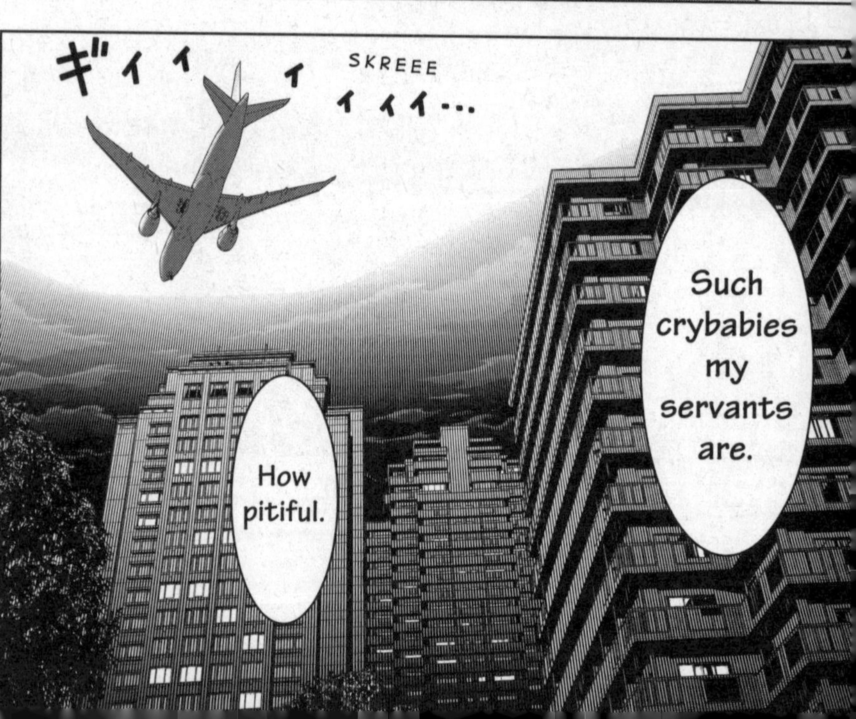
ギイイイイイイ…
SKREEE
Such crybabies my servants are.
How pitiful.

Continued in Volume 15

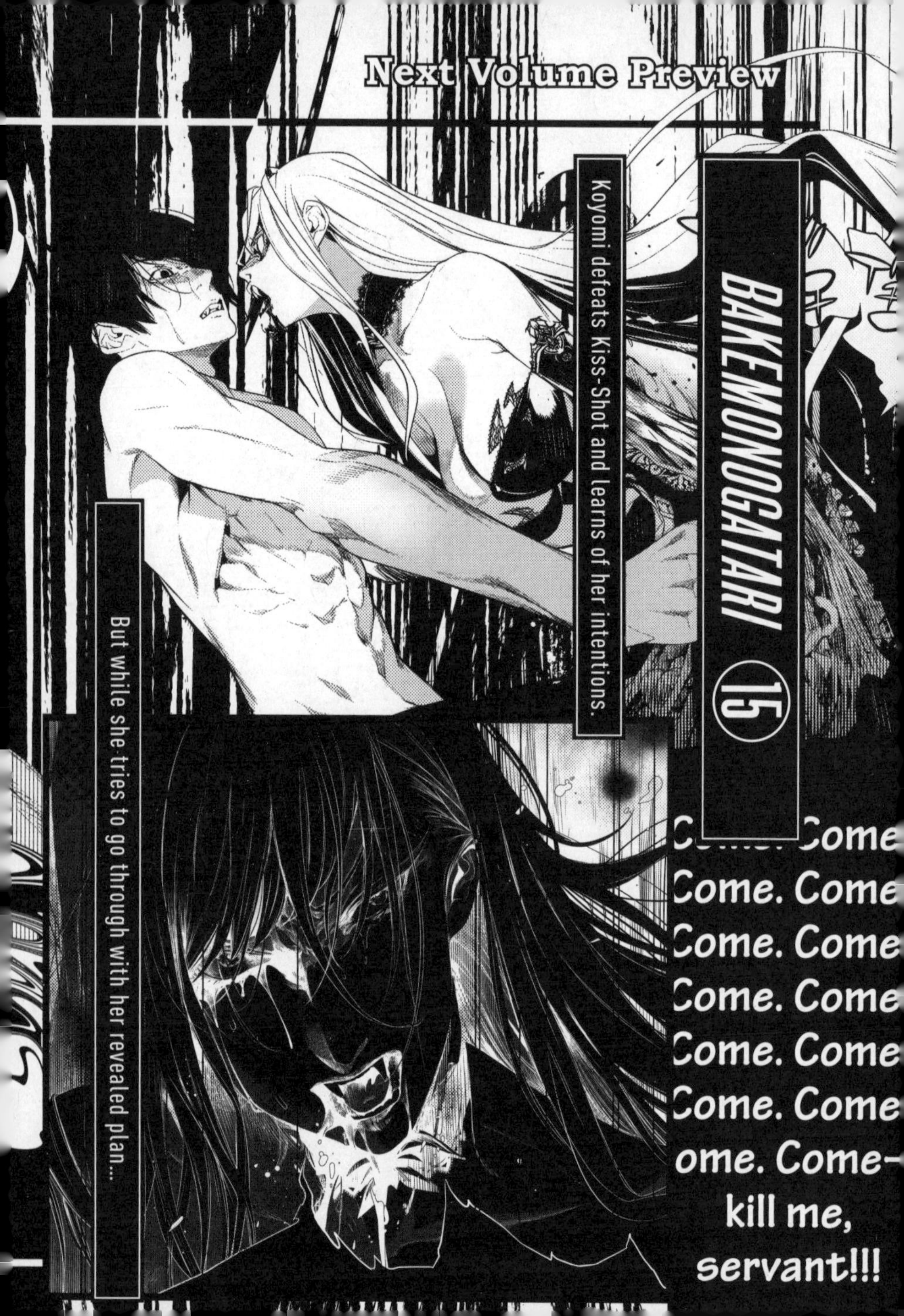
Next Volume Preview
BAKEMONOGATARI 15
Koyomi defeats Kiss-Shot and learns of her intentions.
But while she tries to go through with her revealed plan...
Come. Come
Come. Come
Come. Come
Come. Come
Come. Come
Come. Come
ome. Come-
kill me,
servant!!!